RELIGION IN PRIMITIVE SOCIETY

CROFTS ANTHROPOLOGY SERIES
Alexander Goldenweiser, Editor

RELIGION

IN PRIMITIVE SOCIETY

WILSON D. WALLIS, University of Minnesota

F. S. CROFTS & CO. NEW YORK 1939

MANUFACTURED IN THE UNITED STATES OF AMERICA

To

SIR FRANCIS AND LADY WYLIE

ACKNOWLEDGMENTS

I am indebted to Ruth Sawtell Wallis for a critical reading of the manuscript and the galley proofs, and to Elizabeth Colson for checking and completing bibliographical references. Assistance in the preparation of these materials was furnished by the personnel of Works Progress Administration Official Project No. 665-71-3-69, to whom I am indebted for the typing.

The illustrations on the cover (from a wall of the Jaguar Temple at Chichen Itzá, Mexico) and the title-page (a head from Oaxaca, Mexico) and all those in the text except that of the Toda temple were supplied by, and are used by permission of, the American Museum of Natural History.

W. D. W.

TABLE OF CONTENTS

LIST OF ILLUSTRATIONS

In every department of human thought there is present evidence of the persistence of primitive ideas. Scratch the epiderm of the civilized man, and the barbarian is found in the derm.—Edward Clodd, *Magic in Names*

Many carry the sacred wand, but rare are the Bacchoi.—Dionysiac proverb

The things of which we want the proof are those we know the best.
—Emily Dickinson

CHAPTER I THE SPHERE OF RELIGION

Anthropology has no concern with the truth or falsehood of religion, but is content to identify and describe the forms of religion and their cultural and psychological significance as belief and behaviour.

It is difficult to delineate the field of religion. There is no common agreement as to its boundaries, no consensus regarding the phenomena which it comprises. The religion of one devotee is to another irreligion; the act which one regards as pious, another considers impious; the sanction of a Jew is the sacrilege of a Mohammedan. "Whatever is held sacred by the Romans," remarks Tacitus, "with the Jews is held profane; and what in other nations is unlawful and impure, with them is fully established. . . . The ox, worshipped in Egypt for the god Apis, is slain as a victim by the Jews." Similarly, what the Egyptians called "holy" the Jews called an "abomination," for, as a contemporary remarks, "what is holy to an Egyptian is naturally the opposite to a Hebrew." It is, moreover, easy to mistake the incidental, superficial, or merely formal activities and aspirations of a religious cult for its fundamental drives and abiding purposes. Not what the devotees profess but what their deeds confess is the more significant fact; for action is older than thought, and reflection merely modifies and directs more primary reactions.

The supernatural is a primary and fundamental element in religion, for men spontaneously react to phenomena which they deem supernatural. Religious attitude, that is, emotional, ritualized, or rationalized response to the supernatural, characterizes all cultures and every stage of history. As Hume says, "Look out for a people entirely destitute of religion: if you find them at all, be assured, that they are but few degrees remove from brutes." [1]

Preliterate man conceives a world which is only partly subservient to

1. David Hume, *The Natural History of Religion*, Section XV.

uniform law; in a sophisticated culture the devout may accept nature as defined by science. Thus the man who is distraught by an apparently haphazard nature is religious; and likewise he who rises above its awesome aspect and finds a mystic meaning in its assumed law-abidingness.

> He who can lay claim to art and science,
> Assuredly has religion;
> He who can lay claim to neither,
> Likewise has religion.[2]

To a Mohammedan, religion means Mohammedanism; to a Jew, the Jewish religion; in short, to each, his own cult; yet one cannot understand religion in the large by assuming that all loyalties except one's own are nonreligion or irreligion. One must strive for objectivity when discussing the religions of man and not esteem a system of belief and practice "*religion* when one is within its magic circle, mythology when one has left it." [3]

Religion, then, includes things, persons, times, places, and events which partake of the holy or sacred. The world of the devotee consists of two realms—the sacred and the profane. Thus the concepts of the sacred and reactions to the sacred constitute the distinguishing traits of a religion.

Mohammedanism, for example, differs from Judaism to the extent that its concept of the sacred and its dealings with the sacred differ from those of Judaism. The distinguishing traits of the sacred inhere in the phenomena which characterize it; for sanctity is not consciously imposed upon phenomena but appears to inhere in them. The holy is supernaturally potent; most holy things are at least contingently dangerous; and many are immediately and highly dangerous. The sacred carries a threat. It punishes carelessness and listlessness in religious performance, puts the devotee on edge, and requires caution. It can benefit and it can injure; it rewards proper attitudes and punishes improper attitudes. The sacred can ensure blessings; and it can bring disaster. It must not be approached heedlessly or used carelessly. Its action is automatic and often immediate.

THE SACRED AMONG EARLY SEMITES

The Old Testament furnishes many illustrations of early Jewish concepts of the sacred. The Deity, and everything associated with or attach-

2. Goethe.
3. Andrew Lang.

ing to the Deity, are sacred. No man who saw the face of God could live, not Moses himself, who must be content with a substitute; for power, holiness fraught with dangerous consequences, radiates from the person of the Deity.[4]

The name of God is sacred, for in early thought the name is an intimate and inseparable part of the person or thing which it signifies. Hence priests do not employ the real name of the Deity but use a substitute. The danger in using the name leads to the prohibition against taking the name of God in vain.

Certain individuals are holy and share the qualities which inhere in the sacred. Such are: the king, the Lord's Anointed and his representative in Israel; soothsayer and prophet, who speak impulsively, actuated by a subtle mystic force to whose impulsions they are responsive; priest or priest-magician, who is entrusted with sacrifice and temple ritual, and who communes with the Deity. The Jewish people, the nation, are God's Chosen People and, therefore, a holy people. Many places are holy, especially high places, tops of hills and mountains—"the mountain might not be touched," was said of Sinai—and also clouds and the phenomena of the heavens. Localities, such as the ford at which Joshua crossed the Jordan, or the place at which Jacob wrestled with God, and certain stones, are sacred. Springs are sacred, possibly because the phenomenon of water gushing from the ground, or from rocks, as when Moses struck them, betokens the supernatural; and also because running water is instinct with mystic power. Temple and temple enclosure are concentric holy places with graduated sacredness. Into the outer court women may enter; into an inner court only men may enter; into an innermost court only priests may enter; and at the heart of the temple is the Holy of Holies, a sanctuary which only the High Priest may enter.

Innocent and devout meddling with the Ark of the Covenant, the Holy of Holies, cost Uzza his life. When the Ark was being conveyed to Jerusalem, after David had captured that city and decided to make it his capital, Uzza drove the new cart on which rested the Ark of the Covenant, accompanied by David and all the house of Israel, come to honour it and the occasion. When they arrived at the threshing-floor of Nachow, the oxen which drew the cart stumbled. Uzza took hold of the Ark to stay

4. Similarly, if a Zulu should look upon Nomkhubulwana, daughter of the god Unkulunkulu, face to face, he would be ill and would soon die. Accordingly, when the goddess meets a man, she conceals herself. An Ashanti proverb declares: "No priest may look upon the face of his god and live."

it. Whereupon he was slain by God "for his error." [5] The account implies that Uzza had no impious intention; on the contrary, he acted piously in preventing the fall of the Ark to the ground so that it should not suffer injury or desecration. Whatever the motive, Uzza was "too bold with the Holy Ark." [6] The holy regards not the intention, but rewards or punishes the deed as impersonally as does the live wire, which sends its current as remorselessly through the man who attempts to save an innocent bystander as through him who acts from malice. The potent sanctity of the Ark is again indicated in the verses: "and it came to pass, when the Ark set forward, that Moses said: 'rise up, O Lord, and let Thine enemies be scattered.' " [7] "When ye see the Ark of the Covenant of the Lord, your God, and the priests and the Levites bearing it, then ye shall remove from your place and go after it. Yet there shall be a space between you and it, about two thousand cubits by measure: come not nearer unto it." [8] So potent, so sacrosanct, was the Ark that it caused a grievous plague among the Philistines when they captured it; and when the men of Bethshemesh ventured to look into it, "the people lamented because Jahweh smote many of the people with a great slaughter." [9] The holy, the sacred, may not be approached lightly.

Among Semites of the Arabian desert at least four animals were commonly sacred: camel, ox, mouse, and pig. The pig, a sacred animal among pre-Jewish Canaanites, might not be eaten. Its holiness was responsible for the taboo.

Animals placed in the category of unclean—reptiles, snakes, and crawling things, and those which chew the cud but do not have the cloven hoof—were sacred animals. They were unclean, which really means taboo, because they were holy. To touch them would bring contamination and danger, for holiness is contagious. Hence one who comes into contact with holy things shares their nature and obtains a benefit; or, if he cannot safely partake of the holiness, suffers a mishap—as did poor pious Uzza.

Certain periods of time were sacred, and many ceremonies and festivities were basically calendric. Various seasonal and other periodic feasts of the Jews were instinct with holiness. Some of these came every seven, some every seventy, years: for sacredness attaches to the number seven and

5. *II Samuel*, 6: 3–8.
6. James Howell, *The Parly of Beasts*, 41.
7. *Numbers*, 10: 35.
8. *Joshua*, 3: 3–4.
9. *I Samuel*, 6: 19.

its multiples, especially seven times seven. Thus the seventh day was sacred, that is, taboo. No secular duties might be performed on that day, for it was replete with danger; no enterprise carried on during the seventh day, or Sabbath, would prosper. It was not a day of worship but a day of rest, of abstention; it was unlucky, and any action performed on it might have untoward consequences. It was, therefore, merely practical wisdom to remember the Sabbath and keep it holy; he who did not heed the prohibition would rue his rashness. Sacrifice was deeply fraught with holiness, and, therefore, with danger. A vow, likewise, was holy. Hence one who made a vow must fulfil it; otherwise he would be supernaturally punished.

THE CONCEPT OF HOLINESS AMONG SEMITIC MOHAMMEDANS

Moors use the term *baraka* to connote holiness. Much *baraka* inheres in certain individuals, notably in Mohammed. It is possessed by rulers, sherifs, and sultans. Saints are holy men and have a large measure of *baraka*.

As among Jews holiness may be imparted by one individual to another; as the mantle of Elijah may fall upon Elisha, so among Moors *baraka* may pass from one individual to another.

Numerous places possess *baraka*. Some are indicated by piles of stones, and stones may possess *baraka*. Many plants and trees are holy, especially trees near the grave or shrine of a saint, or near a sacred mosque. In many localities a grove is sacred. Mountains and sea possess *baraka*, and in some places the ground as well. Numerous natural or supernatural phenomena contain *baraka*, particularly a rainbow, lightning, thunder, the moon, an eclipse, the Milky Way.

The horse has *baraka*, and often the saddle shares in this sanctity. The camel has *baraka*, and the greyhound, though most dogs do not have it. Prayer possesses *baraka*; and a pilgrimage to Mecca is regarded as a sacred act.

Baraka inheres in certain numbers and in certain arrangements of numbers. Odd numbers possess more *baraka* than do even numbers. Three, five, and seven are especially potent, particularly the last mentioned. The number forty likewise has considerable potency. There is *baraka* in the mystic arrangement of numbers which gives the sum fourteen, that is, two sevens, whether the numbers are added in vertical or in horizontal columns. In Egypt the magic square consists of numbers so arranged in columns that the sum, horizontally, vertically, or diagonally, is fifteen. Thus:

4	9	2
3	5	7
8	1	6

This magic square is used in China and in India. In India the numbers represent the planets and afford protection against evil planetary influences. A similar magic square used in northern India includes other numbers whose sum is seventy-three.

THE CONCEPT OF THE SACRED IN PRELITERATE CULTURES

Although precisely analogous concepts of the holy are not found in every culture, a distinction between sacred and profane is almost universal. In Polynesia many things are taboo, that is, supernaturally dangerous, or they are *noa*, that is, everyday and commonplace, devoid of supernaturalism. In central Australia *arungquilta* imparts potency to a medicineman; *churinga*, sacred stones at totem centres, are instinct with it. In the New World comparable concepts are Iroquois *orenda*, Central Woodland Algonquian *manitou*, and Micmac *keskamzit*.

The Dakota Indian designates the holy as *wakan*, a word sometimes translated as mysterious, powerful. Wahpeton Dakotas have a comprehensive philosophy of *wakan* and its manifestations. *Wakan* is possessed by stone, which has a hardness and durability not found in any other material. Spider has much *wakan*. It is ubiquitous; it can walk on water and on land; it weaves a net in which it catches other animals; it can pitch up its rope to the limb of a tree and climb up, or climb down backwards, on this rope. No other animal possesses these powers, and no other animal has as much *wakan* as has Spider. Hence, before a man smokes, he offers his filled pipe of tobacco to Spider. He points the bowl of the pipe toward the earth and says: "Spider, I offer you this tobacco." Spider knows everything one says or thinks. Next to Spider in *wakan* is Eagle. Eagle can fly higher than any other bird and by merely extending his wings can stay in the air as long as he wishes. This power can be explained only as due to the possession of *wakan*. Next to Eagle in *wakan* is Wild Goose, the feathers of which, like those of Eagle, have mystic power. Wild Goose knows when to fly south and when to fly north. Wild geese are the only animals which follow a leader; one can hear him issuing his commands. Among trees, birch and ground hemlock have most *wakan*. The oak also is *wakan*. Certain natural, or supernatural, phenomena have or are *wakan*. Such are thunder and lightning, and the beings which cause these phenomena; eclipses; and meteors, or "falling stars." From the last mentioned come the round polished stones which contain the most potent "medicine" or magic.

To an Oglala Dakota, *wakan* implies, among other things, mystic power. The roots of certain plants are *wakan* because they are poisonous. Some reptiles are *wakan* because their bite kills. Some birds are *wakan* because they do very strange things. Certain other animals are *wakan* because *wakan* beings make them so. "In other words, anything may be *wakan*," an Oglala explains, "if a *wakan* spirit goes into it. Thus a crazy man is *wakan* because the bad spirit has gone into him. Again, if a person does something that cannot be understood, that also is *wakan*. Drinks that make one drunk are *wakan*, because they make one crazy. Every object in the world has a spirit and that spirit is *wakan*. Thus the spirit of the tree or things of that kind, while not like the spirit of man, are also *wakan*. *Wakan* comes from the *wakan* beings. These *wakan* beings are greater than mankind in the same way that mankind is greater than the animals. They are never born and never die. They can do many things that mankind cannot do. Mankind can pray to the *wakan* beings for help.

"The most powerful of the *wakan* beings is *Nagi Tanka*, the Great Spirit who is also *Taku Skanskan*; *Taku Skanskan* signifies the Blue, in other words, the Sky. *Iya* is a *Wakan Tanka*, but he is an evil *Wakan Tanka*. Mankind is permitted to pray to the *Wakan* beings. If their prayer is directed to all the good *Wakan* beings, they should pray to *Wakan Tanka*; but if the prayer is offered only to one of these beings, then the one addressed should be named. *Wakan Tanka* is pleased with music. He likes to hear the drums and the rattles. When any of the *Wakan* beings hear the drum and the rattles they always give attention. He is also fond of the smoke of the sweet grass, and evil *Wakan* beings are afraid of the smoke of sage. All of the *Wakan*, both the good and evil, are pleased with the smoke of the pipe. The earth and the rock and the mountains pertain to the chief *Wakan*. We do not see the real earth and the rock, but only their *tonwanpi*.

"When a Lakota [Dakota] prays to *Wakan Tanka* he prays to the earth and to the rock and all the other good *Wakan* beings. If a man wishes to do evil things he may pray to the evil *Wakan*. When *Wakan Tanka* wishes one of mankind to do something he makes his wishes known either in a vision or through a shaman." [10]

Among New Zealand Maoris the *mana* concept plays an important part in interpretations of the world and life. It explains lightning and other startling phenomena. *Mana* is a connecting link between the cult of fire and the cult of heroes. It is responsible for the power inherent in human personality. *Mana* is not identical with magic; the medicineman may possess *mana* or may be devoid of it; and the working of magic is possible without *mana*. *Mana* plays an important rôle in social life. It is inherent in leadership; loss of superiority and prestige betokens loss of *mana*. Personal *mana* has been introjected into physical phenomena, such as lightning, stones, and other objects. The concept varies with culture and has multiform expression. Possibly the concept of *mana* is based on experience which has been interpreted in accordance with the prevailing mental pattern. Some supernatural phenomena, however, do not contain *mana*. A person's shadow or reflection, and a spirit which appears in animal form, are *ata*, the spirit's image or simulation. The tern is the *ata* of the gods, for the gods enter it. An object which a spirit makes a permanent resting-place, such as war club, spear, sacred centre-post, or clan house, is *ata*. *Ata* is responsible for dreams which contain untoward incidents—for example, dreams in which friends or relatives play a part inconsistent with their character. Such dreams are induced by malevolent spiritual beings. When an animal behaves strangely, in a manner not characteristic of its species, it is an *ata* in animal guise; when it behaves normally, it is an ordinary individual. In Tikopia *ata* applies to any object, animate or inanimate, which manifests supernatural power.

Any unusual event Madagascar Sakalavas attribute to the spirit of an ancestor. It is punishing a breach of ancestral custom, or, possibly, merely attracting the attention of the living. Masai *n'gai* connotes the unknown and incomprehensible, manifested in such phenomena as storms and the telegraph. The Naga concept of *genna*, similar to Polynesian taboo, means forbidden under supernatural penalties. *Genna*, which has supernatural sanction, attaches especially to forbidden practices and to holidays observed during performance of ceremonies and sacrificial feasts. It applies to

10. J. R. Walker, "The Sun Dance and Other Ceremonies of the Oglala Division of the Teton Dakota," *APAMNH*, 16: 152–153 (1917). Reprinted by permission of the American Museum of Natural History. (For bibliographical abbreviations used in the present work see page 331.)

the entire social group which is performing the sacrifice, that is, the household or the village, which must temporarily sever relations with other groups. Permanent *genna* applies to certain articles of food. Some *genna* is periodic—for example, that which applies to agriculture; some is occasional, and applies only during a crisis or special contingency—for example, during actual or threatened epidemic. Disregard of *genna* causes calamities and is punished as a social offence. When *genna* rests on a village, no one may work or enter or leave the village. Concepts similar to Naga *genna* are Garo *marang*, Lushai *thianglo*, and Lakher *ana*, each of which refers to something which is forbidden under supernatural sanctions, and may apply to an individual or to a community. The person who defies the *ana* prohibition will die or encounter ill luck. Many of these Lakher *ana* prohibitions are social in their implications. Thus it is *ana* to shift the boundary of another man's field, to throw weeds into the field of another, to steal eggs, or to give birth to a child in the house of another. In Peru *huaca*, a Quichua and Aymara term, attaches to objects honoured by a cult, to lakes, animals, mummies of ancestors, temples, graves, and offerings made at shrines. It is closely associated with the cult of ancestors. *Huaca* includes also household fetishes and amulets, most of which are crystals or small stones of peculiar shape or colour. *Huaca* placed at intervals close to irrigation canals prevents them from leaking and ensures sufficient moisture to maize fields. After the Spanish conquest Peruvians applied the term *huaca* to unfamiliar objects of European introduction, such as sealing-wax or the base of a glass goblet. The *huacque*, or "brother," of the Inca Manco was a miraculous bird called Sun; that of Suichi Rocca, a stone fish; that of Lloque Yupauqui, an idol. The Inca Uiracocha possessed a *haucque* in the form of a gold statue representing lightning. Quichua apply the term *huaca* to the divinity, representations of the divinity, and everything in which a divinity dwells; to "every temple or place which, in native belief, is inhabited by a good or bad spirit; tombs and burial-places; every manifestation of extraordinary beauty or ugliness, the origin of which is outside the normal course of things—for instance, a woman who has given birth to two or more children [at one birth]; an egg with two yolks, monstrous children with more fingers than normal, with deformed limbs, with hare-lip, etc.; the great fountains which spring forth from between the rocks; small stones of various colours encountered in rivulets or on the sea-board; precipitous rocks and high mountains; the Peruvian cordilleras. . . . The term *huaca* was, by the Peruvians, applied to striking phenomena which awakened fear and awe in them, and were therefore, in a general way, regarded as supernatural." [11]

Thus many preliterate cultures conform with Hobbes' interpretation of religious phenomena: "They that make little or no inquiry into the natural causes of things, yet, from the fear that proceeds from ignorance itself of what it is that hath the power to do them much good or harm, are inclined to suppose and feign unto themselves several kinds of powers invisible, and to stand in awe of their own imaginations, and in time of distress to invoke them, as also in the time of an expected good success to give them thanks, making the creatures of their own fancy their gods. By which means it hath come to pass that, from the innumerable variety of fancy, men have created in the world innumerable sorts of gods. And this fear of things invisible is the natural seed of that which every one in himself calleth religion, and in them that worship or fear that power otherwise than they do superstition." [12]

Phenomena which preliterate man does not understand he endows with mystic significance, for they inspire awe.

11. Rafael Karsten, *The Civilization of the South American Indians,* 340 (New York, Knopf, 1926). Reprinted by permission of the publishers: Alfred A. Knopf, Inc.; Kegan Paul, Trench, Trubner & Co., Ltd.; and George Routledge and Sons, Ltd.
12. Thomas Hobbes, *Leviathan,* Chapter XI.

CHAPTER II THE NATURAL AND THE SUPERNATURAL

The beasts are startled and terrified by unusual phenomena.

Tar or whitewash a rat, and its former companions flee in terror.

Deer run in alarm from a stag whose antlers carry a conspicuous foreign substance.

A horse is frightened by a moving vehicle to which no horse is attached —he wants the horse before the cart. A noiseless movement in the grass, a falling twig, startle him, though a train may pass unnoticed. At any unusual noise the mountain lion assumes a crouching, waiting position. "A cord hung with feathers will stop the mightiest droves of wild beasts and guide them into traps. The speeding of a race-chariot and the sight of its revolving wheels will drive back lions to their cage, and elephants are terrified by the squealing of a pig." [1] A horse, the lion's favourite prey, might wander for days in the vicinity of a troop of lions unmolested, "simply because it was blanketed and knee-haltered; while on the other hand, the same family of lions rushed up to my companions' wagons, and in spite of guns, shouts, and fires, pulled down the same nag." [2] Romanes terrified his pet dog by drawing across the floor a bone attached to an invisible thread. The experiment has been repeated with like results. Köhler records the chimpanzee's fear of unusual objects, even small ones; [3] and the Kelloggs found the chimpanzee which they raised in their home "in general wary of the strange and the unknown." [4]

Many species of beasts distinguish between the natural and the supernatural. Horses, so it was believed, refused to go past a certain tree,

1. Seneca, "On Anger," II, xi, translated by John W. Basore, *Seneca: Moral Essays*, I, 191–193 (London, 1928).

2. Gilmore, quoted in John W. King, *The Supernatural, Its Origin, Nature and Evolution*, I, 80 (London, Williams and Norgate, 1892).

3. Wolfgang Köhler, *Mentality of Apes*, 320, 325 (New York, Harcourt, 1927).

4. W. N. Kellogg and L. A. Kellogg, *The Ape and the Child*, 178 (New York, McGraw-Hill, 1933).

in Britain, because "they saw or heard something uncanny there." [5] A horse shies at an opened umbrella or a paper moving on the ground. He reacts to them as men react to the strange, the uncanny—as though they were supernatural. Dogs and cats are alarmed at an unusual noise or appearance and are uneasy until they ascertain the cause. A lion is frightened by an unexpected sound or unfamiliar object. A tiger trembled and roared in apparent fear when a mouse tied by a string to a stick was inserted into the tiger's cage.[6] That the ancient Greeks were acquainted with this type of reaction in animals is indicated in the statement that when Athena revealed herself to Odysseus, "the Gods having the power not to be manifested except at will, the dogs, instead of barking, slunk in whining terror to the back of the yard." [7]

In practically all cultures holiness attaches especially to phenomena regarded as unnatural or phenomenal, that is, as supernatural. Happenings which are out of the ordinary, which are extraordinary, are not regarded with emotional detachment. They elicit emphatic emotional responses different in kind from responses to phenomena which pertain to the everyday and commonplace. Phenomena which the coastal Malay native does not understand are endowed with mystery and magic potency; thus he believes the jungle-dweller to be endowed with supernatural power and unlimited knowledge of the secrets of nature.[8]

In Japan the deities of heaven and earth and their spirits resident in shrines at which devotees worship are *kami*. Human beings, birds, beasts, plants, trees, seas, mountains, and other things which are dreaded and revered because of the extraordinary and pre-eminent powers which they possess, are *kami*. Some are noble, good, or serviceable; but malignant and uncanny things which inspire dread are likewise *kami*. Thus the term *kami*, applied to gods and superior human beings, is not restricted to powers which usually are beneficent, but applies also to malign beings that occasion fear—for example, the fire demons which devour towns. In Japan, as in many other cultures, *Omne ignotum mirifico est*—the unknown is awe-inspiring, for it is replete with mystery.

Japanese *kami* is cognate with Ainu *kamui*, which latter is perhaps the

5. Eleanor Hull, *Folklore of the British Isles*, 133–134 (London, Methuen, 1928).
6. Edward Westermarck, *Early Beliefs and Their Social Influence*, 6–7 (London, Macmillan, 1932). That many vertebrates fear the unknown is pointed out by Mrs. Sidney Webb, in Mary Adams (editor), *The Modern State*, 171 (London, Allen & Unwin, 1933).
7. Odyssey, Book XVI.
8. Walter W. Skeat and Charles O. Blagden, *The Pagan Races of the Malay Peninsula*, I, 563–564 (London, Macmillan, 1906).

older term. Ainu *kamui* is applied to beneficent objects exalted or divine. When applied to evil gods, it designates those which are most feared and dreaded. Among devils, reptiles, and evil diseases it signifies those which are most hateful, abominable, and repulsive. Prefixed to the name of an animal, fish, or fowl, it signifies greatest or fiercest, or most useful for food or clothing. Applied to persons, it may express goodness, respect, or reverence. This ambivalence of the term *kamui*, an ambivalence common in preliterate concepts of the holy, inspired Batchelor's remarks: "As, therefore, the Ainu apply their term for God to such a variety of objects, both to the greatest and highest good, and also to the lowest and most malignant evil—to gods and devils, spirit and matter, reptile, animal, and man—it is not surprising that very much superstition is mixed up with their religion—that demonology is intermingled with their theology, and that evil is mixed with good. Hence, if we find that some of the Ainu ideas of and remarks concerning God and religion are full of contradictions, at one time high and sublime, at another gross and repulsive—as sometimes He is represented as a material substance, and at others as a spiritual Being, now as good, now as evil, and now as indifferent—we shall not be surprised." [9]

Chinese apply the term *chin* to manifestations of the extraordinary in mountains, forests, rivers, lakes, rocks, or hills. Everything mysterious the Todas associate with *der*, which connotes divinity or sanctity. In Melanesia "peculiar or noticeable objects of all sorts, such as large or peculiar trees, prominent rocks, waterfalls, or rapids, are often supposed to be the abode of spirits." Fijian *kalu* denotes the gods and anything great or marvellous. Aruntas dread anything strange or out of the ordinary.

"The Negroes worship everything extraordinary and rare," declares an early African traveller. A Congo Ngala, "who may be courageous in hunting and fishing, is shrinking and timid when in contact with anything mysterious." An egg laid by a hen which has developed the secondary sexual characters of a cock, the Zande regard with apprehension. This "cock's egg," as they call it, is placed near a path in a small shrine similar to shrines erected in honour of ancestral spirits.

In Nigeria, should a large tree fall and crush a passer-by, it is considered the abode of a god and accordingly is worshipped. Indeed, "every striking object in nature is worshipped, not because it is one of nature's wonders,

9. John Batchelor, *The Ainu of Japan: The Religion, Superstitions and History of the Hairy Aborigines of Japan*, 250–251 (New York, Revell, no date). Reprinted by permission of the publisher, the Fleming H. Revell Company.

but because it is thought that it contains the spirit of an evil-working deity. Beneficent spirits are almost unknown to the pessimistic African." [10] The sanctity, that is, apartness fraught with danger, which inheres in the unusual is emphatic in the practice of the Ibo of Nigeria. A goat which climbs on the roof of a house; a cock that crows, or a hen that lays, at night, in an open space; a hen which hatches only one egg out of a nestful; a fowl which pecks at an aka snake; a cow which bears twins; human twins; all are unlucky; and such creatures, including the human twins, are killed. Among the Makololo of eastern equatorial Africa, "everything not to be accounted for by common causes, whether of good or evil, is ascribed to the Deity." Of the Tumbuka of northern Rhodesia it has been said, "almost any object which appears unusual may to them embody the spirit they worship."

The designation of the Zande Supreme Being, *Mbori*, is "a word that accounts for whatever cannot be explained by other Zande notions and indicates incomprehensibility." The Shilluk speak of a foreigner as *juok*, supernatural, "because of the marvellous things he does. He flies through the air or makes a machine that talks, so he is a *juok*. A badly wounded animal that is lost in the grass is *juok*, because it walked off dead and could not be found. *Juok* is the creator of mankind, and the universe, but anything that the Shilluk cannot understand is *juok*." [11] At the boiling springs in the Luenzoro range, between Lakes Edward and Albert, in central Africa, where natives take vapour baths to cure fever or rheumatism, the sound of bubbling water under a rock indicates the presence of an indwelling rock spirit to which people make offerings. When an Ewe of Togoland saw crimson water spurting from a hole which he had dug in the earth, he knew that a spirit inhabited the place and permeated the water. The phenomenon gave rise to a cult. On February 22, 1934, at Bengazi, in Cyrenaica, Africa, "hordes of awestruck natives formed caravans from the lowland to see 'the blanket of Allah' [that is, the snow] which covered the hinterland of the plateau of South Bengazi for the first time in the recollection of the oldest inhabitant. It caused the most reverential reactions of the natives, many of whom prostrated themselves in the fleecy drifts in subjection to Allah's will." Moors say God dispatches angels to conduct the clouds to the place at which they are to send down rain; an angel accompanies every drop that falls from the sky. Without

10. A. F. Mockler-Ferryman, *British Nigeria*, 255 (London, Cassell, 1902).

11. C. G. Seligman and B. Z. Seligman, *Pagan Tribes of the Nilotic Sudan*, 76 (London, Routledge, 1932). Reprinted by permission of George Routledge and Sons, Ltd.

this celestial attendant each drop would kill at least one inhabitant of earth and possibly more.

Eskimo religion is based on the unusual, which is mysterious and unforeseen. Phenomena which are not everyday and commonplace are attributed to an impersonal permeating magical force called *sila*. *Sila*, which may include anything, from the universe to the weather or the intelligence, is not inherently either good or evil, but is fraught with danger to one who does not know how to deal with it. In this respect, like *mana*, it resembles electricity. Every untoward circumstance and every inexplicable phenomenon, such as sickness, stormy weather, unaccountable sound, movement of the compass needle, Copper Eskimos explain as machinations of evil shades or spirits. There is a spirit in the electric battery and in the phonograph—they saw the spirit in the phonograph.

A fetish much prized by a certain Chippewa Indian consisted of a leg of a goshawk, from the outer inferior condyle of whose right tibia there projected a supernumerary leg terminating in two toes, the whole abnormality being about half the size and length of the natural leg and toes. Through this medium the favour of the Thunder God was invoked. Strange phenomena which the Parry Island Ojibwa, of Georgian Bay, cannot explain they attribute to *manidos*, that is, supernatural spiritual powers. Among the Lenape, localities which display curious or unusual natural features are the habitat of spirits. The Great Spirit communicates his will to Choctaws in thunder, lightning, eclipse, meteor, comet, and other supernatural phenomena. To Cherokees anything that appears to be supernatural is suspect, for it is likely at any time to be harmful. The Cayapa of Ecuador believe that "practically all hard objects of unusual form" are the abodes of spirits. Peruvian *huaca* connotes dynamic supernaturalism resident in anything which displays extraordinary qualities, such as a stone that crushes a man, or an albino animal—in short, any freak or monstrosity. A stone which has the shape of a maize ear, potato, or llama confers fertility upon the crop or herd which its form suggests. A double ear of maize or one of unusual shape or colour imparts fertility to the maize crop.

The mysterious lagoons in the Andes are sacred to the Indians of Ecuador, Peru, and Bolivia. Their enormous depth, their black and ice-cold water, and certain strange phenomena associated with them stir the imagination of the natives, who believe the lagoons inhabited by powerful spirits. The Colorados, west of the Ecuadorian Andes, have similar convictions: "the water in some of the mountain lagoons rises and falls with the water in the sea; and sometimes, they say, it bubbles as if it were boiling." [12] Bathing in such lagoons would cause illness. Colorados call them "angry lagoons." They are inhabited by the spirits of malicious sorcerers. Medicinemen, when treating a patient, invoke these demons with incantations.

Maoris have a god of earthquakes, and gods of rainbow, comet, lightning, and other supernatural phenomena. In Hawaii, Pele is a dreaded volcano goddess.

The Oraon show "reverential fear in the presence of certain mysterious supernatural powers and beings, and dependence on and conciliation and propitiation of and prayerful submission to them." [13] In the Malay peninsula the origin of rocks and waterfalls of unusual appearance is attributed to demons. Here, and in Java, most sacred places are solitary hills or spots which "present some great natural peculiarity." In the Malay peninsula and India, sunset, when the atmosphere is replete with mysterious phenomena, is a time of danger. In the former area the yellow glow of the last rays of the sun is especially dreaded. This "Yellow Deity" inspires terror. When it appears, children are called into the hut lest they fall victims to evil influences then abroad. "A great cataract, a difficult and dangerous ford in a river, a spring bubbling up from the ground, a volcano, a high mountain, an isolated rock, a curious or unusually large tree, intoxicants and stimulants, animals of unusual size or appearance, persons suffering from some abnormality, such as albinism or madness—all are looked upon by savages with superstitious regard or are propitiated with offerings." [14]

To Malacca Malays the grave of an albino is an especially sacred place. In Nias an albino child is usually killed; it is a spirit or ghost. The Lenge of Portuguese East Africa kill albinos and other infants who display some abnormality, doubtless because they fear the implied supernaturalism. In the Congo the albino becomes a priest.

Breasted believes the ancient Egyptian derived his first gods from his natural surroundings. Trees, springs, stones, hilltops, birds, and beasts were like himself; or they possessed strange and uncanny powers of which he was not master. "The visible world was first explained in terms of religious powers and the earliest gods were the controlling forces of the

12. Karsten, *op. cit.*, 350.

13. Sarat Chandra Roy, *Oraon Religion and Customs*, 2 (Ranchi, Man in India Press, 1928).

14. Westermarck, *op. cit.*, 6.

material world. A *social* or *political* realm, or a domain of the spirit where the gods should reign supreme, was not at first perceived." [15]

In Egypt "the Lord of Gods came as the north wind." In the Eighteenth Dynasty, Apep, or Apepi, the monster crocodile god who supplanted Set in the pantheon, caused thunder, lightning, hurricanes, sandstorms, rainstorms, eclipses, fog, mist, and darkness. To prevent such calamities priests made large models of crocodiles and burned them at stated intervals in the great temple of Amen Ra, at Thebes. The unusual was a marked element in the sacredness of animals. "Every animal, bird, or creature which was an object of worship possessed some special mark or characteristic which distinguished it from others of its class. Thus the black bull of Apis had a white triangular blaze on his forehead, the figure of an eagle (vulture or hawk?) on his back, the figure of a beetle on his tongue, and had double hairs in his tail. According to Aelian, Apis could be distinguished by twenty-nine distinct marks, which were known to the priests." [16] In Babylonia the god Ramman caused wind, rain, thunder, and lightning. In China earthquakes, eclipses, floods, and pestilences indicated that powers above were displeased by imperial sins. The threatened calamities might be averted by imperial prayers, pilgrimages, or contrite confessions.

Plutarch remarks of Homer: "Where the act is something out of the way and extraordinary, and seems in a manner to demand some impulse of divine possession and sudden inspiration to account for it, here he introduces divine agency." [17] Greeks were frightened when "strange things were seen among them. First of all sweet, fragrant wine ran streaming throughout all the black ship and a heavenly smell arose, so that all the seamen were seized with amazement when they saw it. And all at once a vine spread out both ways along the top of the sail with many clusters hanging down from it, and a dark ivy-plant twined about the mast, blossoming with flowers, and with rich berries growing on it; and all the thole-pins were covered with garlands." A god was aboard, and the pirates "bade the helmsman to put the ship to land." [18]

Unusual phenomena herald important events. In the first century A. D. Jewish apocryphal hope for the advent of the messiah depicts supernatural

15. James H. Breasted, *The Dawn of Conscience*, 18 (New York, Scribner, 1933). Italics in the original.
16. Sir E. A. Wallis Budge, *From Fetish to God in Ancient Egypt*, 67 (London, Oxford University Press, 1934). Reprinted by permission of the publisher.
17. Plutarch, "Coriolanus," *Lives*.
18. "To Dionysus," *Homeric Hymns*.

prodigies: "From heaven shall fall fiery swords down to the earth; lights shall come bright and great, flashing into the midst of men. . . . And God shall judge all with war and sword, and with fire and cataclysms of rain. . . . And then again all the sons of the great God shall live quietly around the temple, rejoicing in those gifts which He shall give who is the Creator and sovereign righteous Judge. For he by himself shall shield them standing beside them alone in his might, encircling them as it were with a wall of flaming fire. . . . And then all the isles and the cities shall say, 'How doth the Eternal love those men!' For all things work in sympathy with them and help them, the heaven and God's chariot, the Sun and the Moon." [19]

According to Tacitus, when, during the first century A. D., the Romans were besieging Jerusalem, "portents and prodigies announced the ruin of the city. . . . Swords were seen glittering in the air; embattled armies appeared, and the temple was illuminated by a stream of light, that issued from the heavens. The portal flew open, and a voice more than human denounced the immediate departure of the gods. There was heard, at the same time, a tumultuous and terrific sound, as if superior beings were actually rushing forth. The impression made by these wonders fell upon a few only: the multitude relied upon an ancient prophecy, contained, as they believed, in books kept by the priests, by which it was foretold, that, in this very juncture, the power of the east would prevail over the nations, and a race of men would go forth from Judaea to extend their dominion over the rest of the world. The prediction, however, couched in ambiguous terms, related to Vespasian and his son Titus. But the Jewish mind was not to be enlightened. With the usual propensity of men ready to believe what they ardently wish, the populace assumed to themselves the scene of grandeur which the fates were preparing to bring forward. Calamity itself could not open their eyes." [20]

During the time of Otho, many prodigies appeared, and there was general panic. "The goddess of victory, in the vestibule of the capitol, let the reins of two horses, harnessed to her chariot, fall from her hand. A form of more than human size was seen to issue from the chapel of Juno. In an island in the Tiber, the statue of Julius Caesar, without any apparent cause, on a day perfectly serene and calm, turned round from the west to the east. In Etruria an ox was said to have spoken; animals brought forth monstrous births; and to these was added a variety of preternatural

19. *Sibylline Oracles*, 3: 650–712.
20. Tacitus, *History*, Book V, 13.

appearances, such as in rude and barbarous ages were the coinage of superstition; and, even in profound peace, made an impression on vulgar credulity, though of late years they have so far lost their effect, that, unless it be a time of public distress, they pass away unheeded and forgotten. Amidst the omens, which seemed to threaten impending danger, an inundation of the Tiber was the most alarming. The waters swelled above their banks, and overflowed the adjacent country." [21]

Plutarch speaks of a rain of blood which signified the displeasure of the gods. At another time, after profanation of the temple of Vulcan, "on a sudden, strange and unaccountable disorders and altercations took place in the air; the face of the sun was darkened, and the day turned into night, and that, too, no quiet, peaceable night, but with terrible thunderings, and boisterous winds from all quarters." [22]

For the Hindu, contact with the unknown contains an element of incalculable power and may bring unexpected good or unforeseeable evil. Hence all things, animate or inanimate, that first come into contact with man are surrounded with an atmosphere of the mysterious and problematic. Their innate powers, *paygun*, occasion apprehension, and measures are taken to ensure as far as possible that new contacts bring weal and not woe. Practically always the potentiality of the unknown, especially critical at first ventures, demands protective measures against inherent potential evil consequences. In the unusual there is *sakti*, or holiness, that is, supernatural power, which averts the evil eye. Thus butter, milk and grain can be protected by an inverted measure; a cock with comb reversed is not liable to the evil eye; dolls hung upside down afford protection to the house and to butter and other comestibles. The evil *sakti* of the evil eye is attributed to many forms of the unusual; hence reversal of the usual negatives these circumambient dangers. A female buffalo which has the appearance of a male, with thick hide or tail, or which has three nipples, or a single horn bending forward, brings evil. Among the Santal, "when something is done or happens, different from the ordinary, without any observable cause, especially when it is of constant occurrence, it is supposed to be due to the 'command' of the higher powers." The Santal have a word for happenings which cause fright by "something not understood and supposed to be supernatural." [23] The sixth book of Manu declares that the *samyasin*, the Brahman ascetic, may not obtain alms by ex-

21. *Ibid.*, Book I, 86.
22. Plutarch, "Romulus," *Lives.*
23. P. O. Bodding, *Santal Folk Tales*, I, 156 (Oslo, Aschehoug, 1925).

plaining prodigies and omens. Important events, such as the birth of a god or even of a man, are heralded by omens. Omens and supernatural portents will reveal the successive reincarnations of the Bhutan Lama. Many portents heralded the birth of Buddha. There were earthquakes and miracles of healing; flowers bloomed and rains fell out of season; heavenly music and sweet scents filled the air; the water of the ocean lost its bitterness and became delicious.

The Vedas picture Agni as a god of fire and the Maruts as storm gods who make rocks tremble and devastate the forest. Ushas, the highborn dawn, shines upon men like a young wife, rousing every living being to go forth to his work. The Asvins, the Horsemen, first outriders of the dawn, are the first rays of sunrise, lords of lustre. The Solar Orb himself, Surya; the Wind, Vayu; the Sunshine, or Friendly Plant, Soma; and many other deities, are invoked in the Vedas, in all about thirty-three gods, eleven in heaven, eleven on earth, and eleven in mid-air. In their totality they are concerned with practically every startling natural phenomenon.

According to Moorish chroniclers portents and mysterious visions preceded the fight with the army of Roderick during the Mohammedan conquest of Spain. When, in 1526, the Moors of Aragon were forcibly converted, an image of the Holy Sepulchre in the Carmelite convent of Saragossa wept for twenty-four hours; and the images of Our Lady of Tobet and the associated angels sweated profusely for thirty-six hours. In 1590 Philip II devoutly begged a portion of the precious exudant, which had been collected and preserved against the needs of a future day. When, in 1610, the Moriscos were expelled, this marvellous fluid, including the portion which had been allotted the sovereign, evaporated.

In early New England, when witchcraft and other superstitions flourished, meteoric appearances and other unusual natural phenomena were revelations from a supernatural source. "A blazing spear, a sword of flame, a bow, or a sheaf of arrows, seen in the midnight sky, prefigures Indian warfare. We doubt," writes Hawthorne, "whether any marked event, for good or evil, ever befell New England, from its settlement down to Revolutionary times, of which the inhabitants had not been previously warned by some spectacle of this nature. Not seldom it had been seen by multitudes. Oftener, however, its credibility rested on the faith of some lonely eye-witness, who beheld the wonder through the colored, magnifying, and distorting medium of his imagination, and shaped it more distinctly in his after-thought." [24]

24. Nathaniel Hawthorne, *The Scarlet Letter.*

When the vineyards and grain-fields of Germany seemed to be supernaturally blessed, the spirit of Charlemagne, German tradition declares, has crossed to them over the golden bridge at Bingen.

In parts of modern Greece storms are attributed to elemental spirits at strife, and church bells are rung to frighten them away. They send the whirlwind. For protection against it men and women mutter "Meli-gala" —"honey and milk"—perhaps a survival of the ancient Greeks' libations of honey to the Furies. A thunderbolt is the "starry ax"; an earthquake is "God . . . shaking his hair." (Ancient Greeks called it the nod of Zeus.) They say "God rains" when we say "it is raining." In times of drought a little girl, who must be an orphan, as being more likely to obtain the blessings of Heaven, is clad in a vesture of leaves and crowned with flowers. Accompanied by other children singing as they go, Perperouna, as she is named for the occasion, makes the round of the village, and at every dwelling people sprinkle a few drops of water on her head as a prayer for rain. Formerly it was common practice during a storm to make passes in the air with a black-handled knife in order to "cut it." There is a peculiar virtue in the black handle; thus a black-handled knife under one's pillow will keep away nightmare.[25] Serbians say the saints met at the gate of heaven to divide the gifts which God had bestowed upon them, and made the following arrangement: St. Elijah took under his care the thunder; "Mary of the Fire" took the lightning and the arrows; St. Thomas, the seal of the clouds; Archangel Michael, the weather of autumn; St. Nicholas, the seas, the rivers, and the ships that sail upon them; St. Saviour, the cornflower; St. Sava, the snow and ice; St. Pantheleymon, the scorching heat of summer; St. George, the flowers of spring. They then began to punish the lawless people of India. They closed (probably with the keys of which St. Peter was the keeper) each of the seven heavens. St. Elijah struck the sinners with his thunder, and the Blessed Maria killed them with lightnings and arrows. This had slight effect. St. Archangel then sent down bad weather; Peter and Paul removed the wine and wheat for three years; St. Thomas sealed the clouds, so that no rain or morning dew watered the thirsty earth; St. Pantheleymon loosed the burning heat to scorch the earth for three years, until the brains of the people boiled, the rocks burned and broke up, and the earth burst into deep crevices which engulfed men and horses. St. Sava sent deep snows and for three years prevented the snow from melting, so that the shepherds lost all their sheep, and even the bees fled. Old

25. Ferriman Ducket, *Greece and the Greeks*, 246–247 (New York, 1910).

Serbians personified the forces and phenomena of nature and worshipped them as gods. Sun, and lightning accompanied by thunder, impressed them deeply. Daybog, or Dagog, who personified sun and sunshine, was giver of life and all good things, god of prosperity, light, and all benefits. Peroon personified thunder and lightning. The London doctor who, on a night of "violent storm and wind," observed, "it is a very fine night; the Lord is abroad," [26] was true to Jewish and Christian tradition.

Hegel regarded fear of "earthquakes, thunderstorms, floods, animals, which threaten with death," as the earliest form of religion.[27] Certainly, as Frazer remarked some two decades ago, "the influence which physical environment has exercised on the history of religion deserves to be studied with more attention that it has yet received." [28] Sir Walter Raleigh has said: "Nature is too much for one; it is impossible not to fear her a little, and so superstition seems natural." [29] But man does not fear nature; rather he fears those phenomena which he considers supernatural. Ferguson makes a keener analysis: "In what depends on the known or the regular course of nature, the mind trusts to itself; but in strange and uncommon situations, it is the dupe of its own perplexity, and, instead of relying on its prudence or courage, has recourse to divination, and a variety of observances, that, for being irrational, are always the more revered. Superstition being founded in doubts and anxiety, is fostered by ignorance and mystery. Its maxims, in the meantime, are not always confounded with those of common life; nor does its weaknesses or folly always prevent the watchfulness, penetration, and courage, men are accustomed to employ in the management of common affairs. A Roman consulting futurity by the pecking of birds, or a King of Sparta inspecting the entrails of a beast, Mithridates consulting his women on the interpretation of his dreams, are examples sufficient to prove, that a childish imbecility on this subject is consistent with the greatest military and political talents." [30]

26. Quoted in James Boswell, *Life of Samuel Johnson*, II, 377. Samuel Pepys records: "Waked with a very high wind, and said to my wife, 'I pray God I hear not the death of any great person, this wind is so high,' fearing that the Queen might be dead." He doubtless recalled the death of Cromwell in a high wind. Elsewhere in his diary he speaks of the fear of death aroused by a high wind.

27. Hegel, *Vorlesungen über die Philosophie der Religion*, I, 220.

28. Sir James G. Frazer, *The Golden Bough* (New York, Macmillan, 1935).

29. Sir Walter Raleigh, in Lady Raleigh (editor), *The Letters of Sir Walter Raleigh* (1879–1922), I, 58 (London, Methuen, 1926).

30. Adam Ferguson, *An Essay on the History of Civil Society*, 137 (Edinburgh, 1767).

Throughout the preliterate world the albino animal is sacred. The source of its sacredness is the awe which the unusual arouses, or the cleanliness or purity typified by whiteness. Animals which have other striking or uncanny characteristics are ominous or sacred. The night is dread as

> The time when screech-owls cry and lean dogs howl,
> And spirits walk and ghosts break up their graves.

The unseemly screech or hoot of the owl which goes abroad at night when other birds keep their perches arouses apprehension in civilized man, at times, as well as in the savage. There is an uncanniness in the cry of the owl, a penumbra of mystery about a bird which ventures forth into the darkness of the night while retiring and respectable birds sleep. Owlish habits suggest evildoers who go abroad in the darkness to do dark deeds while the innocent sleep. This bird of darkness arouses an ominous mood, a tone of melancholy with which its notes lugubriously chime. The ominous character of owl, crow, and raven arises from their inherently untoward characteristics.

The black coat of the raven or crow suggests lowering clouds and a dark day. These birds are not liked; they bring only evil tidings. In all cultures they make a similar appeal, although each culture interprets the appeal in specific fashion. Everywhere crow and raven arouse dismal feelings. Their appearance is funereal. Their black coat presents symbolically the dark side of life. The intelligence of ravens is uncanny. Their savage character and deep, harsh, humanlike voice no doubt partly account for the "vile reputation of the bird, and the sombre superstitions associated with it." That fear of albino and black feathered tribe, of owls which hoot lugubriously and behave ominously, should be found over widely separated and culturally unrelated portions of the globe is not an enigma. Human nature is similar and either spontaneously or under the stimulus of suggestion reacts similarly to like phenomena.

Preliterate and unsophisticated man is not at home throughout the realm of nature and natural forces. He fears phenomena which he does not comprehend. Fear is proportionate to wonder, and wonder is aroused to the extent that he views events as extraordinary, as falling outside the category of the uniformly recurring.

> No natural exhalation in the sky,
> No common wind, no 'customed event,

> But superstition, from its natural cause,
> Construes awry, and calls them prodigies,
> Signs, fatal presages, and tongues of heaven
> Plainly denouncing vengeance.

The specific character of these beliefs varies from one culture to another; but until the categories of sophistication intervene, emotional response to the extraordinary is much the same everywhere. This universal emotional response, therefore, we may regard as primary and as engendering the accompanying animistic interpretations, though the interpretations, in turn, stimulate the emotional response. Many of the specific interpretations of the supernatural are widely spread through contiguous areas and therefore imply considerable diffusion. The diffusion of such interpretations implies, in turn, a common psychological or logical need. Everywhere men stand in awe of phenomena which they do not comprehend.

Diffusion of animistic interpretations of the supernatural is facilitated by a predisposed attitude of attuned emotional response. In most cases the apparent irregularity of the startling phenomenon is the primary reason for regarding it as supernatural.

An intellectual element in the interpretation is indicated by the fact that events which in themselves are actually or potentially injurious—for example, eclipses, with diminution of light, earthquakes, and lightning, which occasionally do damage—are everywhere regarded as untoward and as foreboding ill.

But the inherent untowardness of such phenomena does not account for fear of a rainbow, a will-o'-the-wisp, a comet, phosphorescence, ghosts, and many other harmless supernatural phenomena. The incomprehensible character of the phenomena is responsible for the emotional reaction to them. Even when such phenomena contain a liberal element of potential danger, the fearsome apprehension which they arouse greatly exceeds the actual danger. "Many ghost-forms of spectres, with which no terrible *experience* can be individually connected, are much more uncanny than certain very substantial dangers, which we may easily have encountered in daily life." [31] If

> My heart leaps up when I behold
> A rainbow in the sky,

this may be, in part, because my ancestors have endowed the phenomenon with mystic significance; but it is also, in part, because the phenomenon

31. Wolfgang Köhler, *op. cit.*, 322. Italics in the original.

had an inherent psychological appeal to them and has such appeal to me. As Hume says, "convulsions in nature, disorders, prodigies, miracles, though the most opposite to the plan of a wise superintendent, impress mankind with the strongest sentiments of religion: the causes of events seeming then the most unknown and unaccountable. Madness, fury, rage, and an inflamed imagination, though they sink men nearest to the level of the beasts, are, for a like reason, often supposed to be the only dispositions in which we can have an immediate communication with the Deity." [32]

32. David Hume, *The Natural History of Religion*, Section VI.

CHAPTER III SACRED PLACES

Sacred places derive sanctity from inherent supernaturalism, from association with a sacred god, power, or person, or from performance of a sacred rite. Thus the cave of the naiads had two entrances: one for men, and one for the Deathless Ones, that is, the gods. The latter entrance "is holy indeed. No human foot may trespass there." [1] Persian legend declares that Zoroaster dedicated to Mithra a natural grotto in the mountains of Persia.

Alleged footprints of gods or holy men become sacred. Among the Venda of the northern Transvaal, as in central Africa, natives see in the rocks the footprints of the Creator left there when the rocks were soft. In Samoa two hollow places nearly six feet long in a rock are shown as the spot where Tütii stood when he pushed the heavens up from the earth. In the midst of a level plain at the summit of Adams Peak, Ceylon, stands a rock three feet high, five feet long, and two and a half feet wide, which bears marks resembling a footprint. Here was Paradise, and this impression is the footprint of the first man. Brahmans say it is the footprint of Siva; Buddhists regard it as the footprint of Gautama Buddha; to Christians the depression is the footprint of St. Thomas, or of the Eunuch of Candace, or the Queen of Ethiopia; Moslems regard it as the spot where Adam stood when he was driven from Paradise. Frequently, it seems, when Mohammed stepped on a rock, his foot sank into it and left its sacred impress. The most famous of such imprints is in the rock at Jerusalem from which he mounted for his journey to heaven. Similar footprints attributed to him are exhibited in Damascus, Cairo, Constantinople, and various localities in Mohammedan India. In Persia the footprints are attributed to Imams. Near Mishapur, in a beautiful tree-hidden shrine, a stone bears the huge impress of the foot of the Imam Rida. In a Rus-

1. Odyssey, Book XIII.

sian Orthodox shrine on the Mount of Olives whence Christ ascended to heaven is the imprint of his foot in the rock. A few yards away another Christian sect guards a shrine which contains the imprint of Christ's foot, made at his ascension.

Bethel, "House of God," referred originally to the sacred stone in which the deity dwelt: "Ye shall reverence my sanctuaries." [2]

The ground on which the Tahiti king stood became sacred, that is, taboo; hence he was carried by a bearer who, through contamination of sacredness, also became taboo. In Melanesia the place at which a powerful man was buried, or which a ghost frequents, is sacred and awesome, "never to be lightly invaded or used for common purposes."

To the Jibaro and Canella, of eastern Ecuador and Peru, places and localities are sacred which have something striking in their appearance, are connected with remarkable incidents, or are inhabited by spirits. In many cultures certain places derive sanctity from the unusual character of their natural features. Among Eskimos a locality is sacred by virtue of an inexplicable peculiarity which inspires belief that it is the residence of a soul or spirit. Inordinately bountiful food resources, for example, may imply the presence of supernatural forces or beings. Thus certain localities are sacred because for no evident reason caribou frequent them. Koksoagmiut Eskimos, of Ungava Bay, believe every prominent rock, bay, island, or other local feature the residence of a malignant spirit which must be propitiated by appropriate offerings.

Foremost among sacred places in early historic civilizations are high places—hills and mountains. Among the Canaanites and Jews of Old Testament times many high places were sacred, and on them sacrifices were offered. Abraham selected a high place on which to sacrifice Isaac. A thousand years previously high places were sacred in Palestine. Moses ascended Sinai to receive the Laws; there Yahweh appeared to him in clouds and a burning bush. Breasted refers the "peculiar manifestation of Yahweh as a 'pillar of fire' or a 'pillar of cloud,' and his appearance on Mount Sinai *by day* with 'thunders and lightnings and a thick cloud,'" to volcanic phenomena. Yahweh, he believes, was a volcano god, who resided in Mt. Sinai. "Through the influence of Moses the Hebrews cast out their ancient *els* (local gods) and adopted Yahweh as their sole god. Deliverance from Egyptian task-masters was accompanied by some terrible manifestation of Yahweh's power." [3] Perhaps, while the Israelites

2. *Exodus*, 20: 24; *Judges*, 13: 19; *I Samuel*, 14: 33, 35.
3. James H. Breasted, *The Dawn of Conscience* (New York, Scribner, 1933).

fled, there was an eruption of Sinai, which is a volcanic mountain, and a tidal wave from the accompanying earthquake may have engulfed the pursuing Egyptians. Thus when the Hebrews entered Yahweh's territory near Mt. Sinai, Yahweh delivered them by an awe-inspiring manifestation of his power and favour. But these may be vain surmises.

Zeus haunted the high places in the region inhabited by the Hellenes. The highest ground in Greek cities was usually crowned with his temple, and the summits of the loftiest mountains were sacred to him. "It was but natural for the high esteem in which the god was held to find its expression in the placing of his image or fane on a site physically high, and especially in the case of him whom the worshipper thought supreme."

The Welsh god of the dead, Gwyn ab Nud, showed similar predilection for high ground. Temples of the Gaulish Mercury crowned the Puy-de-Dôme, the Donon, and other elevations. "The choice of the god's seat of superiority seems to have been dictated, at least in part, by his solar origin and connection with the sky." [4] From the mountain-top he ruled the weather; there the clouds gathered before descending as rain to the plains; thence the flashes of the god's lightning burst forth; and thither the mists lazily crept. "Such were the phenomena which the ancient Greeks associated with Zeus." [4] A rich Welsh mythic poem refers to the Celtic Zeus as "blazer of the mountain-top."

Fear of the supernatural prevents the Balinese from climbing high mountains; the heights are reserved for the gods, the middle world belongs to men, and the lower regions of ocean and land belong to spirits of the underworld. The Ibo of Nigeria say the Thunder God frequently strikes tall trees and hill-tops because he is jealous of things which seek to approach his kingdom. Only the birds may venture with safety into the sky realm where he resides. Respect for high places probably inspired the taboo against climbing to any height—for example, up a tree trunk or over a wall or a fence. Civil war broke out among the people when the late chief Oosi built a "storey-house," that is, a two-storey building raised above the ground upon a foundation of piles, and permitted his women to mount the stairs. Isokpo Ibo chiefs were enraged because two men in their village built a "storey-house" and allowed their women to climb to the top rooms. "The chiefs declared that this endangered the safety of the town; for, should Amaoa Onhia, the Thunder God, hurl his bolt

4. Sir John Rhys, *Lectures on the Origin and Growth of Religion as Illustrated by Celtic Heathendom*, 182–183 (London, Williams and Norgate, 1888).

at the offending structure, peradventure he might punish the whole people for this disregard of his laws." [5]

In Africa, Guiana, the Andean region, Mexico, the Southwest of the United States, and the Northwest Coast area and the Northeast Woodland area of North America, sanctity attaches to certain mountains. Among the Okanagon of northern Washington, for example, two prominent peaks in the tribal territory are foremost places at which to acquire the power or guardian spirit. Inasmuch as sacred high places are usually associated with gods or spirits, the absence of sacred high places among many preliterate folk may be due to the comparative absence from these cultures of important aerial gods.

Other natural features may be sacred: valleys, ravines, caves, ocean, lakes, rivers, springs, rocks. There is abundant evidence of such sanctity in early civilizations north of the Mediterranean, particularly Greek and Roman, and in many preliterate cultures. Among the Rengma Nagas of Assam a particularly evil spirit lives in a certain pool which is believed to be bottomless. Among the Ekoi, of southern Nigeria, is a so-called Lake of the Dead, haunted by evil spirits, into whose boundaries no one dares venture. Nothing is allowed to trouble the water, even its outermost edge. The lake and the surrounding territory are thus a refuge for wild game, for no hunter dares penetrate it. Among the Venda the curious formation and unusual character of Lake Fundudzi, northern Transvaal, make it an object of peculiar awe. No one might visit it unless he was under the protection and care of a certain chief. This chief and his kin must take especial care not to offend the spirit dwellers of the lake, who will vent their anger by hurling stones from the lake onto the village. The spirits catch any article thrown into the lake and cast it out upon the bank, where men find it the following morning. Water of this lake placed in a receptacle forthwith vanishes; if sealed up for a day or two, it will burst the container; and it leaves behind it as testimony of its former presence a characteristic curious odour. A person who should wash or swim in the lake would be drawn down into it by the spirits. From beneath its waves comes music, like that of Venda flutes.

Throughout the Woodland area and the Plains area of North America deep lakes and pools in rivers are believed to be inhabited by monsters against which the Thunder Being has eternal enmity.

5. P. Amaury Talbot, *Some Nigerian Fertility Cults*, 58 (London, Oxford University Press, 1927).

The place of worship is usually sacred, particularly the edifice set apart for divine service. In the time of Tacitus, "even a Jew is not admitted beyond the portal [of the temple]. No man, except the priests, has access to the interior parts." [6] A Hindu temple consists of two ritually distinct parts, an inner and an outer part, each with distinctive sanctity. Iron, for example, may be taken into the outer part of the temple but not into the inner shrine. The only exception is the iron trisul of the god Siva, which is kept near his image. Among the Nigerian Ibo only the high priest can enter unscathed the central sanctuary in the temple of the Thunder God: supernatural punishment falls upon any other intruder. At the sanctuary, the sacred bush, or the sacred grove, no leaf may be plucked and no branch broken. When the sacred tree of a compound falls, the family to which it belonged marks the place where it formerly stood; a garden may not be made at that spot. Among the Tallis of the hinterland of the Gold Coast, the *bogar*, or sacred place, which may be a grove, a cave, or a small natural enclosure formed by trees and boulders, may be entered only for ritual purposes and in company of all ritual officiants. The Dahomey temple of Nana-Buluku may be entered only by the greatest and most powerful priests of the cult; for one who puts his foot within its precincts "learns how to speak a thousand tongues at once." Among Zulus the place of sacrifice, the cattle kraal, is sacred. Among the Bechuana, of South Africa, the places at which sacrifices are made are temporarily sacred. Among the Kikuyu an elder who is in a state of anger may not approach the sacred tree and one who on the previous day displayed anger toward wife, child, or a stranger may not come near it. If two elders or their people are having a blood feud, these elders would die if they approached the sacred tree.

In the Society Islands there were seldom any houses in the vicinity of a temple or *marae*. Except on days of feasts or religious ceremonies, an impressive silence, which even the priests and guardians of the temple dared not interrupt, reigned at the sacred precincts. No one would enter this enclosure unless obliged to do so; those who passed it observed strict silence, and uncovered to the waist while yet a long way off. Only priests might enter the temple at any time and might eat the flesh of animals offered in sacrifice or the fruits of the trees within the enclosure. In Hawaii only chiefs and priests may enter the temple enclosure. In Bali no outsider may enter the sacred temple of Tengavan Bah, "a small enclosure under a great Banyan tree surrounded by a wall of uncut stones

6. Tacitus, *History*, V, 8.

roughly piled up. Inside were a few mounds of the same stones, reminiscent of altars." In one of them was a larger stone with, apparently, a natural cavity. "This pile of stones is the only sacred 'essential' place of worship for the Tengavans, who are expert carvers and fine artists." In Madagascar one may not bring within the sanctuary of an idol, which includes a wide area about the idol's abode, any object or animal taboo to that particular idol. The things taboo to a certain idol include guns, gunpowder, figs, onions, a species of small shellfish, a young animal, striped or spotted robes, black objects, cats, owls, and meat which has been given away at a funeral.

In the Pueblo region of the United States, sacredness surrounds the *kiva*, the underground structure where priests prepare for important ceremonies. Among Zuñis, rooms in which sacred objects are kept may be visited only by members of the cult, and they may enter only officially, that is, for religious purposes. With the exception of the War God Sanctuary, which may be visited by any one who wishes to pray for good luck in war or in gambling, a sanctuary may not be visited even for purposes of prayer unless the ceremony is specifically public. A non-member who crosses the threshold of a room where a ceremony is being held is "caught" and initiated into the cult. If he is not qualified as an initiate, he is ceremonially whipped and must make specified payments to his ceremonial "father." In the Plains area the place at which the sun dance was performed retains a degree of sanctity, that is, of taboo, of apartness from the profane. A man will not camp at a spot where the grass has been trampled by participants or where the central pole still stands. In central Australia the vicinity of the place at which the *churinga*, venerated tribal and totemic heirlooms, are stored, is sacred. It is unseemly to quarrel, talk boisterously, or display weapons near by.

Universally, the altar is sacred. Such sanctity is characteristic of Judaism, Christianity, Hinduism, and Buddhism. Among Mayas and Aztecs permanent stone altars in or near the temple were invested with sanctity. The sand paintings of the Navahos which constitute their altar must be obliterated at the end of a ceremony, before sunset, lest their sacredness be profaned.

Sacred tombs of saints, prominent in Mohammedan, Buddhist, and Christian lands, are practically unknown in preliterate cultures. In India earth from a saint's tomb is preserved as a token and tied to cattle that are barren or give no milk. An Indian Mohammedan ties earth from an ancestor's tomb in a copper casket which he hangs from the neck of a sick child. Small cakes, about the size of a match-box, composed of dust from the mosque at Mecca and the tomb of the Prophet at Medina, mixed with water from the well Zemzem or from the holy spring Ain Zubida at Medina, are carefully preserved as curatives. Pilgrims from Mecca and Medina keep their travel-stained shirts because they contain sacred dust from these holy places.

Soil—a certain kind of soil, or soil from a particular place—may be sacred. Thus in Hawaii rich clayey soil from the lower part of Nuuanu Valley, which is forced out of the earth as if by geyser action, is regarded as connected with the goddess Mo-o-inanea, and is eaten and plastered on the hair. In Fiji one may not smite or strike the hole from which clay is taken to be used in making pottery. Among Jicarilla Apaches the clay used in making pipes for the rain ceremony must come from the place of emergence near Taos, and it may be taken only after certain prayers have been said. Peasants of southern and western Ireland regard the portion of the earthen floor of their houses immediately inside the threshold, which they call "the welcome of the door," as sacred, and clay from this spot has curative properties.

The sanctity of holy places usually derives from association with holy things. If celestial beings are prominent in the religion, high places are sacred, for they are literally near the abode of the gods. Hence the sacredness of high places in Mediterranean lands from earliest historic times to the present, and the sacredness of high places in other lands in which celestial beings are prominent—China, Japan, Persia, and India. The comparative absence of sacred high places in North America is in keeping with the comparative absence of important celestial gods. In other preliterate cultures in which celestial beings are of minor importance no great sanctity, and usually no sanctity at all, attaches to high places. In the Old World, diffusion doubtless has been an important factor in the spread of the concept of sacredness of high places. We infer that the sacredness of most high places in historic civilizations of the Old World derives from a common origin. Even so, the trait has spread only into areas conceptually prepared for it, presumably by the prior existence of important celestial beings. It is, of course, possible that the sanctity of high places developed celestial gods; but the absence of an innate powerful psychological appeal in high places, implied by the absence of such religious appeal in most preliterate areas, suggests that their sanctity is derived from the sacredness of aerial or supernal gods.

CHAPTER IV SACRED OBJECTS

Among the more important classes of sacred objects are fetish, idol, medicine-bundle, and garb and regalia used in religious rites.

FETISHES

The term *fetish* was originally employed by the Portuguese to denote magico-religious objects used by West Coast African Negroes. Most African Negro fetishes are small, are individually owned, and are not sold or exchanged. They are intimately associated with their possessor, bring good fortune, and fend off evil.

Their efficacy derives from a magic potency which partakes of the supernatural. Frequently the fetish is not distinguishable in appearance from profane objects. A powerful Ashanti fetish, for example, consisted of a broom resembling in every respect the household broom which sweeps rooms and compounds; indeed, it formerly served this purpose. The priest-medicineman sanctified it by investing it with every kind of taboo. He brought it into contact with every tabooed object, then, standing before it, uttered every proscribed name which ordinarily might not cross his lips, and which no one might utter in his presence with impunity. Thus the broom became instinct with virulent taboo, that is, became holy and a fetish.

The virtue of the Dahomey fetish is specific. It protects, specifically, house, or temple, or market, or field; prevents sickness, or accident; brings success in love, or in litigation; kills an enemy directly, or turns his magic disastrously against him. The virtues of Ganda fetishes are likewise specific and limited. One fetish gives protection against a particular disease; another against the king's wrath; another against being made a sacrificial victim; one ensures fertility; another brings success in hunting. A common type of Ganda fetish consists of an animal horn in which a powerful medicineman has placed herbs, clay, and magical substances, such as the heart of a lion, buffalo, or crocodile. In these fetishes gods accompany the warriors to battle. Some Ganda fetishes are carved or modelled in human form; some are disk-shaped, some crescent-shaped. Wood, herbs, roots, clay, and other material are used in various forms. On the lower Congo people rouse the fetishes to activity by blowing whistles at them, exploding gunpowder near them, or beating them with a stick. If they fail to accomplish their allotted tasks, they are thrown out onto the rubbish heap.

Objects commonly called fetishes are employed in the Pueblo region of the Southwest of the United States, among the Isleta, Hopis, and Zuñis. Fetishes of Zuñi rain priests have great sanctity; in them inhere the welfare of the people. To them and other sacred objects which possess magic properties devotees make periodic offerings of corn meal. At stated times, to pay them special honour, people remove them from their usual resting-places. They are inherently potent and establish contact with more powerful supernatural beings. Zuñi fetishes include *etowe*, fetishes of priests, and accompanying objects; stone images of beast-gods, some the property of a group, some individually owned; feathered ears of corn given to members of the higher order of societies at their initiation; and personal fetishes or amulets of various kinds.

Medicine, paint, feathers, and every article used in the regalia of the *katcinas* are sacred. The *etowe* of priests perform a function in Zuñi life comparable to that of the medicine-bundle in the Plains area. *Etowe* proper consists of bundles of plugged reeds filled with seeds or water; miniature frogs; pots of sacred paint; and a miscellaneous assortment which includes obsidian knives, arrow-points, "thunder stones" (naturally polished round stones which are rolled over the floor during the performance of ceremonies), and rattles of olivella shells. They may contain *miwe* also, objects brought by ancestors of the Zuñis from the lowermost of the four worlds, from which the tribal ancestors emerged. These, "the ones that were at the first beginning," reside in sealed jars in houses in which, so Zuñis assert, they have remained since the settlement of the village. At each mealtime they are "fed" by a woman of the house in which they are kept. From these resting-places they are removed only when taken to a retreat provided in their honour. Masks, too, are fed regularly. Some are "from the beginning." Such masks are tribal property administered in trust by self-perpetuating ceremonial or cult groups.

Zuñis do not lay a ceremonial mask down casually. If there is no special place to receive it, they hang it on the wall.

Each member of the higher or curing orders of the medicine societies possesses an ear of corn wrapped in feathers; this is his personal amulet or fetish and is destroyed at his death. Some men carry pieces of medicine roots or packages of red paint as fetishes; some have pebbles and sticks of black paint from which they seek help in special emergencies, and which they honour with prayer and song. Perfect ears of corn and ears with flattened ends have protective power. Sacred objects are taboo to those who do not "belong" to them. The strength of this feeling varies with the power of the fetish. Only the chief of the priesthood will touch a priest's fetish or enter the room where it is kept. A similar statement applies to the permanent masks and society altars. When those who keep a *Ca'loka* mask move to a new house, they summon the head of the kiva, whose mask they have, to transfer it, for they are afraid to touch it. Corn fetishes, prayer-sticks, and ceremonial garments are handled with great respect.[1]

In Tibet amulets are mainly sentences ascribed to Buddha, but these are supplemented by relics of saints, consecrated grain, miniature images, and other objects.

IDOLS

An idol is a three-dimensional representation of a god or religious power, and in this respect differs from a fetish, which is a medium of religious or supernatural power but not a representation of it. Psychologically there is, perhaps, no fundamental distinction between respect for a drawing of the god and respect for an image in wood, stone, or metal; as a matter of practice, however, only images are called idols. Thus defined, idols are rare in preliterate cultures. They are common in Buddhism, Christianity, and most religions of early Mediterranean cultures; Judaism and Mohammedanism prohibit the use of them. Idols, inasmuch as they are representations of gods, are often treated as though instinct with intelligence and possessed of needs and appreciations characteristic of gods. Hindu priests who minister to idols in the temples wake them in the morning, bathe them, paint their faces, dress them, burn incense and wave lights before them, and present them with flowers, drinking-water,

1. Ruth L. Bunzel, "Introduction to Zuñi Ceremonialism," *ABE*, 47: 502 (1929–1930).

and cooked food, chiefly rice. The food is afterward consumed by priests or distributed among worshippers. In Bali, however, the gods are worshipped only in spirit, and their images or representations are not holy unless it is supposed that the gods temporarily occupy them. There was appreciation of the psychology of idol worship in the Hebrew prohibition against bowing down before graven images, and in Mohammed's command that his followers make no representation of beast or man; for there is a tendency to substitute the image for the god which it represents.

The Chibcha of Colombia had idols in wood, clay, cotton, wax, copper, and gold. To the many idols in the temple priests made offerings to induce them to intercede with Sun or Moon and persuade the god to grant the prayer of the petitioner. Offerings consisted of textiles, emeralds, gold figures of men, beasts, birds, reptiles, or insects, and gold tiaras or other gold ornaments. They were deposited in vases having the form of a human figure, sunk in the ground to the neck, and covered with clay or feathers. When the vase was full, it was removed and the contents buried in a secret place.

Temple idols the Chibcha usually arranged in pairs. Individuals kept private idols in their huts or carried them in small baskets. They guarded the possessor against illness and conveyed other benefits. Idols of wood, pottery, and gold were used also in Antioquia, southern Cauca, and among the Sutagao, south of the Chibcha.

Stone images of gods were made in many parts of Polynesia. In Mangaia there were carved images of the more important deities. Rongo was represented in stone, other gods in wood. These images were kept in the tribal temple, and priests had other images in their houses. Stone images of gods were used in the Ellice Islands. In Fakaofo (Bowditch Island) there were images of the gods, the largest of which, nearly fifteen feet high, was covered with mats.

MEDICINE-BUNDLES

Medicine-bundles, used in the Plains area of North America and in the adjacent Central Woodland area, constitute a special class of sacred objects. They contain various things, such as down of a wild goose, feathers or claws of a crow or other bird, pieces of shrubs or of trees, and, in many cases, a supernatural stone, that is, one which has an unusual shape, was found in a *wakan* spot, or is believed to be a fragment of a fallen star. Songs accompany the use of the medicine-bundle, and apart from them it has no efficacy. Medicine-bundles are individually owned. Among the

RIGHT

The top of the circular altar at Tikal, Guatemala

BELOW

The boulder altar at Quiriguá, Guatemala

LEFT

A Toda temple

BELOW

The singing of the eight traditional songs in a Hopi antelope *kiva*

Blackfoot sale or purchase of them constitutes a major economic enterprise. The objects in them and the songs which accompany them are secured through dream or vision. A Sarsi beaver bundle contained a small bag of buffalo scrotum (filled with dried saskatoon berries), eight rattles, a digging-stick, one beaver skin, one skin of a white muskrat, the tail of a buffalo, the stem of a pipe, two buffalo stones, two elk ribs, the skins of prairie dog, young deer, antelope, sheep, and birds, and a pair of wristlets made from wild cat claws.

CEREMONIAL DRESS

The distinctive dress, vestments, or decorations used during performance of, or preparation for, a religious ceremony are, as a rule, sacred. They may be worn only by the officiant, who usually may employ them only when performing the appropriate rites. When a Toda priest leaves the premises of the dairy, he must deposit there the garment which he wears when performing his services as *polol*, or priest, and resume it when he returns. An Oglala Dakota candidate for the sun dance wears a red shirt made of soft tanned deerskin, a cape made of otterskin tanned with the fur on, two armlets made of hair shed from a buffalo, and two anklets of rabbit skin tanned with fur on. He carries a whistle made from the ulnar bone of an eagle wing and a hoop made of willow withe. When he enters the Sacred Lodge in the ceremonial camp, he is provided with these articles, and also with a pipe and a supply of tobacco that will last through the four days of the ceremony. These regalia would be inappropriate, if not taboo, at any other time.

When the Malay medicineman or priest builds the altar for the preliminary sacrifice at a mine, he wears a black coat. No one else may wear a black coat, and he may not assume this garb on any other occasion. In Ontong Java sacred regalia impart sanctity to priests who wear them, and ordinary men may not go near priests who are wearing their regalia. Priests beat fans to warn of their approach, that others may retire. During the interval when the regalia are removed, as they must be when an ordinary act is performed, such as eating or bathing, the priest loses his sanctity. When the Chinese *sai-kong*, member of an order of priesthood, officiates at religious sacrifices, he wears a square, sleeveless silk garment embroidered on the back. The garment has magic significance; it represents the shape of the earth as conceived in primitive Chinese philosophy, invests its wearer with the power of the order of the world, the *Tao*, and enables him to restore that order.

During participation in sacred acts, an Israelite worshipper wore special garments, washed his ordinary garments before and, for greater safety, after the ceremony, or borrowed for the occasion a garment, which subsequently remained in the holy place. In pre-Islamic times the last mentioned practice was observed at Mecca, in the sanctuary of Al Djalsad, in the cult of the Tyrian Baal at Samaria (*II Kings*, 10: 22), and perhaps at Jerusalem—if the ephod which David wore when he danced before the Ark was a priestly dress (*II Samuel*, 6: 14). The sacred rite might be celebrated without the wearing of any clothing. This was the custom of certain Bedouins at the Kaaba, and Israelites and Babylonians seem to have been familiar with the practice. An Arab who failed to observe any one of the prescribed precautions must, on leaving the sanctuary, abandon his garments, which he might not wear or sell. The motive for the precautions was the concept, common among primitive peoples, that clothing is particularly liable to be impregnated by contiguous influences. Clothing may bring hostile influences into the sacred precincts, or carry the sacred into profane surroundings. Hence Jewish priests must remove, in the inner court, the dress in which they have officiated, "in order that they may not sanctify the people by their garments." [2]

ALTARS

As mentioned in the preceding chapter, the altar is sacred. Zuñis call altars the "sacred" or "taboo." Acoma Pueblo Indians prefer an altar made of wood from a tree which has been struck by lightning, preferably one from Mt. Taylor. When the altar is too old for further use, it is hidden in a canyon or on a mountain, lest it be profaned or dishonoured.

Among the southern Okanagon of Washington, the dance pole used in the winter dance was removed to the woods at the termination of the ceremony and "placed upright against a tree, where it was abandoned." If, while the post was being used in a ceremony, a person with insufficient power touched it, his hand "froze" to it and could not be withdrawn. "If any one, with or without power, foolishly touched it out of his turn, his soul would leave his body and become attached to it." [3]

OTHER SACRED OBJECTS

Among Zulus the instrument used in sacrifice is holy. This is a special ancestral assagai which has been handed down from father to son. Leaves

2. *Ezekiel*, 44: 19.
3. Walter Cline, in "The Sinkaiethk or Southern Okanagon of Washington," Leslie Spier (editor), *General Series in Anthropology*, 6: 147, 150 (1938).

which fall from the sacred Bo Tree in Ceylon are sacred and are carried away by pilgrims as highly treasured objects. Even the silkworms which feed upon them share the tree's sanctity. At Kandy, Ceylon, in a Buddhist temple reposes a tooth of Buddha on a golden leaf enclosed in seven jewelled caskets. In the fourteenth century Sir John Maundeville referred to the plurality of sacred relics in Europe and Syria: "and some men say that the head of St. John is at Amiens in Picardy; and other men say that it is the head of St. John the Bishop; I know not which is true; but God knows. But, howsoever men worship it, the blessed St. John is satisfied." [4] This traveller found four different crowns of thorns preserved as relics in as many places. Each, he explains, was used at a certain stage of the torture. There were also two spear-heads which had pierced the side of the Saviour, one somewhat larger than the other. Of course, not all the devout were aware of these discrepancies; but there is reason to suppose that most of them would not have been greatly troubled had the facts been known to them. A volume could be filled with illustrations of similar practices in Christianity. Thus at Turin, Italy, on May 4, 1931, the holy shroud, known as the "clean linen cloth" which covered the body of Christ after he was removed from the cross, was exhibited to the public for three weeks. The shroud was removed from its jewel-studded marble case in the chapel of the cathedral of Turin and carried into the main section of the church, a ceremony witnessed only by members of the reigning house of Savoy, owners of the garment, high churchmen, and a few guests. The controversy which had raged for centuries over the authenticity of the shroud, and which was particularly violent when it had been last exposed, in 1898, was not resumed.

CONTAGIOUS HOLINESS OF SACRED THINGS

The sacred place imparts added sanctity to the bones of the holy man deposited in it; conversely, the body of a sacred person imparts sanctity to the burial place: martyrs sanctify their resting-places. There is sanctity in the cross, the swaddling clothes of the babe Jesus, the thorns about his brow when he was crucified, the pillar to which he was bound, the stairs which he ascended. A shrine holds the toenails of St. Peter; hair or shreds of clothing of saints are highly prized possessions. Thousands of such precious relics are deposited in European sanctuaries, many of which are important centres of pilgrimage for the devout.

4. Quoted in G. G. Coulton, *Medieval Panorama: The English Scene from Conquest to Reformation*, 441 (New York, Macmillan, 1938).

The Hindu obtains *punya,* or merit, by bathing in a river, particularly when the *sakti,* or virtue, of water is greatest; by entering the precincts of a sacred shrine; by touching a temple or things in contact with divinity. The sight of things which possess power confers *punya*—the sight of images, of even a distant temple spire, of holy men. Contact with power by wearing things which possess power brings *punya* to the wearer. Touching sacred books, the feet of priests, saints, a bridal pair, or the dead, confers *punya.* By applying to his person earth or water from the enclosure in which the tulsi plant grows, a man may acquire *punya;* and seeing and touching certain trees confers *punya.* One may acquire *punya* by seeing and touching a cow; or by sprinkling over his person the urine of a cow, or the water found in the footprint of a cow. By touching or taking things which have acquired *sakti,* sacredness, by virtue of contact with divinity, a man acquires *punya.* Things which contain *sakti* and are capable of imparting *punya* include leaves and flowers used in worship; offerings of food made to a god; the coconut broken before an image; sandalwood paste used in worship; incense burned and waved before an image; lights waved round a god; water in which an image has been immersed.

NAME

The name of the sacred may also be sacred. Thus, although the Egyptian Mohammedan is not averse to taking the name of Allah in vain, he nevertheless is careful not to desecrate it. The name *Mohammed Ali,* for example, the name of the Prophet's cousin, should not be branded on an animal, even though this is the name of the owner of the beast, for the animal might bring the name into contact with something unclean. During the last century Mohammedans objected to the printing of books, for every book contains the name of Allah, and the book might fall into the hands of infidels. Even secular books begin, "In the name of God, the Compassionate, the Merciful." The ink which forms the name *Allah* might not be applied with a brush made of pig's hair, for the pig is unclean. The Koran is especially sacred and is defiled by the touch of Jew or Christian. The writer while travelling in Mohammedan lands suffered expropriation of an English translation of the Koran; its possession by a Christian is resented by the Faithful. The name of the Japanese Mikado is so sacred that it is seldom mentioned, and indeed is not known to a great portion of the public. A few years ago, when a Japanese mayor discovered that he had given his son the name which the Emperor bore, he resigned and, in extenuation of the breach of propriety, killed himself.

To guard against irreverent use of the sacred name of Yahweh the laity ceased to pronounce it. Only the priests at the benediction and, after the death of Simon the Just, only the high priest, and he with bated breath, so as to render it inaudible even to his colleagues, pronounced the "unutterable name." The correct pronunciation of the name was revealed only to the pious and humble. In Morocco, when a Jew has been ill for a long time and all approved remedies have proved futile, ten rabbis meet at the bedside of the patient and bestow another name upon him. This new name he will bear after his recovery. The patient abandons to the evil spirits the name which formed an integral part of his individuality and thus turns away the wrath from the new personality; for the owner of the new name is conceived to be a new personality. In Ethiopian belief the Three Persons of the Trinity existed in the primeval ocean, which had been their abode for ever; but they existed in name only. Each Person of the Trinity acquired his Personality only after reciting his own name.

In the summer of 1913 the monastic communities of Mt. Athos were convulsed by the controversy which the Holy Synod later condemned as the "heresy of the Name of God." The heresy was inspired by a book published by a Russian monk, Ilarion, bearing the title *In the Mountains of the Caucasus*. Ilarion argued that the name of God, being part of God, is divine and should be worshipped. His teaching was welcomed with enthusiasm by the monks of the monasteries of St. Andrew and St. Pentelemon. The Russian Government, fearing that the heresy if not stamped out would spread like wildfire among the ignorant Russian peasantry, suppressed it and deported six hundred of the heretical monks to Russia, where they were distributed as prisoners in various monasteries.

Among the Todas, the powers of the sorcerer depend largely upon a knowledge of the proper words and especially on a knowledge of the names of the four gods. The near identification of the name with the object signified by it explains such customs as the use by Todas when praying, not of the usual names of the gods, but of special *Kwarzam* names; the prohibition against taking the name of God in vain; the custom among old-fashioned people in Lincolnshire at the end of the eighteenth century of making it a "matter of conscience when they read Holy Scripture, or talked on religious subjects, to speak of the 'devil'; but when they had occasion to use the word in oath, or in talk of lighter sort, to be careful to say 'divil.' "

The concept of contagion underlies the sanctity of many sacred objects. Association of ideas generates and supports the concept.

When one thinks of the sacred place, one thinks of the things in it; when one thinks of the sacred service, one thinks of the objects used during its celebration; when one thinks of the objects or the clothing associated with a martyr, one thinks of him and his holiness. Hence the facile extension of holiness: things associated with the holy themselves become holy. Holiness may be more or less circumscribed, more or less concentrated spatially, but it cannot be confined to a mathematical point. It radiates and percolates, and embraces things in its locality, especially those habitually used in religious rites. The temple, and the things within it, are sacred. Inasmuch as sanctity attaches to the edifice, it attaches also to things which are used in the service, such as censer, chasuble, communion cup, altar. Among the Ganda the vessels of the priests were kept in the temple and were sacred. One might not touch them. In some temples, however, the priests poured beer from their cups into those of the people, and those who thus received the beer might drink it with impunity. Religious service is sacred; hence also things used during the service are sacred. So, too, the sacred place imparts sanctity to things in its locality. The underlying concept is contagion, diffusion of sanctity by contact or contiguity.

Contagious or radiant potency characterizes the magico-religious. It is illustrated in Melanesian *mana*, which spreads, by contact, to place, object, or person; in the Eskimo concept of uncleanness; in the Jewish concept of the holiness of sacred things, and likewise in the concept of things unclean, that is taboo. The concept is prevalent in Christianity, and is exemplified in, for example, the ceremony of the laying on of hands.

CHAPTER V SACRED TREES

Some species of trees are endeared to a people because of their remarkable utility. Thus the strong roots of the *Trichillia emetica* tree provide the Lenge of Portuguese East Africa with handles for hoes, and from the wood of the trunk they manufacture large spoons, food bowls, and the sacred goblets used in offering libations to ancestral spirits. The burning bark produces a clear blue flame. With its white ashes, mixed with ashes from another wood, they make a whitewash the whiteness of which is not surpassed by the European commercial product. The dead branches furnish good fuel; the smaller branches provide the sacred brush which is dipped into the magic mixture sprinkled on nuts to drive away evil spirits and sorcerers; and the fruit furnishes food and oil.

From the date palm, to cite another example, Arabian Egyptians obtain bread, honey, wine, and vinegar. From the stones of the fruit, smiths make charcoal; shepherds and herdsmen soften them and mash them into food for their herds and flocks. The natives celebrate in verse and in prose three hundred and sixty uses of trunk, leaves, juice, and fruit of this tree. Little wonder, then, that such trees are greatly respected.

Perhaps Anatole France's reference to the "first image of the gods, a tree," is a wrong conception, but sacred or mystic qualities have been attributed to trees, or to some particular tree or species of tree, from the dawn of history. Crooke suggests that in northern India the sacredness of the tree arises from the fact that the tree embodies many utilities necessary to human life, and many qualities which menace life. Its wood is the source of fire, itself a fetish. Its fruit, juice, flower, or bark supplies food, intoxicants, or poisons, and the latter two suggest demoniacal or magical influences. Some trees develop curious or uncanny forms, which compel fear or adoration. Thus trees which have been struck by lightning or knocked down by inundation, which have fallen toward the south, which have grown on a burying ground, at a consecrated site, at the confluence of large rivers, or by the roadside, which have withered tops, which support an entanglement, heavy creepers, many honey-combs, or birds' nests, may not be used in the making of bedsteads, for they are inauspicious and will bring disease and death. "The step from such beliefs to the worship of any curious and remarkable tree is easy." [1]

In ancient Egypt a tree was apparently sometimes the residence of a spirit. In the Egyptian sky world, the "Isle of the Blest," a tree of life, a "milk-yielding tree," gave sustenance to the soul. Amon was "creator of the tree of life." On a tall sycamore east of the sky, which stood before the doors of the sky, the gods sat. Two sycamores were on the farther side of the sky. These the king took hold of when he had been ferried to the sky world and deposited on the east side of the sky. In late Osirian myth a sycamore grew in the tomb of Osiris and enveloped the body of the dead god, to become the visible symbol of his imperishable life.

In the fourth millennium B. C. the sacred tree was portrayed in the art of Asia Minor and the eastern Mediterranean area, including the Aegean. Seals from the Indus valley, probably made in the third millennium B. C., contain the sacred pipal tree (*Ficus religiosa*) from the stem of which spring the heads of animals. On Babylonian and Assyrian monuments and seals the sacred palm tree is portrayed in various forms, sometimes naturalistically, sometimes conventionally. In cuneiform inscriptions from Susa "cedar tree" is a part of the Deity's name. The bisexual palm was sacred, and its fertilization was a religious rite. The sacred palm tree stood at the "holy place." Its roots, of bright lapis lazuli, planted in the cosmic abyss, marked the centre of the world. Its foliage formed the couch of the goddess Bahu. The god Tamuz dwelt in the shrine under the shadow of its branches, a place which no mortal had entered. An oracle was attached to this sacred palm tree, the "holy tree of Eridu," which was also a tree of life.

In Ezekiel's conception of Paradise the tree is not a palm but a cedar. His concept suggests the sacred grove of cedars described in the Babylonian Gilgamesh epic. The palm tree, which in Egypt, Babylonia, and Assyria was a tree of life, plays a rôle also in Jewish religion: "And you shall take you on the first day the fruit of goodly trees, branches of palm-trees, and boughs of the thick trees, and willows (or poplars) of the brook." [2]

1. W. Crooke, *The Popular Religion and Folk-Lore of Northern India*, II, 85–86 (London, Constable, 1896).
2. *Leviticus*, 23: 40.

The Hebrew word for myrtle is possibly connected with Assyrian *hadasatum*, "bride"; the myrtle was sacred to Astarte, goddess of fertility. The willow (or poplar, or viburnum) grows by the water and thus symbolizes moisture. The tree of good and evil, and the tree of life, in the Jewish Garden of Eden, also imply Babylonian influence. The sacred groves referred to in the Old Testament are probably relics of Baal worship.

Zoroastrians revere the poplar, the lily, the cotton plant, and other plants which turn toward the sun. The devout "make themselves like those flowers in faith and action, high and fragrant." Archangels guard the vegetable world; and to them the lily and the camba are consecrated. The tree Gokart, or white Ham, forestalls decrepitude, revives the dead, immortalizes the living, is the source of all medicines, and a component of the food which bestows eternal life upon all.

In Vannic, proto-Armenian, religion, a prominent object of veneration is the sacred vine, planted by the side of the temple of Khaldis, or in a sacred enclosure of its own. Sar-duris II describes his endowment of a vine, which he consecrated on the north shore of the lake of Van and named after himself. Frequently the vine is planted in the middle of a garden adjacent to the temple.

Herodotus and Aelian say that Xerxes in his important expedition against Greece tarried an entire day in the desert of Lydia, to pay homage to a large plane tree,[3] on the branches of which he hung rich garments, bracelets, and other precious ornaments. On the following day he proceeded on his march but left a soldier to guard the honoured tree. Greeks associated trees and flowers with the worship and ritual of Apollo, and various myths explain the association.

At Ephesus the olive and the oak were sacred to Artemis; and at Delos, a palm tree. Dionysus was a tree god. There were sacred groves at Dodona, and elsewhere.

Among tenth-century Byzantine Greeks olive trees were sacred. When the modern Greeks of Siphinos, one of the Cyclades, cut down a tree inhabited by a spirit, they prostrate themselves humbly and in silence, when the tree falls, lest the escaping spirit chastise them for destroying its abode. The concept suggests the hamadryads of ancient Greece. The religious importance attaching to the tree in ancient Greece is attested by the fact that the oldest image of Artemis, at Ephesus, was placed in the

3. Compare the air in Handel's opera *Xerxes* in which the hero addresses the plane tree, a melody better known as Handel's Largo. (I am indebted to Mr. Theodore McClintock for this reference.)

hollow stem of an elm tree. Pausanias saw the image of Artemis Kedreatis in a large cedar at Orchomenos. Many later sculptors display small divine images on the stem or branches of protecting trees. The third order of men referred to by Hesiod sprang from ash trees. Hesiod, Eustathius says, declared men sprang from oaks, stones, and ash trees.

A tradition associated with the temple of Dodona declares that oaks first gave prophetic utterances. "The men of that day," says Plato, "deemed that if they heard the truth from 'oak or rock' that was enough for them." In their purification ceremonies ancient Greeks used laurel leaves and pig's blood.

Two trees in Rome were given divine honours: the oak of Jupiter Feretrius, on the Capitoline, and the *Ficus ruminalis*, on the slopes of the Palatine.

Cato tells a woodcutter how to escape the consequences of thinning a sacred grove. One must first sacrifice a pig and then beg permission to thin the grove in order to restrain its tendency to overgrowth.

Plutarch speaks of a grove of Marica, in Italy, "which the people hold sacred and make it a point of religion not to let anything that is once carried into it to be taken out."

Among ancient Arabs the tree Dhat Auwat, "that on which things are hung," received divine honours. Weapons and other objects were suspended from it. A sacred palm tree was decked with apparel. At Hahla the goddess Uzza was worshipped in the form of three trees. The garments, rags, and other objects placed on such trees Nöldeke regards as substitutes for sacrifice. Sacred trees to which rags are attached are found at the present day in Arabia, Asia Minor, Syria, and Mohammedan central Asia.

In Morocco rags are placed on trees near the tomb of a saint. To compel the dead saint to grant a request the leaves of palmetto or the stalks of white broom are tied in the vicinity of the grave. The olive tree is sacred, because the name of God is written on its leaves. Trees pray during the day and sleep at night. If they neglect their duties to God and their obligation to pray, they may be cut down and torn up. Hence the trees themselves are responsible for their being cut down and made into a house. A man who tears up a tree without good reason exposes himself to speedy death, or may see his family perish. Trees are respected, and may not be polluted. If the branch of a tree strikes one, one should not swear at it, abuse it, or break it. On the contrary, one should beg the tree's pardon for hurting it, and say: "O Tree, daughter Tree, forgive me!"

In Indo-Germanic lands people transfer diseases to trees. When the pilgrim to the little chapel of St. Therapin, near Acheron, in Mytilene, has recovered his health, before leaving for home he hangs up a piece of his clothing on a tree near the chapel. The traveller Newton saw a bush covered with shreds of old clothes. At the present day the chapel and the tree are the scene of similar observances. The hanging of rags on a tree or bush as evidence of a malady left behind, or as evidence of the suppliant's plea for cure, is a widespread custom in European lands, particularly in central and southeastern Europe. The practice is based on the belief that evil can be transferred from oneself to another object through the medium of the clothing of the sufferer. In Persian legend the tree of the Sun and Moon spoke to King Alexander and warned him of his death. Men who keep these trees and eat their fruit will live to be four or five hundred years old.

As stated above, the sacred tree is found on Indian carvings which date from about 3000 B.C. Much attention was given by the followers of Gautama, the Buddha, to the tree under which he had his vision. This fig tree, the Bo Tree, from the day of the vision or shortly thereafter was treated with considerable respect. It has long since perished; but close by is another great tree which may be its descendant. In Ceylon is the oldest historical tree in the world, planted as a cutting from the Bo Tree in 245 B.C. "From that time to this it has been carefully tended and watered; its great branches are supported by pillars, and the earth has been terraced up about it so that it has been able to put out fresh roots continually." The Vedas declare the sami tree has an evil influence upon the hair. Hindus say the soul of the dead clings to the tree under which the deceased was buried, or which served as the coffin. Hence the saying, "the fathers creep about the roots of trees." Hindus consider it dangerous for a woman to be married a third time; accordingly, when a woman is to be married for the third time, the bridegroom is first betrothed to a tree, which is supposed to die in the woman's stead.

To Nambutiri Brahmans the tulsi or sacred basil (*Ocimum sanctum*) is the most sacred of plants. It contains the essence of Vishnu and Lakshimi; some legends say it is the metamorphosis of Sita and Rukmini. The udumbara tree (*Ficus glomerata*) also is sacred. Under this tree Dattatraya, incarnation of the trinity, performed his ascetic austerities.

Throughout southern India the bel or bilva (*Aegle marmelos*) is sacred to Siva. Kusa grass is sacred and is used in many ceremonies. The *Ficus religiosa* (pipal) is pervaded with the spirit of Brahma and is sacred.

During Puranic times various beliefs grew up regarding the sacredness of the pipal tree. The base of the tree is the residence of Brahmadev, the middle part houses Vishnu, and the topmost part is the abode of Siva. Shri Krishna breathed his last under the pipal tree. The *munja* or *navjot* ceremony is performed at this tree. An embankment is built around it. Barren women encircle the tree a hundred thousand times to induce it to send them a child. A square stone with serpents carved on it is placed at the foot of the tree, and an investiture ceremony is performed, to remove barrenness. An old pipal tree at Prachi, a village near Prabhas Pattan, in Kathiawar, is visited by thousands of persons in the hope that they will be blessed with children; and the desires of many of them are fulfilled. A learned Brahman who dies celibate chooses the pipal tree as his abode. Owing to the extreme reverence paid the pipal tree, it is never cut. Hindus and Buddhists consider it a sacrilege to cut even a branch of it. A Gujarat legend avers that blood issued from a pipal tree when some one tried to cut it. Similar traditions attach to oak and pine trees, which once were sacred in Europe. The pipal is the haunt of good and evil spirits, such as *munja*, elves, jinn, and *vetal*. People worship the tree with a view to propitiate it and to avert its evil influence or wrath. The pipal tree is also the abode of the Fire God. Hence sacrificial fire is created by rubbing a piece of pipal wood against another by means of a device called *arani*. Small pieces of wood of specified trees, called *samidha*, are employed for pouring the ghee used to ignite sacrificial fire. Pipal *samidha* are the best for this purpose.

In Slavonic and Hindu belief trees of paradise produce golden fruit. In the Hindu paradise are trees of precious stones, and trees of gold which shine like fire. They continuously bear flowers and fruit, swarm with birds, are of heavenly smell and touch, and satisfy all desires. Other trees produce clothing of various sorts and shapes. There are also trees on which beautiful maidens grow pendant from the branches.

On the northern side of Mt. Meru are trees which bear sweet fruits and are always covered with fruits and flowers. The fruits are of excellent taste, the flowers fragrant. Some of the trees yield fruits adapted to the tastes of whosoever comes to pluck them. The milk-producing trees yield six different kinds of food possessing the flavour of amrita itself. The trees which yield clothes have in their fruits ornaments for the use of man.

South of Mt. Meru grows the gigantic jambo tree Sudarsana, which touches the skies, and bears fruit 1,115 cubits in circumference. When the fruits fall to the ground, they make a loud noise, and exude a silvery juice. The juice of the jambo becomes a river, and passes circuitously round Mt. Meru to the region of the northern Kurus. "If the juice of that fruit is quaffed, it conduces to peace of mind. No thirst is felt ever after; decrepitude never weakens them." A Jain community in the Nimar district worships a deified tree. The Musahar worship a "forest king" whom they call Banraj, and a female deity whom they call Bansapti, "queen of the wood." By her command trees bear fruit, bulbs grow in the earth, bees make honey, silk-worms breed, and lizards, wolves, and jackals, useful to man, multiply their kind.

Indian pagan versions of Hindu mythology declare that Cusna (Krishna, the eighth and most celebrated avatar of Vishnu) when a boy climbed the margosa tree and sat on one of its boughs. Some Brahmans rested beneath its shade, unaware that Cusna was atop. While they were saying their prayers, a bird of prey, carrying a whale in its talons, perched on the tree, and under this added weight the bough broke. When it was about to fall upon the Brahmans, Cusna, who was near and perceived the Brahmans' danger, grasped the bough, held it up, and told the Brahmans to go away. In gratitude for this favour done by Cusna, Brahmans introduced the devotion of going every day round this tree, invoking the name of Cusna; hence both men and women walk round the margosa tree reciting prayers. They also marry the margosa tree to the sacred fig tree. A daughter of Brahma was transformed into a wind; and because at every breeze the leaves of the margosa tree move and make a harmonious sound, natives believe the goddess, Brahma's daughter, is in the tree, and they adore her. Excrescences from the bombax, the cotton tree, protect one against evil magic. A similar belief prevails in Mexico.

The Todas tie three sprigs of the kaburdri plant (*Euphorbia rothiana*) over the door of a dairy which is being purified. Certain trees which failed to assemble at the call of the god On were cursed and made to bear bitter fruit. The sacred bark of the tudr tree is used when buttermilk is poured out. The keeper of the dairy strikes it three times with a bell. At some Toda ceremonies the bark is pounded and the juice from it is squeezed over the sacred bells. The juice of certain plants is mixed with water and is drunk during the ceremony in which the dairyman's assistant is ordained.

At the Holi festival in northern India a sacred tree is burned. People leap over its ashes to get rid of itch and other ailments, and villagers try to steal one of the rags tied to a sacred tree in a neighbouring village, for such theft is very propitious. Worship of the neem tree propitiates the goddess of epidemics which prevail in summer.

When the Bandavas lost their kingdom in gambling with the Kanravas, the latter promised the former that they would give them back their kingdom if they would live in the forest for twelve years and unknown for one year. After having completed their stay in the forest, the Bandavas remained unknown for one year in the city of Virat. During this year they concealed their weapons on a shami tree. Before taking these weapons they worshipped the tree. In the great battle of Kwinkshetra the Bandavas won a splendid victory; hence they worship the tree on the tenth day of the bright half of Ashvin (September–October). A species of the tamarind tree, called *gorakh chinch,* is associated with the Hindu saint Gorakhnath, and is therefore sacred. Thick evergreen groves are sacred as the abode of a forest god.

The Nagas regard the rubber tree as the home of the chief god. Some believe he dwells underground at its foot. Lhota Nagas believe the chief god lives in the fig tree. Among the Lushai the rubbing together of two boughs denotes the presence of a demon; and the demon must be appeased by the sacrifice of a cock or a hen. The Lai (Laos) of northern Siam often permit a forest to grow freely on a small plain. These are sacred woods, and no one dares profane these sanctuaries. To cut a tree in these woods is a crime that deserves divine punishment, for it would immediately result in the spreading of all kinds of diseases throughout the world. This sacred forest people pass through with great respect mingled with fear, for the forest is peopled with spirits.

Trees occupy a conspicuous place in Chinese, Finnish, Hindu, Persian, Arabian, and other religions; and the worship of Celts and Teutons centred in sacred groves.

Relics of ancient tree-cults are found among Aryan-speaking and non-Aryan-speaking peoples in Europe and Asia. Reminders of holy trees and groves are recorded in such names as *Holyoake* and *Holywood.*

The rowan tree was sacred among Finns. Because of the redness of its berries, it was called Thor's tree, or Thor's (Ukko's) wife.

In the yard there grows a rowan,
Thou with reverent care should'st tend it.
Holy is the tree there growing,

Holy likewise are its branches,
On its boughs the leaves are holy,
And its berries yet more holy.[4]

The plane tree, says Coryat, a sixteenth-century traveller, was so highly esteemed "for its shadow" that the roots of it were nourished by wine. In Gaul, the plane tree possessed the sanctity which attached to the fig tree in the south.

Poles have a superstitious fear about cutting down hollow willow trees, because the devil resides in them. Irish consider it specially unlucky to cut down the white thorn tree. In Irish lore certain trees attain sanctity from proximity to sacred rivers. In early Ireland and Scotland the elm tree is associated with the milk cult.

Apple, rowan, hazel, and oak trees provide longevity, knowledge, and the wine which originally was an elixir that imparted new life and inspired prophetic utterances. In the almost treeless Outer Hebrides the goddess "Maiden Queen" dwells in a tree and provides "the milk of knowledge" from a sea-shell. The megalithic monuments of the British Isles have been attributed (wrongly, we believe) to the influence of the tree cults of Babylonia and Egypt. Trees play an important rôle in Celtic folklore, particularly in the Celtic Elysium. Some trees are golden, some are marvellous in other ways. They have silver branches and golden apples and produce a wonderful music which sometimes causes sleep and oblivion. Laeg, Cuchulainn's servant, describes one hundred and fifty trees which he saw growing in Mag Mell; their nuts constituted the food of three hundred people. The apple which the goddess gave to Conlaech was inexhaustible; when another favoured mortal visited this Elysium, Conlaech was still eating the apple with the goddess. Neither age nor dimness of sight afflicts those who eat of it. Apples, crimson nuts, and rowan berries are the food of the gods. A rowan berry which drops to earth produces a tree; the octogenarian who eats of its fruit is rejuvenated. To keep mortals from contaminating the tree by their touch, the gods set a Fomorian giant to guard it. The berries of a certain dragon-guarded rowan tree contain the virtues of nine meals; they add a year to a man's life, and banish illness. At the source of all Irish rivers are hazel trees with crimson nuts which fall into the water and become the food of salmon. The fortunate man who catches and eats one of these salmon obtains knowledge and wisdom. In Avalon, or Apple Land, the Celtic Paradise, grows the hazel

4. Kalevala, XXII, 221–226 (translation by Kirby).

"tree of life." Gods and men share its life-giving nuts. Beside a sacred pool grow nine sacred hazel trees, the nuts from which are swallowed by the salmon in the pool. Thus these fish acquired their red spots. He who tastes of the juice of the hazel nut acquires prophetic power. Sticks from the tree are used to produce the sacred fire, the "fire from heaven," which in pagan Scotland is connected with the sky-goddess, who thunders from her cloud-chariot and flings down fire-balls.

Tacitus says of the Germans: "Woods and groves are the sacred depositories; and the spot being consecrated to those pious trees, they give to that sacred recess the name of the divinity that fills the place, which is never profaned by the steps of man. The gloom fills every mind with awe: revered at a distance, and never seen but with the eye of contemplation." [5]

Early Teutons said that man was made out of the mystic trees Ask and Emble, which the sons of Bör found on the sea-coast when walking there. In parts of northern England, during a funeral a basin filled with sprigs of box-wood is placed at the door of the house through which the coffin is removed; each person who attends the funeral takes a sprig of the box-wood and throws it into the grave of the deceased. To this custom Wordsworth refers in the lines

> Fresh sprigs of green box-wood, not six months before,
> Filled the funeral basin at Timoth's door.

On the mountain of immortality, in the Japanese land of bliss, Tokoyo no Kuni, the Eternal Land, grows a wonderful tree with roots of silver, a trunk of gold, and fruits of rare jewels. In the Western Paradise the Shin-Shiu, described by a Japanese Buddhist sect, are lotus lakes adorned with gems. On their banks grow trees of gems; in their waters float lotus flowers of various colours. In the heaven described in early Shintoism splendid robes for the use of the fortunate inhabitants hang from sacred *sakaki* trees.

The Ainus say elm trees are inhabited by spirits. By the following process of reasoning the Ainus prove that the elm tree must have been the first tree: Man existed before disease, for otherwise sickness would have had no place to go. Health comes before sickness. Food and clothing are necessary to health, and cooking is necessary in the preparation of food. Fire and the means of producing fire are necessary in cooking. The roots of trees were used for making fire before people had matches,

5. *Germania*, LX.

A Laguna prayer-stick

A sacred doll of the Crow Indians

and bark was used for clothing. These materials came from the elm tree.

In many European ballads and stories the dead manifest themselves as trees. Putting the soul for safety into trees is found in many Indo-European mythologies, and close association between an individual and a tree is found in some preliterate cultures.

When a child is born, the Mentawei of Sumatra sometimes plant a coconut tree. When the child grows up, its soul will be bound to the tree. Andamanese name a child after the tree in flower when the child was born. To this name is prefixed a prenatal name chosen by the parents. The concept of descent from the tree, however, seems not to be involved. The *Ficus laccifera* tree is the habitation of the souls of unborn children. If a tree of this species should be cut down, a storm would result.

At Bruneck, in the Tirol, a great hollow ash is shown from which children are brought. At Asrgan such a tree is called the child-fear-tree. At Nierstein, in Hesse, is a great lime tree from which children for the whole neighbourhood are fetched; and a similar tree is known at Gummersbach.

In Viscaya, sovereignty was vested in a biennial assembly of chosen deputies, who sat on stone benches in the open air under an ancestral oak tree in the village of Guernica, the Basque capital. This tree was the emblem of their liberties. A scion of the parent oak was planted near by to carry on in case the old tree should die.

The following is a Basque song addressed to the tree of Guernica:

The tree of Guernica
  Is beloved
Among the Basques.
  Loved by all,
  Grow and spread
Your fruit over the world.
  We adore thee,
  Holy tree.

It is
About a thousand years since
  God planted
The tree of Guernica.
  Gather round!
  Now is the time.
If you fall,
We shall be lost.

You shall not fall,
  Beloved tree;
If I understand
The magistrates of Biscay,
We shall take a warrant
  With you
That the Basque people
  Live in peace.

Live for ever!
To pray for thee
Let us place ourselves
  On our knees;
And when we have asked
With all our heart,
The tree shall live
  Now and for ever.

Among the Yezidi the plane tree and the mulberry were sacred. In Europe the oak may have acquired sanctity from the fact that it was often struck by the thunderbolts of Zeus, or of Woden. The sanctity of the mistletoe was derived from its association with the oak. The Semnoics boasted a wood of immemorial antiquity and holiness; the Nahanarnah possessed a grove of ancient sanctity. The sanctuary of Nerthus was an island grove. Arminius' forces assembled in a wood sacred to Hercules, and Civilia united his army in a sacred wood. In many of these sacred groves were altars. In the Caucasus at the present day sacred groves afford refuge to criminals and animals. Those who take shelter in them may not be disturbed. In England the cult of the tree survives. At Berry Pomeroy, South Devon, is a famous Wishing Tree. In the park at Rydal, Westmoreland County, grew a haunted tree, celebrated in the lines of Wordsworth:

. . . though truly some there are
Whose footsteps superstitiously avoid
This venerable tree; for, when the wind
Blows keenly, it sends forth a creaking sound
(Above the general roar of woods and crags)
Distinctly heard from afar—a doleful note!
As if (so Grecian shepherds would have deemed)
The Hamadryad, pent within, bewailed,
By ruder fancy, that a troubled ghost
Haunts the old trunk; lamenting deeds of which
The flowery ground is conscious.

Charles II spent a day in hiding in the upper branches of a great oak tree in Shropshire—

> While far below the Roundhead rode
> And hummed a surly hymn.

Hence people wear oak-leaves on May 29; and many public-houses bear the sign, "Royal Oak." Thus sheer association may endear a tree to a people.

In Cairo an aloe is hung over the door of a house, especially a new door or the door of a newly built house. It ensures the occupants long and successful lives, and greatly prolongs the life of the house. The aloe lives for several years without earth or water, as its name, *sabr*, "patience," testifies. Possibly its mystic vitality endows it with sanctity and magic. Egyptian Mohammedans say that at the extreme or most elevated spot of Paradise is a tree, the *Sidr*, or lote-tree, more commonly called *Shegeret el-Muntana*, "Tree of the Extremity," on which are as many leaves as there are human beings on earth. On the leaves are inscribed the names of all living men. Each leaf bears the name of a person and the names of his father and mother. The tree is shaken each year on the evening of the fifteenth night of a certain month, a little while after sunset. If a person is destined to die soon, his leaf is withered: only a small portion of it remains green. If he is to die later in the year, a correspondingly larger portion of the leaf remains green. Among the northern Beja certain trees are not cut down, lest evil should in consequence befall the camels. Sacred trees are found among Mohammedanized Kazaks. Offerings are made to them much as in Mediterranean Mohammedan lands. When a man approaches a sacred tree, he dismounts, places his saddle-cloth on the ground, kneels on it, recites a prayer, and hangs on a branch of the tree a few hairs from his horse or a piece of his clothing. Such offerings ensure happiness, health, and long life.

There is a tendency for the sacred tree to impart sanctity to its immediate locality. Thus among the Lushai a tree which has the pendant protuberance called *thungzang* is sacred, and the adjacent jungle may not be cut. Near Nanders, in the Tirol, was a sacred tree from which children, especially male children, originated. One might not collect timber or firewood from its vicinity; crying or screaming near it constituted serious misbehaviour; quarrelling, cursing, or scolding near by was an offence which called to heaven for punishment.

In some cases the sanctity of the tree derives from a striking or unusual characteristic—solitariness, gnarled appearance, strange excrescence, hardness, toughness, pliability, needles, peculiarly shaped leaves, whisperings of foliage, or giant size. In many cases, however, no peculiarity accounts for the sanctity of the tree unless it is the peculiarity that trees, in some sense not clear to the native, are living things. Seldom does preliterate man have other than mythologic explanation of the sacredness of trees.

CHAPTER VI SACRED ANIMALS

The category of the "sacred" is very elastic and sometimes includes the tabooed, the respected, or the feared, as well as beings which are offered gifts and prayers and receive other attributes of worship. An all-inclusive account of sacred animals would be voluminous, and we must be content to indicate merely a few which play a rôle in various cultures.

The Tlinkit, in effect, pray to the grampus for good luck. The hunter addresses it graciously, for the animal can direct him to the seals. The Mattole revere frogs and white mice and do not kill them. Among Luiseños, the bear and the panther are agents and watchers for a supernatural being. They are usually referred to by sacred double names, as, for example, bear-panther. A chief's oration at the annual religious festival of the Crees concluded with an invocation "to all the animals in the land, and signal being given to the slave at the door, he invited them severally to come and partake of the feast." Birds, buffaloes, bears, or snakes instructed the young men of the Hidatsa Lumpwood military society in their visions. Among Cheyennes all warrior members of a society consider the elk antler sacred; and members of the Coyote society regard the coyote hide as sacred.

Teton Dakotas pray to grey spiders and to those which have yellow legs. Canadian Dakotas attribute supernatural power to Spider. The man who is about to smoke offers tobacco to Spider. The Sias and Hopis of the Southwest respectfully refer to Spider as Grandmother Spider. In these cultures Spider plays the rôle of a god. Algonquins, especially Central Algonquins, have much respect for the mythic great hare, Michabo (Manibozho), but not for present-day hares. Pawnees consider the buffalo sacred, and consecrate deer and buffaloes to Tirawa. Among Menominees and Chippewas the crow is sacred. Among Potawatomis, of the foods used in the initiation of candidates for the Medicine Lodge, the most important is a sacredly raised dog, because the dog was placed in the world to be the companion of man. To Delawares the eagle is a symbol of cleanliness. Among Cherokees, as generally in the Plains area, the eagle is the most sacred bird. The golden or war eagle is especially prized. Pimas receive assistance from various animals in war expeditions. When rain is especially needed, any one may petition for it by means of a "small grey fly that has a large head." The petitioner rubs soot from roof or chimney into the fly's eyes, and says: "Go quickly, little fly, tell your grandmother to send the rain." In a Zuñi ceremonial dance a live turtle is carried; in another sacred observance a rabbit-hunt is part of the program. At the Hopi fire dance, a winter observance, celebrants leap into the fire, and reappear with a live animal. On Santa Catalina Island, Chumash kept and "worshipped" condors; and on the adjacent coast Shoshonean tribes, apparently, had a condor cult. At Isleta the mountain lion, bear, badger, eagle, and "big snake" (rattlesnake) are regarded as supernatural and as powerful helpers. The lion is foremost, and is designated "first helper." The lion and the bear are strong and can help in any way. Their claws are worn in ceremonies. The lion or the bear helper of the Laguna Father lives on the summit of San Mateo (Mt. Taylor); and the bear assists in curing. The badger, the great digger, helps medicinemen dig out of the earth whatever they want; the "power" of the eagle enables them to fly; the snake cleans the village by his sucking or drawing power. Each of these animals is represented in stone fetishes.

Almost the entire local fauna enters largely into Navaho ritual and worship, through the use of skins, feathers, claws, or other parts of the animal. Many animals are represented in the sand drawings, including eagle, deer, antelope, prairie dog, and turkey. In curing, the prayer-stick colours correspond with those of the animal with which it is associated, and the prayer-stick is subsequently deposited near the animal's habitat. The stick is "dressed" for the animal, that is, it is coloured and decorated with plumes, and fed with tobacco, which is symbolically lighted, and then placed in the hands of the patient. Water animals are sacred and are used, at least symbolically, in many rites. The skins of beaver or of otter make highly prized ceremonial headbands, and the fur of beaver or of muskrat decorates some of the rattles used in religious rites. The shells of turtles are medicine-cups. Several birds are sacred and anthropomorphic, and have an associated prayer-stick and sacred name. Navahos do not kill eagles or hawks, for these birds are their allies, but release them after they have plucked the desired feathers. Most waterfowls and shore birds are sacred. With the exception of the turtle-dove, Navahos do not eat these birds. The bat, the crystal-ear bat, the bull-bat or night hawk, and the humming bird are sacred. The crow and the buzzard are sacred, and the buzzard is not molested. Among Yuman tribes of the Gila River sheep are sacred.

Among Aztecs, the coyote, eagle, serpent, and cougar were sacred animals, and temples were erected to them. The priests of Coyote constituted a special group and did not mix with the other three orders of priests. When Cortés was travelling inland on his conquest of Yucatan, he left a sick black horse, Morcillo, in the care of Canek, chief of the island city Tayasal. Almost immediately after his departure the Indians led the sick horse to one of their temples and worshipped it as the god of thunder. After the horse died, an image of it made of stone and mortar was greatly revered. Mayas respect the reptiles found in or near old palaces and temples built by their ancestors; they embody the spirit of Xlab-pak-yum, lord of walls, whose spirit roams there. Some tribes on the banks of the Orinoco, in Guiana, pay homage to frogs which are kept carefully under pots in order to obtain rain or fine weather. Among the Chaima, the Cumanagoto, the Tamanac, and other Carib tribes, the frog is a god of waters. Among the Toba the wild cat is the sacred animal of good spirits.

In Egypt and Ethiopia ibises are said to have killed the winged serpents that tried to invade the country; hence these birds are sacred.

Among the Bari of Mongalla Province, Anglo-Egyptian Sudan, birds are respected. The Lot do not eat jackal flesh, though they may kill the jackal. The Ludara have special reverence for the dog. The Lumbari do not kill their brothers the leopards, and leopards do not kill them; if a leopard kills a Lumbari "accidentally," it will not eat the corpse. The Moje abstain from the heart of all animals; the Moru will not kill or eat the *moru* (rat); the Kanam will not kill the ground hornbill, which they regard as their brother; the Kariak do not kill the wagtail and if they see a member of another tribe kill it they demand compensation as for a brother. Twice a year, in the afternoon, the spirit of the grandmother, which is identified with the wagtail and a snake, is honoured with a meal of beans, because she is the Mother of Food. The wagtail is never harmed, and the snake is sprinkled with milk when it appears in the house. The Kakwa treat the goat of a dead rain-maker with great veneration; it may trespass where it likes and must not be driven away. In time of drought people lead it around the cultivated fields.

Bushmen respect a snake, antelope, or lizard which is near a grave. At Allad and Savi, Dahomey, the crocodile is sacred. Among the Yorubas, crocodiles are Olosa's messengers and may not be molested. They bear to the goddess the offerings which the faithful deposit on the shores of the lagoon or throw into the near-by sedge. Some crocodiles, selected by the priests on account of certain markings on them, are treated with great veneration. Rude sheds thatched with palm leaves are erected near the water's edge for their accommodation. On every fifth day or festival food is supplied to them. Many of them are tame and, as in the Malay peninsula, come for the offering as soon as they see or hear the worshippers on the bank. Fish near the harbour bar at Lagos are sacred to a local sea goddess; a man who should attempt to catch them would be thrown overboard by the other boatmen. Among the Vais the crocodile is sacred; to kill one brings death. It is revered in Annamaboe. Among West African Bantus it comes to the assistance of a fugitive heir and in consequence is sacred. Crocodiles in Lake Tilla are spiritual counterparts of the people. When a person at Tilla is about to die, his crocodile-counterpart leaves the lake and crawls to its last resting-place.

These West African beliefs regarding the crocodile are reminiscent of Graeco-Egyptian concepts that the crocodile is sacred because it is the only aquatic animal that has a thin membrane covering its eyes, and hence can see without being seen. It has no tongue, and like the divine Logos, has no need of speech. It has one hundred teeth, declared equivalent to the number of days in the year. It lures its prey by weeping like a woman, that is, by shedding "crocodile tears."

Among Yorubas honey-bees are the messengers of the god of agriculture, Orisha Oko; flies and mosquitoes are the messengers of Sapatan, the Ewe smallpox god, and of Shankpana, the Yoruba smallpox god. The association, however, does not confer sanctity upon the insects. The Mandingo believe monkeys which gather on the trees in the vicinity of a graveyard embody the spirits of men buried there. Among Yorubas a small black monkey which frequents the mangrove trees is sacred to Ibeji, tutelary deity of twins. They make offerings of fruit to it; its flesh may not be eaten by twins or by a parent of twins. The bandicoot is sacred to the god Ifa because it lives chiefly on palm nuts; these are sacred to Ifa, who planted on a rock a palm nut from which sixteen palm trees immediately sprang. A small bird, *papagori*, is sacred to the god Shango; his worshippers interpret its cry. The killing of the *ajako*, a species of jackal, will, a proverb declares, bring misfortune upon the slayer. The vulture cannot be killed with impunity and rarely is one slain. The god may be part animal in form. Thus the god Aroni is represented in human shape, though with only one leg, and with the head and tail of a dog. The goddess Elusu is covered with fish scales from below the breasts to the hips—an African mermaid. Tribes of equatorial Africa regard the hen as a sacred bird and do not eat its flesh.

The circumstances under which an individual animal may obtain almost reverential respect is described by Baudin: "An ox which I presented to Mepon, the king of Porto-Novo, soon became his favourite. Every day the king gave him a small ration of acacia, and the animal never failed to come each day for his accustomed pittance. On market-days he went about among the crowds of Negroes, never hurting anybody, and the king's favourite soon became the favourite of all. When Mepon died, the ox came as usual for his ration; but not finding his master, he began to bellow. The fetish-priests, not understanding the cause of this, concluded that the genius of Mepon had passed into the animal. From that time it was forbidden to molest him; he was allowed to go wherever he pleased, and he never failed, especially on market-days, to take his usual walk. When he died, in 1883, the king had him wrapped in cloths and rendered him full funeral honours. According to custom, drums, guns, and every instrument capable of making a noise was brought into requisition, the blood of sacrifices and libations of rum were squandered to the great satisfaction of his adorers. Then the ox, followed by a cortege of fetish-priests and priestesses and the populace, was carried in great state on the shoulders of the Negroes, and laid in the grave destined for his reception. He was besprinkled for the last time with the blood of the victims immolated at the tomb, and all was ended. The *manes* of Mepon ought to have been satisfied." [1]

Among the Venda of northern Transvaal, in many important kin groups there is a sacred black bull, called Grandfather, which is regarded as the embodiment of all ancestral spirits. The bull is given the name of the grandfather of the chief who installs it, or the dynastic title of the family whose ancestors it embodies. The bull and the cow associated with him, though sacred, enjoy few privileges not possessed by

1. R. P. Baudin, *Fétichisme et féticheurs* (Lyon, 1884).

other cattle at the chief's kraal. At the harvest festival, thanks are offered to the ancestral spirits collectively. When the bull becomes very old, he is killed, and a new and younger beast, usually a calf of the sacred cow, takes his place. At the ceremony of substitution the head of the family says to the bull: "Oh, Grandfather, you are now too old and we must kill you, because of your age, but we replace you by a younger animal. Do not take offence at our action, but continue to be good to your people." If a sacred bull dies otherwise, people fear the ancestral spirits are angry and they hastily consult a diviner. The diviner usually discovers that the headmen of the kin group are quarrelling, or that an important rite in connection with the ancestors has not been performed. The kin then assemble, select a new bull, and implore the ancestors to enter it and be reconciled with their children. The Ranga of southern Rhodesia, and the Lamba, have a similar bull cult, but it is not usual among southern Bantus.[2]

Ancestors in the male line are represented among the Venda by a sacred bull or by stones; those in the female line are represented independently by a black female goat. The latter is first and foremost the mother's mother, but is also an embodiment of all the mother's ancestors in the female line. The ceremonies connected with it are similar to those conducted for the sacred bull. The king of Urundi possessed a herd of cows, half white, half black, without a spot. The herd was religiously guarded in the kraals near the sacred groves. The hide of such a cow was used to repair the royal drum.

In Dahomey, great veneration is paid the tiger. This does not prevent the people from capturing or killing a tiger, but they must not touch its beard, lest they greatly offend the beast. At Benin, the catfish, a sacred animal in West Africa, was frequently cast in bronze. The Mossi keep several animals in sacred groves. Within the enclosure the animals, which include the crocodile and the leopard, are respected; other animals of the species may be killed. Among the Ibo, the fish in the rivers inhabited by Iyafo, a water-spirit, are regarded as the children of Iyafo and are sacred. Feathers of parrots and certain other birds are placed in an earthenware bowl used to receive sacrificial blood. A Koro group at Itika respect civet-cats, badgers, and brown monkeys. If any one should kill one of these animals, his teeth would drop out. The Awgu, who are members of the Uhuenye group, respect civet-cats as sacred to the local Earth Deity. If a member of the group kills a civet-cat accidentally,

2. Hugh A. Stayt, *The Bavenda*, 243 (London, Oxford University Press, 1931).

he must go to another town, capture two civet-cats of opposite sex, and take them to the priest of Ala, together with the necessary sacrificial offerings.

At Eha-Amufu, there is a river cult, the priest of which is known as the Atama Ebe. Ebe is the spirit of the river and controls the fish, which are regarded as the spiritual counterparts of the human inhabitants of the area. The big fish are counterparts of the principal men of the village group; the small fry are counterparts of persons of no consequence. When a villager dies, a fish dies; when a fish dies, a villager dies.

At Lokpanta leopards are sacred to the kin groups known as Um-Ago and Um-Ohe. If a member of one of these groups should kill a leopard or eat its flesh, he would soon have an untimely death. A man who kills his "brother," that is, a leopard, accidentally, must flee and remain away for a month. He is then permitted to return, but at the first festival of Ala (Earth Deity) he must bring gifts, including a goat. The goat becomes sacred and taboo and is allowed to wander about unharmed. It is given right of way on a road. If it bears young ones, they become taboo, as "goats of Ala." Similarly at Eha-Amufu members of the Um-Ezudu kin group regard leopards as their brothers. A member of the group who kills a leopard accidentally must sacrifice a goat to the spirit known as Ekweesu (an evil spirit). If he finds a dead leopard, he must retreat hastily. If he enters a compound where the flesh of a leopard is being cooked, he must disinfect himself by picking up dust and throwing it over his shoulders.

At Mmako a species of monkey is sacred to members of the Eziobodo group, because their war "medicine" is prepared from this monkey.

In many parts of Polynesia the centipede and lizard are sacred, and are minor divinities. Polynesians offer human flesh to birds believed to be deities incarnate.

Samoans regard certain animals as sacred, and call them *atua*. In one district this may be an octopus; in another, an owl. They are not totems, but people do not eat the animal which is their *atua*. If the food offered to the god Ave I Le Tala is eaten in the night by dogs or rats, the god, for the time being, becomes incarnate in the living animals of that species. The stinging ray fish and the mullet are incarnations of Moso the Strong. If visitors or friends have caught or have brought with them one of these fish, a child of the family is laid in an unheated oven, as a peace offering to Moso for the indignity done him by the strangers. A member of the family who should taste of this sacred fish would be compelled by the heads of the families to drink a cupful of rancid oil dregs as a punishment to stay the wrath of Moso. In one family the god Moso appeared in the form of a pet pigeon, called Tu. Care must be taken when one is carrying water, for should any be spilled, the god would be angry and leave. In another family he was incarnate in the domestic fowl; if a member of the family should eat a piece of fowl, the consequence would be delirium and death. In another family Moso appeared in the form of a cuttle-fish, which none of the family might eat.

In some parts of Samoa, where the cuttle-fish was the household god, if a visitor caught a cuttle-fish and cooked it, or if a member of the family had been where a cuttle-fish was eaten, the family would assemble. A man or woman selected for the purpose lay down in a cold oven, and was covered with leaves, as when food is baked. This symbolic burnt offering averted the wrath of the god. Meanwhile the family prayed in unison: "O bald-headed Fe'e! Forgive what has been done —it was all the work of a *stranger!*" Failing such signs of respect and humility, the god would come to the family, cause a cuttle-fish to grow internally in some member of it, and so be the death of the victim.

Fuailang, originator of the heavens, was incarnate in the sea eel; if one cooked or ate the sea eel, his eyes burned and his scalp was clubbed in punishment. The village god Nonia was incarnate in the cockle. If one ate this shellfish, a cockle would grow on his nose. If one picked up a cockle and took it away from the shore, a cockle would appear on his body. On Hudson and De Peyster Islands the household gods were incarnate in fish; in the Mitchell group they were incarnate in birds and fish. One might not eat the animal in which his god resided.

The bat is venerated by the men of New South Wales and Victoria as a transformed ancestor. In Melanesian myth Spider is a miracle worker. In the Solomon Islands and San Cristoval the frigate-bird possesses a spirit and has supernatural powers. The sacred animal of the Navatusila, an inland tribe in Viti Levu, Fiji, is a fish hawk. It may not be eaten by any member of the tribe. Each group has another sacred animal, such as pigeon, dog, or remba bird, which members of the group may not eat. Among the Minahasa of Celebes, the principal sacred birds are the "foreteller of day," the "foreteller of night," and the "year bird."

Natives of Sarawak, Borneo, have a superstitious fear of the crocodile, which they will not mention by name, but refer to as "the old Grandfather." Several other animals they fear or respect. Among the Achenese the crocodile is sacred, as also in a large portion of the Malay peninsula where the crocodile occurs.

The cow is the most sacred animal among Hindus. Among some Brahmans—for example, the Nambutiri—every hair of the animal is sacred; the urine is holy water; and the dung is the most efficacious purifying substance. In Bombay the cow is the most sacred animal. In her body reside thirty-three images of gods. She is compared with the earth in its sacredness; and when she is pleased she can give everything required for the maintenance of mankind. The Khond regard the tiger and the leopard as sacred. They will not permit a dead leopard to be carried through the village; and they take oath on a leopard skin. Nambutiri Brahmans worship the horse. It is the favourite animal of Kutera, the treasure-god. The horse is worshipped also in the Deccan. The Hanuman or Entellus monkey is sacred among the Behari, who worship it as the deity Mahabirji. Todas devote much time and attention to their buffaloes, and ceremonially bestow much care upon one group of them. These sacred buffaloes are attended by men set apart for the purpose, who comprise the Toda priesthood; the milk of the sacred animals is churned in dairies regarded by the natives as temples. Religious ceremonies accompany nearly every important incident in the lives of the sacred buffaloes. Ceremonies celebrate the birth of a calf; ceremonies accompany the giving of salt to the animals; and ceremonies celebrate other events in the lives of the buffaloes. In Bombay the elephant is divine. It is the vehicle of Indra, the lord of gods; and its head is attached to the trunk of Gampati, the son of Parvati and Siva. Of the fourteen jewels obtained by the gods and demons by churning the ocean, one was a horse with seven mouths. Hence the horse is divine. The male monkey is holy and represents the monkey-god Maruti. The peacock, the favourite vehicle of Sarasvati, goddess of learning, and associated also with Kartik Swami, is respected. The mouse, the vehicle of the god Gampati, is worshipped along with that deity on *Ganesh Chaturthi* day, the fourth day of the bright half of the moon *Bhadrapad* (August–September). The parrot is worshipped by singers who desire to improve their voices and by dull persons who desire to improve their intellects. The hen is worshipped on the last Sunday of the month of Jyeshth (May–June). The mouth of a she-goat and the smell of a horse are sacred. The earth is supported by a tortoise; therefore, when the goddess earth or Prithvi is worshipped, the tortoise also is worshipped. Alligators in a pond at Magar Pir, near Karachi, are worshipped. In many parts of the Presidency Hindus worship them as water deities. Hindus considered the deer holy, and Brahmans and ascetics use deer skin while performing their austerities. The Bharvad worship the goat when they worship the goddess Machhu. The goat is holy for sacrificial purposes. By worshipping the cat a man can win over his opponents. It is a great sin to kill a cat. In the Deccan, on Panchavi day the cat is especially sacred. Black ants also are sacred. The dog is an incarnation of the deity Khandoba, and is respected as the favourite animal of the god Dattatraya. In the temple of Dattatraya Hindus worship dogs. Although most Hindus consider the donkey unholy, certain low-class Hindus—for example, the Lonari—consider it sacred. The lion is sacred because it is the lord of the beasts of the forest and the vehicle of goddesses. The tiger is worshipped with Vagheshvari Mata, for it is her vehicle and the conveyance of the goddess Ambaji. Sanctity attaches to female buffaloes. The bull is respected as the favourite vehicle of the god Siva, and because it is useful for agricultural purposes. Crows are worshipped as representing sages. Hindus consider the eagle the vehicle of the god Vishnu; it is a favourite devotee of that deity. The cuckoo is an incarnation of the goddess Parvati. It is worshipped especially by high-caste Hindu women for a month on the occasion of a special festival, the festival of the cuckoo, held in the month of *Ashadh* (June–July) every twenty years. The swan is the vehicle of the goddess Sarasvati. Its worship ensures success in any enterprise. The cock is holy as the vehicle of the goddess Bahucharaji. The Khasi say the cock assumed responsibility for man and is the mediator between God and man.

Deification of the tiger prevails in some villages of Chodheras, Gujarat, where the people are exposed to the wrath of this animal. Horses and cattle are revered here, but no special worship is offered them.

In Persia dogs, cows, bulls, and oxen are sacred. There is a distinction between common bulls, cows, and oxen, and privileged ones. The latter are protected by magic rites. Ormazd created the dog; hence ill treatment of it is severely punished. To Ainus the albatross is sacred.

In the cults of the ancient Egyptians an important place was assigned to animals. Egyptologists believe these sacred animals were not worshipped. The gods and goddesses were generally local spirits symbolized by the body or head of an animal. The scarab represents a sacred being which entered the body at birth and abandoned it at death; it symbolized or embodied the soul. Its association with the soul may represent a later rationalization, for the Egyptian name of the beetle resembles the word "to be" or "to become." Thus the beetle came to signify all that exists or causes to exist, namely, the self-existent god who brings into being all things that are, especially the heart. The flying scarab represents the sun, which crosses the sky from east to west in a day. The grasshopper, the cricket, the praying mantis, the large stag-beetle, and the ibis were sacred.

Not until about the time of Rameses II (about 1292–1225 B. C.), however, is there evidence of so-called animal worship in Egypt. It arose, Breasted believes, because the poor man could not make proper offerings in the magnificent temples and was forced to find other insignia of his faith. At first, Maspero surmises, only individual animals were sacred, though later the sacredness attached to all members of the species. Accordingly, at first only exceptional and sacred animals were embalmed, those which bore marks of being the incarnation of the god—for example, those which had the stigmata making them an Apis, a Muevis, or a Bacchis. So it was with the geese of Amon, the fish of Hathor, the ibises of Thoth.

Animals which had been sacred to the god and had lived in the precincts of a temple were embalmed. About the end of the Theban period the veneration which had been bestowed upon only a few individuals was extended to the species, at least in those places in which they were venerated as gods. Thus, for instance, at Bubastis and at Stabl Antar, all cats were considered incarnations of the goddess, and after death were mummified and buried. Later whole cemeteries were reserved for animals; and soon they covered as much space as the burying places reserved for human beings. The Apis bull of Memphis was engendered by a flash of light which came down from heaven and impregnated a cow, which gave birth to no more young after she had borne him. This bull was black, spotted with white. On his forehead was a white triangle, on his right side the figure of the crescent moon; on his back he generally wore a red cloth. The priests regarded the bull as the "living repetition" of Ptah, the local god of Memphis.

These bulls were generally emblematic of the gods. In some cases the sacred bull was found only after a three months' search. "He was recognized by certain marks—namely, a crescent on his forehead, a scarab under his tongue, and a vulture upon his back—which the priests undertook to discover." Among Semitic peoples, too, the bull was sacred. Among Babylonians it symbolized strength and became a synonym for hero. Israelites bowed down to worship the golden calf set up by Aaron, having learned in Egypt, Babylonia, or Syria of its sacredness.

The sphinx is evidence that the blending of human and animal characteristics was not considered absurd or fanciful. The combination of the body of a lion and the head of a man showed objectively a possible psychological combination.

Frazer finds the origin of the sacredness of Egyptian animals in totemism and believes the sacredness of cattle a relic of the pastoral stage. In similar manner he accounts for the sacredness of other animals, such as insects and birds. But Egyptologists do not accept this view. They believe the sacredness of the species is secondary and derived. Breasted, for example, says: "the animal-worship which we usually associate with ancient Egypt, as a cult is a late product, brought forward in the decline of the nation at the close of history." In the early period "it was unknown; the hawk, for example, was the sacred animal of the sun-god and as such a living hawk might have a place in the temple." [3]

In the Arsinoite district the crocodile was sacred; it was given geese and fish decked with necklaces and bracelets, and when it died it was mummified. In the classical period several kinds of fish were venerated in Egypt, notably those known as oxyrhynchus, phagrus, and lepidotus. Aversion for these three was general because in popular belief the phallus of Osiris, after his dismemberment, was consumed by these fish. Strabo mentions a fourth fish which was venerated, *Lates niloticus*, which was worshipped at a city named after it Latipolis, in conjunction with a goddess whom Strabo identifies with Athena.

On early coins from the Aegean the sow is an emblem of divinity. Caesar says that in southern Britain it was a crime to eat hare, goose, or domestic fowl. Probably these prohibitions were based on, or gave rise to, the sacredness of the respective animals. In Irish legend the ass and the cow are sacred animals because they kept the infant Jesus warm by breathing on him.

Thus there appear to be various motives for the sacredness of animals. In some cases man is impressed with the magic power of the ani-

3. For a different interpretation of the origin of the animal cult in Egypt see A. Moret and G. Davy, *From Clan to Empire* (New York, Knopf, 1926), and G. W. Locher, *The Serpent in Kwakiutl Religion: A Study in Primitive Culture*, Chapter IX (Leyden, Brill, 1932).

mal; as when the Dakota alleges that Spider has *wakan*, as exhibited in its ability to walk on water as on land, to build a net and capture other insects in it, and to "throw down" or "pitch up" a "rope" and climb up or down on it. Moreover, Spider's uncanny way of appearing almost any time from anywhere impresses him as a mystic ubiquity. Eagle, too, shows *wakan* by virtue of its power to soar above all other birds and to remain aloft as long as it likes by merely extending its wings. Only mystic power, *wakan*, enables it to do these things.

The peculiar markings on an animal are other bases of sanctity, as, notably, in ancient Egypt. Indeed, albino animals are sacred the world over. So, too, animals which are associated with the sacred, symbolically or ritually, become sacred.

Examples of such sanctity arising from symbolism or association are the beetle, in Egypt, which typified resurrection, and so the sun god, who is each day resurrected; and the lamb and the dove in Christianity, symbolic of purity and meekness, and hence especially appropriate offerings in purification ceremonies in the Jewish temple.

CHAPTER VII SACRED PERSONS

"Come not too near me, for else I shall sanctify thee." Those who deal with the sacred are automatically sanctified. The sacred radiates, permeates persons and things and brings them within its mystic influence. The most important classes of sacred persons are priest, priestess, prophet, seer, saint, and pilgrim.

PRIEST AND PRIESTESS

The importance of the function of the priest is a measure of the elaboration of religious rite and ceremony. In most of the simple cultures there are no priests; and when, in these cultures, they exist, they play a minor rôle, to which they impart prestige rather than conversely. Thus priesthood is unknown to the Australian, Tasmanian, Andaman, Vedda, and Bushman cultures and the little developed cultures of the New World. When religious rites and ceremonies are elaborate, the way to priesthood is open. In highly developed cultures, especially when ritual, ceremony, and symbolism are important and religious rites are community functions, priesthood is usually well entrenched. In most North American tribes there is no priesthood; but among tribes of the Southwest of the United States which have elaborate religious ceremonies priesthood is important. Hopi and Zuñi priests, set apart from their fellows during the long period of preparation for public religious ceremonial dances, have a distinctive status. A Zuñi priest, that he may be unhampered in his religious work—promotion and maintenance of the material and spiritual welfare of his people—eschews trivial, irrelevant, and distracting matters. He may not quarrel or dispute, and hence is not appointed to civil office. He may not leave the Zuñi valley during his term of office, though now, to the distress of the orthodox, this prohibition is frequently broken. A man who approaches the gods to make request of them cuts himself off from the world and forgoes distracting activities, that he may concentrate upon compelling the supernatural. Hence the retreat. During the "strictest" retreat, in addition to the usual restrictions, Zuñi priests eat no flesh. On the fourth day, when they again offer prayer-sticks, the food restrictions are lifted, but the priests remain in seclusion for another four days.

In the highly developed Peruvian, Maya, and Aztec cultures, which harboured elaborate religious rites, the priest had a distinctive status. Seminaries trained candidates for the priesthood. At an early age the candidate withdrew from the world and devoted himself to preparation for the priestly calling. The importance of the Peruvian, Maya, or Aztec priest in public life was greater than in any other area of the New World, and religious rites and ceremonies were correspondingly elaborate. Indeed, in both preliterate and historic cultures the public importance of the priest depends on the extent to which religious life is elaborated, specialized, socialized, and made a community affair.

In the simpler cultures of Africa, notably among Bushmen, there is no priesthood, but in many highly developed Negro cultures the priest plays an important rôle. Thus in Dahomey and Ashanti, and among the Ganda, there is an organized priesthood, and priests, trained in seminaries, have complete charge of religious functions. The Ashanti priest undergoes a long period of training which imposes many taboos. Nearly all Ashanti priests and priestesses are qualified for the profession by susceptibility to spirit-possession. When performing ordinary tasks or, more frequently, when attending a religious ceremony, they suddenly and without previous warning hear the "voice of Tano" or the voice of another god, or fall down in a fit, or go into a trance. A fully qualified priest or priestess called in to interpret the phenomenon says, usually, that the spirit of the god "wishes to marry" the possessed person. As a rule, the subject of the fit then decides, sometimes under persuasion, to train for the priesthood. If he so decides, he enters the service of a full-fledged priest of the god whose spirit, he was told, had manifested itself to him. His novitiate lasts three years. The neophyte leaves home and resides with his new master. A married man must separate from his wife and may not cohabit with her until his three years' training has ended. If he is unmarried, he must remain chaste during these three years. Each unit in the period of training lasts a year.

During the first year there are ceremonial ablutions, "bathing with medicine." The priest who trains the candidate gathers leaves from *asoa* and *krampan* trees. The former "strengthen the ankles" (for dancing); the latter "cause his god to stay with him." For seven days he washes in a decoction made from these leaves. *Nsansomo* leaves, mixed with green *summe* leaves and white clay, are rubbed on his eyes "that he may see his god daily." Apparently, however, this statement is not to be taken literally, for a common saying declares: "A priest cannot look upon his god and live." [1] If the spirit of possession does not manifest itself to the novice, the priest presses *nyanya* leaves on the novice's eyes, behind his knee-joints, and on the soles of his feet. The spirit of possession then returns to him. If the novice cannot "hear his god's voice," *afwina* leaves are placed under his pillow. The priest instructor collects leaves from a plant growing over a grave in the "thicket of the ghosts," brings them to the village, and places them in a pot containing eggs and a fowl. The pot is put on the grave from which the leaves were taken. The novice must go alone in the middle of the night to the "thicket of the ghosts" and "bathe" in this medicine. The ghosts beat him—his screaming can be heard; nevertheless, he must bathe. During seven successive nights he goes to the grave and bathes there. The medicine in the pot is then replaced by a tree fungus, "Sasabonsam's hat." With this the novice, as previously, washes himself on seven successive nights. The priest instructor walks along one of the narrow forest paths, plucks leaves from left to right, perhaps keeping his eyes closed while he does so, and cuts off pieces of roots which cross the path. These he places in a pot and over them pours cold water. In this water the novice must bathe three times a day and three times a night for several days and nights. Medicine is made also from pounded bark of *odum;* with this the would-be priest rubs himself. These successive lustrations bring the spirit of possession into the novice.

Bathings at the cemetery ensure contact with spirits of the dead. After the candidate has bathed with the foregoing and many other plants and roots, the spirit of possession visits him from time to time. He trembles visibly while it is in him.

An elaborate system of taboos confines the Ashanti priest of the Supreme Deity. He may not eat carrion, snake, rat, porcupine, wildcat, or monkey. He must wear only white and blue clothes, except when he attends a funeral, at which time he may not wear them. He may not eat food which has been cooked by a menstruating woman, and the plates and cooking utensils which come into his enclosure must be placed in a prescribed position. Certain kinds of wood he may not use

1. See page 3.

for his fireplace. Every fourth day, on the market day of his clan, he must remain at home and meanwhile may not speak to any one until he has performed certain rites. After their performance he retires to his room, pours an offering of palm wine on the ground, and prays to his god. He may not leave his house on Saturday, but spends the time eating and conversing with other priests of his order and with members of his family.

The Ga priest must observe certain taboos. He may not see a dead body; he may not eat before performing certain rites; he may not eat salt, except in water, or fermented food, nor eat before sunrise; and he must refrain from sexual relations.

The Todas of India have an elaborate religious life that centres in the sacred buffaloes, which are in charge of priests set apart for the purpose, who superintend also the sacred dairies to which the milk is taken. The priest has a dairy assistant, wears distinctive garb while on the dairy premises, and is restricted in his associations with laymen. He attains sanctity fitting him for his office by a nine days' ordination ceremony. By drinking water from the leaves of a sacred tree and by rubbing his body with the bark three times seven, seven times seven, and nine times seven times, he acquires ritual purity or sanctification, which enables him to deal with sacred things. He must observe specified rules of diet, sleeping, and dress. He may not cut his hair or nails, cross a bridge, attend a funeral, transact business with a member of the laity, or associate with his wife or other women.

Among the many taboos which hedge the Burmese Buddhist priest are the following: he may not sleep on a place of more than eight fingers' elevation; or on a rug that more than ten men can sit on; or on the skin of a tiger, elephant, or horse; or in a monastery or rest-house with the doors open; he may not exchange his blanket with other monks, novitiates, or nuns; he may not boast of omniscience or of being better than other monks; ask for gifts, except from a robber; use gold, silver, copper, lead, or tin, in any fashion; kindle a fire or send another to kindle a fire; scratch himself on a stone or stump when bathing; adorn himself with wreaths of flowers; and so on through a long list of prohibitions.

A Naga village priest moves amid encompassing taboos. A Mao Naga priest is forbidden the flesh of animals of species offered in sacrifice.

In Bali only priests wear beards. Here, as in China, to wear the fingernails long is a sign of distinction and indicates that the wearer does no manual work. Some priests wear the nails of both hands long, although most well-to-do Balinese wear them long only on the left hand. The life of the Bali priest is strictly regimented and is hedged with prohibitions. His life is considered an arduous one because he must continually think of the gods. He must observe, when eating, many taboos. When he eats with others, he must sit at a higher level than they; otherwise the gods will be displeased. He throws a few grains of rice at hungry dogs because he must share his food with these disguised evil spirits. He may not sit at a public eating-place or eat in the market; while eating he must face east; he may not eat until he has said his morning prayers; beef, pork, and food from offerings are forbidden; he may not touch alcohol. He may not walk under dirty water. Now that many drain-pipes have been built at high points over the roads to connect the rice fields, a priest encounters great difficulties when travelling by motorcar; for the priest must climb over each pipe; he may not go under any of them.

In Buddhist China, boys who are candidates for the priesthood are initiated into religious duties during their seventh year. Their heads are shaved. A special teacher is assigned each novice. When the final consecration is prepared, the novice, in token of willingness to endure hardship, is branded on the head. The branding is sometimes repeated, with the consent of the victim, during later stages of initiation. The candidate is first received into novitiate by simple ceremonies in which he takes the nine primary vows. He then enters, by virtue of further vows and ritual, the state of *lohan*, in which he seeks salvation for himself and for others. The nine primary vows taken by the initiate are: to abstain from killing, stealing, adultery, slander, reviling, lying, jealousy, hatred, and folly. Sometimes other abstinences are added.

In Polynesia the following classes of priests, which constitute a hierarchy, are recognized and designated by special terms:

MAORI	TAHITI
First-grade priest	Great author, or high priest
High-class priest	Author of prayer
Instructor in occultism	Author of medicine
Acolyte	Author of temples (or of temple orientation)
Wizard	Author of houses (or planner and builder of houses)
Junior priest	Author of canoes (or one adept in canoe-building)
Seer	Author of fishing (or authority on fishing seasons)
Wizard	
Lower-class shaman	
Expert in astronomy	

Tahitian priests must be able-bodied, tall, and free from personal defects, for the gods do not find acceptable a man with a blemish, such as a humpback, a bald head, a blind eye, or squinting eyes. They must be deft and sure-footed, for awkwardness in the service of the gods is an abomination.

In most parts of Oceania there is little development of priesthood, but in those parts of Polynesia in which the institution of the sacred temple exists priests have distinctive if not elaborate duties, and enjoy a distinctive status in tribal life. Historic civilizations tell a similar story. In Egypt, Babylonia, Greece, Rome, and Palestine, when religious life developed, priesthood became an important institution; only when ritual, ceremony, temple, and formal regulation of religion developed among the Jews did priesthood flourish. Any one of these phases of religious life is an index of the stage of development attained by another.

Perhaps it is not true that

> He who drives fat oxen
> Should himself be fat,

but it seems to be true that he who deals with the sacred should himself be sacred. Indeed, he will be sacred whether he wishes to be so or not; the sacred adheres to him and claims him for its own. The performer of sacred rites is thereby made taboo, set apart from his fellows. A Jaina monk must observe rigorous celibacy. He may not look at, think of, or touch a woman, or sit where a woman has sat. So absolute is his separation from the other sex that he may not stroke a female animal.

An Egyptian priest must for a period of time abstain from meat, wine, and sexual intercourse in order to ascertain the will of the gods and acquire the gift of prophecy. Before coming into the divine presence the priest shaved his entire body and put on clean garments. This was also court etiquette, and acknowledged the divinity of the pharaoh.

In every culture apartness is an attribute of priesthood. By no people was the apartness of priests emphasized more than by the Romans. The Vestal Virgins might not marry. One order of priests, the *flamines Dialis,* were so holy that no one in the community might have intimate contact with them. The *flamen Dialis* might not touch, approach, or name any animal or object which was unclean, that is, ritually taboo, such as a corpse, a bier, raw meat, beans, a dog, a goat, or a horse. He might not hear the sound of a flute played at a funeral. He was excluded from contact with death and things associated with cult of the dead. He was apart from men; taboos confined him within the realm of the holy. He might not touch anything tied, knotted, or fastened with ring or chain. If he wore a ring, its continuity must be broken. His garments might be fastened only by a safety pin or by some other object in which the continuity is broken. He might not touch ivy, for it has tangled and intertwining branches. He might not walk in a vineyard or pass under a trellis. He must at all times wear his priestly garments; and he might not go bareheaded. At the foot of his bed stood a table of oblations. He must have been married according to the ancient form of *confarreatio*. He might not divorce his wife; and when she died he must relinquish his office. He might not utter an oath. He might not see armed men, or mount a horse. In early times he might not leave the city for a night; in later Roman days he might stay away three nights, but no longer. He might not wear or look at anything which resembled bonds. A man in fetters who entered his house was immediately released, and the chains were thrown through the *compluvium*, the opening of the house, lest the domicile be polluted. A slave might not touch him; hence only a free man might cut his hair. In shaving he must use a bronze razor, not an iron one. For him every day was a holy day, and he might not work or see work performed. When he went abroad, an attendant preceded him to warn workmen to desist from their labours while the *flamen Dialis* was passing by. His was literally a charmed existence, though the kind of existence which he led, instinct with danger to his fellows, may not, to the layman, seem very charming. Every privilege, however, carries responsibilities; and those who deal with the holy must submit to insulation even at the price of isolation.

Among Mandaeans of Iraq and Iran, a religious sect which preserves many Babylonian and Iranian concepts and practices, the boy who is chosen to prepare for the priesthood must be without physical blemish. Thus one who while chopping wood had inadvertently chopped off the end of a finger thereby severed himself from possible priestly function. Because the body must be "pure, sound, and perfect," the function of priest may not be performed by a man who has been circumcised, by one who is impotent, or by a eunuch; and the priest who loses a limb or is robbed of his manhood may no longer officiate. His genealogy, too, must be sound; that is to say, he must be of uncontaminated Mandaean blood, with family lines on both father's side and mother's side ritually immaculate for several generations.

A Kota priest may not eat from vessels used by laymen, and may enter only a certain portion of the house of a fellow-villager. To join in the ordinary social dances would be as unbecoming as, among ourselves, for a bishop publicly to demonstrate the tango. The priest "may have only one wife and may not have intercourse with any other woman." [2] His wife shares his sanctity and hence may not have intercourse with any man other than her husband. Here "the [Kota] principle of the equivalence of brothers gives way before the more demanding principle of the segregation of the priest and his wife from contaminating mundane influences. The brothers of a priest do not have access to his wife." [2] Sexual intercourse with them would impair her sacrosanct nature. The priest may not consort with the wives of his brothers, though other Kota men share their brothers' wives. "The priestly principle is dominant over the fraternal principle because its effective rating, to use Professor Linton's phrase, is higher. That is, the society is more concerned with preserving the purity of the priests than it is in consistently equilibrating the rights of brothers. The priesthood complex has greater potentialities, in this instance, for influencing societal behavior than has the fraternal complex." [2]

If a Toda priest, even unwittingly, passes a village in which there is a woman in a seclusion hut after childbirth, or in expectation of giving birth to a child, the priest loses his sanctity, becomes an ordinary person, and can no longer perform the duties of his office unless reinstated by all the ceremonies necessary for initiation into priesthood. A Chinese *sai-kong* who officiates at sacrificial ceremonies is so instinct with holiness that he must be carried to the altar. Should he come into contact with the earth, his *yang*, or potent maleness, would be contaminated by the female principle inherent in the earth.

A Totonac priest, in the Veracruz region, must be a man over sixty years of age, of unblemished reputation. He must vow perpetual silence; he might speak only when consulted on questions of policy or ritual. He wore fox or coyote skin and abstained from meat. At Tehuacán priests slept on mats, used a stone for a pillow, and even in winter wore only a thin cotton cloak and cotton breech-clout. Except on feast days they might eat only once a day. Their meal consisted of one tortilla per man (about two ounces) and a little *posol*. They might not eat salt, chili pepper, or other proscribed food, except on the feast day which came at twenty-day intervals, at which time they might eat as freely as

2. David G. Mandelbaum, "Polyandry in Kota Society," AA, 40: 577 (1938).

they chose. Every twenty days they pierced their ears, passed sixty reeds through the wounds, and drew blood from their bodies. Serious lapse from piety during incumbency was punished by death.

Most Mexican priests wore long white cotton shirts and over one shoulder a fringed cotton cape. Aztec priests might not cut, comb, or wash their hair. When celebrating religious ceremonies they blackened their faces, hands, arms, and legs. On special occasions their faces were blackened with ashes obtained by cremating a mixture of poisonous snakes, insects, and other animals, including scorpions, tarantulas, wasps, and centipedes. There were different classes of priests, at the head of whom, in Mexico City, were two high priests. Totonac priests were consecrated by being anointed with a liquid composed of crude rubber and children's blood. Crude rubber was a symbol of rain and fertility deities; children's blood humanized the rite and sanctified it.

Chibchan priests inherited office matrilineally, although chiefs were influential in appointments to important offices. During a twelve-year probationary period the candidate received religious and medical instruction and practised various austerities in the seclusion of an isolated hut. When he was inducted into office, his ears and nose were pierced and he assumed gold ornaments. He practised much self-denial, lived abstemiously and in celibacy, performed many penances, slept little, and spent the greater part of the night chewing coca. He was intercessor between man and supernatural powers. In time of drought, for example, several priests fasted, and then went to the top of a mountain, where they burned various offerings, including hair soaked in resin. The ashes which remained were scattered to the winds. There was no priestly hierarchy; theoretically, all had the same status. In the plains tribes to the southeast of the Chibchas, candidates for priesthood were educated in the temples for their future sacred profession.

Some Peruvian priests inherited the office. In many cases, however, the priest had been selected for the office because he exhibited a personal idiosyncrasy, such as epilepsy, was born during a thunderstorm, or had recovered from a lightning stroke. He might marry, but his life was hedged about with many restrictions. Only the divine ruler, son of the Sun, was more revered. The ceremonial robes of a Peruvian priest consisted of a long ungirt tunic and a cape. His head was adorned with a plate of gold representing the sun, his breast with a plate of silver; his garments were richly ornamented with precious metals and jewels.

Each Ganda temple is served by from one to four priests, who live near the temple, are responsible for its care, receive devotees and their sacrifices, refer them to the temple medium, and interpret to them the latter's utterances. Their persons are sacred; and they perform unscathed certain miracles, such as licking a red-hot iron. A man who committed an offence against a priest was killed. In a house near the temple priests kept their sacred vestments, and there they robed. They might not walk abroad in their ceremonial robes, but merely perambulate between temple and house. The laity stood off at a respectful distance while a priest put on his robes and were afraid to touch or approach him. A woman who was a medium of the god, that is, spoke under possession of the god, was separated from the men and must be chaste during the remainder of her life; she was the wife of the god.

In most tribes of northern Nigeria priests allow the hair to grow long, although some Yoruba priests shave the crown of the head. When sacrifice is to be performed, they wear special garments. Thus Bata priests wear baggy trousers and around the waist a piece of cloth, the upper part of the body being naked; the Bata priestess wears a skirt of strips of cotton-cloth thrown over the shoulders, leaving the right breast exposed.

In most tribes of northern Nigeria the priest lives apart from his wives during a religious festival. In the Vere tribe the priest's wives may not approach him during the festival period; a male attendant brings the food which the wives cook for their priest husband. In some tribes he abstains from washing and shaving; in some, he washes and shaves especially for the occasion. The Ekoi priestess (southern Nigeria) must forgo all work and some kinds of food. She may not smoke; she may wash only with palm oil; and she may participate in no dance except the special dances reserved for priestesses.

Among the Ibo of Nigeria, a man or woman whose skin is of the peculiarly vivid red hue occasionally found in that people is thereby marked out as priest or priestess of the Thunder God. The head priest of the Thunder God must eat in a hut which stands apart in the middle of the compound. He may not taste the season's yams until two months after ordinary men are permitted to eat them. Slaves attached to the temple are sacrosanct. They may go into a marketplace and take without payment anything they want, for no one dares touch them. Those who build the temple may not leave the premises until the work is finished. Meanwhile they may not eat coconut, palm nuts, or cassava, but must subsist on cooked yams and soup. The priest of the god Ala, the

Earth deity, must observe many taboos. He may not eat food in another's house, or food which a menstruous woman has cooked; he may not sit on the ground. In some Ibo villages a widow or a tattooed person may not enter the house of a priest of Ala. The priest of the Obum cult may not eat the flesh of a leopard or of any reptile. If the word *dog* is mentioned while he is eating, he must forgo the remainder of the meal. He may not sleep on any other bedstead than one of mud, and he may not cross the boundary of the village. When he is about to cross a river, every one must make way for him and remain on shore until he has crossed.

For some time before he approaches the altar, and while at it, the Ashanti priest must abstain from eating. Indeed, all who approach the altar must be ritually clean, that is, must have abstained for a specified period from intoxicating liquor and from sexual intercourse.

In the Marquesas certain priests, when performing the duties of their office, must wear a hat of coconut leaves and a collar made of a coconut branch. A Mentawei priest may not hold in his hand anything that is burning. His cigarettes are lighted by unmarried men. He may not carry water to the house; he may not feed chickens or pigs. His children do the work that normally is done by a man; if he has no children, he adopts nephews to do the work. A priest's helpers also are sacred and may not feed chickens or pigs; but they may fish and hunt.

A Hudson Bay Eskimo shaman sometimes transmits his power to a successor by laying his hands on the latter's head. Similarly, in many cultures the priest's holiness passes by contact to others. A Hindu saint can transfer power to another in many ways: by giving a remnant of his food; by wetting his finger with the saliva and applying the sanctified finger to the mouth of another; by laying his hand on the head or over the heart of another; by blowing on water and giving it to another to drink. One who washes the hands of a saint acquires *barkat*, inherent power.

Earth from the feet of a Brahman is pure; consequently, when a Brahman guest crosses the threshold in leaving the host's house, a cloth is spread on the ground for him to walk over. Dust thus collected on the cloth is preserved as a curative or is sprinkled over the heads of the other guests. The concept of contagion underlies the Christian ceremony of the laying on of hands and also the dogma of apostolic succession. The healing by touch practised until modern times, an attribute of English queens and kings until the day of Queen Anne, implies a similar concept.

PROPHET AND SEER

Oracular declaration under possession by a ghost is common in Indonesia, Melanesia, and parts of Africa.

To induce trance, the Bali priest uses *pranayama*, breath control, closing each nostril alternately with a finger, inhaling deeply, holding his breath as long as possible, and exhaling through the other nostril. With a blade of grass he inscribes the sacred *ong* in the holy water, prays again with a flower which he drops into the water container, then takes his bell in the left hand and strikes the clapper three times with another flower held in his right hand. His breath, his voice, and his spirit are now in unison with the deity. The priest mumbles his guttural prayers, rings the bell alternately with swift, intricate gestures of hands and fingers, takes flowers at intervals, drops them into the holy water or holds them over the lamp and the incense, then flings them away. He rings the bell more loudly and quickly, then suddenly stops. During the preliminaries, signs of the oncoming trance are gasping, rolling the eyes back, and a tenseness in body movements. When the deity has entered him, he sprinkles holy water and flings flowers toward himself. He touches his forehead, throat, and shoulders with sandalwood powder and assumes the attributes of Siva; he ties a long blade of *alang alang* grass round his head; he places beads over his ears, across his breast, and on his wrists, and his red and gold mitre on his head; recites silently his most sacred prayers and, with apparent physical effort, leads his soul from his lower body into his head, while he holds a rosary of *genitri* seeds and raises his hands slowly upward. This ushers in the complete trance, during which he trembles, rolls his eyes in ecstasy, and pronounces prayers for the world in a deep and strangely changed voice. The water in the container then becomes Siva's water. At preliminary ceremonies for the cremation of the regent of Buleleng's daughter, a small pavilion caught fire near the place at which the high priest was inducing the trance, and the structure almost burned to the ground, while the corpse lay in state. The priest continued his prayer unmindful of the screams of women attendants and of the bustling relatives who were extinguishing the flames. That the possessed man may regain his former personality the priest sprinkles water toward him, drives the man's soul back into his stomach, removes his ornaments, and pins a small bouquet of multicoloured flowers over his hair knot. He then sprinkles the man's relatives and neighbours with the remaining holy water.

In the island of Florida, Melanesia, possession is indicated by sneezing and shaking; the eyes of the possessed man flare, his limbs twist, his lips foam, his body is convulsed. A voice apparently not his own comes from his throat and either approves or disapproves the proposed plan; for he seems not so much to speak as to be spoken from. In the Solomon Islands a man or woman may fall into a trance and speak with the voice of the ghost which declares itself in possession of the medium's body. Sometimes the paroxysms which indicate possession come suddenly. They may be accompanied by bad health or nervous prostration. In Sa'a the wild words and convulsive movements of the possessed man are ascribed to the ghost which has taken control of him; he, with Ovid, could declare: "There is a God within us who breathes that divine fire, by which we are animated." [3]

In the Mortlock Islands, Micronesia, signs of possession are convulsive twitching of hands, violent nodding of head, and other dynamic stigmata. The spirits open the man's mouth and speak through him. The answer given by the spirit, or spirits, is couched in language that is very different from everyday speech.

Possession is a highly developed technique among African Bantus. Among Sutos those who are possessed talk with disembodied spirits and are no longer of this world. The possessing spirit is sometimes that of an ancestor, but more usually it is the spirit of a celebrated chief or a famous medicineman. The medium (usually a woman) asserts that she is possessed by the spirit of So-and-so, and proceeds to deliver the message which has been entrusted to her. Frequently the message carries a threat, and invariably a demand by the possessing spirit for something to be received through the medium. Auditors receive these messages reverently.

In northern Rhodesia men or women may be the medium of spirits of dead kings or chiefs who prophesy through them. The man possessed by the spirit of a dead chief roars like a lion. Women gather about him, beat drums, and shout: "The chief has come to pay us a visit." Sometimes the possessed man prophesies impending war or attacks by lions. During the inspiration he eats only unfermented dough. Women

3. Ovid, *Fasti*, Book VI, 5.

who have the divine afflatus whiten their faces and anoint themselves with flour, which has sanctifying potency. While one beats a drum, others dance and sing. When the exaltation is complete, the possessed woman falls to the ground and begins an uncanny, almost inarticulate chant. Silence falls upon the group, and the assembled medicinemen interpret the spirit's message.

A Ganda inspired by the ghost of the dead king first addresses the royal jawbone, which is brought from the inner shrine and placed on a throne in the outer chamber of the palace where people assemble to hear the oracle. The seer then smokes one or two pipes of home-grown tobacco. The fumes induce the prophetic fit. He speaks with the voice and characteristic turns of speech of the departed monarch. His rapid utterances are so difficult to understand that a priest must interpret them. Through this medium the living king consults his dead predecessors periodically on affairs of state, when he visits the respective sacred temples in which their relics are preserved. On the lower Congo the possessed medium is in a frenzy and shouts. His entire body trembles and undulates, his muscles quiver, perspiration exudes from his forehead, foam appears at his mouth, and his eyes roll. When fully possessed by the spirit, he utters his oracles.

SAINT

A Hindu saint is instinct with sacred power and can perform marvels. He can transfer himself instantly from one place to another; be in different places simultaneously, assume any form, transport devotees great distances in the twinkling of an eye, give the suppliant a view of distant places, make inanimate things animate, show the sun on a moonless night, divert rivers, fly, disappear into the earth, sit on the water, and rest peacefully in mid-air. He controls death and can live as long as he likes. In short, almost all things are possible to him.

PILGRIM

Each year hundreds of thousands of pilgrims visit noted Shinto temples in Japan and climb sacred mountain peaks. Pilgrimages are made also to many places of lesser sanctity. Each district has a circuit of its own. Pilgrimages to a shrine to ask a favour are common among Hindus and the Santal. Crowds of Hindu women travel on foot, sometimes sixty miles, to a Siva shrine. A Mohammedan or Hindu pilgrim who has returned from a sacred place is sacred and is treated with great respect.

Because he is holy, he is dangerous. A Mohammedan pilgrim is feared for forty days after his return. To avoid his curses one must humour him in every way, must not excite him or allow him to work. When he returns from his pilgrimage, he must go to a mosque and wash his face and hands before he enters a house. A week must elapse before he sleeps with his wife. A Hindu pilgrim is similarly sacrosanct and dangerous. Upon his return from a pilgrimage he is received at the village boundary and given milk. Before entering a private house he must pass a night or two in the temple. If he arrives during the day, he must spend at least a few hours outside village bounds before he rejoins fellow-villagers. When he first enters a private dwelling, his feet are washed and grain is thrown over him.

Pious Gallas, doubtless because of Mohammedan influence, make pilgrimages to sacred places, especially Mt. Zuquala, and to the head of the priests and soothsayers, Father of Anointing, who dwells remote from his fellows. These pilgrimages begin in June of each year and may last five or six months. The pilgrims travel only a short distance in one day; from sunrise to sunset they may not cross more than five river beds. After their interview with the Father of Anointing they wear garments of cow hide and return home. They bring blessings to their households. They also enjoy special privileges and distinctions: they pay no imposts, forgo work in the fields, and carry as a badge a long staff tipped with an antelope horn.

Elaboration of religion fosters priesthood, and priesthood is a powerful factor in religious development. Religious traditions reside in the priests, who are responsible for their interpretation and perpetuation. This circumstance gives the priests an added interest in the religious life and concentrates their attention upon it. They develop a theology; and the priestly theology influences religious concepts and practices. The emphasis upon the apartness of those who deal with the sacred increases with elaboration of religion and is perhaps a function also of social differentiation. A simple social organization, such as that of the Pueblo peoples of the southwestern United States, is accompanied by priesthood if the religious life, especially in rites and ceremonies, is elaborate. Also, the society which has social stratification is likely to have a distinct order of priests or priestesses. Such is notably the case in Africa and Oceania and in the higher civilizations of both the Old World and the New. In the Northwest Coast area of North America, however, where aristocracy is entrenched, there is little tendency to award priests a special status—if, indeed, priests can be said to exist in that area.

Saints and pilgrims pertain only to the higher cultures. They are found in few preliterate cultures and are not reported for early historic civilizations. Indeed, Hinduism, Buddhism, Christianity, Mohammedanism, and tribes within their influence have a monopoly of saints and pilgrims.

CHAPTER VIII THE GODS

The gods, personifications of the holy, and frequently anthropomorphic, are foci of the holy and sources of mystic power.

They flourish in some areas in which the predominant magico-religious force is impersonal, as in Melanesia with its mana and Polynesia with its taboo. With the exception of Buddhism, Confucianism, and Taoism, all higher religions entertain the concept of a god; and in later Buddhism there have been many popular movements toward deification. Yet no anthropologist could agree that "the concept of god is certainly one essential element in religious feeling." [1]

Early Greeks had a healthy respect for the gods. "The wrath of god is a sore thing to fall on man. . . . He of a surety is not long-lived that fighteth with immortals, nor ever do his children prattle upon his knees at his returning from war and terrible fray. . . . There is no comparison of the race of immortal gods and of men that walk upon the earth." [2] "Deep awe of the gods checks the voice." [3]

Democritus said that in the atmosphere were beings with forms similar to those of men but far surpassing their human counterparts in size and length of life. Their diverse influences were sometimes beneficent, sometimes malign. Images which emanated from them and appeared to men during sleep or in waking life were later exalted into gods. To Prodicus the gods were personifications of the heavenly bodies, the elements, the fruits of the earth, and, generally, of all things useful to men. Critias declares belief in gods the invention of a politician who employed it as a weapon to deter men from evil. "As the Gods have made the goods of sense common to all, but those of the intellect only

1. Alfred N. Whitehead, *Process and Reality*, 315 (New York, Macmillan, 1929).
2. Iliad, Book V.
3. "To Demeter," *Homeric Hymns*.

to the wise," says Sallustius, "so the myths state the existence of Gods to all, but who and what they are only to those who can understand." Epictetus declares: "The next thing is to learn the true nature of the gods. For whatever their nature is discovered to be, he that is to please and obey them must try, so far as he can, to make himself like them. If God is faithful, he too must be faithful; if free, he too must be free; if beneficent, he too must be beneficent; if high-minded, he must in fact, as one who maketh God his idea, follow this out in every act and word." [4]

The suggestion that religious attitudes create gods and their attributes as truly as gods create worshippers and their attributes dates from the sixth century B.C. "Men," observes Xenophanes, "imagine gods to be born, and to have raiment and voice and body like themselves." Thus "the gods of the Ethiopians are swarthy and flat-nosed, the gods of the Thracians are fair-haired and blue-eyed." Indeed "oxen, lions and horses, if they had hands wherewith to grave images, would fashion gods after their own shapes and make them bodies like their own."

The Ethiop's Gods have dusky cheeks,
Thick lips, and woolly hair;
The Grecian Gods are like the Greeks,
As tall, bright-eyed, and fair.

Ethnography and history confirm Xenophanes' observation that gods reflect the mental attitudes of worshippers. A Maori said: "Gods die unless there are priests to keep them alive"; and to a Maori deity is attributed the statement: "When men no longer believe in us, we are dead." [5]

Thus Gods are made
And whoso makes them otherwise shall die.

The concept of God may embody in a supreme character the best that men have felt and thought. History confirms Ingersoll's gibe, which, in the last analysis, is a compliment, that "an honest god is the noblest work of man." The observations of Epictetus, Sallustius, and Xenophanes are applicable to Christianity. Chrysostom and Luther believe the universe was created by a father and king who now governs it. Their concepts of God reflect their concepts of human government. In other cultures and times the prevalent concept of God conforms with political experience. Asiatic peoples conceived divine government as despot-

4. Epictetus, *Discourses*, II, 14.
5. J. Gudgeon, *Journal of the Polynesian Society*, 15: 27 (1906).

ism. The Old Testament Yahweh is a glorified Oriental monarch, moody and vain, who governs arbitrarily, often without mercy, justice, righteousness, or lawful constraint. The God of medieval Christianity is a feudal lord who by covenants has given his vassals on earth specific rights and duties. The eighteenth-century God of the Enlightenment is a constitutional monarch who reigns but does not govern. The God of Modernism, the *élan vital* of some evolutionists, or the scientist's laws of nature, is deified law or constitutionalism. Nazism unmakes old gods and makes new ones.

The extent to which gods exist in preliterate cultures is largely a matter of definition. Gods are everywhere if one admits into this galaxy personages or beings of diverse types who play the rôle of creator, culture hero, or wielder of supernatural power. There are few gods if one admits to this status only personages of majesty and power to whom respect and reverence are paid and prayer or sacrifice is offered. If the criterion is a god of the type of the Hebrew Yahweh, the Babylonian Marduk, or the Olympian Zeus, there are, indeed, few gods among preliterate peoples. Perhaps, however, we should not be overexclusive in admitting personages or beings to the rank of god, but should recognize that there are many degrees of respect, reverence, love, and fear, that these attitudes vary from group to group, and that we should assign to claimants appropriate status in the hierarchy of gods.

A few examples of preliterate concepts of the gods will indicate how various these are. During the first three periods of creation, say the Central Algonquin Shawnees, Our Grandmother originated nothing bad, but only beneficial things. Evil origins and events they ascribe to her grandson and constant companion, Rounded-side, or to another grandson introduced in some variants, the devil, over whom she has little control. The creator, or creatress, occasionally bungles her creations; though after she has retired to her present residence, her creations or instructions are never bungled. Her grandson, Rounded-side, no longer originates catastrophes, but plays innocently with cumulus clouds. The devil punishes only under her auspices. She tolerates the nonsense of her Silly Boys, but retains firm control of them. She does not, however, continue to create good things; rather she guards jealously her accomplished work, boasts about her power in a way calculated to arouse awe, plays the rôle of policewoman rather than of benevolent deity, and on occasion metes out punishment. The Salivan of Colombia believe in a supreme invisible deity, Puru, the creative power from whom all things visible and all natural forces originated. He rules over men's destinies and sends them blessings or calamities in accordance with their good or bad conduct. Natural forces, wind, fire, earthquake, and thunder, and other forces operative in the natural and the human world, emanate from Puru. Guaigerri, the wind, sweeps over the earth and moves the clouds on which Cuisiabirri, the fire, is seated. The latter causes the lightning, and thus arouses the anger of the sleeping Puivisana, the earthquake, who resides in the dark regions of the earth. His grudge is the thunder, which is so terrible that Chavisana, the water, covers the earth with floods in order to soothe the pains of the fire-stricken deity, who in anger shakes the earth by turning around in his underground bed. This logical sequence of events is ordered by Puru in order that Qurrama Minari, the hidden force of vegetation, may favour men with the benefits of his fruit. Sometimes, however, in order to punish the inhabitants of the earth for their misdeeds, Puru unchains all the elements. Then houses are burned, food becomes scarce, and men are frightened by the anger of Puivisana, who upsets the earth. The above mentioned natural forces are conceived of by the Salivan, not as independent gods, but as parts or attributes of the one everlasting Puru.

The account of creation given by the Tuamotuans of Polynesia describes the body of the creator, Kiho, thus: flattened-crown, wrinkled-brow, observing-eye, obstructed-nose, conversing-mouth, chattering-lips, flower-decked-ears, distorted-chin, descending-saliva, crooked-neck, broad-chest, contracted-hands, grasping-finger, pinching-nails, flexed-side, bulging-ribs, inset-navel, princely-belly, small-of-the-back, twisted-knee, splay-foot. This realistic account may not sound very awe-inspiring. Yet no one may pronounce the name of Kiho in a public place. The high priests intone the sacred name of Kiho in prayer, invocation, or chants pertaining to high ritual. In places where no human being habitually dwells, his name may be uttered. He manifests himself by various names, each of which denotes a specific phase of his activation.[6] The natives say: "Now, this is the reason that people said that the Sky belonged to Tane, because today, in these times of Tane's ascendancy, the sacred name of Kiho-the-all-source has been concealed; the common people could not mention his name; only the chiefs and priests (could do so) upon the sacred platform of the temple at the time of the ceremonial sanctifica-

6. J. Frank Stimson, "Tuamotuan Religion," *BMB*, 103: 35 (1933).

tion of a new king or priest." [7] Inasmuch as neither king nor priest may pronounce aloud the sacred and forbidden name of Kiho-the-all-source in any public place, "inconsequential people said that Tane was the principal god because this supreme God had not been revealed to them." [7]

Tungus conceive Buga as greatest, omnipotent, ever-existing, all-knowing, responsible for the existence and regulation of life. He directs the whole world. He is not anthropomorphic, he cannot be introduced by human will into any object or person, and his appearance is not known. The Batak say that formerly heaven was near the earth and there was constant communication between gods and men. But human pride destroyed the road to the upper world. After the interruption of direct communication with men the gods lost interest in mankind. Now man turns to them only in the hour of need. This concept is strongly reminiscent of implications in the Old Testament. Each of the four gods of the Masai has a specific colour. The black god and the white god are good; the red god is evil; the blue god is neutral. Only the black god has previously been on earth as a man. The Masai are descended from him.

The following classes of gods, if gods they may be called, play an important rôle in many historic and preliterate cultures.

Celestial Beings—These are usually associated with celestial or atmospheric phenomena, particularly thunder and lightning. Throughout Negro Africa there are celestial gods, as also among the Malagasy, whose conceptions are an amalgam of Mohammedan, Indonesian, and other sources. In South Africa, Unkulunkulu, a sky being, is also a culture hero. Australians attribute to Daramulum, who lives in the sky, certain jurisdiction over youths who are being initiated. In North America the phenomena of lightning and thunder are usually associated with a sky being: in Plains and Northwest Coast areas, with Thunderbird; among Canadian Dakotas and Northern Iroquois, with thunder beings. Zeus in Greece, Jupiter in Rome, and Yahweh among the Hebrews play this rôle. In Egypt the sun gods Osiris and Re were the principal celestial powers.

Underground and Underwater Beings—In some areas the god dwells in an underworld from which he controls affairs. Eskimos attribute to Sedna power over sea animals. When an Eskimo has violated a taboo, she calls the seals from the haunts of men, but she may be induced to

7. J. Frank Stimson, "The Cult of Kiho-Tumu," *BMB*, 111: 26 (1933). Reprinted by permission of the Bernice P. Bishop Museum.

release them and permit them to return to the surface waters. The dragon in China, the tortoise in Hindu belief, Neptune and Poseidon in Graeco-Roman culture, and the feathered serpent in the Southwest of the United States are examples of underground or underwater beings with godlike power; to them should be added the gods of vegetation in Mediterranean cultures: Osiris, Demeter, Adonis, and others.

Culture Hero—If being a creator entitles one to a place in the pantheon, in practically every culture there is at least one god. The Prometheus of Greek legend has a counterpart almost everywhere, in his rôle of *Heilbringer*, or culture hero. In Australia, primeval kangaroos gave the landscape its present configuration. In northern California, Coyote is the culture hero; in southern California a bird, in many cases the wren, is the bringer of the culture. In many tribes of western North America Coyote brings fire to man.[8] Quetzalcoatl brought culture to Toltecs; Gluskap to Northeastern Algonquins.

Pantheon and Hierarchy—In Polynesia there are two orders of gods: exalted beings, almost abstractions, who are creators; and lesser gods, usually of human form and associated with a particular locality or family group. To the higher gods temples are dedicated and, in some cases, human sacrifice is offered. The Ashanti recognize four orders of sacred beings: *Nyame*, Supreme god; *Abosom*, gods; *samanfo*, ancestral spirits; and *suman*, fetishes. Ganda gods have been classified as national or tribal gods, local or clan gods, and beast or reptile gods. Most preliterate cultures assign specific powers and sometimes varying degrees of power to their gods or sacred beings; usually, however, they do not formulate classes of sacred beings or assign them a place in a hierarchy. Canadian Dakotas, who assign degrees of *wakan*, or sacredness and supernatural power, to Stone, Spider, Eagle, and other objects or animals, formulate a hierarchy. Four thousand years before the Christian era Ptah was regarded in Egypt as a spirit self-created, self-existent, without beginning, and eternal. "He was the Mind of the Universe, the Cause of Causes, whose thoughts had produced every material thing and being in heaven, earth, and the underworld. The gods were merely forms of his thoughts, and he was therefore God alone." [9] There were

8. For examples of the culture hero in connection with the origin of fire, see Sir James G. Frazer, *Myths of the Origin of Fire* (London, Macmillan, 1930); for the culture hero in general see (Pater) W. Schmidt, *Der Ursprung der Gottesidee*, 6 volumes (Münster, Aschendorff, 1935).

9. Sir E. A. Wallis Budge, *From Fetish to God in Ancient Egypt*, 16 (London, Oxford University Press, 1934). Reprinted by permission of the publisher.

gods over cities or districts, which were under their patronage, on whose inhabitants they bestowed "life, health, strength, victory, and prosperity." There were also nature gods, sun, moon, sky, and Nile, which were of secondary importance, at least in early religious development. Eventually, Re, the sun god, became the greatest god. In Shintoism the sun goddess is head of the pantheon. Of minor importance are the moon god and the star god. Next in importance are gods of storm, rain, thunder, sea, rivers, water in general, earth and its productive powers, food-crops, mountains, trees, fire—the nature gods. Less important gods were once men: rulers, heroes, or men eminent in some art or pursuit. China has gods of soil and grain, a god of literature, a god of war, a kitchen god, a god of wealth, a god of medicine, and a goddess of smallpox. In Greece Zeus was the supreme god; in Rome, Jupiter. Yahweh, originally a local god, became the chief and only god of the Jews. In Christianity the dispute as to whether Christ was equal with the Father in power led to the first great schism. Similar disputes have occasioned subsequent rifts within the fold of Christianity. Few religions place all recognized gods on a plane of equality.

The god is a personification of the holy. In many cultures men acknowledge a plurality of gods, for the holy is as specific as the things which embody or generate it. Belief that all holiness eventually derives from or is subordinate to one god is essentially the concept of a Supreme Being. Exaltation of the god implies, therefore, concentration of the holy in a supernatural personality or being. Strictly speaking, no religion is monotheistic; all are polytheistic, for all attribute holiness to a variety of things or beings. Monotheism is a rationalization, an intellectual unification of former divergence and manifoldness reflected in the more primary emotional attitudes of devotees. Every historic religion bears witness to a trend toward henotheism and then toward monotheism as theology becomes sophisticated; thus logic seems to have been a guiding thread in the development of concepts of the god, though probably followed without conscious recognition of the guidance.

CHAPTER IX CONSECRATION, PURIFICATION, AND CONFESSION

CONSECRATION

Consecration is making things instinct with holiness—literally, at one with the sacred—"the solemn setting apart of persons or things for some particular religious work or use." Many things attain holiness by association or by sheer contiguity or proximity, for sacredness radiates and irradiates. Objects, persons, or places may be deliberately consecrated, that is, set apart from the profane and devoted to the sacred.

Devotion to holiness, which involves formula, ritual, and ceremony, is a public act. When an edifice is consecrated or dedicated, the ceremony publicly and formally transfers the structure to the realm of the holy. Henceforth the building is sacred and must be treated as such; it becomes an approved place for the conduct of sacred ceremonies; and profane activities may not be conducted within its sacred precincts. In western Ireland to use for profane purposes the remains of a destroyed church would bring misfortune. In some districts the land which formerly belonged to the church was highly venerated by the people, who attributed surprising virtues to it.

When an edifice is to be abandoned, given to secular activities, or destroyed, there is, in some Christian sects, a deconsecration ceremony. What has been done must be undone; the sacredness previously imparted must be removed. At the consecration of a Roman Catholic church the cross is planted at the door and is marked repeatedly on the walls to protect against attacks of the devil the sacred place and the faithful who are to worship in it. The water, salt, and oil used for sacramental unction are exorcised; and exorcism accompanies the blessing of bells, crosses, medals, and reliquaries. The Todas of India, who deftly interweave religion and economic interest, ritually sanctify a new dairy. Dairymen are ordained and new vessels are consecrated before they enter the sacred building.

If an especially sacred pot buried in the buffalo pen has been broken, stolen, or tampered with, if a foreigner has entered the dairy, or if the dairyman has used tobacco, the defilement must be removed by elaborate ceremony. A Maori chief and his house are taboo. It is sometimes necessary to summon a commoner or man of lower rank than chieftainship to repair the chief's house or build a new one. The taboo upon the structure is temporarily lifted by special incantation. When the work is finished and the man of lower rank has left the premises, another incantation restores the temporarily lifted taboo. Thus the sacredness of the place is removed, and later restored.

DEFILEMENT OR UNCLEANNESS

The holy and the unclean, each of which imposes apartness, are often a nuisance, for contact with them, even indirect communication with them, is dangerous. Holiness is secular uncleanness and defiles for secular activities the individual whom it envelops. Uncleanness is acquired by touching the dead body of man or beast, by disease, by childbirth, by having one's hands imbued with murder or other noxious crime, by contact with blood, particularly human blood. Proximity to the dead implies association with ghosts, and such association makes one other-worldly. Contact with things funereal or pertaining to the nether world imparts defilement or uncleanness. Sexual intercourse imposes defilement. Hence many preliterate cultures and many historic civilizations demand from participants in religious rites abstinence from sexual intercourse for a specified period immediately preceding participation. A Naga must abstain from sexual intercourse during the night immediately preceding the day on which he sets forth to choose the stone to erect as a monument. From that time until villagers drag the stone into the village, and for a year subsequently, he must observe this taboo, or *genna*. During the first three days of the search for the magic camphor the Sakhai of the Malay peninsula must not bathe, have sexual intercourse, or put oil on his hair. During the Mentawei communal purification ceremony sexual intercourse is taboo, as also during the founding of a village; violation of the injunction is supernaturally punished. In the Plains area of North America abstinence from carnal intercourse is demanded of the man who performs the sun dance, and women who assist must first state that they have never had sexual intercourse. Men who assist must have abstained from sexual intercourse for four days and nights immediately preceding the performance. Similar prior abstinence is demanded of those about to go on the war path. Violation of this requirement is supernaturally punished. The Isleta require continence during the four days preceding a ceremony and the four days following it. Abstinence is observed by participants in the ceremony and by others who wish to enhance its efficacy. Violation of the taboo negatives the efficacy of ritual, and a man who breaks the taboo may be turned into a rock, a log, or a beast.

Zuñis taboo sex relations during the ten days of the winter solstice and the four days following planting of a prayer-stick or participation in dances or other ceremonies. Warriors who have taken a scalp, and widowers, must refrain from sexual intercourse for a year, and then perform a purification ceremony. If a Zuñi is incontinent during the period of the *katcina* ceremony, the mask which he wears will choke him or stick to his face.

In Fiji a woman who makes clay pottery or who is present during its manufacture must observe sexual continence. If a woman is pregnant, but the embryo not yet formed, she may not take part in the operations. If the embryo is formed and the pregnancy is perceptible, the prohibition does not apply. If this prohibition is broken, the clay will crack when being made into a pot.

The sacred oil of the Ceram Laut may be made only by a boy and a girl who are virgin. At Buka Passage, Solomon Islands, abstinence from sexual intercourse during the night preceding the expedition must be observed by the bonito fisherman who wishes a catch. Sexual abstinence is demanded of Yukon Eskimos who participate in the Bladder Festival or in the annual ceremony concerned with the ribbon seal. During the night before he digs the clay to be used in making pots, the Zande (Anglo-Egyptian Sudan) abstains from sexual intercourse. He must abstain also during the night preceding consultation of the poison oracles, and before collecting the poison. A Hehe medicineman must abstain from sexual intercourse the night before he administers medicine which confers invulnerability to gun and rifle bullets. A Lenga married woman who makes oil from the plant *Morordica clematidea* must abstain from intercourse with her husband the preceding night; if she does not do so, the oil will "refuse to come." Chewa hunters must abstain from sexual intercourse the night before they use the medicine made to keep carnivora away from the kraals; otherwise it will lose efficacy. A Zulu officiant in a sacrifice must approach the gods wholly "clean." During the night preceding the sacrifice he must keep away from women and must sleep in a hut in which there are only men and where there is no fire. A devout Jain observes celibacy before an important festival or fast, before going on a pilgrimage, and during twenty days of each month. He advances in holiness until finally he renounces entirely the society of his wife. A Hindu must be chaste before performing rites designed to secure *punya*, or merit, and before offering sacrifice or taking a vow. To acquire *punya* he must be ritually clean. A man polluted by contamination of death or birth cannot enhance his *punya;* and his destination in the next world is determined by his accumulated store of *punya*. While unclean he may not read a sacred book or listen to its recital by another, and may not offer silent prayer. If mourners are ritually unclean, the deceased loses *punya*.

PURIFICATION

In many Christian churches a ceremony of purification is performed after the edifice has been desecrated by a suicide on the premises or by other sacrilege. By an old rule of the English Established Church, still in force, a church in which a murder has been committed must be purified before it can be used again for services. The adhering uncleanness is removed, the status of holiness is restored. Marquesans purify a tabooed house by ceremonial sacrifice of pigs. Purification is usually effected by a physical agency, which frequently has a magical basis in association of ideas. Aleuts obtain purification by burning grass which has been placed close to their persons to absorb their sins. Ancient Peruvians changed their garments or shook from their clothes the adhering invisible dust, standing by the door that the dust might be blown away into the open space about them. Some peoples purify by means of an emetic, a literal purging, of which Plato often speaks figuratively. Rites of purification by emetic were practised by Peruvians, by Zuñis (who had taken scalps) and the Isleta in the Southwest of the United States, and by Yuchis and Creeks in the Southeast Atlantic area. A Creek warrior who has shed blood purifies himself when he returns to camp. The ritual emetic leaves him "in a state of perfect innocence [and] inspires [him] with an invincible prowess in war." The Haida purify themselves by purging the stomach of its contents and drinking alternately fresh and salt water. A Yokut shaman (California) establishes contact with the supernatural power by means of a tobacco emetic. Navahos take emetics on the day of the Mountain Chant ceremony to free them of the spiritual pollution of the bear and the snake and the spiritual pollution of contaminating enemies. Ritual emetics are used by the Kikuyu of East Africa. The Ila use an emetic to drive out disturbing ghosts. The plea in *Psalms*

(51:7), "Purge me with hyssop and I shall be clean, wash me and I shall be whiter than snow," sounds familiar to Christianized Bechuana, of South Africa, who obtain both physical and ceremonial cleansing by use of the hyssop rod and by rubbing from their persons the undigested contents of the stomach of the sacrificed animal.

The most common ceremonial purifying agency is water. During the Bladder Festival, Yukon Eskimo men, to remove ritual uncleanness, bathe twice a day. During preparation for the Ribbon Seal ceremony, held south and west of the mouth of the Yukon, women bathe each morning before taking food to their husbands who are participating in the ceremony. As a cleansing ceremony following mourning observances, Polar Eskimos and those at Chesterfield Inlet wash face and hands and throw away the clothes they have been wearing. After a death in the village, Eskimos of St. Michael, Alaska, before eating bathe in urine to remove any evil influence attaching to them as a result of contamination with death. The sweat bath, performed in a shelter erected for the purpose, is a means of purification. Water is poured on heated stones, and participants take the sweat bath in the steam vapour. The institution of the sweat bath is found throughout nearly all North America north of Mexico, with the exception of the Eskimo and most of the Northwest Coast area, though it is practised by the Tlinkit, the Tanaina of Cook Inlet, and Alaska Eskimos. In many areas the sweat bath is a means of purification or of propitiating spirits; warriors take the sweat bath before going to fight and, in some areas, boys upon attaining puberty. Navahos say "the first sweat-house was built at the Place of Emergence when Dineh came up from the Underworld. It was used then as now, not only as a sweat-bath, but to purify the body after a journey."

A Kwakiutl myth states that a certain man who sought supernatural power purified himself in the river for four days. Three days after a death, every member of the village must bathe. The Haida purify themselves by a mud bath, then wash the mud off from above downward, accompanying the act with prayer. When the aurora borealis appears, the Modoc, shouting, rush into the water and beat it about them to ward off the threatened illness. Before the Pomo initiate the fishing season of the year, they purify the fishing implements in a basket of boiling water which contains plants. After taking the sweat bath, Crows wash their sickness away in the river. Hopis and the Isleta use yucca suds as a purifying agent. At Isleta the hair of funerary attendants is washed on the third day after the performance of their duties. On the fourth day they take a ritual bath in the river. At the solstice ceremonies each participant washes his hands and face in the river. After the rites they ceremonially wash off paint from face and body in the river. Zuñi *Koyemci* priests are bathed in the house of the priests, and later are again washed at the home of their "aunts," the rite being symbolic. The sprinkling of corn meal on their heads is also called "washing." Ritual washing of the head is done by one's paternal aunt. To remove the contamination adhering to the scalp of an enemy, the scalp is ceremonially washed by two men appointed for the purpose. A Maricopa who has killed an enemy must purify himself by bathing; and a ghost who dies in the land of the dead must purify himself by bathing in a certain river. Death in ghostland makes him unclean and other ghosts do not cherish his company. The concept of using water to restore life or as a sovereign healing power is found in the folklore of the Northwest Coast (Kwakiutl, Newettee, Bella Bella, Bella Coola, Rivers Inlet, Chehalis, Coos); in California (Yana, Maidu, Shasta, Achomawi, Paviotso); the Plains (Southern Paiute, Ponca); Central Woodland (Ojibwa); Northern Iroquois (Seneca); Southwest (Pima); and in Siberia.

An Aztec priest baptized, and uttered the words: "May the water wash away all that is evil; may it whiten thy heart." Ceremonial bathing at festivals cleanses from sin as well as from physical pollution.

In Maya ceremony boys and girls, in separate groups, were baptized and purified. White cloths were placed on their heads, and they confessed important sins. The priest blessed them and sprinkled water on them from a short carved stick. The noble who presided over the ceremony then tapped each child nine times on the forehead with a bone, rubbed each child nine times on the forehead with a bone, and rubbed perfumed water on their faces and between their fingers and toes. Later the boys sniffed perfume from a bouquet of flowers, inhaled mouthfuls of smoke, and were given food. Offerings accompanied with prayer were made to the gods, and gifts were presented to parents of participants. Feasting and drinking concluded the ceremony. In Aztec and Pueblo tribes, four days after a death survivors wash the head, for the spirit of the dead lingers four days. In Peru, bathing is a means of ritual purification and also of removing disease.

In the Marquesas men who have engaged in house-building must purify themselves by bathing. In Samoa one who has violated taboo is purified by being sprinkled with coconut water. In Maori purification ceremonies which terminate childbirth taboos, the officiating priest places a twig from a shrub in the middle of a stream, and a twig on each side of the first one. Mother and child are then sprinkled with water from the middle twig, which the priest holds in his hand.

In the evening following the killing of an enemy, an Angami Naga warrior, before eating or drinking, must wash hands and mouth and throw away the water used in doing so, also all water then in his house. The next day, carrying spear and shield, he goes to a spring and bathes. The Shan of Indo-China purify with water the plough with which they do the ceremonial ploughing of the rice fields. In a Mentawei ceremony water is placed on the head of a child to ensure it long life; and a ceremonial washing of the hair initiates the communal purification ceremony.

On the Guinea coast ceremonial washing as a means of ritual cleansing is practised by pregnant women. The Herero vestal virgin who guards the sacred fire sprinkles water on mother and child at the naming ceremony. Among the Rondo, east of Lake Victoria Nyanza, a murderer, or a man who has killed an enemy in battle, must be twice ritually purified by being washed in the river. The West African Ga purify a widow by taking her to the beach and giving her a sea bath during the twelfth week following the death of her husband. The Ashanti purify by sponging or sprinkling with water. A week after the birth of a child the Lenge mother, of Portuguese East Africa, performs ceremonial ablutions at a lake and thus terminates the seclusion enforced by the uncleanness inherent in childbirth. She must wash privately and not at a place where other women are bathing or drawing water. Should she not observe this privacy, the baby will incur the ceremonial misfortune of *Khombo* and perhaps die. A widow must cleanse herself ritually by an ablution. Among the Lenge washing the body is always a ceremonial act: "It is not a mere cleansing of the body; it is almost sacramental in that it is a type of cleansing from the moral defilement of illness, death, and loss. In fact it is an aggregation rite, bringing the person who performs the ablutions once more into the common life." [1] When Bechuana sons return home after prolonged absence, their elders asperse them with "holy water." Among the Mba of northern Rhodesia and among the Suto, a returned warrior is purified by bathing in a stream.

Purification by water was common in ancient Egypt. When the pharaoh went to his kingdom in the sky, he was purified, usually through the medium of water, by libations, or by bathing in the sacred lake located in the blessed fields. The gods, bearing towels and raiment, offici-

1. E. Dora Earthy, *Valenge Women*, 167 (London, Oxford University Press, 1933).

ated at the royal bath. "I am pure; I am pure," says the scribe Nu; "I have washed my front parts with water of libations, I have cleansed my hinder parts with drugs which make wholly clean, and my inward parts have been washed in the liquor of meat. There is no single member of mine which lacketh righteousness." When the deceased had been purified with water, natron, and incense, the soul made before Osiris the above declaration that it had been purified. At the coronation purification ceremony, patterned after the purification ceremony performed for the infant, a priest, impersonating the god, thus addressed the king: "I purify thee with the water of life and good fortune, all stability, all health, all happiness." Before the king entered a temple, he was purified, either by washing his hands in basins provided for the purpose at the temple, or by being sprinkled by the priest. The "water of life and good fortune," and "that which renews life," was procured from the sacred pool which, apparently, was in every temple.

In Babylonia purification was often effected by use of pure water, which must be taken from the Tigris or the Euphrates, or, preferably, from the joint mouths of the rivers, near the Isles of the Blest. The water of purification must be kept in a pure place, "preserved faithfully in the abysses." Apsu, the abyss, was the cosmic sea which underlay the whole earth. On its bosom the earth rested; to it the kings dug when laying the foundations of the palace; and from it came the fresh water of springs and rivers. In every great temple stood the laver, the "great sea," *apsu*, which may have inspired Solomon's "brazen sea." Here, probably, was kept the pure water of purification, the water of Eridu, "the sweet or good city." In default of it the water of wells, if consecrated by prescribed incantation, might be used to purify. The ceremony of washing the hands, accompanied by appropriate incantations, was repeated several times. The detailed accompaniments of the ceremony of hand-washing were numerous; a description of them "would demand a treatise." Usually the Babylonian ceremony of purification did not necessitate bathing the entire person but was accomplished by merely washing the hands. Sometimes, however, head or forehead as well must be washed. In special cases it was necessary to cleanse the mouth or drink water. Occasionally the person was sprinkled. In some cases the ceremony must be performed in a "clean" place—for example, open country or desert. To ensure efficacy of the rite under such circumstances a *bit runqui* was built. Often the *bit runqui*, a "washing house," or chamber of lustration, was attached to a house in the city. To it the polluted were taken and there cleansed in accordance with specified ritual. Priest and suppliant wore special garments of sable hue. Apparently lustration was symbolic removal of contamination, which sometimes involved symbolic transfer, by the medium of water, to some other object. The object to which uncleanness was transferred might be the representation of the cause of impurity—for example, a clay or wax image of the witch who had occasioned it. The image was burned, buried, or otherwise "destroyed," and the uncleanness thus removed from the victim. Before a sick man could be cured, he must be purified; while he was contaminated, medical treatment was ineffective. An Assyrian patient purified himself by washing his feet, hands, and face, and sprinkling his body with perfumed water.

The Zoroastrian Vendidad prescribes the means of getting rid of uncleanness consequent upon contact with a corpse from which the devil has not been driven away by beasts or birds of prey. A disinfectant, cow's urine, sprinkled upon the contaminated person, drives the demon from one lodging place to another, literally from head to foot, until, finally, it escapes from the left great toe, rushing off, with a buzzing noise, to the home of the devils in the north. To ensure this consummation the procedure described above is performed six times. The purified man then rubs himself from head to foot with dry earth and washes in water at three separate depressions in the ground, performing one ablution at the first depression, two at the second, three at the third. The respective ablutions are repeated at intervals of three days, during which time the man is quarantined. Not until the end of the ninth day may he approach fire, water, earth, cattle, or the faithful, lest his impurity, not yet totally banished, spread to them. If, however, the demon was expelled from the corpse by means of dogs or birds of prey, the person who acquires uncleanness by touching the corpse is purified by washing thirty times with cow's urine and water. A field in which a dead dog has lain is unclean and must remain fallow for a year. The ground in which a body has been buried is unclean for fifty years. Running or standing water in which a body has been found is unclean. In Mithraism, honey and water were used in ritual purification of the initiate.

Probably the small light bathrooms at Mohenjodaro, in the Indus valley, dating from about 2500 B.C., were used for ceremonial bathing in connexion with religious rites. Hindus believe that the ceremonial bathing of a king will keep away evil tendencies he otherwise would acquire. Water sprinkled over the *yajaman*, the performer of a rite, by the priests at obsequial ceremonies, destroys evil tendencies of the *yajaman*. Water deprives *paygun*, a man's inherent potentiality, of evil, and averts the evil eye. Orthodox Hindus bathe after contact with the wicked, and rinse the mouth with water after uttering the name of a wicked person. Before they wear clothes returned by the washerman, they sprinkle water on them, as also on articles brought from the market, on flowers before using them in worship, on coals brought for a sacrificial fire, and on the emptied plate on which fire was brought. If a Sudra caste man has touched a well-rope, before a member of another caste will draw water from the well he sprinkles the rope with water. When utensils loaned to a Sudra for cooking or for other purposes are returned, the owner sprinkles them with water. Some Hindus, when they go to a temple, carry a cloth soaked in water which they wring out or sprinkle as they go. At the evening service in the Hindu temple the worshipper receives in the hollow of the right palm about a teaspoonful of holy water. He supports his right palm upon his left one and a portion of his cloth between the two, to prevent the holy water from falling to the ground. Then the devotee, lifting his head, pours and reverently drinks half of this blessed water. He sprinkles the remaining half on his head and returns home rejoicing. It is unholy to lick or sip the water from the hand. Before a Hindu offers sacrifice, he takes water in the right hand and pours it over his fingers. Bathing as a means of purification is prescribed in the Laws of Manu. By bathing in the sacred Ganges or in one of the holy tanks the Hindu is cleansed of every sin.

In Buddhism, purification, or release, is attained by asceticism, fire ritual, or baptism. The last mentioned consists of frequent immersion in water, preferably running water, which is most efficacious in removing impurity. The ritualistic Bharadvaja clan invites the Buddha to bathe in the Bahuka River. When the Buddha asks, "What of the river, Brahmin, what can it do?" the answer is: "Many consider it a means of deliverance and of merit; many people let it bear away their evil deeds." The typical ceremonial bathing is in the river Gaya, at the spring festival of Phalgu. The Suttas, holy books of Buddhism, however, distrust ceremonial purification and emphasize the necessity of following "the path to purity" by developing proficiency of heart and head.

> What boots the Bahuka, or the Gaya?
> For ever and a day his foot may plunge
> Therein, yet are his smutty deeds not cleansed.
> They will not purge the man of passions vile.
> To him that's pure, ever 'tis Phalgu-time,

To him that's pure, ever 'tis Sabbath-day,
To him that's pure and in his actions clean,
Ever his practices effectual prove.
Here, Brahmin, is't that thou shouldst bathing go:—
Become a haven sure for all that breathes;
Speak thou no lies, harm thou no living thing,
Steal nought, have faith, in nothing be thou mean,
So living, what are river-rites to thee? [2]

A Jain who has acquired impurity by touching an outcaste, that is, an "untouchable," sitting by one, or brushing against one, purifies himself by bathing and by changing his clothing, or, if less meticulous, by sprinkling water over his clothes. Village Jains may purify themselves by touching a Mohammedan. If an outcaste passes near a Jain's house or enters his room, the defiled man purifies house or room by sprinkling water on it. If the outcaste brings wood, the Jain purifies the wood by sprinkling water over it. After walking through an outcaste quarter, the Jain purifies himself by bathing or by sprinkling. A meticulous Jain purifies himself by affusion; others are content with aspersion. A similar difference of opinion regarding proper method of baptism is rife in Christendom.

Members of the Kachari tiger totem go into formal mourning when a tiger dies near the village. At the end of the period of mourning, the floor and walls of each house are carefully smeared with freshly prepared compost of mud and cow dung. All articles of clothing and all brass household utensils are thoroughly cleansed in running water; all earthenware vessels except those which are new and have not been used for cooking are broken and thrown away. An elder, acting as priest, then solemnly distributes the "water of peace," of which all in turn drink. Buildings and clothing are liberally sprinkled with this water. The service of propitiation and purification is completed by sacrificing a fowl or a pig, of which all partake in communion.

At the purification ceremonies held by Rengma Nagas the men must wash in water that is absolutely unpolluted. At dawn the males of the village, including the small boys, wash in a stream.

Among Madras lower castes, when a man has committed a serious offence, he and his family must be purified. The walls of his house are sprinkled with water and whitewashed, and the floors are scoured with a mixture of cow dung and water. The family priest then sprinkles consecrated water over the house and each member of the family. Sometimes,

2. *Majjhima-Nikaya*, I, 39. Quoted by C. A. R. Rys Davids in "Purification (Buddhist)," *ERE*, X, 469.

in addition, he brands the culprit's tongue with a gold needle, the more thoroughly to purify him, and, perhaps, to induce repentance.

In Confucian purification rites the sacrificial articles placed in front of the spirit-tablets of Confucius and associated saints may be carried only by those who have attained ceremonial purity, that is, have completed the three days' purification known as *Chai*. Before approaching the altar with sacrificial meats and fruits, candidates must pass through a final ceremony of purification. Clean water is transferred from one vessel to another; in the latter the officiant who is to carry the offerings to the altar washes his hands, and ceremonially dries them on a long narrow strip of fringed cloth taken from a bamboo basket. In Shintoist Japan a man who wishes to be purified procures from the temple a small piece of white paper cut roughly in the shape of a shirt. On this he writes his name, sex, and year and month of birth, rubs the paper over his entire body, breathes into it, and thus transfers to it his sins and ailments. He then takes it back to the temple, where it is deposited on a black table during the purification ceremony. Eventually it is sent away in a boat and is thrown into the water. The underlying concept implies a physical substance or essence which can be separated from a person and put into some place—in this instance, river or ocean—where it can no longer impart contagion. To purify the Mikado clothes are made, as if for him to wear; he then blows upon them, they are cast into the water, and he is purged of all spiritual impurity. In Shintoism sin implies physical impurity, and ceremonial purification with water is an old rite. At every Shinto shrine there is holy water with which the pilgrim washes his hands and rinses his mouth. Water is the common Ainu symbol of purification.

Athenian practices of washing the statues of tutelary divinities and rekindling the fire on the city hearth at the New Year were primarily purification rites. At the Attic Plynteria, held in May, the vestments, and probably also the idol of Athene, were ceremonially washed. The day was *moira*, sacred, taboo, for expulsion of the contagion rendered the circumambient air dangerous.

In ancient Rome, water, fire, and incense had lustral power. Bodily impurity and defilement by a bad dream were removed by running water. Many herbs also purified. Purifying power was attributed to the willow and possibly also to the myrtle used in rites for the dead and at the marriage ceremony. Some sins, however, could not be removed by purification.

At Serabit, in pre-Jewish Sinai, prior to 3400 B.C. much importance attached to ceremonial ablutions. In the principal courts along the approach to the shrines were four tanks or basins at which, presumably, the worshipper washed different parts of the body. As in the Hebrew sanctuary, one large tank was at the north door of the temple, for use in preliminary cleansing. The other three were in the finest parts of the buildings, thus indicating that ablutions performed at them were acts of worship, ritual purification, and not mere physical cleansings. Such elaborate ceremonial cleansing is not a feature of early Jewish ritual, but in *Exodus* (40: 7, 11–12) a laver is provided at the door of the tabernacle. Here priests washed their hands and feet. Later, about the tenth century, the washing of mouth, nose, arms, and other parts of the body was enjoined, much as is now done in Mohammedanism.

Wudu, minor purification, is performed by Mohammedans regularly before each of the required five daily prayers, but it may be omitted if the worshipper is sure that he has suffered no defilement since the last purification. *Wudu* is performed at a tank or reservoir provided with spouts. The man declares that the act which he is about to perform is for purposes of purification, tucks his sleeves above the elbow, and performs three times each of the following acts: washes his hands; rinses his mouth; snuffs water up each nostril, in turn; washes his face; washes his right arm, so that the water runs from palm to elbow; then washes similarly the left arm. Each of the following cleansings is then performed once: he pushes his turban back with the left hand, and passes the wetted right hand over the upper part of his forehead; combs his beard with wetted fingers; inserts the tips of the forefingers into his ears and passes the thumbs around the back of the ears; wipes his neck with the back of the fingers, using both hands; washes each foot up to the ankle, and inserts his fingers between his toes. The major purification with water, the *ghusl,* must be performed in case of conversion to Mohammedanism, before Friday prayers and festivals, after washing a corpse, after blood-letting, and after death.

Ghusl involves the use of more than a specified minimum amount of water. The water must touch every hair and part of the body. Usually it is a plunge bath. If water cannot be secured within two miles or without incurring danger, purification may be effected by dry dust or sand, which, after the declaration of intention, is thrown upon the face and hands. Water used for ritual purification must be clean; hence rain-water is preferred, and is recommended in the Koran: "Remember . . . He sent down upon you rain from heaven to purify you therewith and remove from you Satan's pollution." Dry ground is clean; and any spot may be made ritually clean and fitted for prayer by spreading a clean rug or garment on it. A person who has touched forbidden animals, such as a dog, a pig, or a rat, must be purified, and also his garments. Dishes which have contained wine or flesh of swine must be purified before a Mohammedan may eat or drink from them.

The Mohammedan washes not only before prayer but also before touching the Koran. He washes three times: first, right hand and right forearm; then, left hand and left forearm. While he washes the right hand he says: "O My God, on the day of judgment, place the book of my actions in my right hand, and examine my accounts with favour." While he washes the left hand he says: "Place not at the resurrection the book of my actions on my left hand."

Indian Mohammedans say that water washes away the sins of a Mohammedan but is powerless to cleanse a Hindu of his sins. In proof of this they cite the fact that a horse will drink water in which a Hindu has bathed, but not water in which a Mohammedan has bathed. The explanation, however, takes no account of olfactory discrimination.

Pagan Teutons sprinkled an infant with water as a means of purification. When Copts combine purification rites with commemoration of the baptism of Christ, males of all ages plunge into water. Some churches contain large tanks of water blessed for the occasion, but usually the ceremony is held at the Nile. Before participants plunge into the stream, the priest pours holy water from the church into the river to purify it.

Mandaeans, Semites who live in lower Babylonia, sometimes called Muglitasils, that is, Washers, because of the frequency of their ablutions, or Christians of St. John, because of their tradition that they are descended from disciples of John the Baptist, turn, when they pray, not toward Jerusalem, but toward the north, that is toward the great mountains from which flow the rivers Tigris and Euphrates. The source of these rivers is the world of light, where the Supreme Life, that is, God, lives and reigns. In these waters they bathe morning and evening, especially on Sundays and fast days. They observe also a bathing festival in which all the members of a community go to the river and bathe ceremonially under the direction of their priests, or according to their private rules. Through these immersions in the "waters of light" they receive renewal of life from the Great Life, the Master of the Universe and of all virtues. They could not practise their religion in a region devoid of streams; hence they have always resided in the district near Kurnah, where the Tigris and Euphrates unite. Their "baptism" they term *masbutâ*, because the ceremony takes place in "living," that is, flowing, water. They despise the Christian ceremony because it is performed in "dead," or still, water.

In Morocco water magically removes uncleanness and washes away spells. Thus a young girl, a widow, or a divorced woman who has not succeeded in securing a husband, washes her face and hands in the first water from a freshly dug well and is immediately successful in securing a life partner. Before the fast on the eve of Yom Kippur Moroccan Jews bathe together in the large tanks in the synagogue. Rabbis beat them with sticks to drive away evil spirits. They purify themselves with water on the last day of the Passover.

Marrakech Jews perform the last mentioned rite at dawn in a partly demolished water channel which because of its miraculous origin has supernatural power; and they wash hands and face in the water. Water is taken away in bottles so that the rite can be performed by sick people and women in childbirth who cannot be carried to the place. Water washes away the memory of trouble. The feet of a released prisoner are washed before he crosses the threshold of his house; the water carries away the memory of his punishment. If the man has been in prison a long time, a visiting friend takes away a piece of his shirt or turban, ties seven knots in it, and throws it into running water. The knots tie up the punishment, and the current carries it away.

As mentioned, Mohammedans use earth or sand for ritual purification when water is not available. Hindus use earth as one of the eight media of purification. In times of scarcity, when water must be taken where found, high-caste Hindus purify it by pouring it into a depression in the ground. For Hindus, falling rain is not pure until it has touched the ground. A vessel polluted by impure touch—for example, that of a god, a menstruating woman, or an untouchable—is purified by being buried in the ground for three, five, or seven days.

Hindus fumigate the newborn child with grain mixed with mustard seed. In South America many tribes purify by fumigation with tobacco. Other plants or substances are sometimes used in lieu of tobacco. The Jibaro fumigate newly built houses by burning cedar to purify them from evil spirits and insects. During mourning men are ceremonially purified by smoke of tobacco or of burned termites. The Quichua and Aymara fumigate habitations by burning certain plants, llama tallow, or wild cat skin. Purification by fumigation is practised by the Pima,

Tarahumara, Cora, and Huichol. Witchitas purify by burning sage. After death in the household or as protection against witchcraft, Zuñis burn piñon gum and inhale the smoke as a purifying agent. After childbirth and in medicine society ceremonies they use ashes for purification. Among Mohaves baths and fumigations keep away a disturbing ghost. Yukon Eskimos purify themselves by jumping through smoke. A Mongol of the Ordos desert who has touched a corpse purifies himself by jumping over a fire. The corpse of a Buryat shaman is purified by fumigation with smoke of ledum, thyme, and fir bark. In China, when a man has hanged himself in a house, the pollution is removed by cutting down the beam, burning it, and carrying away and casting into the river the earth or ashes beneath the burned beam.

The Lenge and the Kikuyu of Africa use fumigation as a means of ceremonial cleansing. The Ila and Suto purify warriors in fumes of certain medicine plants burned in a sherd. In Morocco a child is passed three times through the fumes of the incense burner to purify it from contact with a stranger and to destroy the evil results that might otherwise ensue.

A Zuñi form of purification known as "wiping off" consists of expectorating into cedar bark or corn husk, or on a prayer-stick, waving the packet four times over the head in counterclockwise circuit, and throwing it down, or, if healing is the aim, burying it to the east. Zuñis purify also by destroying property or, like the Hopis, by whipping.

Among Navahos the war dance or enemy dance is performed "to purify all who had gazed upon the dead, to drive out enemy ghosts, to cleanse from spiritual pollution." At Isleta pueblo, houses, corrals, plaza, and river are cleansed by the use of eagle feathers with accompanying slicing and discarding motions by the hands. Feathers, bear claws, or cotton wipe or brush out of the body any concealed substance, such as stick, stone, cloth, thorn, or ants. In some tribes uncleanness is removed by rubbing the body with the fat or other portion of an animal. On the Wanigela River, British New Guinea, a man is purified by rubbing spleen and liver of kangaroo on his back. Among the Lenge sweeping the kraal is a ceremonial as well as a physical purification. In many South African tribes blood cleanses from guilt. This belief was a feature of Mithraism. Christianity borrowed the concept from its rival, and the revivifying Blood of the Bull became the cleansing Blood of the Lamb.

In many cultures impurities which afflict or threaten the community are carried away by an animal or a human being. Athenians held each spring the Thargelia Festival, during which two human scapegoats were loaded with the uncleanness of the people, beaten through the streets with certain plants, and then "led out" of the community. The ceremony rid the people of the uncleanness which had accumulated during the year.

Much more famous is the Jewish scapegoat. This was brought forward on the Day of Atonement, when the high priest laid hands on the head of the goat designated by lot, confessed over it, and placed upon it the iniquities and transgressions of the children of Israel accumulated during the preceding year. The goat, burdened with these iniquities, was led away and released in an uninhabited region, carrying the shame and sin of Israel with it. In later practice, to ensure that the beast would not return to the abodes of men, it was pushed over a precipice. The man who led the goat into the wilderness had been in proximity to aggregate uncleanness, and was himself unclean during the remainder of the day.

The institution of the scapegoat flourishes throughout southern Nigeria, where a man lays his hand on the animal and transfers to it his guilt or the punishment which he fears is in wait. At Awka medicinemen lead a goat seven times around the town or the people to be purified and then throw it into the bush or the river as a propitiatory offering to the evil spirits which are harassing the people. The Ibibio drive goats, fowls, and cats into the bush, the animals bearing the sins and troubles of the town with them.

Among Yorubas, Ijaw, and other tribes a man acts as scapegoat, taking upon himself the sins of the people and thereby bringing them good fortune. He is treated with respect and indulgence and receives the best of everything. When the time for his death comes he is paraded through the village. People lay their hands on him and transfer their sins to him. He is then led to a grove and executed. In time of calamity, such as a plague, the Ganda select a man with a physical defect, take him to the border of their territory, maim him, and leave him there to die. He carries the calamity away with him. The Kikuyu have a similar practice.

Rengma Nagas release chickens, as scapegoats, to take away the evil which has attached to those who release them. On the last day of this festival of cleansing each householder has an old man perform for him the following ceremony: The old man holds a cock and prays: "Today's dawn is fair, it is as if a door had been opened. If your wife's relations have spoken ill of you, one with ten fingers and ten toes [that is, the cock] is taking away the evil. Be happy. Be like a tree. Be like a clear spring gushing out from a rock. May all your evil fall upon this cock. And you, fowl, shake all this evil from your wings and tail." The man then waves the fowl nine times. The Oraon sacrifice a fowl to the tutelary deity or spirit of cattle, saying, as they do so: "Now I have sacrificed to thee. Go away, carrying with thee all sickness and sins. Do not afflict us with sickness or other calamities." In northern India a pig, a buffalo, or a goat is driven out into the jungle by excited crowds of people; the animal carries with it the disease which afflicts the community. At Hampi, Hindus celebrate the Kollappanahabba ceremony, similar to the Holi ceremony, at which on the full moon day of *Guari humnivi*, in October, a man hired for the occasion impersonates the demon of illness and evil. He stands in the centre of the village, is beaten and mauled, and is then driven out of the village by a large crowd. Persons who meet him while he is being driven away may not see his face. Members of adjoining villages should not see the pursuers enter their confines. One who meets the noisy rabble should about-face and join in the pursuit of the demon. The expelled man may not return to his village that day and must pass the night in the jungle.

On the Guinea Coast there is an annual purification ceremony, preceded by a feast of eight days, for the driving out of devils, or evil spirits. To ensure that they will not return to the village the women wash and scour all utensils to cleanse them wholly.

Among the Edo of southern Nigeria, a diviner sometimes orders that the disturbing spirits be driven out of the village. People grasp their cutlasses and rush about the village. They then tie leaves to the top of a stick, roast an ear of corn and tie this to the stick, and surmount it with the head of a bush buck. People hold this in their hands, and a procession goes around each house. The stick and its emblems are waved over the heads of the people, and songs are sung bidding the evil spirits depart. Or a chicken or other small animal is waved round the head and thrown through the parted legs. The animal is then transfixed to the midrib of a palm leaf, and this is planted upright at cross-roads or where a path branches from the main road. In Benin a town purification is sometimes ordered, and evil spirits and malign influences are driven out with hatchets and "medicine" supplied by the witch doctor.

At the end of the year Ibo women carry old pots, clothes, baskets, and other articles to a place consecrated to the god Aro and there throw them away. Thus they rid the community of pain and sickness during the coming year. When an epidemic breaks out in a Kikuyu village, central Africa, the elders slaughter a ram, a male goat, or an ewe lamb which has not borne young, cut pieces of meat from the carcass, and impale these on wooden skewers. Men and women then throw them into the bush some distance from the village, and the disease is carried away with the meat. They "put out the sickness" so that it cannot return to the village.

In Wales and the border county of Hereford the soul of the deceased was purified by a "sin-eater." When the corpse was removed from the house and placed on the bier, a loaf of bread was brought out and given to the sin-eater over the corpse; also a maple bowl of beer, which he was to drink; and sixpence in money. "In consideration whereof he tooke upon him the sinnes of the Defunct, and freed him (or her) from walking after they were dead." [3]

So contagious and clinging is uncleanness that Jewish priestly laws are concerned mainly with rites of purification. These restore to normal social and religious status persons or things which have been in contact with, and hence have contracted, uncleanness and thus have become a pollution to men and an abomination to God. Disease, moral obliquity, and infringement of a taboo bring uncleanness. Among Jews as among Greeks, Japanese, and many other peoples, evils were conceived as physical infections that could be caught and transferred. In Jewish law these various contagions, or uncleannesses, fell under the translator's category of "sin." Contagion rather than moral wrong, however, is the underlying conception. "Sin" attaches physically to inanimate objects—for example, the stones of a new altar—and is removed by physical means. The "sin" offering is an offering not for sin, but for inadvertent transgression of certain ceremonial prohibitions. It is required after childbirth, contagion of leprosy, completion of a Nazarite vow, and on other occasions, none of which involves moral sin. As a result of including the moral in the sphere of the religious, the physical means efficacious in removing uncleanness are employed to purify a man from moral defilement or to protect him against the consequences of wrongdoing.

A leper was banished from the community and compelled to go about with garments rent, hair dishevelled, lips covered. If men ap-

3. J. Aubrey, *Remaines of Gentilisme and Judaisme*, 35–36 (London, Folk-lore Society Publication IV, 1881).

proached him, or he them, he must cry out "Unclean! Unclean!" The man who recovered from leprosy must be purified before he re-entered the community. The ceremony of purification consisted of killing a bird over an earthen vessel containing fresh water and allowing its blood to fall into the water. The priest dipped into this water cedar wood, wool dyed crimson, hyssop, and a living bird. He sprinkled the blood-stained water upon the leper and released the living bird which had been immersed in it. The bird flew away, carrying with it the contagion.

Among Old Testament Jews a woman was unclean for forty days after giving birth to a male child and for eighty days after giving birth to a female child. Impurity attaches also to a Mohammedan mother; its duration varies among sects, in most cases being forty days. The Roman Catholic Church observes the Feast of the Purification of the Blessed Virgin Mary; and in the English Established Church there still survives the "Churching of Women" after childbirth. The ceremonies have become a form of thanksgiving rather than purification, but purification was the original motive in the Jewish prototype. In the canon law Innocent III decreed: "If women after child-bearing desire immediately to enter the church, they commit no sin by so doing, nor are they to be hindered." Instead of the Jewish offering of a lamb, a pigeon, or a turtle-dove, the woman makes a money-offering. Now, however, the motive of thanksgiving is emphasized.

"Be ye holy, even as I am holy," applies especially to priests. Thus in the Roman Catholic Church there are elaborate purification rites for a priest who has been defiled accidentally or innocently.

Rengma Nagas hold ceremonies designed to remove from the community the sins and evils which have accumulated during the preceding year. On the third day of the festival all go to the village spring and wash their bodies, clothes, and weapons, to rid them of the impurities which have accumulated during the preceding year. The northern group of western Rengmas have an elaborate purification ceremony every seven years. On the third day of the ceremony all wash in the stream and return to the shelters to sleep. On the fourth day they again wash in the stream.

A purification at the end of the old year, to rid the people of accumulated evils and pollutions, is a common feature of New Year celebrations in China, Indo-China, Indonesia, India, Africa, and ancient Babylonia, among American Indians in the Southeast and Southwest of the United States, and in the higher civilizations of Mexico and Peru.

CONFESSION

Confession of sin purges the soul or removes from the community the stain of guilt incurred by the erring individual or group. An ill Netsilik Eskimo must confess the errors he has committed. If he does not do so, the illness will probably be fatal. Confession was a feature of the prophet dance or dream dance among the Okanagon of Washington. A confession dance was held "whenever an earthquake, falling star, or other cosmic phenomenon frightened the community, or when a man dreamed that doomsday was near. It was continued 'till they got over being scared.' "[4] At their New Year ceremonies the northern Iroquois had a general confession of sins, preceding the ceremony of driving away evil spirits.

Confession is practised by Eskimos from Greenland to Alaska, Northwest Coast tribes, Athabascans, Iroquois, Plains Indians, Chippewas, Pueblos, the Huichol, the Hupa, the Yurok, Luiseños, and Juaneños. A Zuñi witch who confesses is sometimes allowed to go unpunished. Confession was common in ancient Mexico and is reported from Chiapas, Yucatan, Guatemala, and Nicaragua. In South America it is known among the Kagaba and Ijca of Colombia and the Kariri and Tupinamba of Brazil, and was highly elaborated in ancient Peru.

The Aztec penitent, according to Sahagun, addressed the confessor as follows: "Sir, I desire to approach that most powerful god, the protector of all, that is to say, Tezcatlipoca. I desire to tell him my sins in secret." The confessor replied: "Be happy, my son: that which thou wishest to do will be to thy good and advantage." The confessor then opened the divinatory book known as the Tonalamatl (that is, the Book of the Calendar) and acquainted the supplicant with the day which appeared the most suitable for his confession. On the day thus designated the penitent provided himself with a mat, copal gum to burn as incense, and wood whereon to burn it. If he was a person high in office, the priest repaired to the man's house; in the case of lesser people the confession took place in the priest's house.

The penitent, after lighting the fire and burning the incense, addressed the fire as follows: "Thou, Lord, who art the father and mother of the gods, and the most ancient of them all! thy servant bows before thee. Weeping, he approaches thee in great distress. He comes plunged

4. Walter Cline, in Leslie Spier (editor), *General Series in Anthropology*, 6: 175 (1938).

in grief, because he has been buried in sin, having backslidden, and partaken of those vices and evil delights which merit death. O master most compassionate, who art the upholder and defence of all, receive the penitence and anguish of thy slave and vassal." The confessor then turned to the penitent and thus addressed him: "My son, thou art come into the presence of that god who is the protector and upholder of all; thou art come to him to confess thy evil vices and thy hidden uncleannesses; thou art come to him to unbosom the secrets of thy heart. Take care that thou omit nothing from the catalogue of thy sins in the presence of our lord, who is called Tezcatlipoca. It is certain that thou art before him who is invisible and impalpable, thou who art not worthy to be seen before him, or to speak with him." The penitent, after listening to a sermon by the confessor, confessed his misdeeds, after which the confessor said: "My son, thou hast before our lord god confessed in his presence thy evil actions. I wish to say in his name that thou hast an obligation to make. At the time when the goddesses called Ciuapipiltin descend to earth during the celebration of the feast of the goddesses or carnal things, whom they name Ixcuiname, thou shalt scarify thy tongue with the small thorns of the osier and if that is not sufficient thou shalt do likewise to thine ears, the whole for penitence, for the remission of thy sin, and as a meritorious act. Thou wilt apply to thy tongue the middle of a spine of maguey, and thou wilt scarify thy shoulders. That done, thy sins will be pardoned." If the sins of the penitent were not very grave, the priest would enjoin upon him a fast, sometimes brief, sometimes prolonged.

In ancient Peru confession was made, sometimes publicly, sometimes privately, before priest or diviner. There was an official confessor in each village. Confession of a few designated grave sins must be made before the Chief Priest of the Incas. If the sinner did not confess, the entire community would suffer in consequence of his delinquency. Usually confession was made close to a river. In his right hand the confessor held a bundle of esparto grass; in the left, a small stone tied to a string or fitted into a hole made for the purpose at the end of a stick. The confessor sat and summoned the penitent, who came trembling and prostrated himself before the confessor. The latter bade him rise, then admonished him to confess all his sins and conceal nothing. Inasmuch as confessor was also diviner, he knew most of the sins which the man had committed. Confession was auricular and usually secret. A confessor convicted of revealing confessional secrets was killed. The man who confessed must do specified penance, the nature of which depended upon the character of the sins confessed. After confession, the confessor gave the penitent light strokes on the back with a small stone tied to a string, whereupon the penitent, and then the confessor, spat on the bundle of esparto grass. They then threw the bundle into the river and prayed the god to take it down into the abyss and hide it there forever. Bathing in the river absolved the penitent of all sins. Accordingly, when he had confessed, he went into the river to be finally and completely purified of his sins. He stood in the current and pronounced the following formula: "I have confessed my sins before the Sun and Viracocha; as he created me, so he has pardoned me. River, mayst thou receive them, and take them away to the sea, so that they may never appear again."

Confession as a means of ridding one of sickness is found in tribes of western South America whose culture is related to that of ancient Peru. The Aurohuaca of the Sierra Nevada, Colombia, believe sickness a punishment for sins. The medicineman summoned to the bed of the patient does not inquire about symptoms; he makes strange passes over the man and asks in a sepulchral voice whether the patient will confess his sins. If the sick man refuses to confess, the medicineman does not attempt to cure him. If, however, satisfactory confession is made, the medicineman transfers the patient's sins to bits of stone or shell. These are carried high up into the mountains and laid in a spot where the first beams of the morning sun will strike them. The radiant influence drives away the sin and sickness. Similarly, the Ijca of Colombia believe that sickness is cured by confession of sins. A Barama River Carib who has an erotic dream will fall ill unless he immediately confesses the dream to fellow villagers.

Among the Bechuana of South Africa, a sacrifice of atonement must be accompanied by confession; and if the community is suffering by reason of the sin which is being atoned for, public confession must be made on behalf of the entire tribe. If confession is not forthcoming, resort is had to divination to determine the cause of the misfortune.

If an adulterous woman of the Tallis, in the northern territories of Ashanti, does not confess her adultery, her children may be supernaturally killed. The suspecting husband may thrash her to extort confession. Confession is practised in West Africa by sixteen ethnic groups, including Mbara, Gari, Chama, Kpelle, Kissi, Toma, Fanti, Ashanti, Tshi, Yoruba, Asaba, Kosi, Fan, Wili, and Loango. In equatorial and southeastern Africa it has been reported among thirty ethnic groups, including Boloki, Zande, Shilluk, Lotuko, and Lugwari. In Madagascar it was practised by the Antambahoaka; in Malaysia by the Semang and Sakhai; in Malacca; in Sumatra by the Batak; in Nias; in Borneo by the Dyak. It is found among Manus of the Admiralty Islands and Papuans of British New Guinea, at Rossel Island, among the Sulka of New Britain and the Lifu of Loyalty Islands, and in Fiji, Samoa, Marquesas, and Tokelau. In Hawaii confession is "open avowal of fault and apology to the spirit guardian." Confession is practised by the Yurok, the Samoyed, and the Aleutian Atkhan. Confession became an established practice in the Christian church and plays a potent rôle in Roman Catholic faith and in the Buchmanite movement. A Brahman sinner atones for faults by confession to his spiritual director, who specifies the requisite penance. Such suffering for shortcomings mitigates, or, some believe, abrogates, punishment in the next world.

"A sinner who makes a sincere confession," declares a Jaina text, "is like the bearer of a burden, whose burden is taken from him."

Thus confession of sins, which was known in ancient Egypt, Babylonia, Israel, southern Arabia, Syria, Asia Minor, India, and Greece, and among the Hittites, is of wide distribution among preliterate peoples.

Infringement of rules of clean and unclean incurs mystic dangers of taboo; hence these rules must be scrupulously observed. Often the holy is viewed as physical contagion. Individuals are inducted into its realm through contact, and the contagion spreads to objects and localities as well as to persons.

The underlying concept of permeation by contagion is expressed in the belief of the Ibo of Nigeria that the *mana* of the Thunder God passes from the tree which he inhabits into surrounding vegetation, "growing and spreading with each new season's boughs." By taking his food amid the seeds set apart for planting, the chief priest of the Thunder God endows them with special fertility derived from the *mana* of the Thunderer whom he serves. Similarly, uncleanness, or taboo, is contagious, an impalpable essence or effluvium which is contaminating. Its removal by purification necessitates employment of physical agencies and performance of magico-religious rites which operate sympathetically with more or less automatic efficacy. These are the underlying conceptions in most ceremonies of consecration, deconsecration, and purification, in preliterate cultures and in historic civilizations.

CHAPTER X OFFERING AND SACRIFICE

Not lightly do the glorious gifts of Gods yield to force of mortal men.—
Iliad, Book XX

Gifts move the gods, gifts move worshipful princes.—Hesiod, *Doubtful Fragments*, 6

Ever jealous the Gods are, that we men mind their dues.—Odyssey, Book IV

OFFERING

In many tribes offering is made to a supernatural power. Throughout Canada "Indians made offerings at waterfalls and rapids, at passes in the mountains, at trees or rocks that stood solitary, at every place that seemed in any way dangerous or uncanny." [1]

Central Eskimos offer the dried skin of a species of small seal to Kadlu, who uses it to make thunder. The Naskapi of Labrador offer to the spirit in sun and moon a portion of each animal killed. The northern Iroquois sacrifice a white dog. Algonquins break the head of a dog and suspend it from a pole in honour of Michininsi, god of waters. During festivals in honour of certain deities the head of a dog must be presented to the chief of war. Crees hang dogs in honour of the sun; the Illinois, in honour of Thunder. Before a Wahpeton Dakota smokes, he offers tobacco to Spider. In many North American Plains tribes the hide of an albino buffalo is offered to a *wakan* being, usually the sun.

When the Sarsi are about to perform the sun dance, a man gives a buffalo tongue to his wife. She holds it toward the sky and says: "Pity me, my father; I have lived faithfully with my husband." Later she and her husband eat the tongue. When the sun dance has been performed, pieces of skin torn from the body of the performer are placed as offerings at the base of the post by the man who pierced the performer's flesh in preparation for the dance. At the end of the fourth day of the performance the camp circle is moved and offerings at the pole are left there intact. In the Southwest, corn pollen or corn meal is offered to the god or supernatural power.

1. Diamond Jenness, *The Indians of Canada*, 173 (Ottawa, National Museum of Canada, 1932).

Among the Ashanti, offerings, usually accompanied by prayer, are made to a fetish tree. A pot containing water and certain kinds of leaves is brought to the tree. The priest waves the pot several times about his head and utters meanwhile a prayer such as the following: "So and so is ill and does not know the cause; do you, Edinkira, make the sickness return to him who caused it." Or the priest, when making an offering, may say: "O Edinkira! So and so says he went to ask about his head [that is, to consult a god] and the god said he must bring eggs to you; may you receive them and eat (them) and cause him to have strength." [2] The eggs are then broken and rubbed on the trunk of the tree. On one occasion on which an offering, consisting of a fowl, three eggs, and a pot of palm-wine, was brought to a tree, the priest, holding an egg in his right hand, stood by the tree, and made the following prayer: "O Edinkira! Kwaku Abu and Wisiraka who are walking with the White man say they have heard your name and bring wine, and a fowl, and eggs, to behold your face. May you receive them and partake and may they gain strength and not become ill and lie yonder. Do not let them offend the White man on the journey and may their payment be increased." [2] The priest then broke the eggs, one at a time, upon the trunk, and rubbed them over the bark of the tree, saying, as he did so: "[Grant] life to them, stand behind them with a good standing (firmly)." [2] He then wrung the head off the fowl, rubbed the bird's bleeding neck against the tree, and again uttered the last mentioned request. He tore the fowl open, removed heart, lungs, intestines, and liver, and placed them and the head on a small stone at the foot of the tree. He poured wine into a calabash and, as a sign of respect, holding it in both hands, poured it over the trunk, saying, as he did so: "Here is wine from their hands." [2] He then sat down, poured out and drank a little wine, and held the calabash, and those present drank from it. The remainder of the fowl, he stated, might be eaten by the children.

When the Mentawei are about to establish a new village, they make an offering of chicken livers to the wood spirits of the locality.

The *do ut des* theory—I (the worshipper) give in order that you (the deity) may (be induced to) give—is clearly expressed by the Ewe. The prayer which accompanies the yearly offering of yams contains the following supplication: "Today the life-giving yams have been brought

2. Robert S. Rattray, *Religion and Art in Ashanti*, 3–5 (Oxford, The Clarendon Press, 1927). Reprinted by permission of the publisher.

to the city. Here is your part. Please accept it and eat it; do you eat so that we also may eat. Do you see to it that no one who eats yams today will suffer from pains." The prayer of the Thonga of South Africa, which accompanies an offering, does not conceal the utilitarian motive. An example is the following: "You, our gods, you [designating them by name]. Here is our offering. Bless this child and make him live and grow. Make him rich, so that when we visit him he may be able to kill an ox for us. . . . You are useless, you gods! You only give us trouble! For although we give you offerings, you do not listen to us! We are deprived of everything! You [mentioning the gods by name] are full of hatred! You do not enrich us! All who succeed do so by the help of their gods. Now we have made you this gift. Call your ancestors [designating the gods by name], call also the gods of the sick boy's father because his father did not steal his mother. These people of the [designated] clan came in the daylight to buy the mother. So come to the altar! Eat and distribute among yourselves our ox, according to your wisdom."

Zulus, similarly, accompany an offering with a prayer such as the following: "We offer unto you, spirits of our departed relatives, this heart in order that you, who are the chief relations of this patient, may invite all your other spiritual relations to partake of this heart offered to you, even as you did on earth while alive, in behalf of the patient; satisfy yourselves and show kindness unto this patient, your relation, by giving him good health."

Offerings to Greek gods included bread and cakes of various kinds. In many cases the food, after being laid upon the altar as upon the table of the god, was removed and eaten by the priest. The dough and the honey containing poppy seeds, which were offered to gods of the underworld, were wholly consumed by fire. Sometimes cakes were made in a special form. Thus at Athens Artemis-Selene received cakes shaped like the disk of the full moon and decorated with lights; Apollo received cakes in the form of a lyre or of a bow and arrows. Baked dough images of sacrificial victims were common offerings. Those who were too poor to sacrifice an animal substituted an effigy.

In Rome private or public offerings to the gods were of the nature of gift or tribute. They consisted of the common products of primitive pastoral life and agriculture: dry spelt-grits pounded (not ground), with salt, spelt-mush, beans, various kinds of bread and cakes, honey, fruits, milk, cheese, swine, sheep, or neat cattle. In public cults cattle and sheep were preferred to swine, and cereal oblations tended to become mere accessories.

SACRIFICES

Among the Zulus of southern Africa, "sacrifices are offered to the spirits, (1) *to avert an evil*, as in the case of sickness, barrenness of women, serious accidents; when a serpent has visited a kraal, under unusual circumstances; when an omen has appeared. (In cases of sickness and barrenness, the seer or prophet is resorted to, and the sacrifice offered when he attributes the misfortune to the spirits. He is applied to when a serpent or omen has been seen.) A soldier wounded in battle would only pray, if his hurt were slight; but if it were serious, he would vow a sacrifice on his return, naming perhaps the particular beast. If he were too weak, a comrade would invoke the spirits for him. If he were a 'boy' and without cattle of his own, the beast would not be witheld on his return; and sometimes a father will chide a surviving son, if he have not vowed a sacrifice before his brother's death. On the other hand, if a 'boy' were to vow an ox or a cow, not being in great danger, his father would not be pleased, though he would probably sacrifice a goat. (2) Sacrifices to *procure a blessing* are offered after the building of a new kraal; when the army is setting out; by the seer or prophet to procure inspiration; after a burial, to secure the favour of the deceased. Mothers, when their sons are on an expedition, frequently vow a sacrifice in the event of their returning safe; I suspect however that these vows are not always performed, for the prophet sometimes attributes sickness to their non-fulfilment, when the husband becomes angry at his wife's presumption. The natives employed by white men to hunt the elephant sometimes vow a sacrifice, when they are not successful. When Tshaka sent a mission to the Cape, he gave Lieutenant King an ox to sacrifice. Pande has sacrificed to procure rain. (3) *Thank-offerings* are made when a person has enjoyed a long prosperity; as for instance, if he have many children and no sickness in his kraal for some time. When Tshaka's mission returned from the Cape he sent an ox, to thank the spirit for Lieutenant King's safe arrival. Sacrifices are offered when the Zulu army comes home from a successful expedition. Refugees from the Zulu-country sometimes testify their gratitude, for having been permitted to escape, by sacrificing the first beast they earn in Natal.

"The animals offered are exclusively cattle and goats. The largest ox in a herd is specially reserved for sacrifice on important occasions; it is called the Ox of the Spirits, and is never sold except in cases of extreme necessity.[3] The original idea of a sacrifice appears to have degenerated into that of a present of food; the only word to express it is *um-nikelo*, a gift (from *nikela* to give to); when the prophet prescribes a sacrifice, he directs the people to give the spirits flesh; when the spirits are addressed, they are invited to eat; beer and snuff are usually added; and, when a person has no animal to present, he offers these alone. When an animal is to be sacrificed, it is brought into the cattle fold, and there slain, by having an assagai plunged into its side. Just before or after its death the master of the kraal addresses the spirits. If the sacrifice be offered to avert an evil, he might speak to the following effect: 'Eat ye; here is your ox; I give it you. Eat, my father, my grandfather; all ye spirits of my ancestors, eat. Take care of me; take care of my children, take care of my wives; take care of all my people. Remove the sickness, and let my child recover. Give me plenty of children—many boys and a few girls. Give me abundance of food and cattle. Make right all my people.'

"If the sacrifice were a thank-offering for prosperity, he would, perhaps, after having called on the spirits, proceed thus: 'This kraal of yours is good; you have made it great. I see around me many children; you have given me them. You have given me many cattle. You have blessed me greatly. Every year I wish to be thus blessed. Make right everything at the kraal. I do not wish any omens to come. Grant that no one may be sick all the year.' When the animal has been skinned, it is cut into several portions, and the whole (including the skin, head, and blood collected in a vessel) placed in a hut, with beer and snuff. I have been told that a small fire is made, in the ordinary fire-place of the house, and a piece of fat (or flesh) burnt on it.[4] The contents of the paunch, or of some other internal part of the animal, are dashed against the inside of the roof of the hut, and scattered about the kraal. At night, young people alone sleep in the hut, without fire, the duty primarily falling upon the boys. Next day the beef is cooked in the usual way and eaten." [5]

3. "A white man who had a particularly fine ox which became sick, sold it to a Kafir for a trifle. The beast having recovered, he would gladly have purchased it, but the owner, much to his surprise, could not be induced to part with it."

4. "The Frontier Kafirs burn fat in some cases as a sacrifice. A war offering made before a battle is burnt. What remains of the black bull at the Feast of First Fruits is burnt with the skins and bones."

5. Joseph Shooter, *The Kafirs of Natal and the Zulu Country*, 163–166 (London, Stanford, 1857).

Zulus do not lift up the beast for acceptance, as do the Kamba, but point it out to the ancestors as the beast which is to be given them, and describe in detail its colour, horns, and distinguishing traits. If it bellows when slaughtered, this is a sign that the ancestors are pleased with it, for the bellowing expresses the spirit's acceptance of the offering. If the beast does not bellow, this means that the spirits reject the beast. In that case another animal must be slaughtered for the sacrifice, and the flesh of the first may then be eaten. If, however, in the first instance, a beast does not bellow, every effort is made to force it to do so: the assagai is moved about in the wound, or the tail is pulled to ensure the bellowing. The Tembu and Fingo of southern Africa, do not sacrifice a stolen animal, for this would incur the wrath of the ancestral spirits.

The Koryak of Siberia believe that the sacrifice of a deer to evil beings wards off their attack and that a sacrifice to the Supreme Being ensures order on earth. A crude form of sacrifice is practised by Ainus, the Gilyak, and other tribes of northeastern Asia, who imprison a bear in a stout wooden cage and feed it until the time of sacrifice. It is then taken out, shot with blunt arrows, and finally suffocated. The victim is cut up; the flesh is kept in the hut for three days, and is then eaten. Among the Koryak, Altaians, Samoyed, and Ostyak, shamans designate the animal the sacrifice of which will cure a specified disease. Before migrating to a new locality the Samoyed sacrifice a reindeer. Todas, until prohibited by the British Government, sacrificed numerous buffaloes at a funeral; now, only two are killed.

In many areas the laying of the foundation of a building or a bridge is an occasion for sacrifice. Moors sacrifice an animal when they lay the foundations of a new building; if an animal is not offered, occupants of the house will die or be childless. In Syria each house demands the life of a human being or that of a beast. Berbers of Aglu kill a goat when they dig a well. They accompany the sacrifice with the words: "We killed for you, O masters of this water; may you make it easy for us; we shall make it easy for you; may you not cause any difficulty." In Angora a black goat is killed and thrown into the stream when a new millstone is put in place; the sacrifice protects the mill against injury by jinn. The sacrifice of a cock appeases the evil spirit which causes sudden sickness, such as convulsions or epilepsy, and ensures recovery. Chinese respect the cock as the herald of the appearance of the sun and offer its head and blood in sacrifice. Finns sacrificed in sacred groves dedicated to underground spirits of great men of the past and important nature gods. Teutons sacrificed white horses in sacred groves.

Sallustius rejects the *do ut des* theory of sacrifice. He says, in his treatise *On the Gods and the World,* under a section entitled "Concerning Sacrifices and other Worships, that we benefit Man by them but not the Gods": "Since we have received everything from the gods, and it is right to pay the giver some tithe of his gifts, we pay such a tithe of possessions in votive offerings, of bodies in gifts of hair and adornment, and of life in sacrifices. Then, secondly, prayers without sacrifices are only words, with sacrifices they are live words; the word gives meaning to the life, while the life animates the word."

Animals sacrificed to Greek gods were in the main those used as food, including sheep, goats, swine, and neat cattle. Usually individual gods had preferences, and in some cases, distinct aversions. Thus Demeter preferred swine; Poseidon, bulls; Athena, cows. Aphrodite would have no swine. In most cases the gods accepted only physically perfect animals and perhaps only mature ones. The colour of the animals was sometimes prescribed. Seldom were wild animals offered. Only a few gods, those with peculiar tastes, would accept fish.

A Homeric sacrifice specified "sleek kine, that have not felt the goad," or "a yearling heifer, broad of brow, unbroken, that never yet hath man led below the yoke." [6] That there was a feeling of appropriateness regarding the amount sacrificed is implied in Lucian's *Zeus in Tragedy,* wherein Zeus complains that the sea captain, Mesilleus, had sacrificed only one cock to entertain sixteen gods. Olympian gods did not take kindly to the "sixteen to one" doctrine. The last words of Socrates, "Crito, I owe a cock to Aesclepius; will you remember to pay the debt?" shows that the practice of sacrifice had not fallen into complete disrepute in sophisticated Athens even among intellectuals.

Reciprocity is asked by the Aryan sacrificer. "Compassionate father," says the Tanna priest, when he offers first fruits to a deified ancestor, "here is some food for you; eat it, and be kind to us on account of it." A Pahlavi text states that when the guardian spirits are invited to partake of the sacrifice they do so; if they are not invited they go up the height of a spear and there remain. Iranians offered sacrifices to the dead. Their gods sacrificed to one another.

Among the Tobas of Sumatra, horses are offered in a great sacrificial feast for the three gods of the trinity. Each Toba sib has a sacred horse

6. Iliad, Books VI, X.

consecrated to one of these gods. It is the "throne," that is, the symbol of the presence of the divine tribal father among his descendants. The black horse is sacred to Batara Guru, the brown horse to Soripada, the piebald to Mangalabulan. Each sib, as it traces its descent from one or another of the three gods, possesses a black, a brown, or a piebald horse.

These sacred animals are inviolable and non-alienable. They are not confined but graze with impunity where they will. A sacred horse grown old in honourable service is replaced by a young beast of the same colour. At a feast the old horse is sacrificed to the god appropriate to its colour. On a lucky day, selected with the aid of the calendar, the sib members, including the women, assemble in the villages of the head chief, who, as manager of the feast, has obtained a black, a brown, or a piebald young stallion, chosen for its beauty.

The two sacred horses, the intended victim and its successor, are bridled, and the ears of the young horse are decorated with flowers and sweet-smelling herbs.

To the strains of the native orchestra these horses are conducted to the centre of the village, where the men entrusted with the duty of slaughter and evisceration kill and skin the old sacred horse. The pelt is washed and laid over a *rangin,* the crudely cut image of a horse, a tree trunk hollowed out on the underside and terminating in an image of a horse's head. The *rangin* covered with the hide is taken to the chief's house. There, amid a food offering of rice, sacrificial cakes, fruit, white flowers, and the purifying lime juice, the sacrificer offers the hide to the god as a covering for his throne. The hide, sprinkled with the consecrated water, is left in the house for the time being. The people return to the village, where the priest summons the three gods, Mula djadi (the Batak creator and father of the three gods), the nature gods, and the ancestral spirits, for the consecration of the new horse. A man comes forward with a plate of sacrificial cakes and a small sack of rice kernels topped with a chicken's egg or a gambir nut. The priest summons the gods and the ancestors of both sexes up to the seventh generation for the blessing of the people, then sprinkles the young horse with lime juice water. Participants scatter rice kernels over its head and pray: "Our *tondi* is firm, may we remain healthy." The young horse is led back to its stall, through a further shower of rice. "The people return to the house of the chief, where the ceremony ends in music and dancing. The god, stimulated by the orchestra, enters his medium, one of the chiefs, to inform the people that he has received their sacrifice and will give them help. After the feast the horse flesh is divided," [7] and each takes his portion to his village to eat.

A Shinto priest, before making the sacred offerings or chanting the liturgies, must bathe and put on clean garments. The Yashts say that thirty strokes with the *sroashokarana* purge people of their sins and prepare them to offer sacrifices.

The Satapatha Brahmana says:

> The gods lived constantly in dread of death—
> The mighty Ender—so, with toilsome rites
> They worshipped, and repeated sacrifices,
> Till they became immortal.

Insistence that the animal be without blemish is widely spread, as also insistence upon cleanliness in the sacrificer, who likewise must be blameless. The insistence is sometimes carried to the point of demanding fasting from the sacrificer and even from the victim. The buffalo offered by Malacca Malays must be without blemish; after its death its bones may not be broken and its horns may not be used. Hindu gods welcome pure sacrifices only. The Kalika Purana, written under Siva's direction, declares that the man offered in sacrifice must be free from corporeal defect and unstained with great crimes. The animal must be more than three years old and without blemish or disease; the victim may not be a woman or a female animal, for females are inherently unclean. Among the Khond the man destined for sacrifice must fast from the evening preceding the sacrifice, though on the day of the sacrifice he is refreshed with a little milk and palm-sago; before he is led from the village in solemn procession to the place of sacrifice, he is carefully washed and is then dressed in a new garment. The Santal bathe in preparation for performing a sacrifice or making an offering. The sacrificer must first "sanctify himself," as the Santal say. Male members of the household, and particularly the sacrificer, must be abstinent during the night preceding the sacrifice. They may not eat or drink, go near a woman, or sleep on a bed, but must sleep on a mat on the floor. Some groups demand that the sacrificer shall not sit on a stool until he has performed his sacrifice; otherwise the ceremony will be vitiated. Sometimes the wife of the priest must sleep on the floor, "perhaps be-

7. Edwin M. Loeb, *Sumatra, Its History and People*, 91–92 (Vienna, Verlag des Institutes für Völkerkunde der Universität Wien, 1935). Reprinted by permission of the publisher.

cause she, in such cases, may have to come a little nearer to the performance than women are otherwise permitted to." [8] The sacrificed animal should be an uncastrated male, though at the present day female fowl, goats, or sheep are used, provided they are "so young that sex has not commenced to manifest itself." Rengma Nagas of Assam insist that the cow and the bull which are ceremonially killed as a sacrifice be without blemish. The bull mithan must have no teeth missing, no chips off the horns, "no white blotches anywhere, and no whorls of hair except on the back of the neck and behind the ears. On the day of the sacrifice the mithan is kept without food or water." One who offers a pig, in the purification ceremony, says: "This is a fine pig. Its feet are white. Its forehead is white. Its teeth are perfect. This is a lucky day. I am offering the pig to the spirits."

The Zamindar of Bhamr Pahar sacrifice two goats every three years to the bees that infest the hill under which their residence is situated. Among Tungus, animals liked by spirits are kept for a long time before serving as sacrifice. A suckling pig is sometimes taken by the Birarien, raised on special food—the acorn of *Quercus dauricus*—and later sacrificed. In the meantime the spirit becomes accustomed to the animal and "likes it." To give the animal away would bring misfortune to members of the family. The spirits prefer the red deer, *Cervus elaphus*, and chickens.

Herodotus says ancient Egyptians beat themselves while the sacrificed animals were being burned; and Carian dwellers in Egypt cut their faces with knives.

In ancient Egypt the sacrificed animal must be wholly clean. The religious law of the Jews forbade the use of honey or leaven in connexion with vegetable offerings: they ferment, acidify, and spoil everything with which they are mixed. The animal intended for sacrifice must be free from blemish and at least eight days old, that is, untainted with the impurity of recent birth. Consonant with these prescriptions is the concept that the victim must abstain from food for a specified time before it is sacrificed. Moors fast on the day preceding celebration of the yearly sacrificial feast. In several districts of Morocco the sacrificial sheep must fast on the day of sacrifice, or at least on the preceding morning, though food is given it immediately before it is slaughtered.

A Chinese commentator of 541 B.C. says spirits of hills and streams were sacrificed to in times of flood, drought, or pestilence. Spirits of

8. For a comparable motive among the Kota see page 77.

sun, moon, and stars were sacrificed to if there was unseasonable snow, hoar-frost, wind, or rain. De Groot believes that originally Chinese mourners fasted so that they might sacrifice more amply at the tomb; he bases this inference on the fact that the foods forbidden until the end of the deepest mourning were the most important foods at the ancient burial sacrifice.

HUMAN SACRIFICE

Human sacrifice implies a relatively high stage of sophistication; simple cultures are innocent of it. Human sacrifice is the logical outcome of the conviction that, inasmuch as the god is pleased with offerings, the more valuable the offering, the more pleased the god will be. The Mentawei offer human sacrifice when they build a communal house. Northern Iroquois occasionally offered human sacrifice. On the Northwest Coast of North America slaves were sacrificed when the foundations of a building were laid; later, as a substitute, slaves were freed. In many parts of the Plains area a finger or a portion of a finger was sacrificed to the sun; Pawnees sacrificed a maiden to the sun each spring. Sacrifice of a child to the sun is found in Hopi myth, and Hopis are said to have sacrificed a youth at the tribal initiation fire festival. Human sacrifice appears in Sia legend. In the Zuñi myth of the origin of death a child is sacrificed in return for the gift of seeds; and "tales of the former existence of human sacrifice in the pueblos [of Southwestern United States] continually crop up." [9] In the higher cultures of Central and South America human sacrifice reached the acme of its development in the New World. Peruvians sacrificed children and occasionally adults to the sun. Chibchas sacrificed a child to sun and moon. Human sacrifice was practised in Ecuador. On the coast the blood and heart of the victim constituted the offering. The inland Canari sacrificed men to spirits or gods of the underworld and also abundantly to the sun. Mayas offered human sacrifice when a new house was built, and probably the Zapotecs had this practice.

Aztecs were arduous sacrificers and annually offered hundreds of victims, mainly captives, to the sun. Other victims were in some cases unsuspecting. In one ceremony the woman selected for sacrifice was seized while in a temple and beheaded before fully aware of the fate in store for her; in another ceremony a young man chosen for the sacrifice was

9. Ruth L. Bunzel, "Introduction to Zuñi Ceremonialism," *ABE*, 47: 487 (1929–1930).

flower-bedecked, feasted, and fêted for days, and treated as a god, only to meet at the end of his godlike career with sacrificial death. On festival days priests and nobles drew blood from themselves with the spines of the gourd tree. Usually a child was sacrificed, its heart removed, and its blood sprinkled toward the four cardinal points as an offering to the four winds. The priest publicly sacrificed blood from his ears, tongue, and other parts of his body.

Throughout western Africa there is human sacrifice. The motive is sometimes to please the god, sometimes, as in Dahomey, to benefit the soul of a deceased chief or relative. In Dahomey, when inhabitants of a town are threatened by great danger, the usual sacrifice is a newborn infant, or one only a few hours old. It is torn limb from limb and offered to the town god; the dismembered infant is strewn about in the god's temple or place of abode. The child, because it is guiltless of offence, is peculiarly acceptable to the guardian deity, which will then exert its full power to avert the impending danger.

At annual rites, the Nigerian Ibo sacrificed a woman; and sacrificed also a slave at a sacred tree. Among the Ganda thirteen localities were appropriate for human sacrifice. Each locality had its favourite method of dispatching victims. At one shrine they were clubbed to death and their bodies left on the spot for beasts of prey to consume; at another, arms and legs were broken and the crippled men were left for crocodiles to devour; at another, princes of royal blood were starved to death. Thus they displayed local pride and ingenuity in serving their eminently respectable gods, who frequently demanded a liberal offering of human lives.

Human sacrifice is practised by the Winamwanga, south of Tanganyika. To avert a drought, which to these agricultural people is dire calamity, the head chief sends special messengers to capture men, women, or children, to sacrifice to his ancestral spirits. Three or four victims may be necessary. They prefer members of the family of a priest, those who have a squint, mothers who have borne only one child, or pregnant women. The victims are taken to a shrine, where these special messengers kill them by twisting their necks. Their bodies are secretly disposed of. The Senga, to secure rain, sometimes sacrifice a woman. The Mba sacrifice a bull and a slave woman. If the drought is severe, a human victim is taken to Mwaruli, where the high priest keeps him caged in a stoutly woven fish-basket, until preparations for the sacrifice have been completed. Konde chiefs in secret conclave select a boy, make him drink beer until he dies, burn his body, grind it to powder, and distribute this over the district as "medicine" to ensure a good crop.

In the Solomon Islands, Melanesia, human sacrifices are the most effectual means of propitiating an offended ghost.

Kalmucks of Siberia believe that occasionally a child of the chief must be sacrificed to the gods of the river. Nagas offer human sacrifice to secure rain and to increase the productivity of the soil.

In ancient India a pregnant woman was the favourite sacrificial victim. At Hampi is a wall, sacred to women pilgrims, in memory of the time when Nahapurusa Bhistapaya buried his pregnant daughter beneath it to prevent its falling down, as it had previously done several times. The Hindu ceremony of burying an image when the foundations of a house are dug may be a survival of an ancient custom of burying a living person under the foundations. Non-Brahmans use a hideous image made of wheat flour. At the present time the ceremony is performed when the completed house is first entered. An image about an inch long, of earth, silver, or gold, placed in a box of earth, is buried in the south-eastern corner of the central room in a pit a foot and a half deep, which is filled with water. It is inauspicious if the water sinks into the earth without filling the pit. In the box are placed nine kinds of precious stones, five small pieces of different metals, also flowers, darva grass, curds, and cooked rice.

Sacrifice of children seems still to occur sporadically in India, and fear that children may be kidnapped for sacrifice or for burial in the foundations of a structure under way is common. To this day, at certain seasons, a young Oraon, even the sturdiest young man, will not go alone any considerable distance from the village, for he thinks he might be kidnapped and spirited away as a victim for human sacrifice. A festival held in Karnatak, traditionally known as "the festival of children," appears to be a survival of child sacrifice. In a small pond are placed a cradle and an image of a child. An image representing the mother who sacrificed her child at the request of her father, is seated in an adorned *mandap* for twenty days. On the last Monday of the month Sravan it is taken in procession. Siriyal, an ancient king, had dug a tank into which no water came until his daughter sacrificed one of her children and thus secured abundant rain.

Human sacrifice prevailed in several early Mediterranean civilizations. Semites, particularly Phœnicians, indulged heavily in it. Baal was a recipient of many young lives.

The practice was known to Old Testament Jews. When Hiel wished to rebuild Jericho, "He laid the foundations thereof in Abiram, his first-born, and set up the gates thereof in his youngest son, Segub." [10] Sacrifice of children, particularly the first-born, was introduced by Manasseh during Assyrian domination, when many foreign cults found lodgment in Jerusalem. Children were sacrificed at a hearth or fire-pit in the Valley of Hinnon, a short distance from the temple. The victims were sacrificed, by burning, to Yahweh, under the title of Molech. Molech was not a foreign god; the name means "the King," that is, Yahweh. The practice was justified by early commands of Yahweh: "Thou shalt make over to Yahweh everything that opens the womb" and "The first-born of thy sons shalt thou give unto me." In 621 B.C. Josiah destroyed the altars at which children had been sacrificed to Molech, that is, Yahweh, "the King." The command given to Abraham that he sacrifice Isaac suggests survival of human sacrifice. Substitution of the ram which Yahweh caused to appear in the bush close to Abraham may be a record of transition to animal sacrifice. Abraham's adventure was probably suggested by substitutions of animals for men in Sumeria—and Abraham came from Ur, of Sumeria, rather than, as the text states, "of Chaldea." A Sumerian service reminds men of this substitution:

> The lamb is the substitute for humanity;
> He hath given up a lamb for his life:
> He hath given up the lamb's head for the man's head;
> He hath given up the lamb's neck for the man's neck;
> He hath given up the lamb's stomach for the man's stomach.
>
> Give the hog as his substitute;
> Give the flesh for his flesh, the blood for his blood,
> And let the demons accept them.[11]

The Son of Man lifted up as a vicarious sacrifice is possibly a survival of an older practice of offering human lives to God. In Semitic human sacrifice the victim was a young infant and the first-born of the family; a criminal or a prisoner of war; or an important person in the tribe. The first fruits of the field, of domestic animals, and of the human family

10. *I Kings*, 16: 34.

11. Sir Leonard Woolley, *Abraham: Recent Discoveries and Hebrew Origins*, 161 (London, Faber; New York, Scribner; 1935). Reprinted by permission of the publishers, Faber & Faber, Ltd., and Charles Scribner's Sons.

were sacrificed to the deity. The criminal or the prisoner of war had offended the god by his crimes or by fighting against the god's people. An important person was sacrificed to appease the god, avert calamity or plague, or ensure victory in battle. In one instance the king's eldest son was offered as a burnt offering that there might be "great wrath" against his enemies (*II Kings*, 3: 27). Devices which satisfy the demands of the god without the taking of life include the substitution of a model of wax or straw (early introduced into Egypt). Small figures of men cut from laminae of bronze and silver, found under the foundation of a house at Gezer, evidently represent human victims. The sacrifice of a man who is vile, worthless, or crippled may also be a substitution for lives more valuable. The eldest son of a Hebrew family was redeemed, and thus escaped death in sacrifice. "Probably *mutilation* and similar irreparable injuries—especially those involving the loss of male virility or female chastity—were devices to preserve life while sacrificing its joy. *Substitutionary acts* were also performed, in which all semblance of the victims disappeared." [12]

There were offerings of human lives in Crete. Greek mythology implies previous human sacrifice in that culture. In Lacedaemon the oracle required the sacrifice of Helen to put an end to a plague; however, as the sacrificer raised his knife to take her life, an eagle snatched it from him. When Iphigenia was about to be sacrificed, Artemis "snatched her away and transported her to the Tauri, making her immortal, and putting a stag in place of the girl upon the altar." In Roman myth, Decius rode his horse into the great chasm and, by sacrificing himself, saved his fellow-countrymen. Perhaps, too, there is a reminder of former human sacrifice in the ceremonies of the Lupercalia, a purification rite. In the course of it, goats are killed; "then, two young noblemen's sons being brought, some are to stain their foreheads with the bloody knife, others presently to wipe it off with wool dipped in milk; then the young boys must laugh after their foreheads are wiped." [13]

Plutarch says that during the time of Marcellus, when the Romans were preparing against the Gauls, they "put alive underground a pair of Greeks, one male, the other female; and likewise two Gauls, one of each sex, in the market called the best market: continuing even to this day to offer these Greeks and Gauls certain ceremonial observances in the month of November."

12. R. A. S. MacAlister, "Human Sacrifice (Semitic)," *ERE*, VI, 864.
13. Plutarch, "Romulus," *Lives*.

Human sacrifice was offered to Odin, hanging being the common method of dispatching victims. When Vikarr, king of Agdhir, was wind-bound on a cruise, his followers cast lots to learn the will of Odin. The god demanded that one of the warriors be sacrificed to him. Again the lots were cast, and the choice fell upon King Vikarr. "That night Odin, in the form of an old man, Hrossharsgrani (*i.e.*, Horsehair-beard), commissioned the gigantic hero Starkadhr to accomplish his will, and gave him his spear, which to human eyes appeared to be a reed." Next morning the king's councillors decided to proceed with the sacrifice, but to perform it only symbolically. "Starkadhr fastened one end of a calf's gut to the top of a pine sapling that grew near an old stump," then told the king that the gallows and the noose were ready, and begged him to mount the stump, assuring him that no harm would befall him. "The king complied and put the noose round his own neck, whereupon Starkadhr hurled the reed at him, exclaiming, 'Now give I thee to Odin.' Instantly the reed became a spear and pierced Vikarr through and through; the old stump broke down upon his feet; the sapling shot up into a tall tree, dragging the king with it; the calf's gut turned into a stout rope; and thus Odin received his victim." [14]

A story from early Ireland states that the people declared a human sacrifice must be made and the blood of the victim mingled with the soul. When the Druids saw the young man who volunteered for this sacrifice, "they gave counsel to slay him and mingle his blood with the blighted earth and the withered trees, so that its due mast and fruit, its fish and its produce might come again."

The youth declared himself ready for the sacrifice; but, when he was about to be killed, a woman and a cow arrived at the spot, and the woman declared that the innocent youth should not be slain, but that the cow should be slaughtered in his place and its blood mingled with the soil of Ireland.

Human sacrifice to rivers appears to have been common in Celtic Britain and indeed survives to this day in the beliefs of the people. Thus it is common belief that the river Spey demands at least one victim each year. At the end of a seven years' period the river Ribble, or its inhabiting spirit Peg O'Nell, claims the sacrifice of a life. She may be placated by the drowning of a bird, a cat, or a dog; and if one of these animals is not offered to her, she demands the life of a

14. Walter K. Kelly, *Curiosities of Indo-European Tradition and Folk-lore*, 208–209 (London, Chapman & Hall, 1863).

human being. Indeed, the belief is still general that the water-spirit in river, lake, or ocean will demand its toll of human life. The rivers Till and Tweed declare: "Where you drown a man I'll drown two." In western Ireland, it is said, "people will watch a man drowning, not because they are cruel, but because they firmly believe that the sea or river will have its victim, and that it will revenge itself on the rescuer by drowning him in place of the rescued." [15]

The Chinese emperor Tang offered himself as a voluntary victim to stay a drought; but as he was preparing to fulfil the sacrifice, Heaven sent an abundant rain.

Offering and sacrifice are usually inspired by animistic concepts of supernatural power, although they may prevail independently of such concepts. The Eskimo who offers tobacco to the wind, the Breton peasant who makes an offering at a menhir or dolmen, may not be actuated by animistic considerations more than is the man who curses the stone that trips him. An offering or sacrifice may be a rationalized spontaneous response to a stimulus to which primitive man is sensitive. When the supernatural is conceived as a rational being, offering or sacrifice may become periodic, conventional, and elaborate. Early Jews made no periodic offering or sacrifice to Yahweh; only after elaboration of ritual and ceremony, building of a temple, and development of a priesthood, did offering and sacrifice become prescribed, conventional, and periodic. A similar observation applies, with modifications, to the development of sacrifice in Persia and India.

15. St. John Ervine, quoted in Eleanor Hull, *Folklore of the British Isles*, 56 (London, Methuen, 1928).

CHAPTER XI PRAYER

Prayers of primitive peoples are seldom clear-cut and distinct from magic or observance of ceremony, and are seldom a prominent phase of religious life. Logically, prayer presupposes existence of a power amenable to supplication, hence an animistic being. When mystic impersonal power is believed to control men and events, there is, we might suppose, little motive to pray. In spite of these logical presuppositions, however, in many areas prayers are made to impersonal beings, sun or earth, even when, apparently, they are not conceived animistically. Be that as it may, primitive man seldom voices the sentiment

Make firm in me a heart too brave
To ask Thee anything!

Prayer is found in most American and African tribes. Kalahari Bushmen pray to the new moon: "Give us rain, that we may live!" The Nandi of East Africa offer special prayers during war, after cattle have been raided, when a pestilence breaks out, and during harvest or drought. Twice a day the adult Nandi addresses to the Sun God and to deceased ancestors the following prayer:

O! God, do thou thine ear incline,
Protect my children and my kine.

E'en if thou art weary still forbear
And hearken to my constant prayer.

When shrouded 'neath the cloak of night
In splendrous sleep beyond our sight,

And when across the sky by day
Thou movest, still to thee we pray.

Dread shades of our departed sires,
Ye who can make or mar desires,

Slain by no mortal hand, ye dwell
Beneath the earth. Oh guard us well!

In Ashanti, prayer is frequently an accompaniment of offering or sacrifice, and otherwise is seldom made. An example is: "*Kunkuma*, receive this fowl and partake; if any one poisons me (*i. e.*, does something to make me break a taboo) let it have no power over me; if any one invokes my name, in connexion with an evil name, do not let it have any power over me; if any one takes a gun and points it at me, do not let it have any power over me." Another prayer: "The edges of the years have met. I take sheep and new yams and give that you may eat. (Give) life to me. (Give) life to my Ashanti people. (To) women who cultivate the farms, when they do so, grant that food comes forth in abundance. Do not allow any illness to come." [1]

When Zulus of South Africa kill an ox, they pray: "Hear, Unkulunkulu, may it always be so." In behalf of one who is sick they pray: "Hear, Unkulunkulu, may he recover." Another prayer is: "Unkulunkulu, look down upon us; Baba (my Father), may I never stumble."

At the white dog sacrifice, during the celebration of the New Year (in February), Senecas offer a long ceremonial prayer, of which the following is a portion:

Gwa! Gwa! Gwa!
So now this is the appointed time!
Now listen, you who dwell in the sky!
Our words are straight—
Only these can we speak unto you,
Oh you from whom we are descended,
Oh you who dwell in the sky!
You look down upon us and know that we are all children.
Now we petition you as we burn this sacred tobacco!
Now we commence our invocation,
Now we speak of all that you have created.
Now (in the beginning) you did think that men-beings should inherit
the blessings of your creations,
For you did say, "Earth was my birthplace!"
Now we have spoken in this incense [throws tobacco upon the flames],
Oh now inhale the smoke, so listen to our words.
Now we commence, we are all that remains upon the earth.
You behold the places that once were filled but now are empty;
We were unable to change it for you made the law.

1. Robert S. Rattray, *Religion and Art in Ashanti*, 14, 139 (Oxford, The Clarendon Press, 1927). Reprinted by permission of the publisher.

Now you think that there should be two conditions of temperature upon the earth;
One you thought should be cold and one should be warm,
And when the warm season came that Dioh̄e'ko, our substance, should spring from the bosom of the Earth, our mother.
Now we have harvested the Dioh̄e'ko from whence our living is,
For the warm season has gone and we have here assembled.
Now we have made inquiries among all the people and they remember their promises,
For they promised you that they should assemble again at Gaiwanos'kwa gowa'
On the fifth sun of the moon Niskowuk'ni.
So all fulfilled the plan and gathered together in the moon Nis'a, even those here present,
Oh you who were born of Earth, yet dwell in the sky!
Now all have fulfilled the law, for you did plan that the rites should be perpetuated even forever.
Now we are commencing, Oh you who were born of Earth!
Upon the first day the Great Feather dance went through the village for your pleasure.
The honon'diont and their cousins did their full duty.
Now on the next day Ganēo was celebrated; at midday they went through the village,
And you did give us great joy because we performed this ceremony
For you did think that Ganēo should be celebrated upon the earth for thine own self.
Thus did we fulfill your desires, Oh you who were born of Earth, yet live in the sky!
Now on the next day Gagandot was played.
Truly we did fulfill your desires,
Oh you who were born of Earth, you who live in the sky!
You did see all that was done,
Oh you who were born of Earth, you who live in the sky!
In the beginning you thought that you would lay this sacred tobacco by man's side
That men should have an incense with which to send his words up to the sky,
With which to lift his words when the year ended.
Truly we have fulfilled your desires and here we have that basket of sacred tobacco,
Oh you who were born of Earth, you who dwell in the sky!

A northern Iroquois prayer includes petitions to nature's powers:

Hail! Hail! Hail! Thou who hast created all things, who rulest all things, listen to our words. We now obey thy commands. That which thou hast made is returning to thee. The smoke of the tobacco is rising to thee by which it will appear that our words are true.

Continue to listen: The united voice of the people continues to ascend to thee. Forbid all things which shall tempt thy people to relinquish their ancient faith. Give us power to celebrate at all times the sacred ceremonies which thou hast given us.

Continue to listen: Give to the keepers of the faith wisdom to execute properly thy command. Give to our warriors and our mothers strength to perform the sacred ceremonies of thy institution.

We return thanks to our mother, the earth, which sustains us, that she has been caused to yield so plentifully of her fruits. May she not withhold them next year and may we not suffer want.

We return thanks to all the herbs and plants of the earth; we thank them for giving us strength to preserve our bodies in health and for curing us of the diseases inflicted upon us by evil spirits.

We return thanks to the Three Sisters, the main sustainers of our lives.

We return thanks to the bushes and the trees; we thank the winds which banish disease as they move.

We thank the thunderbirds who give us happiness and comfort by having the rain descend on the earth, causing all plants to grow.

We thank the moon and the stars and the sun. May the latter never hide his face from us in shame and leave us in darkness . . .

At sunrise a Havasupai prays:

Sun, my relative, look at us; help us. Misfortune may befall my possessions; perhaps some one will fall sick. You, sun, ward this off. You know how to help us prosper.

He prays also to earth, rocks, trees, water, air, and wind, for health, prosperity, or success.

An example of prayers offered by the Sarsi in the sweat lodge preparatory to celebrating the sun dance is the following:

Old Man, Father, may I be a person favored with a long and happy life. Have pity on me, Father. May I live long on the earth and become an old man. May I live to see the hot sun rise, and may I experience happiness from you. May this woman with her husband reach old age. They have made your house and given you these tongues to eat.

Blackfeet offer on the eve of the sun dance the following invocation:

Great Spirit, our Father, help us and teach us in the way of truth; and keep me and my family and my tribe on our True Father's path, so that we may be in good condition in our minds and in our bodies. Teach all of the little ones in your way. Make peace on all the world. We thank you for the sun and the good summer weather again; and we hope they will bring good crops of grass for the animals, and things to eat for all peoples.

The Blackfoot woman while treating a patient makes the following prayer:

Hear us, Great Spirit, in the sun. Pity us and help us! Listen and grant us life. Look down in pity on this sick man, grant us power to drive out the evil spirit and give him health.

In another prayer the Blackfoot says:

Listen, Sun! Listen, Thunder! Listen, Old Man! All Above Animals, all Above People, listen!

Pity us! You will smoke; we will fill the sacred pipe.

Let us not starve. Give us rain during this summer. Make the berries grow large and sweet. Cover the bushes with them.

Look down on us all and pity us. Look at the women and the little children; look at us all. Let us reach old age. Let our lives be complete. Let us destroy our enemies. Help the young men in battle. Man, woman, child, we all pray to you; pity us and give us good. Let us survive.[2]

From the Wise One Above, Heammauvilio, Cheyennes ask food, health, long life, success, or other desideratum. They ask Earth to bless the growth of things, make the water flow, and keep the ground firm so that man can walk on it. They pray Thunder to bring warmth which will enable berries and all things to grow.

Arapaho prayers at the sun dance contain the usual Plains area request for long life, and profess purity of heart in the petitioner. One of these is, in part:

Here I am again with your people this day. Your lodge is up and it is in order; may we therefore pray aright at your sacred altar because your people in years past have done this. It is your word that this be a reminder of the first man and we ask you to teach us the right way and guide us through this whole ceremony to the last. My grandfather, Light-of-the-Earth, look down on us, poor in spirit and thought!

Crow prayers are "simple expressions of wishes." Some are "fairly elaborate," have rhythm and quality, and are "at least poetic prose." The following prayer is addressed to the sun when one dedicates to that body an albino buffalo skin:

Greeting, Father's Clansman, I have just made a robe for you, now I give it to you, this is it. Give me a good way of living. May I and my

2. George B. Grinnell, *Blackfoot Lodge Tales*, 277 (New York, Scribner, 1917). Reprinted by permission of Charles Scribner's Sons.

people safely reach the next year. May my children increase; when my sons go to war, may they bring horses.

When my son goes to war, may he return with black face (that is, a victor). When I move, may the wind come to my face (so that game shall not smell me), may the buffalo gather toward me. This summer may the plants thrive, may the cherries be plentiful. May the winter be good, may illness not reach me. May I see the new grass of summer, may I see the full-sized leaves when they come. May I see the spring. May I with all my people safely reach it.[3]

As an example of prayer embodied in song with recurrent rhythm may be cited this excerpt from the Pawnee Hako ceremony:

We heed as unto thee we call;
Oh, send to us thy potent aid!
Help us, Oh, holy place above!
We heed as unto thee we call.

We heed as unto thee we call;
Oh, send to us thy potent aid!
Help us, *Hatoru*, giver of breath!
We heed as unto thee we call.

We heed as unto thee we call;
Oh, send to us thy potent aid!
Help us, *Shakurn*, father of strength!
We heed as unto thee we call.

We heed as unto thee we call;
Oh, send to us thy potent aid!
Help us, *h'Uraru*, mother of all!
We heed as unto thee we call.

We heed as unto thee we call;
Oh, send to us thy potent aid!
Help us, *Toharu*, giver of food!
We heed as unto thee we call.

We heed as unto thee we call;
Oh, send to us thy potent aid!
Help us, *Chaharu*, giver of drink!
We heed as unto thee we call.

We heed as unto thee we call;
Oh, send to us thy potent aid!

3. Robert H. Lowie, *The Crow Indians*, 115 (New York), copyright 1935. Reprinted by permission of the publishers, Farrar & Rinehart, Inc.

Help us, *Kusharu,* sacred to rites!
We heed as unto thee we call.

And similarly through six more stanzas.[4]

Aztec ritual and public prayers consisted for the most part of appeals to the gods on the occasion of a religious festival, war, sacrifice, baptism, funeral, purification, or pestilence. They were markedly hortatory in tone. Most of their ritual prayers were long, "obviously the products of a priesthood possessing ample time for pious consideration." [5]

At the winter solstice, the beginning of the year, a Zuñi Bow priest makes prayer-sticks, and offers the following prayer:

My two fathers,
You who dwell in high places [6]
Ma'asewi [7]
Uyuyewi
For you it is the new year.
Since it is the new year,
All the beings that dwell in mossy mountains,
The beings who dwell in shady places,
The forest beings,
The brush beings
Oak being
Willow being [8]
Red willow being [8]
Lanilkowa being [8]
Cottonwood being
Taking the straight young shoots of all these,
These we shall make into prayer plumes.
For my fathers,
The divine ones,
I have destined these prayer plumes.
When my fathers
The divine ones
Take hold of their prayer plumes,
When they clothe themselves with their prayer plumes,
Then all to my children

4. Alice C. Fletcher, "The Hako: A Pawnee Ceremony," *ABE*, 22, Part II: 286 (1904). Reprinted by permission of the Bureau of American Ethnology.

5. Lewis Spence, "Prayer (Mexican)," *ERE*, X, 196.

6. "The gods of war, whose shrines are on mountain tops. The phrase might also be rendered as 'those who guard the housetops.' "

7. "The Keresan name for the elder of the two gods of war. His Zuñi name, which is esoteric, is Matsailema. According to Mrs. Stevenson he is the younger brother. Both this name and that of Uyuyewi were unknown to the interpreter to whom the prayer was read, but her father, who carves the image of the younger brother, knew the names."

8. "The identifications are uncertain."

Long life,
Old age,
All good fortune whatsoever,
You will grant;
So that I may raise corn,
So that I may raise beans,
So that I may raise wheat,
So that I may raise squash,
So that with all good fortune I may be blessed.[9]

The Kwakiutl have, among many prayers, the following:

MORNING PRAYER TO THE SUN

Look at me, Chief, that nothing evil may happen to me this day, made by you as you please, Great-Walking-to-and-fro-all-over-the-World, Chief. —Hâ.

PRAYER OF A WORKING MAN TO THE SUN

Look down upon me, Walking-all-over-the-World, and have mercy on me. Protect me that nothing wrong may befall me in my work, for I pray that I may succeed easily in what is desired by me, Great-Walking-to-and-fro-all-over-the-World, Chief, Father, and have mercy and listen to my prayer to you, Great-Praised-One, Chief, Father.—Hâ. Now he will do it that way.

PRAYER OF A SICK MAN AND HIS RELATIVES TO THE SUN

Please, look upon me, Chief, Great Father, and have mercy and protect us against our sickness, (me) and my relatives, and pray, make us well, Great-Walking-all-over-the-World, for you are making in every way this world that you made, Great-Walking-to-and-fro-all-over-the-World, Father.—Hâ. (Answers the Sun.)

MORNING PRAYER TO THE SUN

O Great Chief, Father, pray look down upon these men made by you, that nothing wrong may befall me this day, for you do as you please with us, Great Chief, Praised-One, Great-Walking-all-over-the-World, Chief. —Hâ.

PRAYER TO THE SUN AT SUNRISE

Welcome, Great Chief, Father, as you come and show yourself this morning. We come and meet alive. O protect me that nothing evil may befall me this day, Chief, Great Father.—Hâ. (The man himself then answers, in place of "Walking-to-and-fro-all-over-the-World, the Sun, the Chief.")

PRAYER TO CHIEF SUN

Look down upon these who came from you, Great Father! Look down upon these men made by you, Great Father, and protect those who came from you, Chief, Great Father.—Hâ. Now he will do it that way.

9. Ruth L. Bunzel, "Introduction to Zuñi Ceremonialism," *ABE*, 47: 668 (1929–1930). Reprinted by permission of the Bureau of American Ethnology.

PRAYER TO THE SUN WHEN A CANOE IS CAUGHT IN A GALE AT SEA

Press down the sea in your world, Great Chief, Father, that it may become good, that your world may become right on the water, Great Father.

SONG OF A WOMAN WHO DREAMED ABOUT THE SUN

Don't let us hesitate to dance with our Lord, The-One-to-whom-we-Pray, haai' haai' haai'a haai' haai' haai'.

You to whom we pray, haai' haai' haai' haai' you to whom we pray, haai' haai', you to whom we pray, haai' haai' haai' haai', our Lord, the One-to-whom-We-Pray.

PRAYER WHEN OVERTAKEN AT SEA BY A GALE

Stoop down on the sea for me, Summer-Woman, our dung on the sea, Summer-Woman, our bad smell on the sea, Summer-Woman.—Hâ. (The man himself answers.)

PRAYER OF A MAN WHO FOUND A DEAD KILLER WHALE

Oh, it is great, how you lie here on the ground, Great Supernatural One. What has made you unlucky? Why, great and good one, are you lying here on the ground, friend, Great Supernatural One? Why have you been unlucky, friend, for I thought you could never be overcome by all the Short-Life-Maker-Women. Now you, great and good one, have been overcome by the one who does as he pleases to us, friend. I mean this, that you may wish that I shall inherit your quality of obtaining easily all kinds of game and all kinds of fish, you Great Supernatural One, friend, you, Long-Life-Maker. And also that you protect me, that I may not have trouble, Supernatural One, and also that it may not penetrate me, the evil word of those who hate me among my fellowmen, and that only may penetrate themselves the curses of those who wish me to die quickly. I mean this, friend, only have mercy on me that nothing evil may befall me, Great Supernatural One. Wâ, I will do this (says the man answering on behalf of the one he found dead).[10]

The bargaining element in prayer is evidenced in the Haida petition, "I give this to you for a whale; give one to me, Chief."

At Isleta, New Mexico, the large bunch of prayer-feathers is referred to in folktales as "pay"; presumably they are conceived as compensation to the spirits for gifts asked of them.

In many parts of Polynesia, where the gods are exalted, much attention is devoted to prayer. Tahitians pray before building a new house.

We find in Polynesia a type of prayer in which the congregation, by responses, identifies itself with the priest in his request and thus reinforces the supplication. An example from the Ellice Islands is:

10. Franz Boas, *The Religion of the Kwakiutl Indians*, Part II, 182–184 (New York, Columbia University Press, 1930). Reprinted by permission of the Columbia University Press.

PRIEST
O Thou who dwellest on high.
Look down on all your people
Bring up the vegetation on shore
That it may come up
To be your gift
To this congregation,
And dost thou look down on us with favour from above?

CONGREGATION
Favour!

PRIEST
And chase down from above
A school of whales
As your gift
To this congregation.
And dost thou look down on us with favour from above?

CONGREGATION
Favour!

PRIEST
Bring up a crowd of turtle,
A shoal of flying-fish,
A shoal of bonito,
As your gift
To this congregation.
And dost thou look down on us with favour from above?

CONGREGATION
Favour!

PRIEST
Chase hither from the south-east
A school of whales
As your gift
To this congregation.
And dost thou look down on us with favour from above?

CONGREGATION
Favour! [11]

Among the Tuamotus the following prayer hymn is one of the many offered to the Creator God, Kiho-the-all-source, by Tane:

11. Robert W. Williamson, *Religion and Social Organization in Central Polynesia,* 109 (Cambridge, Cambridge University Press, 1937). Reprinted by permission of the Polynesian Society, New Zealand.

Awake in the Eternal Night!
Arise in answer to the supplication of Tane who does here address Thee,
Thou through whom all plant life has evolved!
Thou the upholding hand of all living trees!
Thou the gleaming Star!
Bestow Thy divine power upon Tane, O my guardian God!
Awake! O Source-of-propagation of the Earth!
Awake! O Source-of-propagation of the Skies!
May my difficult task receive Thy aid!
O Kiho! Turn Thy Face toward me! [12]

A note of abstraction and a strain of grandeur are contained in the Tuamotu hymns of adoration sung by the three clans to Kiho-the-all-source, an abstraction and a grandeur which recall Cleanthes' "Hymn to Zeus" and the exaltation of some of the stanzas of *Proverbs:*

The First-Cause has existed forever in the remoteness of Time,
The First-Cause has existed forever in the remoteness of Space, beneath Havaiki.
He is the Overlord inspiring deep awe and reverence.
He is the Author of these prodigies:
The Lower-world of Night,
The Upper-world of Light,
The region of the far Skies above.
Thy several clans dwell in Thy Universe acclaiming Thee Source-of-all.
O Majesty! O Divinity!
Belong of right to the Creator—

These bournless waters of which we sing, changelessly flowing beneath Havaiki, belong to the Creator.
They are the Welling-waters-of-the-Lord-and-King;
They are the sacred waters of the God supreme.
From within the utter depths of this dark flood arose
All the land of the World-of-Night,
All the lands of the World-of-Light,
And the Skies above,
That the clans of Thy Created Universe behold (all these, Thy several Spheres),
While the multitudes of living creatures hail Thee, proclaiming Kiho the Source of All.

Thy countless myriads dwell in Tua-raki, Land-of-ever-radiant-light-of-dawn,
While we, Thy vassals, acclaim Thee Source of All.

I, Fariua-a-Makitua, say to you that this is the conclusion of the highest teachings of the ancient esoteric lore concerning the emergence of

12. J. Frank Stimson, "The Cult of Kiho-Tumu," *BMB*, 111: 27, 44 (1933). Reprinted by permission of the Bernice P. Bishop Museum.

Kiho-the-all-source (from the Void), and the prodigious deeds that he performed here (in his Universe).
It is finished.[13]

The Lakher of Assam who is about to sacrifice a pig intones the following prayer:

Oh, *Khazang,* I sacrifice this pig to you. Accept it without anger and be pleased with us.
Grant me sons and daughters, and let them be clever and comely.
Bless my pigs and cattle, and cause them to multiply.
Watch over me in illness and save me from death.
Enable me to shoot many animals, and give me good crops.
Bless me in all my works and deeds.
Watch over my whole family and keep us from harm.
I cannot pray to you as well as my father and my mother did, but if I have made omissions, forgive me my mistake.[14]

Most peoples, like the Chinese, have a feeling that improper or unseasonable requests should not be made of the supernatural being which controls events. "Persons who recklessly ask favors should not be treated with the consideration to which they would otherwise be entitled," says a Chinese commentator who wrote before 500 B.C. "Prayers for rain should be offered in spring and summer only; not in autumn or winter . . . because the moisture of growing things is not then exhausted; neither has man reached the limit of his skill." Spring and autumn are appropriate seasons for prayer because "time is then pressing, and man's skill is of no further avail . . . because without rain just then, nothing could be made to grow; the crops would fail, and famine would ensue. But why wait until time is pressing, and man's skill is of no further avail? Because prayers for rain are the same as asking a favor, and the ancients do not lightly ask favors. . . . The inspired men of old who had any request to make of God were careful to prefer it in due season. At the head of all his high officers of state, the prince would proceed in person to offer up his prayer. He could not ask any one else to go as his proxy."

Eighteenth Dynasty Egyptians "confessed their reliance upon the power and goodness of their God, and prayed to him day and night in the forms of words which came not from the formal, official language

13. *Ibid.*
14. N. E. Parry, *The Lakhers,* 363 (London, Macmillan, 1932). Reprinted by permission of Macmillan & Co., Ltd.

of an olden time, but from their hearts, and they used the language current in their day among the people generally."[15]

In most preliterate cultures prayer is not so much a spiritual communion with the god as a definite request for aid. Curiously, in preliterate cultures, its development is apparently not related to the development of anthropomorphism. In the New World it flourishes in regions in which anthropomorphism is feeble. The Mediterranean cultures seem to be the only ones in which the development of anthropomorphism is correlated with the development of prayer.

15. Sir E. A. Wallis Budge, *From Fetish to God in Ancient Egypt*, 316 (London, Oxford University Press, 1934). Reprinted by permission of the publisher.

CHAPTER XII RITUAL, CEREMONIAL, AND SYMBOLISM

RITUAL

Ritual, the standardized and socially approved technique for dealing with the incalculable element in life's critical situations, involves organization, art, and traditional rules of concerted behaviour. It regulates the flow of religiously focused emotions and canalizes "impulses that well up and forth from human hearts, to meet in public worship as in some main river, some broad stream of tendency navigable for mankind in general." [1] It is an instrument of religion and also an organ of social welfare, for every people consider their religion good and salutary. Ritual is invoked when "the comfortable certainties of the daily round fail us, and action must nevertheless be taken in a spirit of 'never say die.'" [1]

Zuñi life, for example, is oriented about religious observance to such an extent that ritual is virtually a "formal expression of Zuñi civilization. If Zuñi civilization can be said to have a style, that style is essentially the style of its rituals." [2] "The essence of Hehe religion," it has been said, "is not belief, but ritual." [3]

In ritual there is safety; departure from it is fraught with danger.

According to Livy, when the pious King Tullus inadvertently performed some holy ceremonies incorrectly, he was struck down by lightning sent by Jupiter. When the Romans were engaged in public divine worship, a herald preceded the magistrates or priests and proclaimed in

1. Robert R. Marett, *Sacraments of Simple Folk*, 5–6 (Oxford, Clarendon Press, 1933).
2. Ruth L. Bunzel, "Introduction to Zuñi Ceremonialism," *ABE*, 47: 509 (1929–1930).
3. S. Gordon Brown and A. M. Bruce Hutt, *Anthropology in Action: An Experiment in the Iriñga District of the Iriñga Province, Tanganyika Territory*, 166 (London, Oxford University Press, 1935).

a loud voice, *Hoc age*, "Do this (you are about)!" He warned the people to "mind whatever sacred action they were engaged in, and not suffer any business or worldly avocation to disturb and interrupt it; most of the things which men do of this kind being in a manner forced from them, and affected by constraint. It is usual with the Romans to recommence their sacrifices and processions and spectacles . . . for any slight reason. If but one of the horses which drew the chariots called Tensae, upon which the images of the gods were placed, happened to fail and falter, or if the driver took hold of the reins with his left hand, they would decree that the whole operation should commence anew; and, in latter ages, one and the same sacrifice was performed thirty times over, because of the occurrence of some defect or mistake or accident in the service." [4] Bantus insist upon precision in ritual. In each clan a master of ceremonies demands meticulous accuracy in the performance of ritual. The rites must be correctly rendered. Indeed, the fact "that rites have a much longer life than the theories that give them birth, is abundantly shown in the history of human behavior; and this magical conception of the function of ritual helps us to understand the secret of their superior longevity." [5]

Ritual, the prescribed manner of performing a religious act, is the routine of religion, whether in prayer, offering, ceremony, or other regularized manifestation of religious zeal. So conceived, ritual is an important phase of religious activity, for religious acts are not performed willy-nilly, but follow a predetermined procedure which elicits "the solemn intoxication that comes of intricate ritual faultlessly performed." [6] To ensure safety and efficacy almost all traffic with the supernatural is ritualized. Thus, among the Congo Ngala, when one curses an adult relative, one rubs the thighs, bends toward the ground, turns one's back upon the person who is being cursed, and shouts: "Be accursed!"

Among the Crows the routine of lighting the pipe, usually directed by a war captain's son, is ritualized. After the pipe is emptied, the lighter holds it out and says: "Take your pipe." The two men designated then hold it. The owner draws his left hand down the lighter's shoulder to the latter's hand, then takes the pipe away. The lighter, meanwhile, prays that they may live until a specified season. The distribution of

4. Plutarch, "Coriolanus," *Lives*.
5. W. C. Willoughby, *The Soul of the Bantu*, 396 (New York, Harper & Brothers, 1928).
6. Dorothy L. Sayers, *The Nine Tailors*, 19 (New York, Harcourt, 1934).

A Blackfoot ceremonial pipe

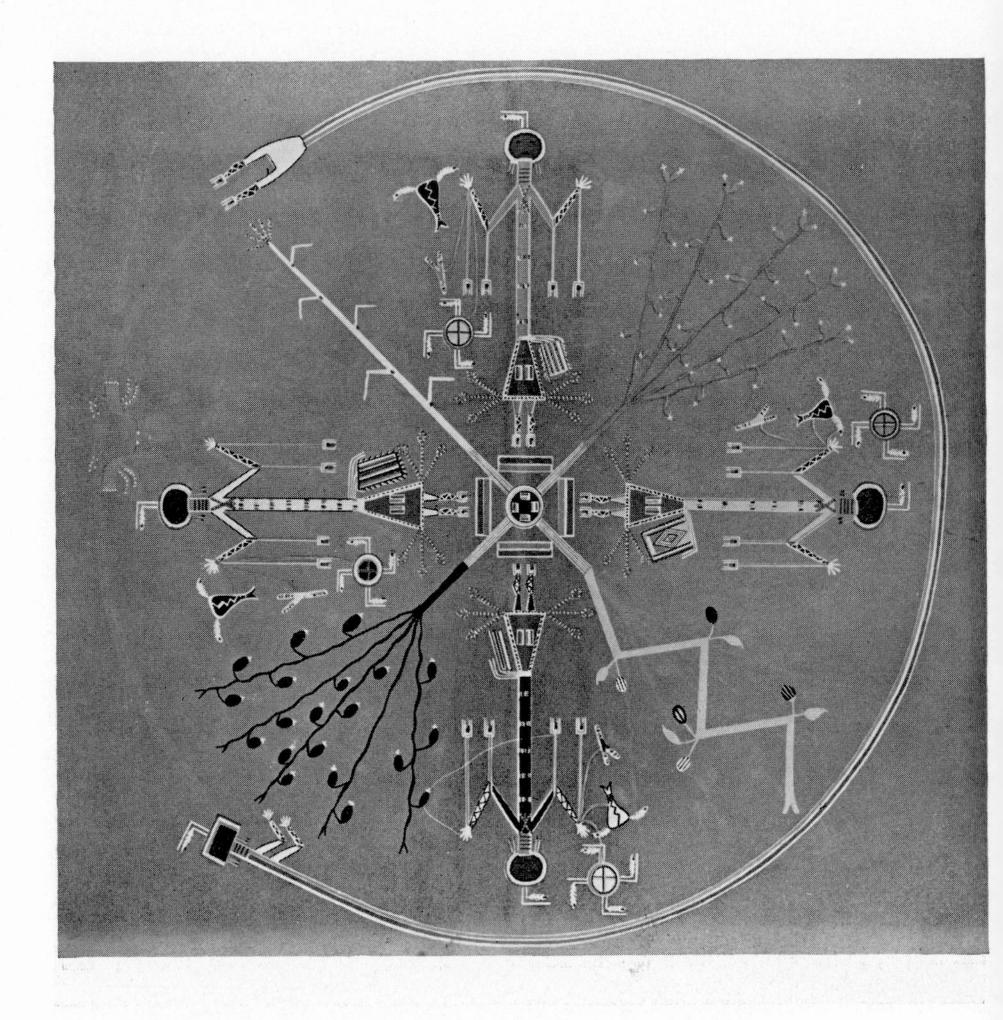

The third dry painting of a Navaho mountain-chant altar

food, which is among the lighter's duties, likewise is conventionalized. The distributor of food crosses his arms, so that the recipient to the right of him receives a portion from the giver's left hand, and conversely, the person to his left receives from the donor's right hand. Thus acts that with us are purely routine and matter-of-fact, with preliterate man often are ritualized. He performs them in a prescribed manner, as for example, in preparation for and conduct of a war party, and even in smoking. A Crow, for example, before smoking, points the pipe upward, then toward the ground, and toward the four quarters of the compass, and prays meanwhile to the winds of the cardinal directions. One can distinguish between the form and the content of religion, but, in preliterate culture, they are inseparable; religion, therefore, cannot be adequately described in terms of mere content.

The emotional heightening generated by situations of stress and risk to individual, family, or community, fosters rituals which in turn intensify the affective tinge peculiar to the sacred. Concepts preserved and transmitted by generations of seers or priests are embodied in legends and myths which quicken a sustaining emotion. Ritual at feasts, festivals, religious processions, and dances intensifies the emotional appeal of the occasion. Sometimes artificial stimulants—for example, the fermented liquor used in Oraon religious ritual—create or intensify religious emotion.

Zuñis secure ritual blessings by inhaling. A man inhales from all sacred objects in order to derive benefit from their *mana*. At the conclusion of a prayer or chant, attendants inhale, holding their folded hands before their nostrils to inspire the sacred essence of prayer.

When an Isleta Pueblo Indian practises the ritual of breathing to secure supernatural aid, he breathes on his clasped hands, with the left hand folded over the right, the thumbs parallel. When the priest supplicates the Mother on the altar he waves the ceremonial feathers first toward the Mother, then toward the audience. He breathes on his clasped hands, moves them in a circuit, and says: "The water people send all of you long life and health." When the runner asks help from scalps or from the sun, he makes a similar gesture. In another ceremonial supplication the hands are held cuplike and moved to and fro, as though the suppliant were drawing something to himself. The Isleta use also an antithetical motion of discarding. In this exorcising movement the palms are passed across each other quickly with slicing or scissorlike movement. Eagle feathers are used during the rite; one feather is tapped against another at a right angle. Eagle feathers are carried by the person who conducts another to a ceremonial place—for example, when the "Father" leads the patient to the society's room. During this ceremony the Father crosses the feathers, and the patient grasps them by the tips. The Father then swings them over his head, while the patient holds them in proper position behind the Father. Sacrosanct objects, especially corn fetishes, are held in the right hand, which rests in the crook of the left arm, the left forearm resting over the right forearm. The ear of corn and also the eagle feather are sometimes held by the butt or tip in both hands; the supplicant then breathes upon them to obtain aid. As among most Pueblo peoples, bare feet and flowing hair are appropriate during the performance of ritual.

A Lenge spits when he offers sacrifice. In the Ndau division of the tribe, the sacrificer does not spit but claps his hands. When the priest of the Supreme Deity rises in the morning, he must go to the sanctuary of the god and there wash his hands and face with water from a basin. He then takes three swallows of it, expectorates, invokes the names of the god, and says: "I seek no one's death. But if some one desires to kill me, then he himself will die." This ceremony he repeats in the evening. On the market day of his clan, every fourth day, he again performs specified rites and makes a ritual prayer. Each Saturday morning he paints himself with white ochre, puts on a white dress and around his forehead a band. These he wears until evening, and associates meanwhile only with members of his priesthood or of his family.

The most important activity in the everyday life of Bali priests is the performance of a domestic *maweda*, or ritual, every morning, on an empty stomach. Every fifth day and on days of full and new moons, the *maweda* is essential and more replete. The priest then wears the full regalia of important occasions. He must first purify himself thoroughly by reciting cleansing *mantras* to accompany each action of his morning toilet. He washes his hair, rinses his mouth, polishes his teeth, and rinses his mouth again; washes his face, bathes, rubs his hair with oil, combs it, and then dresses. At each act he recites a short *mantra*, as also for each garment put on. On a high platform his wife has arranged his paraphernalia: trays with flowers (night-blooming flowers if it is a nocturnal ceremony); gold or silver vessels containing grains of rice and sandalwood powder; his holy-water container; a silver sprinkler; a long-handled ladle; his prayer bell; an incense-burner; and a bronze oil lamp. In baskets to one side of the place at which the priest will sit are the attributes of Siva that he will wear during the ceremony: a bell-shaped mitre of red felt with applications of beaten gold, topped by a crystal ball, the "shimmer of the sun"; and a number of strings of seeds (earrings, bracelets, neck and breast beads) ornamented with pieces of gold set with phallic lingas of crystal. When the priest has seated himself cross-legged among these paraphernalia, he purifies his person. He lays a prayer cloth over his lap, places his hands on his knees, mumbles a formula, and asks Batara Siva to descend into the water-vessel and into his body. He stretches his hand over the incense smoke, uncovers the tray in front of him, mumbles the *mantra asta mantra* (the hand-cleansing formula), rubs the palms of his hands with a flower and sandalwood powder to wipe out impurity, recites a formula for each finger as he passes it over the palm of the other hand, holds flowers over the incense smoke, then flings them away, and says: "Be happy, be perfect, be glad in your hearts."

Toda dairy ritual prescribes rigid daily routine for the dairy priest. He rises early, steps outside, salutes the sun with hand raised to forehead, washes his hands and face in a special vessel which stands in front of the dairy, takes water in his right hand, pours it into his left hand, and conveys it to his mouth.[7] After rinsing his mouth he ties up his hair in prescribed fashion, bows to the threshold of the dairy, enters, and recites a formula. He transfers fire from the ordinary fireplace to the sacred fireplace, doffs his cloak, and dons a special loin cloth. He then recites a prayer, kindles three pieces of wood at the sacred fireplace, and with them lights the lamp. And so on through a long list of prescribed activities of which the above are only the beginning.

RITUAL IN PRAYER

One not merely prays, one prays in a specific manner; one not merely makes an offering, one makes it in a prescribed way; one not merely discharges religious obligation, one discharges it in a preordained fashion. Ritual, essentially regularized routine, is requisite to the success of a religious act. It is objectified and has efficacy *per se*. Zuñi prayer is not the spontaneous outpouring of an overburdened soul but is essentially repetition of magic formulas. Prayers are the essence of the ceremony, and, like fetishes, are sacred and powerful in themselves.

7. "He who pours sesamum seed and water on his head from a right-hand *sankha* destroys all the sins of his life."—Varaha Purana

Even in higher religions and in the most personal religious act, namely, prayer, there is usually a dominant and delimiting ritual.

Thus during prayer the Jewish worshipper spreads out his hands to indicate his plea for divine mercy and help; and inasmuch as kneeling is a mark of homage to a superior, it is the proper attitude for worship. In Egypt and Babylonia, and among Old Testament Jews, the palms are extended outward in prayer. The gesture has been interpreted as a conventional substitute for "stroking the idol," but there seems no sufficient justification for the inference. During prayer Homeric Greeks looked up to "wide heaven," "lifted up their hands," [8] and sometimes knelt. Early Romans and early Jews stood and faced east, but subsequently adopted the kneeling posture. Romulus, says Plutarch, prayed with hands stretched out to heaven. Plutarch [9] says it was the custom of the Romans to turn to the right after adoration or prayer. Originally Christians stood during prayer; this practice persists in some churches —for example, the Greek Orthodox. Kneeling was probably not prevalent in Christian worship until medieval times, when it was adopted as a result of the feudal custom of kneeling in homage. In most present-day Christian churches prayer is performed in kneeling posture, with eyes closed, hands folded or crossed, head bowed. In some sects the suppliant stands; in some, his closed eyes are turned toward the heavens. Closing the eyes during prayer has been supposed to be based on fear of seeing the god who was invoked—"For gods revealed are hard to look upon." [10] Procedure varies from one sect to another and from one individual to another, but for each individual and for each sect there are prescribed attitudes and postures without which prayer cannot be offered in confidence or with conviction of propriety. Copt prayers, apparently influenced considerably by Jews and Mohammedans, are largely ritualistic. The Coptic Church prescribes prayer seven times during the day. The first prayer is at daybreak, the second at the third hour, the third at the sixth hour, the fourth at the ninth hour, the fifth at the eleventh hour, the sixth at the twelfth hour (that is, at sunset), the seventh at midnight. For the Mohammedan the regulations are no less binding than for the Christian. He stands with face toward Mecca and five times touches the ground with his forehead while he prays. Hindus, however, say the efficacy of prayer is destroyed by contact with the

8. Iliad, Books VII, VIII.
9. "Camillus," *Lives*.
10. Iliad, Book XX.

ground. During prayer a Hindu may not sit on the ground. His prayer-rug is sacred grass, deer-skin, or, if he is an ascetic, panther-skin or tiger-skin. An Indian Mohammedan, like his Mediterranean brethren, uses a prayer-carpet or a cloak; he may pray on bare ground only in a spot on which the sun has recently shone. A Buddhist, similarly, follows conventional procedure. In offering prayer to Dharmes, the chief god, the Oraon faces east, the direction of the rising sun. In India the common form of supplication is to hold the hands, palms pressed against each other, in front of the face. When a Brahman makes to the sun the offering known as *arghyas*, which consists of water, rice, sandal oil, sesamum seed, white flowers, and durra grass, he holds the right foot back over the left, lifts the spoon to his forehead, and empties it toward the sun, after reciting the Gayatri verses. If no water is available, he may use sand. In the Survopasthan ceremony the man faces the sun and stretches his arms upward toward it. When ceremonial purification is taken by means of bathing and putting on clean garments, there follows a recitation during which the devotee must make certain gestures and movements. The tips of the four fingers touch the thumb, as in counting, then the palm of the other hand; one hand is then laid over the other; the fingers touch the chest over the heart, the head, the eyes, and the hair, in that order. The right hand is passed round the head and smites the left. An *ashtadal*, or eight-cornered figure, is drawn in red powder; and frankincense, red ointment, and red flowers are offered to the sun.[11]

When the Maria Gond, of Bastar, India, prays, he first bends forward to the earth, presses his palms flat on the ground, belches, and beseeches the god to save from sickness and adversity those who have brought the offerings of mangoes. He then bows his head to the ground, rises and faces the sun, standing, and with folded hands calls upon the sun to be a witness to the fact that the ceremonies have been performed. When ancient Persians worshipped the sun, they laid the hands upon the mouth and then raised them in adoration. There appears to be an echo of the practice in *Job:* "If I beheld the Sun when it shined, or the Moon walking in brightness; and my heart hath been secretly enticed, or my mouth hath kissed my hand." Some students of folk-lore see a survival of this custom in the European habit of kissing the hand in salutation or in farewell.

11. R. E. Enthoven, *The Folklore of Bombay*, 32–33 (Oxford, The Clarendon Press, 1924).

As mentioned, Mandaeans when they pray turn toward the north, that is, toward the great mountains from which flow the rivers Tigris and Euphrates, at whose source God lives and reigns.[12] They hold the head erect and keep the hands close to the body or employ them in a ritual gesture, as when touching or knotting a portion of their religious garb, or they hold the open palm upward.

Among Parry Island Ojibwas, of Georgian Bay, one who prays for healing from an ailment faces the setting sun, naked.

In the Plains area of North America and in the Southwest of the United States the suppliant faces the sky, the rising sun, or one of the cardinal points, usually the east, the place of the rising sun, and, in most Plains tribes, extends the right hand in front of him while he prays. When Omahas pray toward the clouds during a thunderstorm, they stand with arms elevated and hands outstretched, palms down. When Cheyennes pray to the Wise One Above, they uplift the hands and gaze skyward. The Dakota who offers prayer to Spider holds the bowl of his filled pipe toward the ground while he voices his supplication. At each sunrise the northeastern Yavapai prays to the sun, holding his right hand edge up, arm raised to a horizontal position and pointing toward the sun. A western Yavapai stops at a pile of stones and twigs which marks a place for prayer, usually sits down, plucks a fresh sprig, brushes his body, and says: "Keep sickness away from me. Give me medicine power from the rock to keep away illness." He then places a sprig on the pile and lays new stones on it. The Havasupai prays to the sun at sunrise, and draws his hands down over his face as he does when ceremonially brushing away evil. The Zapotec prays toward the cardinal directions or facing the altar, and makes with the outstretched hands, palms inward, the gesture of drawing the spirit toward the worshipper's mouth.

During prayer the Thompson River Indian extends the arms above the head, thrusts them forward, then gradually brings them together and lowers them toward the legs, the palms of the hands directed outward and toward the power or personage to whom he makes appeal. In another gesture, designed to attract to oneself the power prayed to, the arms are slowly thrust forward, brought above the head, then drawn back until they reach the chest; the palms of the hands are turned toward each other and brought close to one another, the fingers slightly curved. The usual procedure during prayer, however, is to raise and

12. See page 106.

lower one arm above the head while holding the other horizontally across the chest; the extended arm is slowly lowered with the fingers curved, until the hands are opposite each other. They are then placed on the chest, one over the other. The suppliant heaves a deep sigh and inclines his head and body forward.

The Okanagon devotee makes signs with his hand as though attempting to attract attention from above, then sends his thanks upward. When the Coast Mewuk prays, he raises the right hand and stretches it toward heaven. When the Haida prays to the moon, he looks up at it, blows a breath, and utters tersely, "Teech! Teech!" that is, "Life! Life!" Usually the suppliant retires alone to the woods, to a running stream if one is accessible, rubs his face with a prickly bush, lays aside his blanket, stands erect naked, with arms extended, and gazes at the moon.

The words and gestures which accompany his prayer depend upon the object desired. When he prays for salmon, he rubs the backs of his hands, looks upward, and utters the words: "Many salmon! Many salmon!" When he prays for deer, he carefully rubs each eye; when he prays for geese, he rubs the back of his shoulder and utters in a singsong tone the conventional formula; when he prays for bears, he rubs his sides and legs vigorously with both hands, and wears round his head a piece of red blanket adorned with feathers. "These practices in prayer no doubt have a meaning; for instance, a steady hand is needed in throwing the salmon spear, and clear eyesight in finding deer in the forest." [13] When a Tanaina prays to the supreme being who lives in the Pole Star, he stands with legs outstretched and right hand raised. When he prays to the being in the constellation of the Little Bear, he holds up a hand. Aleuts go at daybreak to the water's edge and with open mouth raised toward the eastern sky wade into the water until it comes up to their knees. They then pray, as the sun rises, "O beloved Light, you see me wakeful, strengthen me!"

The Malay priest who offers the invocation at the mine stands and places his hands on his hips or behind his back. No other may stand thus, and he may not assume that attitude on any other occasion.

During the ritual prayer which the Gilbert Islander makes to the setting moon, he claps his hands together once, postures with arms and torso, then flings both hands out at arm's length, palms upward toward

13. Gilbert M. Sproat, *Scenes and Studies of Savage Life*, 209 (London, Smith Elder, 1868).

the setting moon. During certain prayers Hawaiians gesticulate or clap the hands. During other prayers, at a given signal the people stand and hold their hands outstretched toward the sky for a half-hour, continuously. At other times they make suitable responses after each petition; and sometimes they sit in profound silence throughout the prayer. In the Marquesas the man who offers prayer sits cross-legged.

When the Zande prays, he takes water in his mouth, spurts it out near him, and addresses to it a ritual prayer. Again he spurts out water near him and makes another conventional prayer. The Kamba looks toward the east, then closes his eyes and utters the prayer. The Ibo of southern Nigeria raises his hands to the heavens and rubs them together. When Naron Bushmen pray to the moon, they sit on the ground and hold the hands out, palms upward, toward the moon. When the Cape Bushman prays to the new moon, he raises the right hand. Among the Bechuana, of South Africa, one invokes the supreme being by looking upward; wetting the forefinger of the right hand with spittle, drawing it between the forefinger and thumb of the left hand and then pointing it toward the clouds; laying hold of the chest; grasping the big toe and wetting it with spittle; or striking the thigh and throwing toward the sky dust or a piece of reed or of wood.

The Kitara of central Africa stands in the open and prays with hands and eyes raised toward the sky. Practically all Bantu peoples greet disembodied spirits, as they greet living chiefs, by clapping the hands. Sutos utter also a shrill ululating cry, of a kind common among the women. Kongos chant the virtues of the spirits to accompaniment of drum, harp, and trumpet, concluding their praises by clapping the hands—a conclusion as indispensable as our amen. Bantus usually intone oral prayers. In some tribes the worshipper prostrates himself in the dust; in some he shows deference by kneeling and touching his temples or other part of his head with earth; in some he sits upon his heels; in some he prays standing; in some he merely claps the hands.

Thus ritual regulates the most personal and intimate relations of the individual with the supernatural power.

CIRCUITS, SUNWISE AND COUNTERSUNWISE

When a religious or ceremonial act involves processionals or the handing around of an object, there is usually a prescribed procedure. In many areas this is sunwise; in some areas it is countersunwise. Among Micmac, when the bark of a tree is to be used as medicine, it is cut from "the place toward sunrise" in the direction of the sun at noon, that is, sunwise. In the game of *Waltés,* however, the play goes counterclockwise. The Parry Island Ojibwa walks sunwise around the plant before he plucks the leaf or root which he will use as medicine. He observes the sunwise circuit in the ceremonial smoking, by pointing the stem of the pipe first toward the east, then to the south, west, and north. The door of the ceremonial wigwam faces east, and all movements within the wigwam are sunwise. If the wind changes against the sun, that is, blows from the south toward the east and then shifts toward the north, there will be a storm; if it shifts sunwise, there will be fine weather.

Chippewas follow the sunwise circuit in their *midewewin* ceremony. When the priest is about to smoke, he takes a whiff and points the stem toward the east, another whiff and points the stem toward the south; and so to west, and to north. Women proceed clockwise when removing bark from the birch tree and when fastening a stretched hide to the frame in preparation for tanning. The flute which the Foxes use in one of their ceremonies they point toward the east, south, west, and north, that is, in sunwise circuit. The appropriateness of clockwise circuit among the Tanaina is implied in their belief that, if a small animal brought home as a pet runs counterclockwise, blood will run from the mouths of the people and they will die. In dancing and at all ceremonials the Lillooet follow the sun's course, and pass the pipe sunwise at gatherings. A Bella Coola mourner, to rid himself of a troublesome ghost, on four successive days creeps through the clefts of four small trees, making a sunwise circuit. When Salish women drink for the first time after their marriage, they must turn the cup four times in the direction travelled by the sun. Throughout the Plains area of North America ritual acts are sunwise, for the sun, as one faces it in the northern hemisphere, swings southward through an arc in clockwise direction. When men are gathered in a tepee in a circle for the performance of a rite and the pipe is passed round, it is handed sunwise, with sometimes a variation in procedure.

During the sun dance the suppliant faces the sun from its rising to its setting, and dancers move in a circle in this direction. Crow braves, when in the sun dance lodge, must walk clockwise. Clockwise circuit was followed in the 1870 ghost dance ceremony. In the owl dance of the Crows, although the main body of dancers moves clockwise, a few participants form an arc of an inner concentric circle and shuffle in counterclockwise direction. When Mandans give a young child a name, they hold the child up and turn it clockwise toward each of the cardinal points. Sunwise circuit is used by Pawnees when the child is ceremonially admitted to the tribe or introduced to the supreme being, Tirawaatuis. When Hidatsas have castrated a colt, they lead it round in a circle, sunwise. Sunwise circuit is followed in Navaho ritual in the Female Shooting Life Chant. In their ceremonies Navahos move with the sun from east to south, to west, to north. Proceeding counterclockwise will bring bad luck and is associated with evil magic. When a medicineman leaves for home, he turns toward the south, in clockwise direction, for evil spirits and witches turn counterclockwise, and bring untoward consequences.

Among the White Mountain Apaches of Arizona, the scheme of the four cardinal points permeates all rituals, even in dreams. The sequence, beginning with the east, is clockwise, a rule of motion which holds for everything which rotates, they say. When the northeastern Yavapai kill a bear, members of the hunting party hold bows and arrows vertically and dance sunwise about the body of the animal. Barama River Caribs who are being initiated into the mysteries of the cult dance in a circle sunwise.

Sunwise procedure is followed by central Eskimos and by the Siberian Yukaghir and Yakut. The Koryak take the sunwise direction when they carry round the house the stuffed skin of a recently killed bear; they then send the soul of the animal away in the direction of the rising sun. Sunwise processionals are the rule in Mediterranean and Indo-European civilizations. An Egyptian Mohammedan who visits the tomb of a saint walks round it sunwise. The reverse direction, as among Navahos, is taken when a magic curse is invoked. To make food beneficial, pious Mohammedans stir it sunwise; and at table they pass dishes in this direction; a Mohammedan will not partake of a dish passed countersunwise. Moslem pilgrims at Mecca walk about the Kaaba with the right hand toward it, sunwise. Hindus and Indian Mohammedans obtain religious virtue by encircling a saint's tomb clockwise. At Murarram, Indian Mohammedans make a sunwise circuit of the *alawa* pit which represents a grave. The Afoshi of northern Nigeria dance in sunwise direction. Sunwise ritual is observed in Haiti voodoo when the officiant bows toward the respective points of the compass—first to east, then to south, then to west.

The Ibo, in their summer dances, move in counterclockwise circuit. A counterclockwise procession is taken in a Dahomey religious dance.

The Tanaino, of the Northwest Coast area of North America, have a counterclockwise dance. Southern Okanagon shamans perform a counterclockwise circuit to ensure the health of attendants and save the lives of those who are threatened with death. Among Quinault Shakers the circular dance is counterclockwise.

The Parry Island Ojibwa who wishes to work evil magic walks countersunwise around a plant before he digs up its root. He then summons the evil supernatural beings from east, north, west, and south, instead of sunwise, as normally. Or his "medicine" in the form of an owl perches on a tree near a hunter's camp and turns sunwise, praying to the evil spirits in each of the cardinal points to injure a specified man. In this event the victim will procure no game and his family will starve. To secure the medicines which he has placed under a subterranean rock the malicious medicineman walks around it four times countersunwise. Similarly a corpse can be made to rise from the grave.

Countersunwise direction is taken in ceremonial celebrations in the Southeastern part of the United States, by Pueblo tribes of the Southwest, and by Aztecs. Hopis ritually run in counterclockwise circuit. The Hopi boy who is being initiated for participation in hunting faces the cardinal points, in turn, counterclockwise. On Mimbres bowls, however, geometric designs—if interpretation is correct—go clockwise. Among Jicarilla Apaches, to complete a clockwise circuit about a buffalo was to court disaster; the animal would probably charge the hunter and gore him. Maricopas note the counterclockwise movement of the Dipper about the Pole Star. Possibly their counterclockwise ritual was not inspired by this phenomenon but rather turned attention to it. The ceremonial countersunwise circuit which characterized the ancient Aztecs is common among modern Zapotecs. At Mitla Christianized natives who make prayers at the four directions of the cross observe the Aztec circuit. Before the bowl of pulque was drunk, it was raised toward east, north, west, and south. This countersunwise circuit is observed when "calling the corners" to cure fright. The omen bird flies around the corners of the house in countersunwise circuit. The circuit of the procession of the *Calenda* and that of Easter Sunday night are, however, in deference to Christian practice, sunwise.

Sunwise ritual characterizes the folk customs in many parts of the British Isles, where doubtless it is a pagan survival. In Colonsay, before people undertake an important enterprise, they encircle the church sunwise. Here, as in the Orkneys, the Shetland Islands, and Iceland, the crew, when starting on a trip, always turn the boat sunwise. In Elgin a procession at a baptism or at a marriage proceeds sunwise. Thus, too, a bride is led to her future spouse, and a consecrated fountain is approached. In Beltane, herdsmen dance three times round a fire, sunwise; at Dipple, bearers of a corpse encircle the churchyard walls of the chapel sunwise. Lochsiant well, in Skye, cures many complaints, provided the patient goes sunwise thrice round the well while he drinks the water. A wooden trencher floating on the well of Shadar, in the Isle of Lewis, foretells the fate of the patient. If it turns sunwise, he will recover; if it turns in the opposite direction, he will die. In the Highlands of Scotland one walks three times sunwise round the person whom one wishes well. This is "making the deasil." In Strathfillan, Perthshire, people are cured of insanity by being made to go three times deasil round a certain pool and then being plunged headlong into it. A Highlander who goes to bathe in a consecrated spring or to drink water from it must approach it from the south side and go from east to west, following the course of the sun. The coffin is taken about the grave deasil; the rope placed on a house or a straw-stack is taken round sunwise; when going to a house the visitor should go round it deasil to secure luck in the object of his visit; after milking a cow the dairy-maid should strike it deasil with the shackle and say, "Out and home." This ensures the cow's safe return. When the marriage party leaves the church, it goes round it deasil. When one is choked by food in the œsophagus, a sympathizer says, "Deasil! It is not grudging it that I am to thee!" [14]

Sunwise circuit in early Ireland is referred to by Cormac in one of the earliest sources for that culture.

On the island of Iona was a "stone of judgment" or of "doom," containing three hollows, in each of which was a white stone or ball. Those who visited the island were expected to turn each of those three balls thrice round the way of the sun. On the Eve of St. Michael the islanders took their horses to a small green hillock surrounding a cairn or cromlech and led or drove them sunwise about it.

To ensure that the king of Breifne would do right by his people, the crozier of St. Maedoc was carried sunwise round the king at his coronation. It was carried thus round his warriors when they went into battle;

14. *Deasil* is derived from *deas*, right hand, and *iul*, direction. Literally, therefore, it means "in the right-hand direction," that is, with the right hand toward the object, and etymologically has no reference to the sun. The etymology, of course, does not tell us whether this meaning is primary or is secondary, derived from an older practice based on the apparent motion of the sun southward from east to west.

if it was turned against any in the contrary way, they would be cursed. Indeed, on one occasion this king forced the nobles, unknown to themselves, to go countersunwise round Tara in order to destroy the chances of an O'Rourke who sought the kingship; and, in consequence, no one of that line ever succeeded in obtaining the throne.

The river Boyne, in Ireland, is said to be named after a goddess who lifted the stone which concealed the waters of a spring out of which the river flowed, and thrice walked round it left-hand-wise, daring it to injure her. There streamed forth, wrathfully and vengefully, a river which despoiled this daring goddess of her thigh, her arm, and an eye, as, too late, she fled before it to the sea. St. Patrick consecrated Armagh, and St. Sana consecrated Scattery Island, by walking sunwise with their followers round these respective sites, thereby providing traditional ecclesiastic precedent for sunwise ritual. In Ireland, when one walks in a graveyard, it is proper and customary to go "with the sun," that is, with the right hand toward the centre of one's peregrinations. In the Hebrides animals are led sunwise round a sick person.

In Cornwall, "when a convalescent goes out for the first time he must bring his bodily functions into harmony with Nature by moving in a circle and with the sun; for if, on setting out, he goes from west to east, he will experience a relapse."

Perhaps it was through a custom of facing the sun that certain preferences for the left over the right arose in China. For when one faces south, the portion of the heavens through which the sun moves, east is on the left and west on the right. In ancient texts reference is always made to left before reference to right, if the two are associated, as, for example, "on one's left and/or right." People sitting on one's left are interrogated before one questions those on one's right. In military affairs preference is given the left; in ritual court matters, however, the right has the honorific place, and in ancient China the right was the honoured position. In China and Japan, when one drinks tea, the cup is given a complete turn clockwise between the first sip and the last.

Sunwise processional is made by bride and bridegroom during the Iraq Mandaean marriage ceremony. To secure *barkat* Hindus encircle a crow-pheasant sunwise. When food has been served at mealtime, a Brahman sprinkles water round the dishes clockwise to keep the spirits away. Water is sprinkled in this fashion in other Brahman rites also—for example, round offerings and the sacred fire. Clockwise circuit, *pradaksina*, is made in the worship of all deities, with one exception: to avoid crossing a water-channel before an image of Siva, one reverses the circuit of his image at the channel. The pole on the threshing-floor, the central pole of a marriage booth, and a sacrificial fire are encircled sunwise. Bricks in an altar are laid in "sunwise order," and this order is observed whenever five articles are arranged in cross-formation. Water is sprinkled on the cardinal points in sunwise circuit, and dancing when a monsoon is delayed is sunwise. Sacred things are encircled sunwise. The sacred books of Hinduism, the Institutes of Vishnu (63: 26–33) and Manu (4: 39), give a long list of objects which must be passed so that the object is on the person's right, as in sunwise circuit. Sunwise circuit is taken by the pilgrim when he makes solemn perambulation round temple or shrine, and by cattle when they tread out the grain.

The Brahman moves thus round the altar. Priests sprinkle from "left to right," that is, sunwise, for thus the ocean flows round the world. The Buddhist prayer-wheel and sacred dancers move sunwise.

In building the altar, Buddhist workers go the "rightward (sunwise) way; for this is (the way) with the gods, and thus, indeed, yonder sun moves along these worlds from left to right." Chips of wood for sacrifice are strewn "from left to right (sunwise) for that is (the way) with the gods." In Tibet Buddhist pilgrims encircle the tombs of holy men in sunwise direction. Visits to Stations of the Cross in Roman Catholic churches are taken sunwise. The altar is in the eastern end of the church or cathedral and the priest and the worshipper face east, the direction of the rising sun, while performing sacred rites.

It is now the custom at convivial gatherings in the Old World—we cannot vouch for the New in this matter—to pass the bottle round sunwise. A photograph of "Dons in a Senior Common Room after Dinner" published in the London press in 1937 shows a neat contraption consisting of a railed trolley from which the port decanter crosses the gap between diners at the fireplace and makes its circuit sunwise. Thus does academic innovation bow to ancient custom, religiouswise. In Homeric days, it appears, countersunwise circuit was observed at banquets: "Up with you in turn from left to right, fellows, the way our wine goes round," was the admonition to Penelope's contesting suitors.[15] At the banquets of the Celts serving boys went from right to left in helping the guests, and the merit and honour of a warrior were indicated by his place from right to left, that is, by his distance to the left from the place of highest honour. Japanese pass things from left to right—for example, in dealing

15. Odyssey, Book XXI.

cards and in playing other games. Europeans deal cards clockwise, and most European games which involve circuits go sunwise.

Passing things in countersunwise direction, for which there is an old English and Scotch word, *withershins*, that is, *wider Schein*, "against the sun," smacks of evil magic. Thus witches, when taking oath of allegiance to the devil, pass thrice round an object countersunwise, or withershins. In India, when offerings are made to the dead, countersunwise direction, *prasavya*, is taken in sprinkling the water—as also in removing evil, in waving things to avert evil, and in witchcraft and sorcery to counter evil influences. Stones representing Vetal are placed countersunwise. In worship a Hindu woman goes round a pipal tree clockwise, but counterclockwise as well as clockwise when she desires issue. In Babylonia the numbering of the twelve spaces in the square-shaped and in the wheel-shaped horoscope chart proceeded counterclockwise. Possibly there is influence from Babylonia in the Indo-European concept of the malign magic in the counterclockwise circuit, although the fact that it is a reversal of the proper circuit would seem sufficient to account for its untowardness.

REPETITION

Often ritual involves a specified number of repetitions. In the Orkneys after the birth of a child a fir-candle was whirled three times round the bed of the mother and child in order to avert evil influences. Or the nurse waved an open Bible three times round the bed, in the name of the Trinity. When the newly-baptized infant was brought home from the church, the mother or the nurse waved the child through a flame and repeated three times: "Let the fire consume thee now, if ever." "Three noble, sacred things: groves or temples, felid or poets, rulers," is an old Irish saying. Again: "Three dead things that are paid for only with living things are an apple tree, a hazel bush, and a sacred grove." The motive of three is common in present-day folk-lore of Europe and India. Thus in Scottish folk-lore a woman bears three sons, a mare casts three colts, a hound litters three whelps, and three trees sprout up in the garden at the same moment.

Among Hindus and Mohammedans the ritual number is three. To invoke the blessings of God, the Mohammedan raises his hands three times after prayer. Three recitations of the Koranic verse *Kul Hwallah* are the equivalent of one recitation of the entire Koran. Mohammedan purificatory ablution involves washing the hands thrice, gargling thrice, taking water in the nostrils three times, washing face and feet three times. To avert or transfer evil, articles are waved thrice round the stricken person. When making a *yantra*, a "restraint," the Hindu repeats three times the *mantra* which invokes power. A Hindu's word repeated three times must be accepted as true, for the repetition speaks for past, present, and future. An extract from the Veda must be recited with three specific accents, known as *udatta, unudatta,* and *svarita*. A *mantra* recited without accent would kill the utterer as if it were a thunderbolt hurled at him.

In Mexico, parts of South America, and a large portion of North America, the ritual number is four, a frequent accompaniment of ceremony. Ancient Egyptians used the number four symbolically and ritually. The four Eastern Horuses were solar genii. Each rite that obtained entrance to the sky world was performed for each of the four Horuses in succession. Thus four considerable utterances were built up, each containing an account of the things done by each of the four Horuses.

So completely does ritual pervade religious ceremony and celebration that an adequate account of it would include nearly every religious performance; the order is prescribed; one may not reverse it or depart from it. Its efficacy depends as much upon following routine as upon performing the several acts which comprise the formal religious complex.

CEREMONIAL

Ceremonial is the picturesque, artistic, and dramatic element in religious observance, the æsthetic and dramatic trimmings of ritual and observance, their decoration and adornment. It develops apace with elaboration of religious observance.

In America north of Mexico ceremonial is most highly developed in the Southwest of the United States, where religious rites are detailed and prolonged. It was a prominent feature of the highly evolved religious life of Mexico and Peru. Similarly, in the historic civilizations ceremonial accompanies elaboration of ritual. In the simpler Christian cults—for example, among the Quakers, Primitive Methodists, and Presbyterians—there is little ritual or ceremonial; in the Greek Orthodox and Roman Catholic Churches, as in the Church of England, elaboration of ceremonial accompanies elaboration and prolongation of ritual. Thus the canonization of Sir Thomas More and Bishop John Fisher, in St. Peter's, in 1935, was accompanied and accomplished by elaborate ceremonial. At eight o'clock in the morning the papal procession began to file into the

RIGHT

A Navaho sand-painting of the god of the whirlwind

BELOW

A headdress worn by a Zuñi dancer impersonating the god of the rainbow

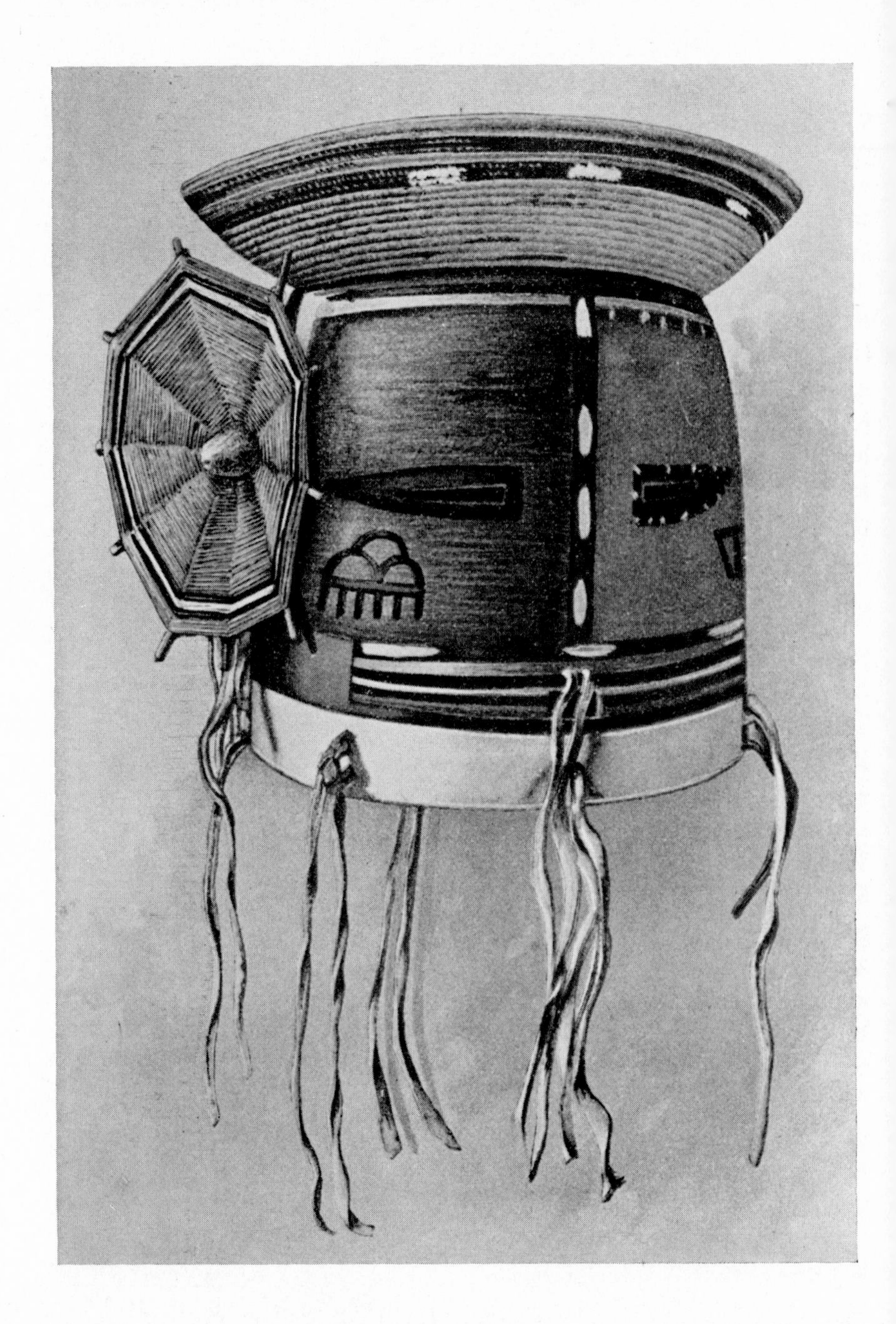

A Tusayan Katcina mask, with squash-blossom appendage and rain-cloud symbolism

church. An hour later the Pope, on the *sedia gestatoria*, the ceremonial portable chair, made his entry. He was dressed in full pontifical robes; wore his triregnum, or triple crown; in his left hand held his shepherd's crook; with his right hand dispensed blessings upon the faithful who knelt while he passed. His appearance was heralded by a blare of the famous silver trumpets of the Vatican. Then followed the intoning by the Sistine Choir of *Tu es Petrus*, "Thou Art Peter," accompanied by frenzied applause from the assembled throng. Ahead of the Pontiff walked in double file fifteen Cardinals with ermine cloaks over their scarlet robes. At their head a white-surpliced acolyte carried aloft the spear-headed cross. Behind the head of the Pope were two flabelli, semi-circular ostrich feather fans, supported by long poles. A long procession of high church dignitaries followed, headed by the new Archbishop of Westminster. Thus began an elaborate ceremony.

SYMBOLISM

Symbolism plays a prominent part in the Skidi Pawnee Hako ceremony. Blue beads are symbolic of raindrops and of the sky, the dwelling place of Tirawahut, "that great circle of the powers which watch over man." A straight groove, painted red on the ceremonial stick, is "the path along which the spirits of all the things that are to be put upon this stick of ash may travel as they go forth to give their help during this ceremony." The groove is red "because the passageway is red through which man's breath comes and goes to give him life. The sun, too, is red, and the groove represents the straight path whereon the sun shines, the path which man must travel if he would live in peace and prosper. The teachings of this ceremony make a straight path along which if a man walks he will receive help from the Powers." Green represents vegetation, the covering of Mother Earth. Eagle feathers are glued to the stick because "the eagle flies near to *Tirawa*." The owl, woodpecker, and duck are utilized, for these birds are leaders: the eagle is chief of day; the owl, of night; the woodpecker, of trees; the duck, of water. Sticks from the plum tree are used, "because this tree is prolific in bearing fruit." [16]

Among Chippewas, white symbolizes east; green, south; red, west; black, north. Among Navahos, white, the mantle of dawn, symbolizes east; blue, the robe of azure sky, south; yellow, the raiment of sunset,

16. Alice C. Fletcher, "The Hako: A Pawnee Ceremony," *ABE*, 22, Part II: 32–44 (1904). The quotations in this paragraph are reprinted by permission of the Bureau of American Ethnology.

west; and black, the blanket of night, north. Each point of the compass is symbolized by an object. White shell beads and rock-crystal symbolize east; turquoise, south; haliotis shell, west; black stones or cannel-coal, north. Colour symbolism is highly developed in the Plains area of North America, the Pueblo region, and Mexico.

A ceremonial belt used in Arapaho religious rites contains straight lines and crosses; straight lines symbolize straight paths and a good life; crosses symbolize stars, which bring good life, and especially the Morning Star, the Father of Mankind. In the dancer's yellow belt, vertical green lines symbolize sunbeams, four crosses are the Four Old Men referred to in prayers, a red notch represents the people, the paint signifies the earth. The otter skin which covers the lance is the earth, the red skin signifies paint, the red paint represents life and symbolizes the wish that the children of the tribe may attain ripe old age. At the bottom of the lance, hair from a horse's mane symbolizes advance against the enemy; yellow tips of eagle feathers represent the rays of the sun entering the tepee in the morning through holes over the door. Each portion of dance and decoration has specific symbolism. A sacred "wheel" represents a water-snake and the water which surrounds the earth, and symbolizes meekness. The blue beads round the neck of the serpent represent the sky, symbol of purity and friendship. Four incised markings represent the Four Old Men who symbolize the four points of the compass, the world quarters, and also summer, winter, day, and night.

Teton Dakotas find symbolic meaning in roundness. Shields are round, the sun is round, the earth is round, the moon is round, the sky is round like a bowl. Tepees are round and are pitched in a circle. The circle, therefore, or roundness, has mystic significance. The symbolism used in the Oglala Dakota Sacred Bow ceremony portrays prayers for protection or for power to offset opposing forces. Oglala Dakotas believe the circle sacred because the Great Spirit caused everything in nature to be round, except stone, the implement of destruction. Sun, sky, earth, and moon are round like a shield; the sky is deep and circular like a bowl. All that breathes is round, "like the body of a man," and all that grows from the ground is round, "like the stem of a tree." Inasmuch as the Great Spirit has caused everything to be round, mankind should regard the circle as sacred, for it is the symbol of all things in nature, except stone. The circle symbolizes the edge of the world, and therefore the four winds which travel about it. It is also the symbol of a year, for day, night, and moon go in a circle above the sky. The circle, therefore, is a symbol of these divisions of time, hence the symbol of all time, as well as of the tepee and of shelter. For this reason, Oglala Dakotas say, they make their tepees circular, their camp circular, and participants in all ceremonies form a circle. An ornamental circle without segments symbolizes the world and time. A circle filled with red symbolizes the sun; one filled with blue, the sky. A circle divided into four parts symbolizes the four winds; one divided into more than four parts symbolizes a vision. A half circle filled with red represents a day; filled with black, the night; filled with yellow, a moon, or a month. A half circle filled with many colours symbolizes a rainbow. Arikaras say the circle of the world is a unit of four segments; and the sky above it is a dome. Hence, "in the structure of the lodge there shall be four main posts, and about these a circle of twelve shorter posts, all supporting the domed roof." Many paint or otherwise represent a circle on tepee, shield, or robe. The mouth of a pipe should be moved in a circle before the pipe is formally smoked.

Early in the history of ancient Egypt everything good was associated with daylight; everything evil, with the darkness of night. In the Old Testament, purity and innocence are typified by white, which represents light and signifies brilliance, beauty, and moral uprightness. Black, the opposite of white and its negation, signifies death, humiliation, and mourning. Blue, the colour of the clear sky, represents revelation. It was the first of the colours used for the curtains of the sanctuary; to remind them of Yahweh, Jews wore a fringe of blue on the edge of their garments. Red, the colour of blood, suggests war, bloodshed, and guilt. Purple, the mark of royalty, signifies dignity and honour. Green, the colour of growing plants, symbolizes hope and resurrection; it is also the symbolic colour of the moon, a luminary resurrected the third day after its disappearance at the end of every month. The appropriate colour of the Oraon chief god, Dharmes, is white, the colour of the sun; hence, the fowl or goat sacrificed to him must be white.

Figures and designs, realistic or geometric, frequently serve as symbols of the faith. Thus early Christianity used symbolically the fish, the lamb, and the labarum. The Greek letters *alpha* and *omega*, signifying the beginning and the end, are frequently used in a symbolic sense as metaphor or as decoration. In Buddhism the swastika is a symbol of eternity. In some cultures—for example, ancient Rome—the unending circle has a like symbolic meaning. The ring used in the Christian marriage ceremony is a survival of that concept.

In ancient Egypt the eye, typifying the wounded eye which Horus sacrificed in his father's behalf, came to symbolize all sacrifice. "Every gift or offering might be called a 'Horus-eye,' especially if offered to the dead." With the exception of the sacred beetle or scarab, it became the most common and most revered symbol in Egyptian religion. The myriads of eyes, in blue or green glaze, or cut from costly stone, which characterize museum collections, and are gathered by modern tourists, are survivals of the inspiration of this ancient story of Horus and his devotion to his father.

A number may be used symbolically—for example, four in ancient Egypt, Indo-European civilization, and most of North America; seven in ancient Egypt, Judaism, Mohammedanism, Hinduism, and Christianity; and three in India and Europe. Thus the Oraon ceremony of examining rice-grains to discover the cause of trouble and the means of defeating it is performed as follows: a man "draws a diagram on the ground with the coal-dust, rice-flour and hearth-flour in the shape of three concentric parallelograms with their eastern arms wiped off." The outermost lines are made of the earth from the hearth and thus are reddish; the intermediate lines are made with rice-flour, and thus are white; and the innermost lines are made with coal-dust, and thus are black. The figure represents three concentric compartments which open toward the east. In the innermost compartment three handfuls of rice are placed in as many separate spots. Over each handful of rice they place a *tulsi* leaf and a piece of *rasni* root, and cover them with a circular plate made of *sal* leaves. Close to the diagram and toward the southeast they place a potsherd which contains fire, a piece of copper, and a lighted earthen lamp; and they lay a *gulaichi* flower and a *bael* (*Aegle marmelos*) leaf on each petal-like compartment of the outermost and innermost lines of the diagram. The woman for whose benefit the ceremony is performed circumambulates the diagram three times, commencing the circuit at the lamp and ending it there. She then bows down before the diagram, sits on the *sal* leaf plate which covers the three handfuls of rice in the innermost compartment of the diagram, and presses the palms of her hands together. Celebrants then place three *gulaichi* flowers strung on a reed and some *arua* rice inside her folded palms.[17]

In ancient Egypt there were four pillars of heaven, four winds, four elements, each with a god, and four rudders of the boat of Re, the sky god. Heaven and earth were divided into four parts. The ritualistic num-

17. Sarat Chandra Roy, *Oraon Religion and Customs*, 285–286 (Ranchi, Man in India Press, 1928).

ber four occurred in the four altars, the four lamps or blazing torches, the four rudders, the four vessels of blood, the four vessels of milk, the four mud bricks, the four pillars or sons of Horus, the four spirits, the four glorious gods, and the four cardinal points, and in other contexts. Magical formulas were recited four times.

Seven also was sacred in ancient Egypt, Babylonia, and Greece. In Egypt there were the seven Hathors, the seven Ariti, the seven cows and their bull, the seven gods of the Lake of Fire, the seven souls of Re, the seven-headed serpent, the seventy-seven gods, the seventy eyes, the seventy ears, and the two and forty (that is, seven times six) assessors in the Hall of Judgment. In the Roman period spells were recited seven times. "The seventh day [of the Jews]" said the uncomprehending Tacitus, "is sacred to rest, for on that day their labours ended; and such is their natural propensity to sloth, that, in consequence of it, every seventh year is devoted to repose and sluggish inactivity." [18]

Orientation by fours, prevalent in the Plains area of North America, the adjacent Central Woodland area, among the northern Iroquois, in the Southwest of the United States, and among the Mayas and Aztecs of ancient Mexico, is thus described by an Oglala Dakota: "Dakota grouped all their activities by fours. This was because they recognized four directions: the west, the north, the east, and the south; four divisions of time: the day, the night, the moon, and the year; four parts to everything that grows from the ground: the roots, the stem, the leaves, and the fruit; four kinds of things that breathe: those that crawl, those that fly, those that walk on four legs, and those that walk on two legs; four things above the world: the sun, the moon, the sky, and the stars; four kinds of gods: the great, the associates of the great, the gods below them, and the spirit kind; four periods of human life: babyhood, childhood, adulthood, and old age; and finally, mankind has four fingers on each hand, four toes on each foot, and the thumbs and the great toes of each taken together are four. Since the Great Spirit caused everything to be fours, mankind should do everything possible in fours." There are also four great virtues: bravery, generosity, truthfulness, and begetting children.

Arapaho sacred numbers are four, five, and seven. Seven is much less frequent than four. Arapahos sometimes say that four is the older number, seven the newer. Objects, names, and conceptions, ceremonial and mythic, are frequently seven in number, episodes in traditions occasion-

18. Tacitus, *History*, Book V, 4.

ally, ritual actions seldom. Five occurs only as based on four: it is the summing-up of four, spatially the centre of four. The idea of five as *per se* a significant number is foreign to Arapahos. Five is common in ritual, perhaps more usual than four; but its relation to four, especially as a visible spatial expression, is usually clear. Four, the primary symbolic number, is associated with the circle; indeed the concept of four is almost invariably inherent in the idea of the circle. The association may be suggested by the four quarters determined by the sun, but the connexion extends to human matters. A circle is "a four-sided or four-ended thing," as "four-determined and four-containing." Rhombus, rectangle, and cross are equivalents of the circle. "Where we think geometrically, the Indian thinks symbolically; where we are realistically visual or spatially abstract, he is pictographic." [19]

Many can sympathize with Pepys in his sentiments regarding the proper way to receive the sacrament: "Sir W. Batten told me how Mr. Prin among the two or three that did refuse today to receive the sacrament upon their knees was offered by a mistake the drinke afterwards, which he did receive, being denied the drinke by Dr. Gunning, unless he would take it on his knees; and after that, by another the bread was brought him, and he did take it sitting, which is thought very preposterous." [20]

To vary the ritual is sacrilegious; to reverse it is diabolical and subversive. In medieval days saying the mass backward was a means of working evil magic. Thus the Mass of St. Secaire was said in an old abandoned church from eleven o'clock at night until midnight. The priest read the mass backward, and used no wine, but drank water from a well into which an unbaptized infant had been thrown. He made the sign of the cross on the ground with the left foot, rather than, as in religious ceremonies proper, with the hand in the air. The man for whom the mass was said in this fashion would wither away and die. In Vedic ritual mispronunciation or omission of a word vitiates the entire ceremony and endangers the officiant. Among Zuñis—and this applies equally to many other cultures—efficacy of formula depends upon absolutely correct repetition. "Every word, gesture, bit of regalia is part of the charm. Hence, the great perturbation in Zuñi if a dancer appears wearing a feather from

19. A. L. Kroeber, *The Arapaho*.
20. The *Diary of Samuel Pepys*, I, 167 (London, Everyman's Library, 1912).

the shoulders instead of the breast of the eagle, if a single gesture before an altar is omitted, or if the words of a prayer are inverted." [21]

In most religions ritual is bolstered by the equivalent of that

> . . . great text in Galations,
> Once you trip on it, entails
> Twenty-nine distinct damnations,
> One sure, if another fails.

When religious celebration becomes more complex, greater attention is paid to ritual, and there is greater insistence upon accuracy in routine and upon following prescribed formula. Pharisees cannot flourish where there is no elaboration of rite or ritual. Although the New Testament disparages ritual, early Christianity developed or adopted many ceremonials. In holy places, devotees perform sacred rituals, recite sacred formulas, receive holy food, and with ceremonial washings are cleansed from sin. Christian rituals developed as efficacious means of pleasing and appeasing God and securing his favours, temporal and eternal.

21. Ruth L. Bunzel, "Introduction to Zuñi Ceremonialism," *ABE*, 47: 492 (1929–1930).

CHAPTER XIII FAST, FEAST, AND VISION

To participate in or obtain control over the supernatural it may be necessary to undergo privation; hold feast or festivity to induce ecstasy; have dream or vision. Frequently fast, feast, and vision are closely related. Feast and fast may complement one another; or one alone may bring the vision which places the individual in communication with the supernatural. Fast, feast, and vision have emotional repercussions.

In ancient Peru the pilgrim must fast twenty days before he was admitted to the sacred temple of Pachacamac. Only after a year of fasting may he ascend the highest terrace upon which the temple stands. Fasts, involving strict limitation of diet, including abstinence from all condiments, such as red pepper, are prerequisite to ceremonial purity. At Isleta, New Mexico, there is ceremonial fasting for four days, complete abstinence from food and drink. During this time the faster may kill no animal, "not even a fly or a spider." The initiate who is entering the medicine societies must abstain from wheaten dishes and eat only cakes of blue corn meal, must made from a wild water-plant, and corn meal tamale. Comparable fasting is practised by Zuñis. During the last night of their performance Zuñi *koyemshi* priests may not partake of food or drink, may not talk or sleep, and from sundown to midnight of the following day may not remove their tight-fitting masks. Fasting is prescribed for the Chippewa youth who wishes to secure his spiritual animal companion, or *manitou*, in a vision. Meanwhile he must live in solitude apart from his fellows and the camp. Similar withdrawal and meditation in solitude are practised in some Plains tribes. Aztecs indulged in festivals more amply than in privations. Privation and solitude are the portals through which the Australian medicineman embarks upon his career. In an isolated cave or secluded shelter *iruntarinia* spirits come to him in the darkness of night, remove his intestines, and replace them with a new set. His personality is remade, his career in the realm of the supernatural is launched. The old self is gone, a new one acquired; new experiences and powers lie before him.

In the Plains area of North America the sun dance is the conventional means of securing a supernatural vision. The performer, usually, has had a vision in which the Sun or some other supernatural power has told him to organize and on a designated day lead a war party, and has specified the number of scalps he will secure. If the would-be performer is too old or otherwise physically incapacitated, an abler-bodied man may substitute for him. Frequently he is told in the vision that he will have long life, the greatest boon to mortal man. The vision through which Pawnee priests receive instructions regarding the Hako ceremony often comes during sleep, but appears also when they are awake. Through visions, Pawnees say, the ceremony in its details has been acquired. Birds, animals, and products of earth represented in the Hako communicated with man by visions. During the song of invocation these personified visions in their dwelling-place above hear the summons, descend to earth, go to the door of the lodge, and there pause. They then cross the threshold and "walk within"; they move about, fill the lodge, and touch all the people. They then "walk away" and ascend to their abode on high. The visions thus repeat the sequence of movements which characterize the Hako party when it enters the lodge. The accompanying song is:

Holy visions!
Hither come, we pray you, come unto us,
Bringing with you joy;
Come, Oh come to us, holy visions,
Bringing with you joy.

Holy visions!
Near are they approaching, near to us here,
Bringing with them joy;
Nearer still they come—holy visions—
Bringing with them joy.

Holy visions!
Lo! Before the doorway pause they, waiting,
Bearing gifts of joy;
Pausing there they wait—holy visions—
Bearing gifts of joy.

Holy visions!
Now they cross the threshold, gliding softly

Toward the space within;
Softly gliding on—holy visions—
Toward the space within.

Holy visions!
They the lodge are filling with their presence,
Fraught with hope and peace;
Filling all the lodge—holy visions—
Fraught with hope and peace.

Holy visions!
Now they touch the children, gently touch them,
Giving dreams of joy;
Gently touch each one—holy visions—
Giving dreams of joy.

Holy visions!
Ended now their mission, pass they outward,
Yet they leave us joy;
Pass they all from us—holy visions—
Yet they leave us joy.

Holy visions!
They, the sky ascending, reach their dwelling,
There they rest above;
They their dwelling reach—holy visions—
There they rest above.[1]

Pawnees distinguish between day visions and true dreams and, unlike many peoples, do not consider visions a form of dreams. Dreams are brought from the realm of the gods above by birds, which then return to ethereal regions.

Vision or dream interpreted as supernatural plays an important rôle in North America from Mexico to British Columbia, between the Rocky Mountains and the Great Lakes region. It is highly developed in much of this area, with the exception of the Pueblo region of the Southwest, where its rôle is less emphatic than in nomadic tribes of the Southwest and the Plains area. Among the Crows—and this applies with modifications to most Plains tribes—the general course of sacred ceremonies and also their details, such as specific songs and methods of painting, are derived from visions. "Through them it was possible to rise from abject poverty to affluence and social prestige. Even war parties were, at least

1. Alice C. Fletcher, "The Hako: A Pawnee Ceremony," *ABE*, 22, Part II: 318–320 (1904). Reprinted by permission of the Bureau of American Ethnology.

in theory, wholly dependent on them; for a man organized one only when prompted by a vision or when dispatched by another man who had received such a supernatural communication." [2]

The Peyote cult, which originated in Mexico and entered this country through the Southwest, was a liberal bestower of visions. Those who ate of the peyote bean, or "button," experienced ecstatic visions in which, frequently, superhuman power was bestowed by a supernatural being. Dr. Heinrich Klüver, who experimented upon himself on two occasions, found that peyote gave him conviction of almost unlimited power. He felt, he said, that he could lift the heavy oak table by him with his little finger and, although he appreciated its massiveness, throw it through the window. He knew the wall of the room was made of brick and cement; yet he felt that, should he care to do so, he could put his foot through it. Peyote rites differ from one tribe to another, but the following description of Wisconsin Winnebago practices characterizes their fundamental nature. The cult was introduced into this tribe about 1895. In the early days the ceremony began with a prayer from the man who had brought the cult to the tribe. This was followed by an introductory speech. The leader, accompanied by a drum, then sang a peyote song. Another speech followed. At its conclusion drum and other regalia were passed to a man to the right. He, in turn, made a speech, sang a song, and passed the regalia to the leader. In this fashion four men continued the service throughout the night. When one grew weary, another took his place for a while. At intervals the performers stopped to eat or drink peyote. About midnight the effects of the peyote became apparent in some participants. The man who felt its influence rose and delivered one or more self-accusatory speeches, made formal confession, shook hands with those present, and asked forgiveness for offences.

A Winnebago thus describes the fast and its benefits: "I never fasted much. I fasted only three times, and believe I never fasted for more than two days at a time. However, I never was blessed with anything (*i. e.*, any object). I knew, however, that I came from the home of the Thunderbirds (*i. e.*, that I was a reincarnated Thunderbird). My spirit father and mother were Thunderbirds. The Thunderbirds are beings whose glance can penetrate any object. For that reason I also can do it. For instance, I have seen a man through a tree. This I did once during a thunderstorm when a man had sought shelter behind a tree. When I was

2. Robert H. Lowie, "The Religion of the Crow Indians," *APAMNH*, 25: 323 (1922). Reprinted by permission of the American Museum of Natural History.

ready to go down among the human beings (to be reincarnated) I was given the power to overcome my enemies in battle. And this I have actually done. All the Thunderbirds have small war-clubs. I also had one when I came. Whenever I went on the warpath I made myself a war-club and used only that in battle. I believe I was invulnerable. I knew I could return to the Thunderbirds, whenever I became tired of living among human beings. I thought I knew all this and that I had these powers. For that reason when I ate peyote I still held on to these beliefs for a long time, thinking that when I returned to the Thunderbirds inasmuch as they are above it would be the same as going to everlasting life, as the Peyote people said. Finally, one night, at a peyote meeting, in thinking about these things, I resolved to give them up. I could, nevertheless, not bring myself to do it. Then the peyote began to strangle me; at least I thought so. I also had the power of causing or stopping rain. All that I had to do was to offer tobacco to the Thunderbirds and make my request." [3]

Of the many tribes which adopted this religion none accepted it until after the tribal culture had disintegrated under White influence and the tribe had been confined to government reservations, where the Indians mourned the loss of aboriginal freedom and the passing of the old culture.[4]

Siberian and Eskimo shamans are especially subject to visions in which they see wraiths or thinly materialized spirits, whose voices they hear, and with whom they converse.

Frequently the religious life deliberately creates the preconditions of emotional stimulation. Feast, fast, and vision stimulate a psychological state which makes the devotee susceptible to religious ecstasy. They break the humdrum of everyday existence, enhance the aspirant's sensitiveness to the supernatural, and are avenues to religious inspiration.

3. Paul Radin, "The Winnebago Tribe," *ABE*, 37: 300–301 (1915–1916). Reprinted by permission of the Bureau of American Ethnology.
4. See Chapter XVIII.

CHAPTER XIV SUPERNATURAL SANCTIONS

Religion may impose sanctions which influence conduct and therefore have ethical import. Thus a Teton Dakota man who meets a lone woman in the woods does not molest her; she may be the supernatural Deer Woman, whose human lovers suffer immediate loss of speech, followed by death. Similarly, the North Queensland native is most circumspect in his conduct toward a woman encountered in the bush; blindness not due to obviously traumatic causes is supernatural punishment for raping a married woman. Transformation into a beast is sometimes the supernatural punishment visited upon the guilty or his relatives. Aleuts believe that incest is punished by the birth of a monster with walrus tusks, or of a child with a beard or other disfigurement. The French Canadian believes that if a person does not partake of the sacrament for seven years he will turn into a *loup-garou*, a shapeless animal without head or limbs, or perhaps into a wild-cat, a hare, a fox, or a black hen. At night he is obliged to range through woods and deserted places. The Yukaghir of Siberia believe that parents who mistreat their children are supernaturally punished. Should a Dakota who has no right to do so paint a horse in the *wakan* manner, he will encounter misfortune, perhaps fall ill, be slain by the enemy, or have his neck broken by being thrown from a horse; the horse is *wakan*, and in one's treatment of it the proprieties must be observed.

Violations of custom are sometimes supernaturally punished. Thus a rich man among the eastern Rengma Nagas, of Assam, who set up a stone monument after the custom of the Angami Nagas rather than after the custom of his own group, was a short time thereafter killed by a tiger close to the village fence "where no one would ever expect a tiger to penetrate. This has always been regarded as a punishment for starting a new custom, and no one has followed his example. His stone has fallen, and is still to be seen near the southern edge of Meluri village."[1]

The Hindus and Santal, to obtain their wishes, make vows, a practice followed by the Old Testament Jews. The Congo Ngala make vows, particularly in behalf of some one who is ill; for example, a man may vow, "I will not eat fowl until my father recovers from his illness." Should his father die, the man will thereafter be obliged to abstain from eating fowl. Among the Bechuana of South Africa, when two men make a solemn covenant, an animal is killed as a sacrifice, and the two men grasp each other's hand while their hands are covered with pieces of the stomach of the sacrificed animal. Oath, blessing, and curse, words or formulas uttered with supernatural sanction, are potent. The prohibition against taking the name of God in vain is based on fear of using his name, because of its inherent danger. For a similar reason the Canadian Dakota Indian will not sing his medicine songs or perform the ceremony which accompanies them unless he is about to use the medicine-bundle to which they pertain. Should he do so to no purpose, the *wakan* being would be displeased because, when it responded to its name, it would learn that it was not wanted. The man who indulged in this procedure would merit and receive supernatural punishment.

BLESSING

The blind Isaac, having blessed Jacob, could not revoke the blessing even when he learned that Jacob had deceived him by pretending to be Esau. When God spoke, it was so, and similarly when man spoke under supernatural sanction. An ancient Egyptian blessing with magic potency was: "Whoever seeth this book and acteth in such wise that my Ka [double] and my Name become permanent among the favoured ones [of Osiris], the selfsame thing shall be done for him after his death in return for what he hath done for me." The blessing, a supernatural sanction which confers religious beneficence on its object, is rare in preliterate cultures. However, in a ceremony of the Rengma Nagas of Assam, an old man, holding a cock, utters the following blessing: "Today the dawn is fair. Today the sunset is fair. Your wife's father blesses you. Your mother's brothers bless you. Your father's sisters bless you. All bless you. May you grow like a plantain shoot," and so on. In Manus, Admiralty Islands, a father invokes a blessing upon his son, such as: "Let his mouth not err, his speech be straight and true." The blessing and the curse of a dying man are found among the Swahili, the Kikuyu, and the Rondo, in East

1. J. P. Mills, *The Rengma Nagas*, 199 (London, Macmillan, 1937).

Africa. Inasmuch as blessing and curse are exceedingly rare in preliterate cultures, outside East Africa, their presence in that region is probably due to diffusion from Euro-Asiatic cultures, which have influenced East Africa in other respects.

CURSE

The curse, which invokes supernatural punishment, derives efficacy from the spoken word. An ancient Egyptian curse was as follows: "If any man belonging to any foreign land, whether he be Black, or Nubian [Kushite], or Syrian, removeth this book, or any thief steal it and carry it away, funerary offerings shall not be made to their bodies [mummies]. They shall never plunge themselves in cool water. They shall never snuff the breezes [of the north wind]. Neither son nor daughter shall arise from their seed, their names shall never be commemorated upon earth by means of children. They shall never see beams of light of the Disk." Ancient Greeks dreaded "an old man's curse."

If, in Tanganyika, a Hehe father curses his son, the ancestral spirits are angry with the son, who thereafter cannot eat in the household without risk of illness and death. Until the ancestral curse is ritually removed, he may not eat with his kin. The Zande father emphasizes his curse on a son by slapping his own sides. When a Zande buries medicines, he places a conditional curse upon the thief: "May misfortune come upon you, thunder roar, seize you, and kill you. May a snake bite you so that you die. May death come upon you from ulcers. May you die if you drink water. May every kind of sickness trouble you. May the magic hand you over to the Europeans so that they will imprison you and you will perish in their prison," etc. Among the Chagga of Uganda, a parental (presumably, a father's) deathbed curse "makes a man a pariah by heaping maledictions not only upon him but also upon any one rash enough to associate with him." The Edo of Nigeria visit a contingent curse on a thief by placing on the head of a girl a small bowl which contains cowries and other emblems of the god Ake. The man who has lost the property accompanies the girl, rings a bell, and shouts: "The one who took my fowl, if he does not bring it back, may the Ebo kill him." The Congo Ngala sometimes utter a contingent curse, such as, "May I be cursed if ever I eat food cooked by you!" In such event the curse must be formally removed before one dares engage in the action covered by the curse.

The curse of an older relative is a recognized sanction among the New Guinea Arapesh. It is occasionally used by a violent and aberrant person.

"The mother's brother's curse has been rendered nugatory as compared to its use by other tribes of the area because among the Arapesh the same mother's brother who put it on need not be the one to remove it." A curse of the Manus, Admiralty Islands, declares: "The words go on the air and do their work." The Dusun of North Borneo have such curses as: "may you fall dead"; "may you be seized by a crocodile"; "may you remain childless"; "may your children die"; "may your plantation be destroyed." Occasionally parents curse their children; "and a Dusun is of nothing more afraid than to be cursed by his parent." When a Samoan found that his bananas (or coconuts) had been stolen, he shouted two or three times at the top of his voice: "May fire blast the eyes of the person who has stolen my bananas! May fire burn down his eyes and the eyes of his god, too!" The thief who heard this trembled, for Samoans dreaded these imprecations. In Tonga a curse imposed upon one who had disregarded a taboo would cause his death within a year. The Polynesian who declares, "Bake your grandfather till his skin turns into cracknel, and gnaw his skull for your share," or, "Dig up your father by moonlight, and make soup of his bones," or utters similar curses of a more indelicate character, is offering not merely insult but supernatural ill as well, for good measure.

The hummingbird is the messenger of the Takelma medicineman, sent to work evil. When it is heard near one, its mission is to take away some of one's hair, probably to be used in sympathetic magic to harm the owner. To thwart this design the endangered man utters the following protective curse: "Mayest thou die with my hair which thou pullest out of the side of my head! In this house mayest thou rot with it!" The Wintun of California utter the curse "May the grizzly bear eat you!" or "May the grizzly bear bite your father's head off!" Each Ponca clan possessed a pipe which would punish a man by acting successively upon parts of his body. When a man was to be punished, the chiefs of the clan assembled; the pipe was filled by the leader, and was smoked in turn by each chief. When the leader took the pipe to clean it, each chief concentrated attention upon the offender. The officiant then poured some of the ashes upon the ground and said, as he did so: "This shall rankle in the calves of the man's legs." He then twirled the cleaning stick in the pipe, removed more ashes, put them on the ground, and said: "This shall be for the base of the sinews, and he shall start with pain" (in the back). He designated, in succession, each portion of the man's anatomy until he "finished the man." Needless to say, the offender "died soon after." To augment the power of the curse a Mohammedan scatters earth when he curses.

In Balkan lands, where the curse is much dreaded, such forms are heard as "May my milk poison you!" This is the most terrible curse a woman can visit upon her son, even though he be old. It is also common to injure a man by cursing his father and mother—possibly Mohammedan influence. In 1916 the Greek Orthodox Church promulgated against Venizelos a terrible curse: "Therefore against the traitor Venizelos we have invoked the following injuries: the ulcers of Job, the whale of Jonah, the leprosy of Naaman, the bite of Death, the shuddering of the dying, the thunderbolt of Hell, and the malediction of God and man. We shall call for the same injuries upon those who, at the forthcoming elections, shall vote for the traitor Venizelos, and further pray for their hands to wither and for them to become deaf and blind. Amen." People placed their curses upon stones and hurled them into one of the curse-pits dug at various places to receive them. In Albania a curse may lie upon a family for generations and, finally, annihilate it.

ORDEAL

Ordeal is a widespread method of identifying the criminal. Among the Haida, if suspicion of causing sickness rests upon the slaves, all of them may be bound hand and foot and thrown into deep water. The slave who floats high harbours the mouse by means of which illness has been visited upon the victim. Medicinemen of the Parry Island Ojibwas of Georgian Bay, Ontario, build a fire and station the accused man by it. If he is guilty, the sticks in the fire will become snakes and will kill him.

In the Arosi district, San Cristoval, Melanesia, the favourite ordeal is to heat stones red hot and have the accused hold them in his hand; if he is innocent, no harm results. Ainus test the innocence of an accused man by compelling him to thrust his hand into a kettle of boiling water or hold in his hand a hot stone. If uninjured, he is innocent; injury proclaims his guilt. Or he may drink a cup of water and throw the cup over his shoulder. If it alights right side up, he is innocent; if it does not, he is guilty.

Ordeal, usually by drinking poison, is found in many African tribes. In Dahomey ordeal consists of drinking poison, licking a red-hot iron, pulling a seed out of boiling water with the fingers, or washing the body with water which contains crushed cowrie-shells. The guilty man who submits to the last mentioned ordeal will have an eruption of sores. If the accused is unscathed, he is innocent. When the ordeal goes against the accused, he may appeal to the special ordeal, at which the priest opens the beak of a cock and compels the bird to swallow a mixture of pulverized bark and water. If the cock dies, the man is guilty.

Among the Ga, to decide whether the accused has practised witchcraft, one partly severs the neck of a fowl and allows it to run about in its death-throes. If the fowl dies breast upward the accused is not guilty; if it dies breast down, the accused is guilty. An Ovimbundu medicineman works himself into a frenzy by dancing, then tosses up a charm and catches it in a basket. If the little horn decorated with wax and red seeds stands upright, the accused is guilty. If, however, the little image with a small cowrie-shell on its head stands upright, the accused's innocence is proclaimed. Or the accused may drink a potion which has been stirred with an antelope hoof. If the draught acts as an emetic, the man is innocent; if it acts as a purgative, he is guilty. In some Angola tribes the accused drinks the potion, then stoops and runs under several arches of bent branches. If he stumbles while running through this archway, he is guilty and is forthwith clubbed to death. When there is a dispute as to who was the killer of game, the Chagga of Uganda subject their dogs to an ordeal. Each disputant feeds his dog a portion of the contested meat. The dog of the master who made false claim will be harmed by the meat. This is taking the ordeal by proxy. In Uganda the person who is unable to rise after drinking the ordeal potion is known to be guilty. Sometimes a heated spade is passed over the legs of accuser and accused; he whose skin comes off was in the wrong. Or a vessel of fire is applied to the chest; if it raises a blister and sticks to the place like a cupping-glass, the man is guilty.

The Kitara, in Uganda, administer poison to accuser and accused, or to fowls which represent them. Or they rub a red-hot iron down the legs of the two litigants. The iron will not burn one who is innocent. Another method used to extort confession consists of placing a small pot, containing a little fire, over the navel of the accused. When the air in the vessel shrinks, the flesh around the navel, if the person is guilty, is drawn up into the vessel. Often the excessive pain causes the guilty man to confess his guilt. Another ordeal, the bead test, ferrets out a thief who has concealed himself in a crowd. The medicineman lays a bead on the eyebrow of each person suspected and pronounces a magic formula. If the man is guilty, the bead will go into his eye and pain him considerably; if he is innocent, the bead will fall to the ground.

The Ganda use the poison ordeal, and also a less popular test known as Mukasa's test. The latter consists of heating a piece of iron or the blade of a hoe and passing over it a bunch of grass which each disputant brings forward. If the heated iron burns one bunch of grass and not the other, he whose bunch burns is considered guilty.

The Konde prepare small pieces of dough and place each piece in a cup, there being as many cups as there are suspected persons. Into each cup is put a small amount of poison. Each of the suspected men, who have not been permitted to witness these proceedings, then selects a cup and drinks the potion. He who selects the cup in which the dough has not absorbed the poison is guilty. When inheritance is disputed, a small amount of dry flour is placed in each cup. The claimant who selects the cup in which the moisture from the dough has penetrated to the dry flour is the rightful heir. In another ordeal the medicineman selects for each man a piece of bark of the *mwafi* tree, raises the pieces and then allows them to fall to the ground. If one turns round when falling and the other falls without turning, this indicates that one of the men is guilty. Next day the medicineman places these pieces of bark in the poison which is administered to the disputants. The one who is innocent will vomit the poison.

In Calabar, Guinea Coast, the accused must swim across a creek near the town; if the man escapes the sharks he is innocent. In Benin ordeal may consist of (1) piercing the tongue of the accused man with the greased feather of a cock. If the quill passes easily through the man's tongue, he is innocent; if it sticks in his tongue, he is guilty. (2) The accused must extract seven or nine cock's quills from a clod of earth; if the quills come out easily, the man is innocent; otherwise, he is guilty. (3) The priest squirts into the accused's eyes the juice of certain green herbs. If this does not injure his eyes, he is innocent; if they become red and inflamed, he is guilty. (4) The priest sticks the tongue of the accused man with a red-hot copper ring. (5) He is cast upon a certain river; if innocent, he will be wafted to the shore; if guilty, he will sink. (6) He removes a shell from the bottom of a vessel of boiling water. If he does not burn his fingers, he is innocent; otherwise, he is guilty. This "fire" ordeal is employed to detect a thief. (7) Boiling palm oil is poured on the accused's hands.

On the Bonny River, Nigeria, the ordeal consists of driving nails into an idol; the guilty person hesitates, for he will be condemning himself to supernatural punishment. Thus this is practically equivalent to refusing to take oath. The Kwotto, of Nigeria, take the ordeal by swearing by the *gwaska* tree and then drinking a potion made from the bark of the tree. The man, if guilty, will die; if innocent, he will vomit the poison. Or he may appeal to the spirit of a fetish which consists of a fruit of the *giginya* tree attached to a rope and buried about three feet underground. The free end of the rope is attached to the wrist of the accused. If he pulls the fruit out of the ground without tightening the rope about his wrist, he is innocent; if the rope tightens, he is guilty. Or the accused may swear by the "thunderbolt" and then drink water from a receptacle which contains one of these stones. If he is guilty, he will subsequently be killed by a falling thunderbolt. Or recourse may be had to the spirit of the Benue River. The man drinks the water from the river, and asserts his innocence. If he is guilty, he will drown in the river when bathing or canoeing.

The Hehe ordeal consists of picking a stone out of boiling water or licking a red-hot hoe. The severity of the burn and the rapidity of healing indicate degree of guilt. The Bechuana of South Africa use the ordeal of boiling water or of treading on a slender calabash. If the calabash breaks, the accused is guilty. The Bena of East Africa use the poison ordeal. Among the Masai a tribal elder gives the accused man blood to drink. The accused then states: "If I have done this, may God kill me!" If guilty, he will die as a result of drinking this potion; if he is innocent, no harm will befall him. The rite appears to be a combination of ordeal and oath.

Somalis take the ordeal by holding in the hand for about ten seconds a red hot iron knife; if the man is burned, he is guilty. Or he picks pebbles or beans out of a vessel of boiling water. Another method is to hold glowing coals of fire in the hands; or the ordeal of the duel is resorted to, in which accused and accuser throw spears at each other. The Bari ordeal includes drinking powdered ivory scraped from a bracelet and mixed with water; for murder, drinking some of the grave dust mixed with water. The last mentioned is common among Anglo-Egyptian tribes of the Mongalla Province. When an accusation of poisoning is brought against a man, the rain chief may dip his iron bar into a mixture of flour and water and give it to the suspect to taste; or, if "medicines" are found in the possession of the accused, he may be compelled to drink them.

The Fajulus of the Anglo-Egyptian Sudan take the ordeal by stabbing the *kir* tree, by breaking the feather of the *kongo* bird, or by drinking powdered ivory. To track down a poisoner and bring her to justice, when a particular person is strongly suspected, they force the accused to interlock the fingers of both hands. An egg is placed in the palms, so that when it is squeezed the force of the compression passes along the major axis of the egg. If the egg breaks, the woman is guilty. If several persons are suspected, a corresponding number of stones are collected and placed on the ground to form a circle, in the centre of which a stake is driven into the ground. A chicken is tied, by a wing, to the stake by means of a string as long as the radius of the circle. The chicken's throat is cut, and the stone on or beside which it dies indicates the perpetrator of the crime.[2] The Kukus drink water from a medicineman's vessel; if innocent, they vomit; if guilty, they die. The ordeal of boiling water is used by the Zande. If one who submits to it is burned, he is guilty; if he shows no traces of a scald, he is innocent. The more usual form of ordeal, however, is to give poison to a chicken. The Bechuana, of South Africa, who practise the ordeal of thrusting the arm into boiling water, have also an ordeal which consists of treading under foot a calabash, or drinking vessel, on the mouth of which two crossed sticks previously charmed by the medicine-man have been placed. If the accused breaks the calabash when he steps on it, he is guilty; if he does not break it, his innocence is proclaimed. Bushmen of the Namib desert divine the guilt or innocence of the accused by a smoke column. If the column of smoke divides, there are several guilty persons; if the smoke rises vertically, the accused are innocent; if the entire column of smoke veers toward one person, it indicates his guilt.

In Madagascar the common ordeal, called *tangena*, consists of swallowing three pieces of a fowl killed for the purpose. Those who have done this then take an emetic. Those who vomit the skin are innocent; those who do not are guilty. Sometimes the poison is given to two dogs or to two fowls, and the result is similarly determinative of the guilt or innocence of the persons represented by the animals.

Among the Philippine Ifugao the ordeal consists of pressing a hot knife against the palm of each litigant. The knife will not injure an innocent man. Or the contestants may be required to remove without undue haste a pebble from the bottom of a twelve-inch deep jar filled with boiling water. Disputes regarding boundaries of rice fields are usually settled by a wrestling ordeal. The boundary is fixed at the point where the defeated wrestler is thrown. Some low castes in Madras resort to the ordeal of plunging the hand into boiling ghi (clarified butter) after a short

2. L. F. Nalder (editor), *A Tribal Survey of Mongalla Province*, 205 (London, Oxford University Press, 1937).

religious ceremony in the temple. A Hindu trial by ordeal utilizes water. The Bhil subject a suspected witch to water ordeal. The witch is tied in a sack and thrown into the water. If she sinks, she is guiltless; if she raises her head above water or swims, she is guilty. When a Kachari girl is suspected of unchastity, she and her sisters must eat uncooked rice which has been buried during the night by the side of the family's sacred *siju* tree. Early next morning the rice is carefully disinterred and some is given to each grown-up girl to masticate. Fear paralyzes the secretory glands of the offender, there is marked diminution in flow of saliva, and she cannot masticate her portion. In Persia a woman suspected of infidelity, who swore she had been faithful, was thrown into a tank. If she swore falsely, she instantly sank to the bottom, but if truly, she floated. In Arabia a certain type of mirror was used by which one could determine a woman's chastity. If the mirror remained clear when her form was reflected in it, she was chaste; if it became dim, she was guilty.

A few decades ago a cadi at Khartum administered to accuser and accused a potion containing the ink dissolved from a piece of paper on which verses from the Koran had been inscribed. The accused man after drinking the potion fell backward and died forthwith. The mullahs of Al-Azhar University, in Cairo, when consulted on the matter by Lord Cromer, gave it as their opinion that Allah had killed him by means of the holy words of the Koran.

Democritus describes a root which, made into pills and swallowed in wine, will make the guilty man confess. The ordeal is referred to in Sophocles' *Antigone*, in which the guards who have been sent to watch the body of Polynices say, in denying neglect of duty: "We were ready to take up the red-hot iron, to walk through the flames, and to make oath before the gods that we were neither guilty nor privy to it." In medieval Europe ordeal was imposed by use of hot irons, boiling liquids, combat, or lot, or by throwing the accused into water. Through Christian ordeals run the concept of struggle, of appeal to chance or supernatural salvation, and a belief in miraculous manifestation of truth. Ordeal was used in South Slav districts until well into the nineteenth century.

In Cornwall, when a petty offence had been committed, the people involved gathered about a table-stone called Garrack Zans; each person took a stick of fire from the burning pile and spat on it. If he could extinguish the fire in this fashion, he was innocent; if not, he was guilty. Possibly this is a modification of the older fire ordeal when the accused must hold fire in the hand or walk over heated ploughshares.

OATH

When war honours were disputed among the Crows, the two rival contestants took oath in the following fashion: Each man placed a knife in his mouth and pointed it toward the sun, then uttered some such formula as the following: "It was I who struck the enemy. Sun, as you looked down, you saw me strike him. Hereafter when I meet an enemy, may I again overcome him without difficulty." Or the oath-taker might say: "I struck the coup, you [referring to the sun] saw me. May the one who lies die before winter." In another oath-ordeal lean meat was impaled on an arrow which was placed on an old dry buffalo skull, the tips of which were painted red. Each claimant, in turn, "raised the arrow, pointed his right index finger at its head, touched the meat with his lips, and pronounced the oath. If both took the test, the people could not at once determine the merits of the case. But if some misfortune befell one of them after the ordeal, he was considered the perjurer and his opponent then justly claimed the contested honor." [3]

Before Omaha scouts went to their posts, they were summoned to the Sacred Wand tepee, where every man was obliged to smoke. The act was equivalent to taking oath to obey custom and do one's duty even at risk of life. A leading man then addressed them. He dilated on the responsibilities of scouts and reminded them of the necessity for a truthful report: "their words would be heard by the unseen powers, which never permitted a falsehood to go unpunished." The man who made an untruthful statement would be struck by lightning, bitten by a snake, injured in the foot by a sharp object, or killed by the enemy. Among some Plains tribes, when the statements of a man who recounted his war deeds were challenged by an auditor, the claimant must place his hand upon a shield and solemnly repeat his claim. If under these circumstances he spoke falsely, he would be supernaturally punished, probably by the enemy on the next war path. In some tribes the man would say: "The *wakan* beings know that I speak truth." This statement was equivalent to a conditional curse, that is, to an oath. When Oglala Dakotas are preparing for the sun dance, maidens who desire to participate in it sit in a circle round the director of the ceremony, and the people assemble about them. The herald shouts the names of the maidens in turn; the young woman whose name is called must stand and declare that she has never

3. Robert H. Lowie, *The Crow Indians*, 217 (New York), copyright 1935. Reprinted by permission of the publishers, Farrar & Rinehart, Inc.

had carnal intercourse with a man. If her declaration is challenged by a bystander and she is silent, her silence is interpreted as confession; if she repeats her declaration, she must bite a snake skin or the effigy of a snake. If, after this, her accuser is silent, her declaration is considered true; if the accusation is repeated, the challenger also must bite the snake skin; otherwise his challenge is considered a falsehood. If he bites the snake skin, the decision on the truth of the respective declarations is held in abeyance until a snake bites one of the two disputants, which it surely will do, and thus decide the issue.

A Teton Dakota takes oath by picking up an arrow, a knife, and a gun which have been placed alongside one another in the camp for the purpose. While holding these he makes his assertion. If a man who takes oath in this fashion swears falsely one of these weapons will kill him. A Cheyenne oath consists of rubbing the hands over a tobacco pipe, pointing at the medicine-arrows, and declaring: "Arrows, you hear me; I did not do this thing." A more solemn oath involves use of a buffalo skull. The skull is painted with a black streak which extends from a point between the horns to the nose; a red line encircles the eye-sockets; on the right cheek is a black round spot, signifying the sun; a red half-moon decorates the left cheek; eye-sockets and nasal orifices are stuffed with grass. Against this skull, which represents the medicine-lodge, are placed a gun and four arrows which represent the medicine-arrows. The man who takes oath places his hands on these objects while making his declaration. Similar supernatural sanctions are found among other Plains tribes.

A Menominee says: "You contradict me. I do not lie, but tell the truth only, as the Great Spirit hears me telling you the truth, and this earth hears me." Or: "This is the solemn truth. At this time all the powered gods hear me tell the truth and this earth hears me tell the truth."

Among the Poncas there were once rival disputants for war honours. The Keeper of the Record said: "I shall leave the question of the truth of this story to the Thunder to decide. We shall know within the year which one of these men has spoken the truth." During the ensuing summer the horse on which one of the disputants was riding fell and killed him. He was supernaturally killed because of his false assertion.

The accused Chukchee swears by the sun or by the bear. Negritos of the Ulu Selama region of the Malay peninsula take oath as follows: "If I lie may a tiger seize me; may a rotten tree fall on me!" Similar oaths are taken by the Sakhai and some Indonesians. The Orang Dusun of North Borneo and the Behrang Sakhai demand from a presumed liar the following oath: "This is the sun that I swear by! If I lie, may a crocodile eat me when I go down to the river; and when I travel on land may a tiger eat me, or may I be struck by a falling tree." In Madagascar, when opposing armies wish to ratify peace, each side kills a bull and sends to the other party a piece of the animal's liver, which they eat in the presence of witnesses from both sides, declaring that if they assert falsely the liver shall make them burst and other misfortunes shall befall them. In some parts of the island oath is taken by a pool in a ceremony during which participants strike the water with tree branches and a spear.

If Hawaiians "gave their oath and did not fulfill it, it came back to punish the one who uttered those words and also the one to whom the oath was made." [4] When a Samoan's veracity was questioned, he touched his eye as assurance that he spoke truth. "It was as if he had said, 'May I be cursed with blindness if what I say is not true!'" An accused man held a piece of grass in his hand while taking oath. The grass indicated a silent additional imprecation that all his family might die, and that grass might grow over their habitations, if he swore falsely. On Upolu, Samoa, in case of concealed theft the people assemble before the chief; each, in turn, invokes vengeance upon himself if guilty. If each denies guilt, the chief terminates the inquiry by shouting: "O Nafuma! Have compassion on us, let us know who it was, and let speedy death be upon him." An impersonal supernatural power will ferret out and punish the culprit. A New Britain oath carries the heavy imprecation: "If I am not telling the truth, I hope I may shake hands with my mother-in-law."

In Nigeria a man invokes a god to smite him with death or misfortune if he lies under oath. If no misfortune comes to him within a year, he is dismissed and the man who brought the charge is punished. The oath of friendship is taken before witnesses and often is accompanied by a ceremony in which each party to the oath washes the other's feet. An Ibo suspected of murder took oath as follows: "Igwe-Ke-Ala, if I know how the dead man met his death may you take my life, that I may accompany him to the land of the dead. But if I am wholly ignorant of what befell him, then do you pronounce my innocence." If the man was innocent, the declaration was greeted by a sound resembling thunder and the place was enveloped in smoke. Then the voice of Igwe declared: "Hold up your right hand. I declare you to be innocent." Thus the oath was to some extent an ordeal. Among the Ibo at Awka, when two

4. E. S. Craighill Handy, "Dreaming in Hawaii," *Essays in Anthropology presented to A. L. Kroeber*, 125–126 (Berkeley, University of California Press, 1936).

men who have quarrelled wish to restore amity, they take the oath: "Whichever sees a thing that can kill us if he does not tell the other let the *alose* kill him." The two men then eat kola together to symbolize the new bond which unites them. Also two villages may establish amity through oath taken by representatives of the villages. Each goes to a place midway between the two villages and carries *oglisi* leaves with him. The initiator of the ceremony picks up sand and says: "If we in all our town see anything which will kill you, and do not speak out, let the *Ajana* kill us." He then puts the sand in the leaf, the two men exchange these leaves, take them home, and there hang them up. Other asseverations with supernatural sanction include: "I will not give you poison: if I do, may the *alose* kill me; if I sell one of your family who takes refuge with me, may the *alose* kill me; if you give me goat or fowl or cow, and I injure it wantonly, may the *alose* kill me; if I want to take your wife and give her to another without repaying the marriage price, may the *alose* kill me." When a Kwatto takes oath, he touches a knife, arrow-head, or ax-head, sometimes also a "thunderbolt," that is, a stone supposed to have fallen to earth in the lightning, or by drinking water in which one of these objects has been placed. If he swears falsely, the spirit associated with these objects will kill him immediately or when he comes into contact with the object.

A Nankanse oath (Ashanti hinterland) takes the simple form "My father and an arrow" or "My father and smallpox," referring to a specific calamity which overtook one's ancestor and which one calls down on oneself if one swears falsely. When an Ashanti takes oath, he strikes the earth with his hand. One who swears falsely will be punished with death. Among the Tallis, in the hinterland of the Gold Coast, a novice who is being initiated swears: "If I tell anybody, may I die!"

The origin of [Ashanti] "oaths" and their meaning to-day may be traced to a time before the advent of kings or chiefs, when each family was a separate self-contained and organized unit, governed by its head—the senior maternal uncle. In these days, of which a dim tradition still survives, the outstanding events in the life of these family groups were the death (by accident) of the head of the family, or some hurt to his person—to an arm, a leg, or a hand. Thus it came about that these greater or lesser tragedies, which were first of all subjects that were wholly taboo, came later, by a process at which we can only guess, to be used by the members of the household as a means of obtaining something which was otherwise unobtainable, or of justifying an action which could not otherwise be justified. "If you do not do so and so, or if you continue to act thus, or if you do not give me such and such a thing which should be mine, may that accident that once befell grandfather's leg, or head, or arm repeat itself." Thus spoke the aggrieved member of the communal hearth; or more briefly—and this came to be the recognized formula—"I mention grandfather's leg (etc.) if you do not do such and such a thing."

Three possible lines of action were now open to the person to whom these sacred words had been addressed. First, he could comply forthwith with the demand, and not take any further action in the matter; any possible evil results were thus immediately nullified—in fact none were possible, because the contingency, the happening of which would alone put the sanction into operation, actually never occurred. The person using the formula thus readily and simply obtained what he desired. There the matter ended.

Secondly the person thus adjured, if he considered the demand made (on the threat of a repetition of a misfortune following non-compliance) unjust, might perform the required action, but simultaneously (or later on) invoke the same calamity and bid the person who had "sworn the first oath" upon him to show good cause for having done so. Yet a third line of action was possible. He might refuse altogether to agree with, or to obey the order and would answer the demand by saying, "If I do what you demand, then may the calamity you have invoked happen." [5]

A Masai warrior takes oath by drinking a mixture of bullock's blood and milk, saying as he does so, "O Engai, I drink this blood, and if I have stolen these cattle, this blood will kill me." Touching the earth when one takes oath is also found in eastern Africa. Dinkas take oath on a spear. One who does so dare not lie. The Bari of the Anglo-Egyptian Sudan swear by the door-posts of the cattle kraal, by the roof of the house, by the head of a daughter, by jumping over a spear, or, recently, by licking a spear. Benas take oath by tearing the king's robes or breaking an object belonging to him. One known to swear falsely is killed. "In effect it was a conditional curse, he who took it saying by implication, 'If I am the man responsible for this act of blasphemy and treason, let me perish at the King's hands.' " A Galla swears "by my hand"; or by saying "may the chief die"; or "by the flesh of my father"; or "by the hand of my father." These forms of oath are found among other Ethiopians, as also "may God kill me"; "may I become ill"; "may I be afflicted with diarrhœa"; and other specific contingent maledictions. Other forms are: "God knows"; "the earth knows"; "God sees me"; "may I lose my guardian spirit." Gallas also dig a deep and narrow pit into which they place spears. They then cover the pit with an animal's hide, sit round it, and take oath, de-

5. Robert S. Rattray, *Religion and Art in Ashanti*, 205–206 (Oxford, The Clarendon Press, 1927). Reprinted by permission of the publishers.

claring that, if they do not perform their agreements, "they may be thrown or fall into such a pit, that they may be pierced through with a lance and their bodies may be hidden, so as to remain unchanged." The Hehe have an oath: "If I break this peace, may the spear-points straighten out and kill me." The witness at a trial takes oath: "I say this before God, and if I lie, may I die by snake-bite or lions!"

Western Somalis swear by a stone, by God, or by spittle. The asseveration for the last form of oath is "much spittle." The oath-taker chews a certain kind of grass, utters these words, and then spits out the grass. When swearing by a stone, the common form of oath, the man who puts another on his oath places beside him a stone. The oath-taker touches the stone and says: "As sure as this is a stone." Throwing the stone backward over the head while taking the oath increases the solemnity of the oath. In Bagirmi, the Sudan, Mohammedans take oath on the leaf of the *Habita arab* tree, or that of the *Acacia albida;* and this oath is as sacred as one taken on the Koran. When Kambas take oath, two men sit knee to knee, bareheaded. Over their heads are held their respective weapons by men who serve as sponsors or guarantors. One guarantor declares that his man has sworn to be the other's friend and that the weapon which he, the guarantor, holds, cannot be used against that friend. To this assurance the other makes response in similar words. A Jakri swears on a bundle of sticks.

Most Naga disputes are settled by oaths which leave arbitration of the matter to the deities. Nagas take oath by severing a cat in two. The man who swears falsely will be supernaturally punished by the feline, which Nagas highly respect. Lhota Nagas take oath on a spot intimately associated with the deity of the wind. If a man has sworn falsely, the thatch roof will be blown from his house. Some Hindus, though not Brahmans, take oath before an idol in the temple. In support of his case the man places his hand on the head of wife or child, swears to the truth of his claim, and invokes terrible penalties on wife or child should his oath be false. The essential feature in many Hindu rites associated with marriage is taking oath. The Hindu takes oath also by stepping over a child or holding a child, saying as he does so, "if I do this I will be drinking the blood of my child"; "a child is near me"; "I will hold a child in my hand"; or, "if I do this I will eat my child." Sometimes the child is taken to a temple and laid before an idol. Before the Santal takes oath, he salutes the sun as he would bow to a superior. If he takes oath before the council which sits in the afternoon, he salutes the sun and then bows toward the place of the rising sun. Usually the oath contains a promise to speak the truth and an assertion that Chando is observing the oath-taker, to whom the latter is responsible. The Santal have several other forms of oath in which the swearer calls down on himself a contingent specific curse, with a visual symbol of the consequences of perjury. For example, he may, like the Konde, stand upon a leopard skin and say that if he does not speak truth may a leopard destroy him; if the dispute is over a boundary, he may take earth from the disputed land and keep this on his head during his asseveration, the implication being that if he speaks falsely the land will become a curse to him.

In India the cotton tree and other trees are occupied by deities who superintend the affairs of a district or a village. These trees exert a restraining influence. A man may be taken to them and compelled to invoke vengeance upon himself or those dear to him if he swears falsely. This sanction compels men to be habitually and conscientiously truthful.

Balinese employ "little" and "big" oaths. The former bring minor misfortunes upon the perjurer. If one perjures by the "big" oath, his descendants to the third generation will be cursed by dreadful calamities, though the curse can be averted by means of an expensive neutralizing formula purchasable from a dishonest high priest. Taking oath is, however, a serious and dangerous performance accompanied by elaborate ritual. The man who is about to take oath comes into the temple with all his relatives, including the small children. He is bareheaded and wears white clothes, symbolizing cleanliness. He sits cross-legged among the offerings, holy water, and incense, and faces the high priest, who reads the text of the oath in a loud voice, and enumerates the calamities that will befall the man and his family if he swears falsely. The priest tears into strips the palm-leaf on which the text of the oath has been written and places these in a jug of holy water. The man drinks the water, makes obeisance with a flower, and is sprinkled with the remaining water; and the pot is dashed to the ground and broken. Perjurers and their accomplices shall be confounded by every evil and be struck by lightning. When they go into the forest, they shall become entangled in the creepers, lose their way, run here and there, but not find the right road. Tigers shall attack them. They shall dash against the rocks, their skulls shall split open, and their brains shall spill out. "On the crossroad they shall be crushed by falling trees. In the fields they shall be struck by lightning from a clear sky, be bitten by poisonous serpents, and torn to bits by the horns of buffaloes. They shall fall into deep rivers where pointed stones will cut their chests open, their bones will be dislocated, and the blood flow from their veins. Their corpses shall sink to the bottom of the waters. When they are at sea they shall be attacked by crocodiles. The Sumdang-Aal and the Peh fish shall bite them and the poisonous sea-serpent Lempe strike them, and sea-monsters swallow them. In their houses they shall be the prey to all sorts of sickness and they shall die unnatural deaths. No one shall help them, and during their sleep they shall die while dreaming, they shall die standing up, they shall die while eating or drinking. Neither they, nor their children, their grandchildren, nor their great-grandchildren, shall again be men on this earth. They shall reincarnate as maggots, clams, worms, and serpents. Such is the curse upon perjury as is ordained by Ari Tjandana and Angasti, and the Eminent Gods of the East, North, South, West, and Center. . . . They, their children, grandchildren, and great-grandchildren shall know no further happiness from now on." [6]

The Chinese, kneeling in front of a candle, takes oath: "I tell the truth and the whole truth. If not, as this candle is blown out" (he then blows out the flame) "may my soul be blown out."

During the sixth and fifth centuries B.C., in the colony of Jews at Elephantine, Upper Egypt, oaths were sworn by the altar,[7] and by Anath-Yan and Kherem-beth-el. Anath was a goddess associated with Yalue (Yahweh), and Bethel probably was the name of a deity.

Among Old Testament Jews the oath was a petition that evil might befall one who spoke falsely under oath.

"Abhorred Strife," says Hesoid, "bare Oath who most troubles men upon earth when anyone wilfully swears a false oath." Zeus appointed his daughter Styx to be the great oath of the gods. "Leto swore the great oath of the gods: 'Now hear this, Earth and wide Heaven above, and dropping water of Styx' (this is the strongest and most awful oath for the blessed gods)." [8] Thus even the gods take oath. Calypso swears, to the advantage of Odysseus: "Bear witness now, Earth, and spacious Heaven overhead, and the river of Styx that slideth downward (which oath is the greatest and most terrible in the use of the blessed gods) how in this counsel I intend no sort of evil against you." [9] Horse-racers suspected of having taken unfair advantage in a race must, when challenged, take oath in

6. Krause, quoted in Miguel Covarrubias, *Island of Bali*, 68–69 (New York, Alfred A. Knopf, 1937). Reprinted by permission of the publishers, Alfred A. Knopf, Inc., and Cassell & Company, Ltd.

7. See *Matthew*, 23· 10.

8. "To Delian Apollo," *Homeric Hymns*.

9. Odyssey, Book V.

special manner. Thus Antilochos was challenged: "Come thou hither and as it is ordained stand up before thy horses and chariot and take in thy hand the pliant lash wherewith thou dravest erst, and touching thy horses swear by the Enfolder and Shaker of the earth (*i.* e. Poseidon) that not wilfully didst thou hinder my chariot by guile." [10] Oaths touching the matter of love, however, says Hesoid, do not draw down the anger of the gods if they are violated. Chivalry has considerable antiquity. Agamemnon says: "And if aught that I swear be false, may the gods give me all sorrows manifold, that they send on him who sinneth against them in his oath." [11] Belief in the efficacy of a name and uttered formula is prominent in the use of oath in legal procedure. Lycurgus' declaration that the oath is the "bond which keeps the State together" implies that the oath was a well-established social instrument. Aristides took oath, in the name of the Athenians, by "flinging wedges of red-hot iron into the sea, after curses against such as should make breach of their vow." The Greek word for oath, *horkos*, "barrier," apparently signifies a barrier that limits subsequent freedom of word or action, a barrier over which the gods keep watch.

By invoking the gods in oath the man who takes it binds himself to another before the gods invoked as witnesses. For this reason each people and each town invoked its appropriate gods. Some gods were invoked only for a specific purpose, and the form of oath varied. Usually the place at which it was taken was marked by a sacred stone. Ordinarily a sacred place, such as a temple, was selected. In the Areopagus were a "stone of crime" and a "stone of accusation," before which oath was taken. When taking oath the man looked upward and stretched his hands toward heaven. Sometimes he placed his hand on the altar, perhaps to ensure contact with the invoked god. Usually a sacrifice accompanied the oath. The god invoked in a false oath punished the insult; a wrong had been done him. Vergil speaks of "the Stygian lake, by whose divinity the gods dread to swear and violate [their oath]."

Celts, Teutons, and Greeks took oath by heaven, earth, sun, fire, moon, sea, land, day, night, and other natural phenomena. In old Norse legend an oath was exacted from fire and water, iron and all metals, stones and earth, trees of the forest, diseases and poisons, four-footed beasts, birds, and serpents; these were made to swear that they would not injure Balder. When the Abkhas of the Caucasus take oath, they eat a sacred substance:

10. Iliad, Book XXIII.
11. Iliad, Book XIX.

"the perjured person cannot possibly escape the avenging god whom he has taken into his body and assimilated." Here, too, oath and ordeal seem combined.

An old Irish oath was taken by "the sea and land, the sun and moon." Such an oath was binding "so long as the sea surrounds Ireland."

In western Ireland oath was taken on one or more oval stones, pebbles naturally waterwashed or artificially shaped and very smooth, which were usually to be found in the small missionary churches. They were highly venerated by the peasantry as having belonged to the founders of the churches, and were used for a variety of purposes, including the curing of disease. A stone in the churchyard at Caslredermot is called the "swearing-stone"; and at Fladda-Chuan on the altar of the chapel is a round blue stone, always moist, on which oaths are taken. In the island of Iona there was preserved in the cathedral until 1830 a black stone on which solemn oaths were sworn and agreements ratified.

SANCTIONS AND CONDUCT: PRELITERATE RELIGIONS

In preliterate cultures sanctions of conduct are usually magical rather than religious, based on fear of supernatural consequences rather than on pious devotion. Among Kaffirs, for example, the dominant regulators of conduct are custom and automatically efficacious magic. In so far as religion influences conduct, it is often degrading rather than elevating. Disrespect for old women, to cite an instance, is correlated with religious beliefs. In the future life women play a subordinate part; their spirits cannot cause much trouble to survivors; therefore little account is taken of them. Social behaviour reflects religious attitude, and vice versa. Men wish to be praised, flattered, fed, and waited upon; after death their desires will be the same; for death does not change personality. After a calamity, the visit of a snake to a kraal, or a vivid dream of a dead relative, men sacrifice an ox to propitiate the offended spirit. Whites sometimes call this a sin-offering. The chief sin confessed over the slain ox is, however, the people's past failure to praise sufficiently the man whose ghost disturbs them. Drought, sickness, and other great calamities they attribute to a neglected ancestor who complains, through a dream, that people have not praised him enough of late. There is no ethical import in these religious sanctions. The only vices deliberately punished by Thonga gods are sexual excess, transgression upon the rights of a priest, and offences involving social hierarchy. For the first mentioned offence the guilty man is killed by his fellows. To other sins the gods appear to be indifferent. They mete out neither rewards nor punishments in this life or the next. On the Gold Coast and in Ashanti, in the worship of gods, numerous as they are and assiduously as some are cultivated, there is little which can influence social conduct. Ashanti gods are worshipped for their own sakes, or for the sake of the worshipper; most of the worship appears to have no reward or purpose other than its own fulfilment.

Yoruba worshippers attribute to their gods marriage and posterity, and the tastes, wants, weaknesses, and vices of humanity. "There are wicked gods, drunkards, adulterous gods, liars, thieves, deformed and grotesque gods. There is no crime, debauch, or cruelty which their history does not contain. Thus the unfortunate Negro, instead of finding in his religious beliefs a means of regeneration, sees therein examples and motives of perversion. The same corrupting influence is met with in their practices of worship, which is naturally in accordance with the divinities to whom they address themselves."

The Supreme Being cares little for the circumstances of men; his attention is directed to them only by special invocation. "He resides in a wonderful dwelling above the sky, and commits the care of earthly affairs to a race of beings, such as leopards, snakes, locusts, crocodiles, and also to inanimate objects, such as stones, rags, cowries, leaves of certain trees, and, in short, anything and everything." Dahomeans have a salutation, "God helps him who works," or, as we say, "God helps those who help themselves." But, as Bouché points out, their religious beliefs are without apparent influence upon their ethics; the Dahomean lives as if God did not concern himself with human beings, or as if God did not exist. Brunet and Giethlen, similarly, find that all the Dahomean's ideas, moral and immoral, are personified by idols and physical objects; the supernatural, the beliefs concerning spirits, jinn, witchcraft, magic, and so forth, they hand over to a fetish doctor whose behaviour the investigators regard as a mock comedy adapted to their curious superstitions.

Among Zande the Supreme Being is a "very vague influence and is not considered a guardian of moral law which must be obeyed simply because he is its author." Even so, the words that accompany the prayer which a certain Zande old man makes to the Supreme Being indicate a high ethical standard in the god. The man states that he has not stolen, has not committed adultery, bears no man ill, and would fain live in charity with his neighbours. "Even if I possess witchcraft in my belly . . . may I not harm the gardens of any man. May the mouth of my witchcraft cool; let it rather vent its spleen on those animals in the bush that daily dance on the graves of my kinsmen."

Fortune lists sixteen commandments implicit in Manus religious sanctions, though not formulated by the natives. They include: "Thou shalt not have sexual intercourse with any but thy legally married spouse; excepting, in past history, in the case of a man with a prostitute woman captured from an enemy people. Thou shalt not fail to meet thy economic obligations on the prearranged date; thou shalt not fail to co-operate economically with thy kin in their economic exchanges; thou shalt not fail to recognize by economic exchange thy affinity to families that are connected with thine by marriage, even upon the other plane. Thou, being a woman, shalt not resent thy husband's economic solidarity with the women of his kin by making charges of incest against him and them. Thou, being a woman, and a widow, shalt not desert thy children and remarry; if thou breakest this law thou shalt not take thy children to thy new house, for they belong to the house of their father and to the surviving kin of that house. Thou, being a junior, shalt not disobey the elder of thy kin." [12] These religious sanctions reinforce tribal ethics.

Tongans believe in a power and intelligence superior to that of human beings, able to control their actions, acquainted with their inmost thoughts. This power is impersonal and non-ethical, though capable of being turned against a culprit. The supreme god of the Lakher of Assam rewards with long lives and riches those who speak the truth, act always according to custom, and are kindly disposed toward their neighbours, who "speak kindly"; and they punish with short lives those who are proud and quarrelsome and oppress the poor, abusing their power, and are boasters.

In messianic religions of aboriginal North America the ethical element is prominent. The Delaware prophet who appeared at Tuscarawas in 1762 exhorted his tribesmen to cease from drunkenness, wars, polygamy, and the medicine song. The last mentioned he declared a means of communicating with evil spirits. The Shawnee prophet, Tenskwatawa, who promulgated his doctrine in 1805 and 1806, like the Delaware prophet taught lofty personal ethics, chastity, brotherly love, abolition of bickerings, kindness to children, abstention from lying and stealing. The Potawatomi messianic cult of 1882 adopted the code of ethics contained in

12. Reo Fortune, *Manus Religion*, 345–346 (Philadelphia, American Philosophical Society, 1935). Reprinted by permission of the American Philosophical Society.

the Mosaic Ten Commandments, and in addition prohibited the drinking of liquor, gambling, and horse-racing. Wovoka, the Paiute prophet who introduced the ghost dance religion which spread rapidly through the Plains area, was directed by God to tell his people to live in peace with Whites, work, refrain from lying and stealing, and cease quarrelling; they must discard practices which savour of war; if they should faithfully obey these instructions, they would finally be united with their friends in that other world where there would be no death, sickness, or old age. Among most Plains tribes who accepted the ghost dance religion, the injunction "When your friends die you must not cry" was interpreted as forbidding the killing of horses, burning of tepees, destruction of property, cutting of hair, and gashing of the body with knives—practices characteristic of aboriginal Plains mourning.

With effective emphasis Zuñi priests tell backsliding members of their clan the story of Mitsi, who became careless, neglected the sacrifices, resigned his priestly functions from mere laziness, and was duly punished by the offended deity. Zuñis and Hopis believe that if prayers are to be answered, a man must speak "with one tongue," that is, sincerely; if prayers are not acceptable, no rain will fall and the people will starve. He must be gentle, and speak and act with kindness to all; the gods do not heed those who speak harshly. In the Plains area truthfulness and chastity, especially the latter, are required of those who prepare the sun dance regalia; their violation is punished by the Thunders.

Sanctions with ethical import play a subordinate part in preliterate religion. Seldom are they the injunctions of the gods, but usually are based on fear of misfortune consequent upon breaking a taboo or departing from approved ritual. In most preliterate cultures the ethical element in religion is exceedingly attenuated if, indeed, it exists at all. "Religions of more advanced peoples commonly regulate social relations by sanctioning the code of laws. Not so with the Eskimo religion. The requirements which it imposes constitute a distinct system of duties and taboos, quite apart from the code of justice. The morality of the Eskimos in purely mundane matters, on the other hand, is influenced by religion only in one way: by the fear that the spirits of the ancestors might be offended if the traditional code of justice were not adhered to. Whether the soul of a person after death will go to a happy or an unhappy place depends scarcely at all upon whether he has been law-abiding according to the civilized code. Actions involving worldly morality are rarely specified as entailing punishment in the after world. Only in isolated instances are theft and homicide, for instance, taken into account in this connection; and it seems that adultery never is. Thus, the regulative force of religion operates chiefly in a different way among the Eskimos than among civilized peoples. The greatest importance is attached to the manner in which a person dies and to the extent to which he has observed the religious taboos. Strict compliance with these taboos is regarded as a moral duty, however; for the violation of them will anger the spirits and bring calamity upon *the whole group*. Confession in the event of breaking them is required. But they seem to a civilized person, at least on first sight, largely arbitrary and extraneous to the well-being of the group or of the individual in his after life. Hence, it must be concluded that the folkways of the Eskimos do not appear to embrace in any broad sense enforcement of worldly morality through religion." [13] The Eskimo's religion has only the faintest suggestion of a concept of divine justice. Restrictions and requirements pertain to material things rather than to ethical ideals. Punishment for noncompliance with taboos comes through depletion of the necessities of life. All supplies—for example, foods, furs, fuel—are dispensed by spirits. Privation and ultimately death may be inflicted upon the living in punishment for what is to us a trivial offence.

Lord Balfour's statement that a world without God is a world in which aesthetic and ethical values are greatly diminished seems "sublimely indifferent to the fact that aesthetic and ethical values have nowhere been so high-pitched as in China and Japan where for centuries past God has been almost a negligible quantity." [14] Many other peoples manage their ethical code without the aid of religion. Thus the Lhota Naga religion teaches no moral code; "yet many, many Lhotas lead clean, straight, honest lives and are ever ready to help a lame dog over a stile. It is true that virtue in this world is vaguely believed to be rewarded with happiness in the next, but this belief weighs little with a Naga, who rarely turns his thought to what is in store for him after he dies. Whatever it be which causes so many Lhotas to lead virtuous lives it is not their religion." [15]

13. Edward M. Weyer, *The Eskimos*, 230–231 (New Haven, Yale University Press, 1932). See also pages 378–379. Reprinted by permission of the Yale University Press and Methuen & Co., Ltd., publishers.

14. Herbert A. Giles, *Confucianism and Its Rivals*, 264 (New York, Scribner, 1915).

15. J. P. Mills, *The Lhota Nagas*, 121 (London, Macmillan, 1922).

SANCTIONS AND CONDUCT: HISTORIC RELIGIONS

Historic religions contain many ethical elements. In early Rome, with some offenders, those who suffer the penalty of *Sacer esto*, for example, the gods will not make peace. In the late republic the distinction between material and spiritual purity is clearly drawn and consistently adhered to. The Oriental religions which invaded Rome contained many elements which made for righteousness. "The concept of divinity as a kindly providence which cares for the individual and exacts the same good qualities from man, the unremitting devotion demanded of the devotees, the sense of moral pollution and a longing for moral purification, the shifting of men's eyes from the material gains of this world to the ideal rewards of the next—all these and many other things gave to the Oriental cults distinct and positive ethical and spiritual values." They demanded self-restraint, moderate asceticism, and unceasing struggle in support of righteousness against evil. Members of these religious bodies regarded themselves as brothers, and the head of the society as a father. During the second, third, and fourth centuries A. D., these Oriental religions contributed to the higher moral and spiritual life of the Roman Empire. Contemporary champions of Christianity do not allege that devotees of these Oriental cults showed moral degradation. Indeed, pagans and Christians of the fourth century held similar standards of morality, and a change from one faith to the other required little readjustment of moral principles or practices. The Greeks "in their religion inherited undeveloped and unmoral gods; they developed not simply the picturesque figures of the poetical Olympos, but the grand and almost monotheistic conception of deity which was embodied in the Zeus of Pheidias and still lives for us, apart altogether from the more metaphysical speculations of the great philosophers, in such literary monuments as the Odes of Pindar, with their scornful repudiation of any myth which would attribute unworthy conduct to the just rulers of the universe." [16] Hesiod declares in his *Works and Days* that Zeus punishes those who practise violence and cruel deeds. "Often even a whole city suffers for a bad man who sins and devises presumptuous deeds, and the son of Cronos lays great trouble upon the people, famine, and plague together, so that the men perish away, and their women do not bear children, and their houses become few, through the contriv-

16. Herbert J. Rose, *Primitive Culture in Greece*, 229 (London, Methuen, 1925).

ing of Olympian Zeus. And again, at another time, the son of Cronos either destroys their wide army, or their walls, or else makes an end of their ships on the sea." To princes is given the warning: "Mark well this punishment: for the deathless gods are near among men and mark all those who oppress their fellows with crooked judgments, and reck not the anger of the gods. For upon the bounteous earth Zeus has thrice ten thousand spirits, watchers of mortal men, and these keep watch on judgments and deeds of wrong as they roam, clothed in mist, all over the earth. And there is virgin Justice, the daughter of Zeus, who is honoured and revered among the gods who dwell on Olympus, and whenever any one hurts her with lying slander, she sits beside her father, Zeus the son of Cronos, and tells him of men's wicked heart, until the people pay for the mad folly of their princes, who, evilly minded, pervert judgment and give sentence crookedly. Keep watch against this, you princes, and make straight your judgments, you who devour bribes; put crooked judgments altogether from your thoughts. He does mischief to himself who does mischief to another, and evil planned harms the plotter most. The eye of Zeus, seeing all and understanding all, beholds these things too, if so he will, and fails not to mark what sort of justice this is that the city keeps within it." Plato states, in the *Laws*, that religion is an essential bulwark of law and morality; one who possesses a sound and vital faith in the gods cannot voluntarily sin. The conscious sinner must deny either their existence or their providence, or believe that divine justice can be corrupted by sacrifice or prayer. In the *Republic* he deprecates assignment of low human motives to gods and declares the reading of Homer derogatory to the morals of youth. But the religions of Greece had already ceased to have an ethical lesson for the Greeks if, indeed, they had ever possessed one. Ennius (169 B.C.), who has been called the Roman Homer, repeats the sentiments of Thrasymachus:

Gods there are, I've always said it, and that will always be my view;
But they little reck, I reckon, of what we race of mortals do,
For if they did, the good would flourish, the bad would perish, which is not true.

According to Sir William Ramsay, religion in ancient Anatolia was far more intimately associated with social and family life than in modern European nations, every act of the individual, good or bad, joyous or mournful, moral (from our point of view) or immoral, being equally presided over by a divinity and, as it were, done under divine sanction.

Here is no flavour of ethics, no hint of righteousness rewarded. The Vedas contain emphatic ethical elements. Men engrossed in Vedanta philosophy "are not likely to fall victims of the ordinary temptations of the world, the flesh, and other powers. The Vedanta law of morality does not ask us to act without motives, but asks us to serve humanity, without any selfish desires, or petty interests, without envy or jealousy, regardless of party or personality. . . . The Vedanta, no doubt, asks us to act according to our conscience, but at the same time it guides the conscience so far as a general ethical system can do this. The Vedanta recognises that loyalty to humanity at large does not mean what it meant to the Cynics of ancient Greece, disloyalty to the narrower conceptions of family and city. It declares that the highest ideals can be realised only through loyalty to the smaller ideals of family, country, and so forth."

In ancient Egypt, from time immemorial righteousness and right-doing were pleasing to gods and to men, and wrong-doing and evil deeds were an abomination. Even so, ethical attributes are not a marked characteristic of early Egyptian religion, even in its monotheistic form. Re bestowed material rather than spiritual gifts. "His cult was gross and material, and the benefits which the Egyptians hoped to receive from him were material: virility, fecundity, robust health, and abundant offspring, both human and animal. The cult of the solar disk Aten was even more material still, although many of its blood-thirsty rites were curtailed or suppressed by Amen-hetep IV. As men expected Re to give them great material prosperity on earth, so after death, in heaven, they relied upon him to provide them with drink and apparel, and unstinted gratification of their carnal appetites. In no prayer to Re can be found a petition by the suppliant for spiritual gifts, or any expression indicating his need of divine help for his soul." [17]

In ancient Babylonia the attitude of the Deity toward men depends upon their qualities. Only the wise man is acceptable to the gods. Inasmuch as religion is essentially knowledge, of necessity the intellectual interest enters largely into piety. The ideal first man is the "keenly sagacious" Atrahasis. The will of the Deity must be ascertained; piety consists in submissive and unflagging performance of ritual. The afflicted king inquires whether his sufferings are the consequences of ceremonial dereliction or of moral wrong-doing. In the conception of Deity right-

17. Sir E. A. Wallis Budge, *From Fetish to God in Ancient Egypt*, 11 (London, Oxford University Press, 1934). Reprinted by permission of the publisher.

eousness and capricious wrath are not differentiated; there is no distinction between sin and ritual error. Murder, theft, and spitting at a holy place are regarded as possible causes of disease; invariably the source of disease is sin. Atonement for transgression is effected by and closely associated with repentance, and especially with the use of incantations. The man who offends the Deity by transgression is recompensed with evil, the devout man with good. The concept of God has no ethical tinge. Yet the gods demand adherence to moral standards. Priests cite the importance of ritualistic errors, but suggest the possibility that misfortune was sent in consequence of moral transgressions, such as lying, stealing, defrauding, maliciousness, adultery, coveting the possessions of others, worldly ambitions, injurious teaching, and other misdemeanours. The gods punish misdoing as severely as neglect of their worship or as indifference to demands of ritual.

In the worship demanded by the Old Testament, purity of heart is not a dominant note. This was true especially in the early history of the Jewish people, as shown, for example, in *Amos*. In the eighth century B.C. or earlier the relation of Yahweh to Israel was not ethical but realistically pragmatic. The Jews were Yahweh's people, and Yahweh was solely Israel's God. "You only have I known of all the families of the earth: therefore I will punish you for all your iniquities. Can two walk together except they be agreed?" Thus Yahweh to Israel. As it was Israel's duty to worship Yahweh, so Yahweh, in turn, was under obligation to protect Israel. Worship consisted of ritual and sacrifice; to their due discharge the morality of the worshipper was irrelevant.

In the New Testament forgiveness is meted out only to him who shows forgiveness. Not so in the Old Testament. On his deathbed David displays an unforgiving spirit when he exhorts Solomon not to allow the aged Joab to go down to the grave in peace. He instructs Solomon to deal similarly with Shimei, whose life David had promised to protect.

Saint and sinner indulge in resentment and personal vengeance. "Vengeance is mine, saith the Lord, I will repay"—but vengeance was not left to the Lord.

Evidence of the transition between the ethics of the Old Testament and that of the New is found in the apocryphal book *Testaments of the Twelve Patriarchs* (109–106 B.C.). It is replete with ethical teachings, concerned especially with the vices of lying, envy, hate, lust, and covetousness, and with longsuffering, truthfulness, love, purity, generosity, and other virtues. Its verses contain such sayings as: "Love the Lord and your neighbour"; "Love the Lord through all your life, and one another with a true heart." Its lofty ethical injunctions suggest, if they do not attain to, those of the New Testament. As a result of Greek influence, Alexandrian, as distinct from Palestinian, Jews, held a doctrine of predestination, and regarded the fate of the soul in the next world as determined during its pre-existence. At death it entered immediately upon a final reward of blessedness or of torment. Hence the afterlife of the soul was regarded as mechanically fixed for good or evil through all eternity.

In the New Testament the blessings of the future life and the spiritual goods of this world are for the humble, the lowly, the righteous, the pure in heart. One is not conquered if one has the will to submit. The meek will inherit the earth, for he who humbleth his spirit is already triumphant. He who is spiritually victorious cannot be overcome by earthly assailant. A spiritual heaven can be achieved on earth, good can eventuate from evil, righteousness can transform earthly misery into happiness. Spiritual reward is not postponed to the next world, though the heavenly reward is inexpressibly grand, beyond earthly realization. The virtues rewarded on earth and in heaven are ethical. There is little stress on ritual or formula; virtuous life is at a premium, bigotry and nationalism are contemned. The service of man is the service of God. "Neighbour" no longer connotes Jew, but any fellow-man with whom contact is possible.

In most preliterate cultures religion has few ethical implications. Few preliterate peoples conceive a personal or anthropomorphic power in control of events and human destiny. Yet among some primitive peoples there are many social implications in attitudes toward gods who control material things. Historic religions, on the other hand, carry many ethical sanctions; they have encouraged, within limits that have grown ever wider, man's social, altruistic, and human proclivities, and have condemned anti-social and self-assertive tendencies. That the Christian religion has promoted ethics there can be no doubt.

CHAPTER XV THE LIFE AFTER DEATH: PRELITERATE CULTURES

DEATH REGARDED AS UNNATURAL

Death is mysterious and uncanny. It is not natural and was not part of the original plan of the Creator. Ancient Jews regarded death as punishment for the sin committed by Adam and Eve in the Garden of Eden. Probably the initial account stated that they should eat of the fruit of the tree of life, and so attain immortality; but the serpent deceived them, and they ate instead of the fruit of the tree of the knowledge of good and evil. In consequence, the serpent, which sheds its skin annually and so renews its life, attained the immortality which God intended for man. Formerly, in Moroccan Mohammedan tradition, people did not die absolutely, but lost consciousness for a while and then revived. The jealousy of Lalla Fatima Zohra, daughter of the Prophet, was responsible for a change in this plan. After a child of her rival had died this temporary death, she went to the Prophet and said to him: "Father, the dead should not come back to life again." The Prophet loved her dearly and prayed God to make death absolute. Accordingly the child of her hated rival did not revive. When, however, her own sons had been slaughtered, she rushed to her father and cried: "O Father, do not the dead live again?" The Prophet replied: "Daughter, thou asked of me that death should be final, and I prayed God for it. Thou must bow to his will. Thy sons will never come back again." Since that time the dead have been dead for ever.

The Efe, Congo pygmies, say that in the beginning there was no death. Muri-muri, the creator, gave a pot to Toad and bade him handle it with care, and not break it, for death was in it. Should the pot be broken, Muri-muri warned, all men would die. Toad went his way and presently met Frog, who offered to carry the pot. At first Toad hesitated to give over his burden, but the pot had now become very heavy, and eventually he handed it over to Frog, with a warning to be careful with it. Frog hopped away with the pot, and let it fall. It broke into fragments, and death escaped from it. Thus death came into the world.

Many preliterate cultures conceive the pristine condition of man as one in which there was no death. The concept is found in Polynesia and in many African and North American tribes. In some cultures only death from obvious cause is natural.

The ethical significance of the emotional response to death, and the rationalistic interpretation of the phenomenon, is the theme of the remainder of this chapter and of the following one.

CULT OF THE DEAD

Many students of comparative religion attach much importance to the cult of the dead. Some regard ancestor worship as the earliest form of religion or as a stage in the development of all higher religions. The term *ancestor worship* is, however, largely a misnomer. Even in the higher religions there is seldom worship of ancestors, though there may be a cult of the dead, that is, ceremonies, rites, offerings, or prayers, designed to ensure the comfort of the deceased, enlist their aid, or thwart their malice toward the living. In Greece, Rome, Indo-Irania, China, and Japan the cult of the dead reaches its highest development. Among preliterate peoples the cult of the dead is most highly developed in Negro Africa. It is strongly entrenched in Polynesia and is present in many other preliterate areas. The cult of the dead is probably based ultimately upon fear of the ghost, a fear which is apparently spontaneous. In many preliterate cultures measures are taken to prevent the return of the ghost or ensure that it will not harm the living. Precautions consist of breaking the bones of the body so that the ghost will not wander; carrying the corpse over a stream which the ghost will not recross; taking it to its resting-place by devious paths which the soul cannot retraverse; or taking it out of the dwelling through an opening made for the purpose in the side of the structure, and then closing the opening. In South Africa, among Bushmen and Bantus, the entire village moves after the death of one of its members.

"Do not abandon me unwept and unburied lest I be the pawn to bring upon you God's wrath."[1] The soul needs food and utensils in the next world; hence in many areas food, drink, implements, and

1. Odyssey, Book XI.

utensils are left on the grave or are buried with the dead. This practice is common in North America, as may be seen in Indian and Eskimo burial grounds at the present day. Among Omahas and Poncas, if one touches the food left at a grave, the ghost snatches it away, paralyzes the mouth of the thief, and twists his face out of shape for the remainder of his life; or he is pursued by the ghost, food loses its savour, and hunger ever after haunts him. Spirits of men who have died of wounds float toward a cliff which overhangs the Missouri River near the Santee agency in Nebraska. There they cut upon the rocks pictures that portray the manner in which they died. A line indicates the spot at which disease or wound caused death. After making this record the spirit flies off to the land of the hereafter. In prehistoric Mimbres Valley culture, in the Southwest of the United States, the pottery buried with the dead was punctured, that is, "killed," presumably to allow the ceramic soul to escape and join the soul of the deceased. Similar practices and motives are widespread.

In western and central Africa at annual ceremonies slaves or captives are killed that their souls may serve the soul of the deceased monarch in the next world. The Ashanti have annual festivals, days of commemoration of the dead, designed to help ghosts across the Volta River, on the banks of which they wander until assisted over by these offerings. Among the Dinka every significant act, individual or social, is watched concernedly by ancestral spirits or by less familiar spirits. The Bari of the Anglo-Egyptian Sudan call the spirits of the dead, which dwell beneath the earth, nephews of God. They powerfully affect human destinies; their anger must be appeased with sacrifices, their favour courted with gifts. Twice a year, in the morning, a cow or a goat is sacrificed to them, and if sickness visits a family, sacrifice is made in the morning and in the evening. If "sickness" visits the people or the crops, the rain chief appeals to his ancestral spirits to avert the calamity.

Zuñis regard the dead as bestowers of rain and all blessings. Rain which falls on the fourth day after a man's death is usually attributed to the deceased and gives consolation to the bereaved. "Worship of the dead is the foundation of all Zuñi ritual. The dead form part of the great spiritual essence of the universe; they are the part which is nearest and most intimate." [2]

A Hindu can obtain salvation after death and ensure that of his an-

2. Ruth L. Bunzel, "Introduction to Zuñi Ceremonialism," *ABE*, 47: 483 (1929–1930). Reprinted by permission of the Bureau of American Ethnology.

cestors only by means of offerings made by a son, a son's son, or a son's son's son lawfully begotten in marriage. "Heaven is not for him who leaves no male progeny," declares a text. The fate of ancestors depends upon offerings made by the living. This belief is found among Chinese, Greeks, Romans, and many other peoples.

BELIEF IN LIFE AFTER DEATH

Religious sanctions of conduct are of varied character and efficacy. The efficacy of curse, oath, or blessing inheres in the automatic power of the uttered word. Reading or quoting the holy book, Koran or Bible, has automatic efficacy. So have written formulas, such as Mohammedans wash from a board and drink in order to imbibe their power and virtue. Even churchgoing may possess automatic efficacy. Of all sanctions, however, belief in rewards or punishments in the next world has generally been considered most potent. To grow weak in character because there is no prospect of immortality seemed, to Spinoza, "not less absurd than for a man, because good food will not preserve his body forever, to betake himself rather to poisons, and stuff himself with deadly potions. Or it is as if, because a man find the Mind to be neither eternal nor immortal, he should therefore prefer to be a fool and to live without Reason. But all this is so absurd that it scarcely deserves consideration." In this point of view, however, Spinoza was unique in his time.

Sir Thomas More, perhaps the most enlightened Englishman of his day, and one of the most liberal men of his century, declared that "if dread of hell were gone, very few would fear God." His defence of hell is as follows: Since fear of God sends folks to Heaven, which is of all things most to be desired, it follows that Hell is really a blessing in no disguise. "God in that thing, wherein he may seem most rigorous, is marvellous merciful to us, and that is, which many men would little ween in that he provided hell. For I suppose very surely that many a man and woman too, of whom there sit some now, and more shall hereafter sit, full gloriously crowned in heaven, had they not first been afraid of hell, would toward heaven never have set foot forward." [3]

Winstanley is of other mood. He asserts that there is no heaven or hell beyond life. Belief in them has been used by possessors to keep the dispossessed in servitude. "The Younger Brother, being weak in spirit,

3. Sir Thomas More, *Dialogue of Comfort*, quoted in Claude E. Shebbeare, *Sir Thomas More, a Leader of the English Renaissance*, 130–131 (London, Harding and More, 1930).

and not having a grounded knowledge of the Creation, nor of himself, is terrified, and lets go his hold in the Earth, and submits himself to be a Slave to his Brother, for fear of damnation in Hell after death, and hopes to get Heaven thereby after he is dead. And so his eyes are put out, and his Reason is blinded. . . . And indeed the subtle clergy do know that if they can but charm the people by this their divining doctrine, to look after riches, Heaven and Glory when they are dead, that then they shall easily be the inheritors of the Earth, and have the deceived people to be their Servants." Mably is convinced that, if men were not certain of rewards or punishments after death, they would not act morally. Hence belief in life after death is essential to the existence of society. Rousseau considers belief in future bliss of the good and punishment of the evil a socially essential dogma, to be imposed on all citizens under penalty of banishment. Samuel Johnson is convinced that "if it were not for the notion of immortality [a man] would cut a throat to fill his pockets." John Stuart Mill attributes considerable ethical efficacy to belief in postmortem existence. G. Stanley Hall affirms that belief in a future life, even a meagre faith, if it includes belief in rewards and punishments, gives inestimable support to morality and makes it easier to die than to swerve from the right.

To test the validity of these views let us examine the beliefs which various peoples entertain regarding postmortem existence of the soul and the manner in which these concepts affect or may affect conduct.

PRELITERATE CULTURES

The Araucanians of southern Chile do not believe in hell. At death good spirits take corporeal form and go to a land of plenty which evil spirits may not enter. Here they are waited upon by their wives, who preceded or will follow them. In this afterworld social distinctions are preserved; poor people and immoral women go to a land which is cold but supplies plentiful food and drink, though of poor quality. Ancient Peruvians recognized distinction of fate for souls of good and of bad, but the character of the distinction is not recorded. The Onagua of northeastern Peru believe the souls of good medicinemen go into the water to live; the souls of evil medicinemen are condemned to dwell in the bush. The souls of other people, in the form of flowers, live in heaven. The Tupinamba say that paradise cannot be entered by the souls of men who were effeminate and lazy and did not defend their native land.

Only the souls of virtuous women are admitted, the "virtuous" being spouses of braves who have killed and eaten many enemies.

Souls of fortunate Mayas reside in paradise under trees; spirits of young children spend the time flitting from flower to flower in the form of humming-birds. Those who lived a good life have a happy fate in the next world. Their abode is free from sorrow and pain; they spend the time feasting and dancing or repose in the shade of a huge tree which grows in the centre of the afterworld. Those who lived a bad life go to Mitnal, a region beneath the plane inhabited by good souls. There they are subject to Hunahau, prince of demons and ruler of the region. Through endless existence they are condemned to such tortures as hunger, exhaustion, cold, and sadness. Suicides go to heaven, where they are under the special patronage of the goddess Ixtab, represented in the codices with a rope round her neck. Many Mayas committed suicide under trivial provocation, or when depressed. Conviction that a good place in heaven was reserved for them may have fostered the practice. Belief in a different fate in the next world for good and bad is not attributable to teachings of early friars. The good fate awaiting suicides is not in accord with Christian teachings, and is not consonant with the attitude found in most parts of the New World. Some groups of Eskimos, it is true, provide postmortem rewards for suicides; but most peoples consider self-murder heinous and regard it with abhorrence.

Aztec warriors killed in battle go to the eastern paradise of the sun, where they beat on their shields to greet the rising orb, escort him on his journey to the zenith, then descend to earth as humming-birds, or other bright-plumaged birds, and dwell amid flowers. Women who die in childbirth go to the western paradise of the sun, carry the celestial orb on a litter of bright feathers from zenith to horizon, and descend to earth as moths. Persons who drown, are struck by lightning, or die of certain diseases, such as dropsy or leprosy, go to the terrestrial paradise Tlalocan, home of the god Tlaloc, where food-producing plants and flowers flourish in perpetual summer with miraculous fertility. Those who die of other disease or of old age make a difficult journey to Mictlan, the underworld, where the god Mictlantecutli presides. They pass between two clashing mountains, run the gauntlet of a great snake and a huge lizard, traverse eight deserts and as many hills, and encounter a wind filled with stone knives. After four years of terrible hardship and risk, the soul reaches a great river which it must swim across. For this passage it requires the assistance of a red dog, such as was kept in the household for the purpose and killed at the funeral of a member of the family. This underworld is lighted by the sun on its return to the east. Infants who die untainted by sin Tonacatecutli receives in a special paradise. Here, as humming-birds, they flit from flower to flower. The souls of those who died a peaceful death live in a sombre and obscure region.

Among present-day Zapotecs the only influence of the belief in life after death is on one's treatment of dogs. If one mistreats dogs, the dog of the next world will imperil the ghost's passage across the river which separates this world from the realm of shades. Zapotec dead cross a broad river at whose bank stand a white dog and a black one. When the white dog is asked to carry the soul across, he refuses, and says his coat would be soiled. The black dog will carry the soul over unless the person during his lifetime has treated a black dog brutally or refused it food. At Mitla some identify this river with the arroyo between the town and the old burial place in the churchyard. The abode of the soul in the next world is a large unnamed pueblo. There life goes on as in this world, and in the same body. Zapotecs at San Dionisis say the white dog will ferry the soul across the underworld river if the soul carries soap and will wash the dog's coat. The Mazatecs of Oaxaca like to own black dogs, for black dogs swim with them across the wide river which the soul must cross. The Mixe of Tepuxtepec say the dead travel eastward for three years to a lake across which they are carried by a black dog. White dogs are at the lake-shore, but refuse to carry souls across. Hence a black dog which steals is forgiven, and these Indians never beat a black dog. At Jalisco natives believe that beating a black dog or refusing it food may result in refusal of the black dog to carry the ghost across the river. A miniature figurine of a dog, with a burden basket on its back and a piece of food in its mouth, is cast into Lake Chapala.

Yucatecs recognize a paradise in which souls of the dead rest in the shade of the mythical Yaxche tree. As among Mayas, those who hang themselves attain future happiness.

The Cuna of Panama describe a nether world in which the righteous are rewarded and evildoers punished. Some of its many custodians—those, for example, who cause rain—take an active part in the earthly life of man. Chibchan souls (Colombia) travel to a land in the centre of the earth. To reach it they must cross in a boat made of spider's web. Hence spiders are not killed. Life in the next world is similar to life on earth, but the post-mortem status depends to some extent upon the manner of death. Men killed in battle and women who die in childbirth are particularly well favoured. Barama River Caribs are said to have no belief in life after death except that souls become hovering disliked ghosts. Shades of the dead go to no special realm. The Lengua believe that souls lead in the next world the same kind of existence which they led in this world. A tall man is tall there, a short man short; a kindly-disposed man has a genial temperament in the next world. Those who were feared and respected in this world receive the same treatment from souls in the next world that they received from men on earth. The spirit of a child remains a child.

The Otomacs of Guiana say that after death the body turns into stone, the material from which it originally sprang. Caribs believe that after death virtuous and brave men inhabit a delightful place in which there are no storms on the sea, game is abundant, and the fruits are always ripe. They have beautiful wives, and their captives are very handsome. They constantly go to war, and crush with their heavy clubs the heads of Arawaks, whom they invariably defeat. The lazy are banished from this paradise. They live far beyond the mountains in great misery and constantly till the soil, for they are slaves of the Arawak dead.

Netsilik Eskimo souls go to one of three post-mortem regions. The "place one can always return to," the Village of Eternal Homecoming, is in the sky, a land of pleasure with plentiful play and merry jests. The houses stand in long rows. The snow around them is trampled hard by the feet of the many happy ball-playing people. These souls are referred to as "those who live above us," or as "those who have been taken up to the sky." Only clever hunters and women with beautiful tattoos go there, for the spirits of the air desire women who do not shirk the suffering which brings beautification. In this region there is always good hunting. The moon spirit, who lives among these souls, helps them to hunt. Some say that souls who go to Qutlivut, as this region is called, are taken there by the moon spirit, and that souls which reach the sky become stars and live with the moon spirit. The moon spirit wishes the living to see what a beautiful country this sky region is, and sometimes tries to snatch them away from earth and take them to it on his sledge.

Some say the game animals in this region are mainly land animals, and that the sky is a great plain with many edible juicy berries. Caribou graze in large herds and are easily killed.

When sky-dwellers wish sea food, the moon spirit takes them to the sea and helps them to hunt the sea animals. While hunting they play various games, as do people on earth who are happy and have sufficient meat. Consequently in this sky-world one hears only songs intermingled with laughter. A shaman who visited the region heard an old woman who was taking part in a game and could not keep up with the other participants cry out: "If only I had known that one ought to die young!" She said this laughingly when the others ran from her. "The same happens on earth: people who go on hunting-trips leave behind them the old women who cannot keep up; but then they do not laugh; then it means death; there you see the difference between similar things in the sky and on earth. Everything is only happiness and fun for the dead. But the words of that old woman gave mankind important tidings, for now we know that we will forever remain at the age we have reached when we die."

Another land to which souls of the dead go is called Nuqumiut, the land of "those who always sit huddled up with hanging heads." This land is close to the surface of the earth, but under it. To this region go men who were lazy and who were therefore poor hunters, and women who are not tattooed, who would not suffer a little in order to be pretty. "There was no energy in them when they lived, and that is why they now, after death, hang their heads, and their chins are pressed down on their breasts. They are always hungry, for their only food is butterflies. They always sit on their haunches with bowed head and closed eyes; only when a butterfly comes flying over them they lift their heads slowly and snap at it, just as young birds open their red mouths after a fly. And when they do, yellow dust flies from their neckbands as from a bursting puff-ball. Thus they always squat down with drooping head." A shaman who went to this land saw a spirit slowly lift its head when a butterfly was hovering over it. "Slowly he lifted his head, the head that otherwise never looks upwards, and at the very same moment smoke came from his throat like yellow dust from a puffball. This is the life after death in Nuqumiut," where souls "live in hunger, idleness and sluggish apathy, just as they spoiled their lives on earth."

The third land is in the underworld, far beneath this second world.

Its denizens are called "those who live down there," or "those who live below." "There is no definitive rule as to who goes down into the underworld. They are the same kind of people as those who go up to the sky. . . . At both places there is only joy, prosperity and abundance, except that the seasons are different from the seasons on earth, for when we have summer they have winter, and their summer is our winter."

Netsilik Eskimos say that, if the individual observes faithfully all the taboos, his soul will take the right path to the afterworld, and life there will be lived happily and without dangers. If the death taboo is broken, the soul stays on earth and becomes an evil spirit to trouble the living: it "does all it can to persecute those that are to blame for its life after death having been ruined."

Among the Koksoagmyut Eskimos of Hudson Bay, the place to which the soul goes depends upon the conduct of the person on earth and even more upon the manner in which he meets death. Those who die of starvation and women who die in childbirth go to the region above. They are not in absolute want but have a few of the luxuries enjoyed by those who go to the world beneath. All desire to go to the lower region, whence they can communicate with the living, a privilege denied those who go above. If death is the result of natural causes, the spirit spends a probationary period of four years in the grave, then dwells on earth. During this probationary period the grave is visited, food is offered, songs are sung; the offerings—oil, flesh, and tobacco for smoking and chewing—the donor consumes at the grave. Clothing is left near the grave, that the spirit may clothe itself anew when funerary garments have decayed and disappeared. Articles for the deceased's immediate use are placed with the body in the grave. Dependence of the dead upon the living is an incentive to treat one's fellows kindly, especially near kin, though fear of the ghost may inspire the offerings. In Baffin Land one of the two souls which every Eskimo possesses goes to one of the "land of the souls." There are three heavens, superimposed; the highest is brightest and best. Those who die by violence go to the lowest heaven. Those who die from disease go first to Sedna's house, where they remain a year. Sedna restores their souls to health, then sends them to the second heaven, where there are many whales. Apparently only light souls leave Sedna's house and ascend to the second heaven. They are strong and healthy.

People who commit suicide go to a dark place where they walk about with tongues lolling. Women who prematurely gave birth to a child go first to Sedna's abode and dwell near by in the lowest world, under the sea. Some souls go to Tukey-chwen, a place of which no description is vouchsafed. On the western coast of Hudson Bay some souls go to a lower world, some to an upper world. The former place is the abode of Nuliayoq, a creature corresponding to Sedna, and of her father Anatalik. It is comfortably warm. To it go the souls of those who have transgressed taboos, and Anatalik punishes them. Souls of the good and of suicides go to an upper region where they play football with a walrus skull; the skull is alive and manifests by its chattering the pleasure which it derives from the game. The Northern Lights are these spirits at play.

The religious doctrines of Copper Eskimos bring little comfort. "Life would be hard enough if they had none but natural forces to contend with, forces that they could see and estimate. But mysterious and hostile powers, invisible and incalculable, and therefore potentially all the more dangerous, hem them in, as they believe, on every side, so that they never know from day to day whether a fatal sickness will not strike them down or a sudden misfortune overwhelm them and their families —from no apparent cause, it may be, and for no conceivable reason, save the ill-will of these unseen foes. Young and old, the good and the bad, all alike are involved in the same dangers, and alike share the same fate. Death rolls back the gate, not of a happy hunting ground, or of a heaven of peace and happiness where friends and lovers may unite once more, but of some vague and gloomy realm where, even if want and misery are not found (and of this they are not certain), joy and gladness at least must surely be unknown. It is little wonder therefore if the mind of the average Eskimo is deeply tinged with fatalism. Life would be unbearable indeed with this religion did he not possess a superabundant stock of natural gaiety and derive a joy from the mere fact of living itself. The future holds out no golden promise, not even the hope of a life as cheerful as the present one; so the native banishes as far as possible all thoughts of a distant tomorrow, and drains the pleasures of each fleeting hour before they pass away forever." [4]

Among Bering Strait Eskimos, shades of shamans and of those who die by accident, violence, or starvation go to a land of plenty in the

4. Diamond Jenness, *The Life of the Copper Eskimos*, 190 (Ottawa, 1922). Reprinted by permission of the National Museum of Canada. Similarly of the Haida, Sproat says: "All the people live in constant apprehension of danger from the unseen world."

sky where there are abundant light, food, and water. Those who die from natural causes go to an underground land of the dead. To this realm go also shades of dead animals, where each species lives in its own village. In this underground world shades depend entirely on offerings of food, water, and clothing, made by kinsfolk during the festivals held to benefit the dead. Even in the land of plenty, shades are made happier if remembered with presents at these festivals. A painful existence after death awaits bad shamans, thieves who have stolen from fellow-villagers, and people who break certain taboos. If no survivor makes a festival for the deceased or names a child after him, he is forgotten, cannot return to the festivals given in honour of the dead, is poor and friendless. Herein lies incentive to treat one's fellows graciously, lest after death one's soul be neglected and perish in solitude and want. Greenland Eskimo witches and bad people go to the upper world; those who have performed a great and heroic action, or have suffered severely in this life—for example, men who die in seafaring and women who die in childbirth—go to the world below. The deceased's comfort depends largely upon offerings from survivors. The moral effects of such beliefs may be considerable. "The rules and customs concerning property, position, and what represented the administration of justice, evidently bore a close relation to their religious belief. The customs according to which an individual became a member of a family, partaking of its reputation as well as its means of subsistence, were supported and confirmed by the belief that the souls of ancestors remained guardian spirits to their descendants, having left them their amulets and *serrats* as a kind of pledge. The same idea must be regarded as having formed the principal foundation for the avenging of blood. The social institutions in connection with the local conditions leaving still ample room for arbitrary acts of violence, the fear of vengeance by ghosts, *kivigtoks, angliaks, serrats,* amulets, and *tupilaks,* must have powerfully contributed to prevent weak and helpless persons being wronged. By the custom of naming a child after a deceased person, it was intended to secure rest in his grave for the latter. The child, when grown up, was bound to brave the influences which had caused his death. If, for instance, the deceased had perished at sea, his successor had only so much greater an inducement for striving to grow a skilful kayaker. As to the funeral rites, the treatment of the body being considered in some way to influence the state of the soul after death, it was generally placed on the floor, for the purpose of guiding the soul on its road to the underworld; but in the case of malefactors, the body was dismembered, and the separate limbs were thrown apart." [5] In most Eskimo groups, however, compliance with or violation of taboo is not rewarded or punished after death. The destiny of the soul is more likely to be determined by the manner of dying than by the manner of living. Religious outlook is little influenced by belief in deferred punishment of sin.

The Haida entertain concepts of the next world similar to those of the Eskimos. There is a region for shamans, another for those who die of hunger, where they will continue to suffer its pangs, and an upper realm for those who die a violent death. Souls of the drowned live with the killer-whales; those who perish by violence go to Taxet's house in the sky, whence rebirth is difficult but, for the adventurous soul, not impossible; those who die of disease go to the Land of Souls, a shoreland beyond the waters. It has innumerable inlets, at each of which is a village, as in the land of the living. The dying man can choose the village which he will inhabit in deathland. Another Haida belief holds that good souls go to heaven, where it is light, and bad souls to a land of darkness. The bad soul is tortured continually and must observe the guardian of this afterworld feasting on the soul's body. In a third region, a domain of death, the soul remains twelve moons. If the soul is not regenerated during this period, it returns to earth, is reborn, and remains there until ready for heaven. Very bad souls are reborn as beasts or as fish and suffer great torture. They are told to attack strangers but spare fellow-tribesmen. They enter animals whose size varies from that of a bear to that of a mouse. Occasionally they enter the fin-back whale. The mice which these souls inhabit are large enough to house an adult's soul and small enough to live in the stomach of a man of another tribe whom the reincarnated soul would harm.

The souls of good Tlinkit go to a paradise above; witches and wicked are reborn as dogs or other beasts. The soul of the wicked goes to a cold desolate country, where it remains until it is sorry for its bad deeds and wishes to make reparation for them. It may then go to a better land above, "Life Above." Those who fall in war go to the region above where Tabit is the chief. Those who die of sickness go to a region on the plane of the earth but beyond its borders. In some Tlinkit tribes, souls who have made no friends while on earth linger painfully on the bank of the river which they must cross in shadowland, for there are no canoes

5. H. Rink, *Tales and Traditions of the Eskimo*, 63–64 (London, Blackwood, 1875).

of predeceased friends to take them across the water. If, however, the soul has many friends in that ghostland, at his call they hasten to him to take him across. Meanwhile they make inquiries about the welfare of those who still live on this earth. The souls of those whose bodies have been cremated are warm and comfortable, but the souls of uncremated bodies shiver in discomfort.

Here, then, is motive to treat one's fellows well, lest there be no well-disposed souls to assist one in the next world. Also, there is the belief that the treatment of the corpse, that is, cremation, will affect the comfort of the soul in the next world.

The Salish believe that the soul goes to the spirit world, after leaving its clothing behind in a beautiful spot covered with grass and flowers. "A chief meets and admits the dead to their respective places in spiritland. There are two rooms, the door of each is kept locked. In one room are those who were bad." They quarrel and fight, and reptiles of different kinds crawl around among them. "They live on raw reptile flesh. Their chief sits with a huge frog in front of him. He cuts up pieces of the flesh with a large knife. In the other room everything is beautiful and pleasant and clean." These people sing and pray. Some are on their knees praising God. All wear the hair reaching down to the shoulders. "Only those enter here who are pure in body and mind."

Nass River tribes believe that the spirit travels by one of two roads: a red, smooth one, to the right, or a dark, rough one, to the left. The dark road leads to a bridge, beyond which is a rendezvous of the poor unfortunates, who continually call across to the more fortunate for food and water to appease their hunger and thirst. We are not told whether the concept has ethical significance.

The Quinault afterworld recognizes no distinction of lot between virtuous and vicious. The dead live precisely as do people in this world, though they speak a language which even the shaman cannot understand. They have no bones, though they have flesh and blood. Their houses and villages are like those of tribesmen on earth. Some say husbands and wives live together, but children dwell in another village. In the older Salish culture the good go to a celestial land of bliss and joy, the bad to a less desirable place of obscure character. In the matrilineal culture which has spread from the Coastal region and permeated the Salish there is no distinction of lot; all lead the same kind of existence in the next world. The soul of an Athabascan Déné-Dindjié, of the lower Mackenzie, goes to the land of shadows. In the southwest, at the springing of the celestial vault of the sky, is a wide opening through which flows the river of the sky, on the banks of which dance continually the souls of those who have not been burned by their enemies. The souls of those burned by their enemies are excluded from this place, and wander about disconsolately. Chipewayan souls travel in a stone boat to a beautiful island which abounds in game. The good reach the island safely. When the souls of evil men are within sight of the island, the stone boat in which they travel sinks, and they struggle forever in the water.

Souls of the Dwamish, near Puget Sound, go to a very pleasant underworld far to the north. There is neither reward nor punishment for earthly deeds. All Nusqually souls go to the same spiritland in the underworld and share the same fate.

Squally-absch souls and also living medicinemen maintain constant communication between this world and the underworld. Otlas-skio, land of souls, has waving forests, grassy plains, and running streams. Villages patterned after the ancient type are beautifully located; the woods are filled with game and singing birds; brilliant flowers enliven the landscape and perfume the balmy air; the streams are filled with salmon. The dead meet friends and relatives who have preceded them, and spend eternity in pursuit of pleasures dear on earth. Before reaching the world of the dead the soul must cross a river; the passage is as easy for the bad as for the good. Bella Coola spirits go to the realm above, where there is neither reward nor punishment. Here as elsewhere in the Northwest Coast area, the fate of the soul depends upon the nature of the individual's death. Souls of men killed in warfare go to a realm above; if they die unavenged, the ascent is difficult. After sojourn in the first realm of the dead the soul dies and enters a second realm.

Cree souls must cross a slender and slippery tree laid as a bridge across a rapid stream of stinking muddy water. Northern Saulteaux describe the hereafter as a region in which two paths lead to the sky. One path is traversed by souls of the good, who travel it immediately after death, as fast as a bird can fly. The other path is traversed by evildoers on foot. They go slowly and at last arrive at an evil place from which there is no escape. Sometimes, as a warning to themselves, and to others as well, souls of the bad who reach this place are allowed to return to earth. Thus people know about the hereafter. Good people do not return from the next world. Reid says the Saulteaux soul travels thirty to sixty days, or even more, before arriving at the entrance to the next world, where it must cross a deep river. A good man easily makes the crossing, but a wicked man, after each attempt, comes out on the side from which he entered. Until the soul reaches the river, it is dependent for sustenance on friends in this world. Hence for several weeks after a man's death his friends when they eat throw a portion of the food into the fire. The spirit of the food consumed in the fire nourishes the soul on its post-mortem journey. Thus in effect it may pass through hell before reaching the place of bliss. The soul of a good and brave chief has in the next world a preferred chance for honours among souls of tribesmen. Bad spirits congregate along the bank of the river which separates them from the abode of the happy; they see spirits of the good enjoying themselves in sunshine; spirits of the bad, enveloped in darkness, shiver with cold. "To give the good Indian a sharper relish for the bliss in store for him, he has had to pass the days, before referred to, in journeying through this country for a period after death, which is supposed to be shorter or longer as he has been more or less deserving. When he arrives at the river, he sees its shores crowded with the unhappy spirits, vainly attempting its traverse; he makes his attempt, succeeds, and looking back must be overjoyed by his good fortune. He is immediately surrounded by his departed friends, who welcome him to the happy hunting grounds, and convey him in honour and triumph to a council with the Great Spirit."

Among Sauks and Foxes the soul journeys toward the realm of the Great Spirit. If he has led a good life, he has little difficulty in reaching it; if he has not, he encounters many trials. Eventually he reaches this land, where all kinds of game are plentiful and the time is spent dancing and sleeping. Originally there were two Great Spirits. One died, went to another world, and is now the Evil Spirit which secures the souls of children who die too young to find the good path. He takes them to his village and deprives them of their brains so that they will not have sense enough to leave him. When the Good Spirit saw this, it sent an eagle to peck a hole in the head of every young child as soon as it died and conceal the brain of the child until it was of suitable age to travel. The eagle then returns its brain, and the child has sense enough immediately to leave the Bad Spirit and find the good path.

Among the Lenape (Delawares) a delightful paradise awaits the good, namely, those who have been kind to their fellows and have done their duty by them. Those who have done evil in this world are excluded from this happy land. No other punishment, it seems, awaits them. In this heaven for the good, life continues much as on earth, except that there is no pain, sickness, sorrow, work, or worry. The Munsi (Delawares) locate the Land of Spirits in the southwest, in a land of good hunting. Here the wigwams of the spirits are always neat and clean, and happiness prevails. Between this world and the afterworld flows a river which the soul must cross on a slender foot-log or in a canoe.

Chippewa souls go south to a region on the shores of the great ocean. Before they arrive at their destination, they must cross a stream, on a large snake which serves as a bridge. Those who have died from drowning never succeed in crossing this stream; they are thrown into the water and there remain for ever. The souls of persons who were in lethargy or trance reach the edge of the stream, but the snake threatens to devour them and prevents them from passing over. They return to their bodies and reanimate them.

In the land of souls all are treated according to merit. Those who have been good are free from pain; they have no duties to perform, their time is spent in dancing and singing, and they feed upon mushrooms, which are abundant. Souls of bad men are haunted by the phantoms of the persons or things which they have injured. If a man has destroyed much property, the phantoms of the wrecks of this property obstruct his passage wherever he goes. Souls of those whom he wronged avenge themselves. A soul which has crossed the stream cannot return to its body. Yet the Chippewas assert that the souls of the departed visit the abodes of their friends and invite them to the other world, thus forewarning them of approaching death. Parry Island Ojibwas, of Georgian Bay, believe that the souls of those who have not died before their time, have not been sorcerers, and have received proper burial, dwell happily in the next world. The souls of sorcerers, however, perish on the journey to the next world. The souls of those who died before their time, and of those who were not buried, linger on earth near their old abodes, and are scarcely distinguishable from their earthly shadows.

Souls of Hurons who have died in war, by drowning, or by other disaster, have in the spirit world no communication with other souls. A man must see to it that he dies properly. Souls of northern Iroquois who gain great riches and lose humility cannot stand or walk upon the sky-road of the spirits. Only the poor and meek can travel skyward; the poor cannot do so unless they have been humble and virtuous. "It is better to be poor on earth and rich in the sky-world than to have earthly riches and no heaven." These phases of the belief were emphasized by the prophet-reformer, Handsome Lake, who possibly introduced them into the aboriginal code. New England Algonquins are said to have believed in a happy spirit world where dwelt the gods and the souls of great and good men. Souls of the wicked might not enter; they wandered without rest or home. Woods says of Massachusetts Algonquins: "Yet do they hold the immortality of the never-dying soule, that it shall passe to the South-West Elysium concerning which their Indian faith jumps much with the Turkish Alshorn [Koran], holding it to be a kinde of Paradise, wherein they shall everlastingly abide, solacing themselves in oderiferous Gardens, fruitful Corn-fields, greene Medows, bathing their tawny hides in the cool streams of pleasant Rivers, and shelter themselves from heats and cold in the sumptuous Pallaces framed by the skill of Natures curious contrivement; concluding that neither care nor paine shall molest them, but that Natures bounty will administer all things with a voluntary contribution from the overflowing store-house of their Elysian Hospitall, at the portall whereof they say lies a great Dogge whose churlish snarlings deny a Pax intrantibus to unworthy intruders: Wherefore it is their custome, to bury with them their Bows and Arrows, and good store of the Wampouyeage and Mowhackies [wampum and tomahawks]; the one to affright that affronting Cerberus, the other to purchase more immense prerogatives in their Paradise. For their enemies and loose livers, who they account unworthy of this imaginary happiness, they say, that they passe to the infernall dwellings of abamocho, to be tortured according to the factions of the ancient Heathern." [6] Although these early accounts cannot be trusted in detail, they are probably correct in assigning to these Indians belief that the character of the life after death depends on the manner of life on earth.

An early source states that the Gaspesians, that is, the Micmacs, believed that, when the soul of the deceased reached the realm of souls, the wicked "danced and leaped with great violence, eating only the bark of rotten trees, in punishment for their crimes, for a certain number of years indicated by Papkootparout: that the good, on the contrary, lived in great repose at a place removed from the noise of the wicked, eating when it pleased and amusing themselves with the hunting of beavers and of moose, whose spirits allowed themselves to be taken with ease. Such is the reason why our Gaspesians have always observed in-

6. Woods, *New England Prospect*, 34 (1629).

violably the custom of burying with the deceased everything which was in their use during life." [7]

Seminole worthy souls go to a land where existence is ideal. Feasts, dances, and ball games are always in progress. Unworthy souls meet eternal destruction. The trip to the sky country occupies four days. Along the way are many temptations for the unwary, particularly appetizing food. The soul must cross a river by means of a slippery log, which is guarded by a dog. If the person has led an evil life, the dog shakes the log and the soul falls into the subjacent stream, where it is devoured by an alligator or a great fish. A Choctaw soul travels far to the west, to a long, slippery, barkless, pine log, which stretches from one hill to another over a deep and dreadful river. The good pass safely over to a beautiful paradise; the bad fall into the watery abyss and dwell in a dark and wretched land, victims of unremitting hunger. The Cherokee land of the dead is a forest with foliage of caressing shade, carpeted with soft leaves and fine needles from majestic pines; verdant groves waft sweet perfume on gentle zephyrs. In this happy hunting-ground the soul finds the wigwams of those who have preceded it. It lives with these predecessors for ever, never grows old, and constantly develops new capacities. Apparently all souls have the same fate.

The Winnebago soul crosses a slippery swinging bridge. If, during the wake following a man's burial, any of the invited warriors exaggerates the deceased's achievements, the soul will not be able to cross the bridge but will stumble and fall into the abyss of fire beneath. In most Winnebago clans there seems to be no interest in post-mortem rewards of virtue. In the Thunderbird clan, however, the travelling ghost addresses Earthmaker as follows: "Earthmaker, my father, you know very well the kind of life I have led." Earthmaker answers: "You have done well, my son."

Crow eschatology contains no suggestion of reward for the good or punishment for the evil. All have the same fate in spiritland. Cheyennes anticipate no reward or punishment in the next world. The character of Mandan existence in the next world depends, however, upon the life lived in this world. Souls of brave and kindhearted Mandans continue the occupations which they followed on earth, eat similar foods, have wives, and enjoy the pleasures of chase and war. The good reach the ancient villages of their ancestors by means of a lake which the wicked, because of their burdensome sins, cannot cross. This distinction in fate

7. Christien Le Clerc, *Relations de la Gaspesie*, 327–328 (Paris, 1691).

has been attributed, perhaps without sufficient reason, to White influence. Hidatsas promise the good man reward in the next world for valour, self-denial, and ambition. The soul of a brave man is honoured; that of a coward, despised. Some say the ghosts of those who commit suicide occupy a separate portion of the village; otherwise their condition is that of other residents. Those who have been useful to the tribe —for example, warriors and good hunters—pass with ease over the narrow footway which leads to the next world, and arrive safely at the ancient village; worthless persons slip off and are carried by the stream below into oblivion.

Sapona souls are conducted by a broad road along which they travel in company for a considerable distance. Finally the road forks into two paths, one level, the other stony and mountainous. Here a flash of lightning parts the good from the bad; the former are hurried away to the right, the latter to the left. The right-hand road leads to a charming country where spring is everlasting and every month is May. The year is perpetually young and so are the people, particularly the women, who are as bright as stars and, incredible though it seems, never scold. In this delicious sojourn are deer, turkeys, elk, and buffaloes innumerable, perpetually fat and gentle, and trees loaded with delicious fruit throughout the four seasons. The soil produces corn spontaneously, a product so wholesome that those who eat of it are never sick and do not grow old or die. Those who would enter must first pass examination at the portal.

The left-hand path, rugged and uneven, leads to a dark and barren country where winter reigns eternally. The ground is covered with perpetual snow, and icicles cumber the trees. The inhabitants are ever hungry. Their only food is a variety of bitter potato, the consumption of which gives them dry gripes and produces a crop of ulcers malodorous and excruciatingly painful. The women are old and ugly and have pantherlike claws with which they punish men who offend them. They talk much in tones exceedingly shrill that occasion exquisite pain to the ear; the ear-drum is so tender that every sound wounds to the quick.

At the end of this path sits a dreadful old woman on a monstrous toadstool. Her head is covered with rattlesnake tresses; her glaring white eyes inspire terror in all who behold her. She pronounces sentence of woe upon the miserable wretches who appear before her tribunal. The condemned are given to harpies like turkey-buzzards, which fly away with them to the place above mentioned. When they have been tormented for a specified number of years, the duration depending upon the degree of guilt, they are driven back to this world, that they may mend their manners, and merit after their next death a place in the regions of bliss. Though the literal correctness of the account may be questioned, there was doubtless a native concept of rewarding the good and punishing the bad.

Omahas say that at the fork of the path of the dead, which path they identify with the Milky Way, sits an old man, wrapped in a buffalo robe; when the spirits of the dead pass along this path, he directs the steps of good and peaceable people toward the short path which leads directly to the abode of their kin. The contumacious he allows to take the long path, over which they wearily wander. This discrimination in the treatment of good and bad Fletcher and La Flesche attribute—wrongly, we believe—to White influence, as also the belief—which we consider aboriginal—that there is a log across a chasm over which the dead must pass; the good experience no difficulty in making the crossing, but some of the bad find the log so unstable that they fall off and disappear. The spirit of a murderer vainly seeks his kin; he for ever searches, weary with futile wanderings. The spirit of a suicide perishes utterly immediately after death.

Omaha and Ponca good ghosts join the good; evil ghosts, the evil. The soul of a dead Kiowa travels over the Milky Way, "Road of the Dead," to the spirit village situated in the western heavens. It must cross a river on the other side of which the predeceased relatives of the soul await it. The soul of a Kansa who was brave or a good hunter walks in a pleasant path; the soul of a bad man or a coward, in a rough path. The soul travels far. Survivors, therefore, bury with the body moccasins, food, and other articles to serve the soul on the journey. Many persons who have revived had been, during their apparent death, to strange villages in which they were not well treated; they therefore returned to the flesh.

Accounts of the eastern Dakota concept of the world after death are not always consistent. Among early writers Ames says the Dakota "country of souls" is a vast prairie, in which there is game in profusion, and where the spirits dance day and night, partake of every delight, and know neither toil nor trouble. Mrs. Eastman says "they have a vague idea of a future state; many have dreamed of it. Some of their medicinemen pretend to have had revelations from bears and other animals; and they thus learned that their future existence would be but a continuation of this.

They will go on long hunts and kill many buffalo; bright fires will burn in their wigwams as they talk through the long winter's night of the traditions of their ancients. Their women will tan deerskin for their moccasins, and their young children will learn to be brave warriors by attacking and destroying wasps' or hornets' nests; they will celebrate the dog feast to show how brave they are, and sing in triumph while they dance round the scalps of their enemies." Neil says: "They have a fear of the future, but no fixed belief in relation to the nature of the future punishment. The Dakotas are generally taciturn on such topics. The more simple minded believe that a happy land exists across a lake of boiling water, and that an old woman sits on the shore holding a long narrow pole, that stretches across the water to the earth. Warriors who can show marks of wounds on their flesh can walk the pole with security; also infants, whose blue veins are a passport as good as war marks. Others slip into the boiling water. Their theology makes no difference between the condition of the thief and liar and the correct and good man. Those who commit suicide are thought to be unhappy. They believe that a woman who commits suicide will have to drag through another world that (pole or tree) from which she hung herself in this, and that she will often break down the corn in another land by the pole or tree which dangles at her feet and for this will be severely beaten by the inhabitants of the spirit land." Forbes states: "Others have told that they believed in the transmigration of spirits, the soul or spirit not always returning as a human being, but sometimes as a grizzly bear, wolf-dog, etc. . . . If a woman commits suicide (men, they think, do no such foolish and cowardly act) the cord by which she hangs herself (the mode of 'suiciding') is left suspended, for the spirit of the deceased will remain there hanging. When a murderer is buried, he is placed face downward and something tied across the mouth, seemingly to keep the spirit there confined; but if forever, or for a time, I could not learn. It is the same with the soul of any very bad man—it does not leave the place where is placed the 'remains,' but hovers constantly around them, and of a dark, still night is heard to whistle the notes of a death song, detained from entering that pleasant 'southern country.' " [8] And General Sibley: "I have no reason to believe that any Dakota, among the very many with whom I have conversed on the subject, was ever deterred from the commission of a crime by a fear of punishment in another world,

8. William H. Forbes, in *Collections of the Minnesota Historical Society*, 6: 415–416 (1894). Reprinted by permission of the Minnesota Historical Society.

nor have I been able to satisfy myself that their impressions of a future state are anything but shadowy, uncertain and unsatisfactory."

After a long journey a Menominee disembodied spirit reaches a swift river which it must cross before it can arrive at the village of the dead. The only bridge over this stream is a slippery log which, though it does not rest on the water, sways with the current. A huge dog, chief of earthly dogs, guards the log. He decides whether the soul may venture the crossing.[9]

This Cerberus does not allow a person of evil life to come upon the bridge, or those who in their lifetime have abused or maltreated dogs or wolves. The soul which has been allowed to pass may slip off the precarious bridge. If it falls into the water, the swift current carries it downstream for ever. When the last barrier has been successfully passed and the soul has safely arrived on the other shore, the old inhabitants, apprised of its advent, pour out of the village of the dead with shouts of welcome, congratulate it on its safe arrival, and escort it to the village, whose inhabitants enjoy eternal happiness, feasting, and games. All are radiantly clad, their faces brilliantly painted with vermilion. In that land is no war, pestilence, want, or sorrow.

After death the souls of good Blackfeet congregate at a designated locality far from the camp. Here they live in shadow lodges, fight shadow enemies, hunt shadow buffaloes, and live a life patterned after that of this world. Shadows of bad people linger near the place of death. They envy the living, prowl about their lodges, and inflict upon them both physical and mental illness. Another Blackfoot account states that after death souls scramble with great labour up the sides of a steep mountain whose summit rewards them with the prospect of an extensive plain abounding with every variety of game, and interspersed with new tents pitched in agreeable situations. While absorbed in contemplation of this pleasant scene they are descried by the inhabitants of the happy land who, wearing new skin clothing, approach and welcome those who have led good lives. Bad Indians, who have imbrued their hands with the blood of tribesmen, are told to return to the place whence they came, and are thrown down the steep sides of the mountain. Women

9. The New World concept of the bridge we consider aboriginal, although some ethnologists attribute it to Christian influence. It is difficult to believe that Christian missionaries would introduce it. The concept is found in northern California and in the Northwest Coast, Central Woodland, Plains, and Southeast areas. This practically continuous distribution suggests pre-European diffusion. The concept of a bridge is found also among Netsilik Eskimos, who say the way to the moon's house lies over a bridge which consists of a live bearded seal.

guilty of infanticide do not reach the mountain; with branches of trees tied to their legs they hover round the scene of their crimes. Melancholy sounds heard in still summer evenings, which Whites ignorantly ascribe to screams of goat-suckers, are the moanings of these unhappy murderers.

The Piegan believe that the souls of the good are separated from the souls of the evil. The good dwell in a land lighted by the sun, whereas the evil wander into a darkness from which there is no return; and the degree of darkness is proportionate to the weight of their crimes.

The Gros Ventre spirit world, a barren region in the north where shades whistle and speak and whence they sometimes come forth to hold intercourse with the living, offers no reward for virtue, no punishment for vice. The souls of northern Shoshones who have died by violence travel in a different direction from that taken by the souls of those who have died a natural death. The latter go to the land of Wolf and Coyote. After death the soul rises to Wolf's house, where Wolf washes and revives it. Spirits of Indians are darker than those of White men and are very small. While rising they resemble clouds. Halfway up they are met by a spirit descending on horseback, who escorts them to their future abode. White men probably go to a different country.

Two roads lead from the Hopi grave to the region below. One, the straight way, joins the path of the sun into the underworld. A branch trail debouches from this straight way and goes past fires to a lake or large body of water. At the fork of the road sits a *tokanaka*; when the breath-body arrives here, this chief looks at it, and, if satisfied, says: "You are very good, go on." The breath-body then passes along the straight way to the far west, to the early Sipapu, the underworld whence it came, the home of Muiyiuwi. When an evil breath-body comes to the fork in the road, the chief says, "You are bad," and conducts it along the crooked path to the first fire-pit. A second *tokonaka*, who sits here, throws the bad breath-body into the fire. After a time it emerges purified; for it was not wholly bad. The chief then says, "You are good now," and carries it back to the first chief, who accepts the breath-body and sends it along the straight road to the west. If the soul on emerging from the first fire is not sufficiently purified, it is cast into the second fire-pit. If it emerges from the latter thoroughly purified, in the opinion of the judge, it is immediately transformed into a *ho-ho-ya-üh*, a prayer beetle. All the beetles in the valleys or among the mesas were once evil Hopis. If after coming out of the second fire-pit the breath-body is still considered evil by the chief, he takes it to a third fire. If no evil remains in it when it emerges from this pit, it is metamorphosed into an ant. If the breath-body is not purified by these three fires and there is still evil in it, the chief takes it to the fourth fire and again casts it into the flames, where it is utterly consumed, the only residue being soot on the sides of the pit.

Zuñi souls go four days after death to Katcina Village. There is some doubt whether uninitiated or women are admitted to this land of the dead. In several folk-tales, however, souls of women join the souls of their husbands. Medicinemen, at least those who possess the ultimate power of "calling the bear," join the beast priests at Cipapolima, in the east. This is probably the Keresan Shipap, or Sipapu, the place of emergence of the tribe and the abode of the dead. Only those who have committed incest are punished after death. Sia souls of the wicked cannot enter the lower world, whither souls of the good go, but are destroyed in fire. Pimas describe the next world as a place of continual rejoicing. There is neither reward nor punishment for conduct in this world. Jicarilla Apaches who were not witches go to an underworld where they are happy amid all comforts. Those who have been witches go to another portion of the underworld, separated by a partition from the land of the happy. Here are poisonous and inedible plants, and dangerous animals. Lizards are the only food for such souls. Each night they listen to the merriment of happy souls beyond the wall, and with their stone knives dig a passage-way under it. They almost succeed in completing the passage-way; but each morning the rock which they have penetrated closes and again presents a solid front. Maricopas recognize no distinction of lot in the next world for good and bad. The only souls not welcome to ghostland are those whose bodies have been buried and not cremated. They smell bad, are not welcome, and must live on the north side of the land of the dead. Here they wander, carry their coffins on their heads, and search for a shady spot wherein to repose. When tired of carrying their coffins, they place them on the ground and sit on them. Twins and the deformed, however, do not go to ghostland after death, but hover near their villages until reborn.

Among Mohaves the shadow soul of a man whose chin has not been tattooed will not go to the land of the dead but will enter a rat-hole.

Northeastern Yavapais appear to attach no importance to the life of the soul after death. The location of the country to which it goes is known only to shamans. In the western Yavapai land of the dead, souls are happy and spend the time dancing. Dead relatives greet the newcomer. The soul of an untattooed woman may not enter there; its destination is unknown.

Maidu souls separate from one another at the end of the Milky Way. The good turn to the left and pursue an easy and comfortable road which leads to the land above, a flowerland where Wonomi, the Creator, lives. He feeds the souls from a small basket filled with precious foods which satisfy every desire. Evil souls go by a dark and dismal route to an unknown bad place. Some reach heaven; but their abode is not as pleasant and agreeable a valley as the land in which good souls reside.

The Achomawi soul goes over the Milky Way to the underworld, where life is delightful. The spirit may return to earth and appear to men in dreams. It leaves the body immediately before death, then stands for a while and watches the people. The soul of a good Karok goes to the "happy western land," beyond the great ocean.

Souls of bad Pomos return to earth and enter coyotes. Some, however, say they fall off a bridge which all must traverse, or are hooked off by a raging beast at the farther end; only the good make a safe crossing. The soul of a Mattole bad man goes into a grizzly bear, cousin-german of sin and wickedness.

When a Tlelding dies, a little bird flies away with his soul to spiritland. If he was a bad man, a hawk catches the bird and devours it, soul and feathers; if he led an upright life, the bird which carries his soul reaches spiritland.

Some Gilyak souls are transformed into birds and gnats, and finally into ashes. Those who die a violent death go to a sky region called Tlo. The Koryak describe a lower world which houses the dead, the *kalan*, and other inhabitants who live apart from the *kalan*. Yakut souls live much the same kind of life as do men on earth, and communicate with the living through the mediation of shamans. Tradition records the killing of annoying young men by the "ancient people," that is, the dead.

Tungus souls in *bun i*, the soul world, need and desire food, clothing, and many other things. Perhaps they need them even more than do the living, for the country which they inhabit is inhospitable and cold. Souls worry about the people left behind in this world. Beyond *bun i* is a place from which souls never return. Souls of very bad people go to this realm. One who has lived a very bad life may be refused admission; in that event it becomes an errant *s irkul*. Or it may be left in *bun i* to expiate its sins. It may be killed or incarnated in an animal of low standing—for example, a mule or an insect. The souls of people of good conduct may be admitted to *uyiski*, where there are some "spirits' masters," instead of to *bun i*. Rich people also are admitted to the lower world.

In the Santal afterworld, it seems, men and women have a hard fate that is independent of the kind of life led on earth, with the exception that men who have learned to chew tobacco are allowed some respite from the otherwise unremitting toil. Chando bonga makes them work very hard. Women must pound the fruit of the castor oil plant with a pestle; from its seeds he makes human beings. They work throughout the entire day, though women who have young children get a little respite to suckle their babies. Because the souls of men are allowed time off to chew tobacco, the Santal learn to chew; for in the next world they will not be allowed to stop working in order to smoke. Frogs guard the water and drive away all who come to drink; hence drinking vessels are buried with the corpse so that the soul will be able to run quickly to the water, fill the vessels, and escape with them. A man who during his lifetime has planted a pipal tree will be compelled in the next world to pick up the leaves which have fallen into the water and are spoiling it.[10] Those who have committed certain sins are immersed in dung in a nether world. Those who were married more than once will be reunited to their first spouses, irrespective of subsequent marriages.

In the Naga afterworld men die six times, women five times, then turn into clouds. A man killed by a Naga is his slave in the next world. The soul of an Angami Naga who has lived according to tribal standards becomes a star. The Tanghul, a division of the Manipur Nagas, say the ghost goes to heaven by a path over the crest of Sirohifurar. By the gates of heaven flits a woodpecker, symbol of restless vigilance. Thin ghosts cannot force their way in. It is incumbent upon the living, therefore, to provide a buffalo for the funeral feast, that its mighty soul may open the massive gates. Close to the gates of heaven a crowd of ghosts whose living kin are too poor or too stingy to sacrifice a buffalo await the arrival of the ghost of a rich man. The Deity judges them. Another account states that the Deity of the spirit world sits inside the door and observes approaching spirits. After judging them he sentences thieves to the left-hand road where there are worms and everything dreadful. Good

10. Cecil H. Bompas, *Folklore of the Santal Parganas*, 410–411 (London, Nutt, 1909).

spirits go by the right-hand road, which is "clean." Subsequently good and bad spirits meet near the banks of a river.

The Nagas at Jessami say there is a heaven above for the good and a region below for the wicked. A Mao Naga soul must strive in combat with the Deity—take the kingdom of heaven by violence. If the ghost wounds the Deity or scores a hit, he fares well; if he fails in this endeavour, he is enslaved for ever. Another Deity sorts out the dead according to merit and the manner of death. Heaven has many mansions. In one compartment are herded together those who have died in battle; in another, those who in life have split their ears; in another, women who have died in childbirth.

Maram Nagas say heaven lies to the west, and is divided into many compartments. Whether any of its inhabitants are ear-marked by fate we are not told. Quoireng Naga ghosts go to a heaven in the northeast.

Western Rengma Naga souls find the realm of the dead an exact replica of this world. Men marry the wives whom they had on earth, and here are reborn to them their same earthly children. "Those who were poor here are poor there, and those who gave Feasts of Merit here give them again in the world below. Those who were unmarried here remain so there. Thieves and wicked men remember their sins and are unhappy, and the good live in joy." Eastern Rengma Nagas believe the dead return to the ancestral home of the tribe, though their fate is now forgotten.

In Athikhi, the land of the dead of the Lakher of Assam, the spirit finally dies; the soul of a chief becomes a heat mist, and the soul of a poor man becomes a worm. The heat mist rises to heaven and vanishes; the worm is eaten by a chicken, and its existence is terminated. Thus in that afterworld the rich remain rich, and the poor continue poor. To attain the most pleasant abode, which they call Peira, is difficult. To enter it one must kill, if a man, a certain wild animal, in a list which includes elephants, tigers, bears, and rhinoceroses.

Kabui souls go to an underground world where they are met by ancestors who introduce them to their new habitation. Life in this underground world is an exact duplicate of life on earth; those rich on earth are rich there, and the poor remain poor. Heaven is a replica in minutest details of the mundane world. Most Kabui souls live on after death much as before, though some enter an animal. Cattle owned in life are the source of riches to the ghost. Most Kabui souls go to a designated hill, but the spirits of those killed accidentally go nowhere. Thieves are troubled in the land of the dead, presumably by their consciences. The Manipur Kabui soul goes to an underground world where it meets its ancestors, who acquaint it with its new mode of life. A man's murderer becomes his slave in the next world. Souls of the good Marring go above, souls of the bad to a place within the earth. Those who have died in some extraordinary manner flit about between heaven and earth in aerial regions. The Khond describe a god of judgment who dwells on a high rock surrounded by a black river. Up this rock souls of the dead climb with much effort and await his decision. The good live in the sun or are reborn in the tribe. Priests reveal the identity of the person reincarnated in the newborn child. Misfortune awaits the wicked, who are reborn as diseased persons. The Oraon have no heaven. Unfortunate people become unhappy ghosts, and have nowhere to lay their heads. The Lushai ghost is reborn as a hornet, and later assumes the form of water. If this water, as dew, falls on a man, it is reborn as his child. Good Golo souls go to heaven; bad souls are burned by Mah, whom God employs for this purpose.

The Lhota soul goes to an underground heaven where everything is exactly as on earth. Families are reunited, and the life on earth is relived. Death comes here, too, and then the soul goes to a second heaven, under the first one. It again dies. Some souls of the thrice-dead return to earth as butterflies or house-flies; some remain dead. Toda souls pass over a bridge of thread stretched across a river. Those who have led wicked lives fall into the river and are bitten by leeches. They must spend among dwellers in swamps a probationary period which varies with the magnitude of their offences. Spirits of the good go directly to heaven. Selfish, jealous, grudging people, and those who have committed offences against the sacred dairy, are most likely to fall from the bridge. Eventually all spirits reach heaven. These concepts, like similar ones in southeastern Asia and Oceania, suggest Iranian influence.

In Indonesia there is generally punishment or reward after death for the life lived on earth. The soul of a murdered Dyak cannot enter the portion of heaven known as Kong-kong, but remains in another region where it spends the time fighting and killing. Women who have died of disease go to Kong-kong; those who have died in childbirth are consigned to the region to which the souls of murdered men go. Long Ghat women tattooed with conventional designs on hands, feet, and thighs will, after death, bathe in the heavenly river Teland Julan, and gather the pearls which lie on its bed. Souls of those only partially tattooed must remain on the bank and watch their more fortunate tribal sisters reap a rich harvest. Souls of women not tattooed on any part of the body may not approach the banks of this treasure-stream. Similar beliefs are found among the Kenyan, the Klemantan, and the Batang Kayan. Souls of the Dusun of British North Borneo live on Mt. Kinabalu, a mountain 13,600 feet high. Their further fate is not detailed. Kayan souls may inhabit beasts or birds. Their afterworld punishes the bad and rewards the good. The good are men who have taken heads or have died on the battlefield, and women who have died in childbirth. These go to Bawang Daha, "Lake of Blood."

The soul of a native Dutch Bornean must cross or go round a hill of fire. Souls of the good are cunning and escape the flames; souls of the bad blunder over the hill and are horribly burned. They recover from the injury, however, and are not destroyed. The place to which the soul of an Iban, or a Dyak (of Sarawak), goes depends upon the manner of death. Those who die a natural death go to the ordinary abode of the dead; those who die in fine weather have an easy journey. The soul of one who dies in wet weather passes through a place of perpetual rain. Children who die before they are weaned go to a different place from that of adults.

For each Iban a house is prepared in the nether world. Those who die well, that is, in their beds, go to Mandai. Those who are killed in battle go to a country of perpetual warfare where there is no rest from alarms, sharpening of weapons, and strife. Suicides who have taken juba poison live apart from others; their habitation is thickly covered with juba climbers; they live a lonely, mournful life; their hair is dishevelled and they bite their finger-nails. Those who drown as a result of the capsizing of a boat dwell by the side of a waterfall. Those killed by a fall from trees are perpetually constructing a climbing rope. Those who die of an epidemic are houseless, sheltered only by a leaf hut, and are outcasts in the land of the dead. The Achehnese say that, if a cock approaches a person and gives vent to a peculiarly shrill cry, it is because the bird hears the dead screaming in their graves while they suffer castigation at the hands of the angels. This reminds the individual of the punishments in store for him and he angrily chases the cock away. In Bali a woman who dies without children must carry a gigantic worm sucking at her useless breasts.

The afterworld of the Semang of Mabakka, Malacca, offers no distinction of fate for the good and the evil. Souls of Malanus go to another world where, after a long life, they again die and later live as worms or caterpillars in the forest. The belief appears to have no ethical flavour. The Semang soul must cross a flimsy rope bridge which spans a boiling sea. At the farther end is a horrible monster, the sight of which so frightens the timid and wicked that they fall from the bridge. They swim in agony in the boiling waters until a god graciously lowers his great toe to enable them to climb out. This motive, presumably of ultimate Iranian origin, is found also in Polynesia.

The Sakhai soul leaves the body by the whorl of hair at the back of the head, passes to the west, and attempts to enter heaven through a gate. It cannot enter here, and goes around another way, in the course of which it must cross a bridge over a cauldron of hot water. Yenang takes the souls out of this cauldron and burns them to ashes, then weighs the ashes. If they are light, the soul passes into heaven; if they are heavy, the souls must be burned again, until light enough to enter heaven. This concept is strikingly like Hopi belief.

The souls of the Menik Kaien or Kintak Bong, Negritos of the Malay peninsula, leave the body through the big toe and go to the edge of the sea, where the sun descends. Seven days later the souls of the good are escorted to an island, Belet, to which they cross by means of a green switchbacked bridge, Balan Bacham, which spans the sea. Souls of the good eventually enter the pleasant land Belet, where they pluck flowers, rice, and fruits. Souls of the bad inhabit another place, in view of the abode of the good. They call to the spirits in Belet to help them reach the wonderful Mapik tree, which bears luxuriant flowers and food, but these good spirits take no notice of them. Negritos of Grik profess to be ignorant of the fate in store for the soul. They do not know whether it is happy or unhappy; there is, it appears, no reward for the good, no punishment for the wicked. The Blandas and Besisi, of the Malay peninsula, say that souls of the good, or wise, go to the Island of Fruit Trees, which, apparently, they identify with the moon. It is reached over a fallen tree-trunk that serves as a bridge. Souls of the wicked fall from it into a lake or boiling cauldron. This misfortune, however, overtakes only those who are frightened by the big dog that sits at the parting of the ways.

The Mantra soul must cross a bridge as narrow as the cutting edge of a knife, and at the end of it leap over a kettle of boiling water. If it makes the leap successfully, it lands in a paradise, an island of fruits, where the soul eats the shadows of fruits. If, weighed down with its sins, it fails to make the leap successfully, it falls into the kettle and there boils and stews until its sins have fallen from it. From time to time the god lifts the soul out of the kettle and inspects every side of it to ascertain whether it has been purified. If he finds it not wholly clean, he drops it back into the seething water. No blemished soul may enter paradise. The Kubu of Sumatra have the same belief.

The social status of souls of the Katchin of Burma is a duplication of their status on earth, with the exception that souls of thieves, liars, adulterers, murderers, and other vile sinners are thrown into a cauldron of boiling water. The concept of hell does not occur in their mythology and appears to have been introduced comparatively recently, probably by the Shan. The Chin believe that the bad go to dark caverns in which they become animals like those whose entrails they there eat. The village of the dead is divided into two worlds, one for the happy, and one for wretches who die unavenged. They must bide their time till their murder is wiped out in blood; otherwise the slain becomes the slave of the slayer.

In many parts of Oceania rewards in the next world depend upon the manner of death, the wealth expended upon funeral rites, or the tribal status of the deceased. In Manuea, Ellice Islands, good souls go to a land of brightness and clear water in the heavens, bad souls to a land of mud and darkness. The good are those whose friends have given a grand funeral feast; the bad are those whose stingy friends have provided nothing at all. (In Nias "bad" denotes those who have no sons to conduct funeral rites, and also adulterers, thieves, and murderers.)

The Samoan soul sometimes returns to earth as a moth. The home of the dead is near the island of Savaii; the souls of inhabitants of other islands pass there by sea on their way to the underworld. The land of the dead, under the sea, is a lovely place which bears rich fruits and beautiful flowers. Salefee, whither commoners go, is under the earth; it is the home of the family of the cuttlefish god, and a pleasant abode. A soul journeying to the land of the dead may have an opportunity to turn back and re-enter the body. If it sticks to a coconut on the western extremity of the island from which it leaped into the sea, it can return. Such has been the experience of a man who recovers from illness. As mentioned, souls of common people go to Po, or Salefee, under the earth; and, as in Tonga, souls of chiefs go to Bulotu, home of the gods. In the Marquesas upper-class souls go to a celestial island which abounds with every delightful thing; lower-class souls go to Po, beneath the earth, a less desirable abode of the gods. The soul may travel to the next world as a dragon-fly. In Mangaia and Rarotonga (Hervey Islands) souls of men slain in battle go to paradise. Other souls dwell beneath, in Po, where they are occasionally covered with excrement dropped from the region above by the souls of the blessed. In the Society Islands souls of chiefs and important persons, that is, those who could afford an expensive funeral ceremony, go to Rohutu-noa-noa, one of the homes of the gods. Other souls go to Po, in this region a very tolerable place. In Ponape the fate of the soul in the next world is not influenced by conduct on earth, except as regards dancing. A good dancer passes over the bridge which leads into the next world; a poor one is dragged away to a place of woe. Good dancing is the only guarantee of a life of bliss in the hereafter. Good Niue souls go to Aho-hololoa, of Aho-noa; the bad, to Po. The latter, which is in the direction of sunset, toward the original home of the ancestors in the west, is a land of darkness or night. There is a second heaven above, Motu-a-Hina. Savage Island souls go to Maui, a subterranean abode. Their paradise is Sina, a bright land in the sky.

In New Zealand souls sometimes return to earth as butterflies. They reside beneath the earth in Reinga, where there are neither blessings for the good nor punishments for the wicked. They are not immortal; eventually they die and are non-existent. Souls spy upon surviving kin to ascertain whether they observe the taboos. Spirits of warriors and other great men watch especially over the fortunes of the tribe. In time of war they attend the army, direct its movements, and give advice or warning to living kinsmen. During the conflict they hover over the combatants and instil courage into fighting kinsmen. There seem to have been vague concepts that chiefs go to heaven after death, and people of inferior rank to an underworld, Po, Night.

Tahitians describe the next world as a beautiful place, an elysium in which the air is salubrious and plants and shrubs are abundant, highly fragrant, and in perpetual bloom. Areois, the nobility, and others of high estate follow unceasingly amusements and pursuits to which they were accustomed on earth. Food is abundant and is indulged in freely. Destiny has no relation to moral character or conduct; the same fate in the next world awaits kind, generous, peaceful men, and the cruel, parsimonious, and quarrelsome. Chiefs go to a god high in the mountains; others, to Po, a land of obscurity. Tonga souls go to Bulotu, where their status depends not upon their conduct in this life but upon their social rank. Lower-class souls dissolve with the body and their sentient existence terminates. The island to which upper-class souls go, like that of Tahitians, contains every useful and ornamental plant; these are perfect and perpetually bear rich fruits and beautiful flowers. The atmosphere is pervaded with delightful fragrance; when fruits or flowers are plucked, others immediately take their places. When a hog or a bird is killed, another living hog or bird is forthwith substituted. The land of the dead is an island northwest of Tonga. Hawaiians say the dead dwell in an underworld where they dance the *hula olapa* (not the modern *hula hula*), feast on shadowy food, and lead a drowsy existence. In the Tuamotus there is no assignment of realms to souls of good and evil. Commoners go to Havaiki-of-twilight-gloom and nobles to Havaiki-the-source, the latter an illuminated region.

In Yap there is no distinction of fate for souls. On Merir, West Caroline Islands, when the ghost of an evil man arrives in the land of the dead, Ruko, god of the sea and of this ghostly underworld, allows the other ghosts to hunt it as though it were a wild beast and to kill it. We are not told what constitutes an evil man.

The abode of bliss of the Gilbert Islanders is not attained by souls of the impure, dishonest, or cowardly. These are cast out into a place of everlasting nightmare, impaled on stakes, or thrown down to writhe eternally in the company of lost souls. Marshall Islanders, however, provide no punishment in the next world for sins committed in this one. In the Marianne Islands those who die a natural death go to paradise to enjoy the trees and fruits which grow there in great abundance. The Philippine Tinguian religion contains no punishment or reward in the next world. Bagobo souls continue in the Land of the Dead the kind of existence which they led on earth. After death the Ainu soul appears before the tribunal of God. The Creator is the judge of all men; the goddess of fire is the chief witness for or against them. Those accounted worthy go to a happy land above, the land of the gods. The wicked go to a wet underground place where they will be for ever unhappy and perhaps frozen in a block of ice. Whether the punishment will be literally fire, ice, or swamp, the Ainus are not sure.

Natives of southeastern Australia say that spirits of the dead go westward toward the setting sun. When they saw White men coming over the sea from that quarter, they thought them reincarnated deceased natives. Andrew Lang assures us that the Australian "Byamee is now (like the Fijian Ndegei) 'fixed and frozen to permanence' on his crystal rock in the land of rest," and that "the souls of those who keep his law go to him, the wicked go to Eleaübah Wundah, the native Inferno." This concept reflects Christian influence. Before contact with Europeans, Australians and Tasmanians promised no rewards or punishments after death. From several Australian tribes has been reported belief in reward of the good and punishment of the bad in the next world; but the beliefs are so similar to the Christian concept that one must infer European influence. The concept of reward of the good and punishment of the evil in the next world has not been reported from Australian or Tasmanian tribes which have not previously been within the sphere of European influence.

When a Fijian dies, his spirit enters a rock on the road from Savusavu Bay to Labasa and travels seventy or eighty miles west of the island. When the soul arrives at its destination, it throws reed spears at a *balawa* tree until a spear strikes the tree. The soul may then rest. A man who has not killed a human being is condemned to beat with his bloodless club a heap of muck—for a Fijian the worst of punishments. Hard is the fate of a man in the next world if he did not while on earth help some other to paradise by a blow on the head. The strength and health of the soul in the next world are determined by the constitution of the body at the time of death. Hence a timely voluntary death guarantees one against a decrepit or crippled soul life in the next world. In the Eastern Islands of the Torres Straits those who neglect deceased kinsfolk are visited with strong winds, sent by angered ghosts, which destroy their gardens and houses.

A ghost shows resentment if its living children are neglected or wronged, or if land or chattels of the deceased are taken by those who have no just claim to them. Such beliefs, if efficacious, should deter wrongdoers and keep the survivors in the paths of righteousness which lead to earthly prosperity and peace of mind.

Papuans speak of a tree, invisible to mortal eye, in the Astrolabe Range, in and around which dwell in happiness those who have lived good lives on earth. Before the wicked can reach this tree, they must pass through sickness, pain, and trouble, but eventually they are gathered beneath its branches. Natives know this account is true, for those they loved and lost have returned and told them of the tree and its inhabitants. There is a spirit world for souls of women and children; another for the spirits of men who failed in life, that is, who displayed no marked prowess in chase or war; another for souls of murderers; another for souls of victims of crocodiles. Souls of Ipi men who die in battle go directly to the sky and dwell with Hiovaki, god of war. Among Koriki only souls of brave warriors and great hunters of wild boars enter Mapua, which is ruled by the god Kaina.

In most portions of Papua the spirit of a murderer is an outcast from the abodes of other spirits. It dwells in a bog-like swamp from which it continually attempts to escape, and where it is sucked down until only the top of its head is visible. By extraordinary effort it struggles upward, but when about to step out of the bog is again sucked down. Arms, hands, and fingers grow long and gnarled like the roots of the mangrove tree. The spirit, in a vain attempt to escape, flings them over the surface of the swamp. Its cries and moans sound like the whining of the wind. Those who wish to assist it are afraid to approach. It rises and sinks for ever, its eyes bulging under the agonizing struggle. On the Wanigela River the soul joins its forefathers in an underground world where it lives a life of ease. New Guinea Monumbo souls go to a place where they dwell without work or suffering and which they can quit when they will. Occupations enjoyed on earth are continued after death without interruption. Sometimes souls play shabby tricks on the living; sometimes they help them in many ways, particularly in war and chase. Tunlec ghosts can return, roam about, and bring good or evil to the living, especially friends and kin. If the living are on good terms with souls of the departed and other spirits, these powerful beings bring good luck in trade and voyages. The Kiwai assign the same fate in the next world to good and bad alike; all go the same road to the same place. Life there, though similar to life on earth, is an easier existence. The Bukana and Jabim expect neither reward nor punishment in the next world. Spirits of southern Massim dead live in a land in which there is plenty to eat. No sickness or evil assails them. Those wealthy in this world are wealthy in the next world; the poor are poor. Each community has its local habitation in that world as in this one. The spirits can join fighting expeditions, as they have done on earth, but one who is killed there is destroyed for ever. Death may visit any or all in that spiritland, and terminate existence. Life in the other world is a faint shadow of life in this world.

Northern Massim souls go to Tuma, a small island about ten miles northwest of the Trobriands. There the spirits of the dead descend into an underworld. A path leads them to the abode of shades, presided over by Topileta, who first sent men into the upper world, and who bids the shades take with them their totem animals. All souls come at last to Topileta and share alike in the life of the underworld, whether they have been good or bad, strong or weak, on earth. Chiefs retain their worldly authority; common people remain their subjects.

Among the Baining of New Guinea, there is no distinction of fate for the good and the evil. The mightiest and the richest go to the shadow realm where the weak and the poor dwell. The old become young, and the young become infants. There they live a happy life for ever. In Lesu the ghost emerges from the mouth of the dying individual, and continues to live in some vague unknown manner. There are no rewards or punishments in the afterlife. The magic spells suggest that there may have been in the past a more coherent theory of the afterlife which has since been lost. "In the war and fishing magic particularly there are invocations to the ghosts of the dead clan relatives to assist in fishing and in weakening the enemy. As if to reward or pay back the same ghosts after a fishing expedition, some taro and fish are left in the *liga* for them. The smallness of the quantity left makes the act an obviously symbolic one. From the magic it would therefore seem that the Lesu man believes that the ghosts of his clan members live on indefinitely, and are able and willing to assist him if properly invoked. Whether this is a remnant of an ancient ancestor cult cannot be determined from the present evidence. Mortuary rites, which would be expected to throw some light on this problem, give no help. For, today at least, the mortuary rites have no effect on the dead man, his ghost, his double, or anything connected with him." These rites give prestige to the survivors who conduct them.

In the Gazelle Peninsula, New Britain, at the entrance to the happy isles each ghost is asked three questions: "Who are you? Where do you come from? How much shell money did you leave behind you?" If he left much money, he is free to enter the realm of bliss, where he will pass the time with other happy souls, smoking, eating, and enjoying other sensuous delights. If he left little or no money, he is banished from the earthly paradise and sent home to roam like a wild beast in the forest and to batten on leaves and filth. With bitter sighs and groans he prowls about the villages at night and seeks to avenge himself by frightening the living. To stay his hunger and appease his wrath, kin or friends sometimes supply him with food. If someone takes pity on him, gives a feast in his honour, and distributes shell money to the guests, the ghost may return to the islands of the blest. Hence the poor do well to leave many friends, and especially friends of means.

In the Solomon Islands distinction is made between powerful ghosts and weak ghosts, those who have, and those who do not have, *mana*. The help of the former is sought, and their wrath is deprecated; from the latter nothing is expected, and no condescension is due them. The ghost of a distinguished man retains in greater activity and with stronger force the powers which he possessed in life; his ghost, therefore, is powerful; while he is remembered, his aid is sought and he is worshipped. Ghosts of the insignificant remain insignificant; after, as before, death, they are nobodies. Ghosts of common people turn into red ants and are food for ghosts which possess *mana*. A man admonishes an indolent son: "If you do not bestir yourself and accumulate property, you will be merely a red ant in the next world."

At Bougainville Straits, in the western Solomon Islands, there is neither reward for the good nor punishment for the bad, save in so far as future life prolongs the good or evil of this life. The dead are feeble counterparts of the living; ghost life is a continuation of physical life and differs from the latter only in intensity. Death, therefore, merely ushers the soul into another phase of continuous existence, a portion of which is spent in this world, the remainder in the next world. The dead work in gardens, dance, marry, and have children. They visit the abodes of the dead in other islands, and sometimes marry and settle in an island other than their first place of abode. Over each village is a chief, a man who had been a chief while on earth. In many respects, however, the dead do not profit from earthly experience: life is begun anew. A grown man may learn from an infant who had died previously and had acquired more experience than he in the world of shades—how to kill a turtle in spirit-land, for example; for in that world the predeceased infant is senior to the man who on earth had been his senior and had outlived the child.

In Lau, Solomon Islands, souls of the dead go to Ramos Island, by canoe, and thence to the island Momulu. Here the presiding ghost examines arriving souls to ascertain whether they are tattooed. Tattooed souls are placed on a platform; those not tattooed must go on all fours, like pigs. The presiding ghost inquires whether they met death through sickness or through evil magic. They are disposed of according to their answers. The Kwara 'Ae, of Lau, say the home of their dead is at Ramos

Island, to which place the souls swim. Ghosts which cannot swim haunt the local beaches.

In Savo, spirits of the dead vanish in the crater of a volcano. Santa Cruz souls foregather at Natepapa, then go to the volcano Tamani, where, after renewal by fire, they reside. In Malekula the dead are set adrift in canoes with provisions; their souls go to a crater in Ambrum. In many Melanesian islands spirits of the dead go to a volcano. On Lepers Island a shark awaits ghosts on their way to Benoi, land of shades, and bites off the noses of those who flouted custom and did not kill pigs at the funeral celebration. At Bogotu, Ysabel, souls pass over a bridge consisting of a narrow tree-trunk. There Balafuguis, the Master-Spirit, examines their hands to ascertain whether they display the conventional mark of the frigate bird which admits them to his company. If the mark is not there, he hurls them from the bridge into the gulf beneath, where they perish. On Duke of York Island, northern Melanesia, the rich are rich in the next world, and the poor are poor. Ghosts of miserly people are punished by being knocked against projecting roots of chestnut trees, and punishment is meted out to those who have infringed social etiquette. Otherwise, belief in life after death has no ethical implication. In New Ireland, there is no belief in future reward or punishment. In the Torres Straits, Banks Islands, and the northwest islands of the New Hebrides, the underworld is called Panoi. In the New Hebrides and Banks Islands a man's fate in the next world depends to some extent upon his rank and liberality in the *sukwe* society. In the Banks Islands one who has killed another without cause or by charm, and thieves, liars, and adulterers, are not admitted into the shadowless Hades in which there are flowers and the empty semblance of social life. Should the ghost of a murderer attempt entrance, the ghost of the victim confronts it and drives it away. Souls of the wicked go to a place where they drag out a miserable existence; they quarrel, and are restless, homeless, pitiable, malignant; they wander back to earth, eat the foulest food; their breath is noisome. Out of spite at the happier fate of mortals they eat men's souls; they haunt the graves and woods for this purpose. According to another version, wicked souls are dragged to their doom and cast into a great pit, a Sea of Filth, where they lie without power to move hand or foot. At the destruction of the world they will die. Souls of those who have hanged themselves and of women who have died in childbirth cannot enter heaven. Souls of those killed in battle are carried by the war god Rasim to his special heaven, where they may continue to fight. At the gate of heaven two rocks which clash and rebound prevent the souls of the wicked from entering. The god Olaitin enables souls of the good to enter between these two rocks without being crushed.[11] In the haven of the good, souls live in peace, harmony, and heavenly contentment. Souls of chiefs and noblemen maintain in the next world the dignified superiority which they enjoyed on earth. Those who have distinguished themselves in life by statecraft or by warlike exploits become after death guardians of their respective clans.

The New Hebrides soul passes through six stages of existence. At the gate of Hades, at the western end of the island, it meets Seritan, the cannibal executioner, and his assistants. If it cannot answer the questions asked of it, an assistant cuts out its tongue, cracks open its head, and twists it back. Some souls are allowed to pass unmolested. In Malekula the soul has three deaths. In the first place of postmortem abode the soul regulates the supply of pigs for the people on earth and feeds on the ghosts of these pigs. Souls of Bowditch Island kings and priests dwell on the moon. Common people go to an outer region where there are many delights, including much dancing and merrymaking. From this land their ancestors went to the land of the White people, where they were reincarnated as Whites. In the Trobriand Islands the *baloma*, the main form of a man's spirit, goes to Tuma, a small island ten miles to the northwest. The *kosi*, another form of the spirit, leads a precarious existence near the usual haunts of the dead man. In the spirit world the ghost dies again. Meanwhile the *baloma* keeps in touch with the world of the living. He visits it and is visited, mainly in dreams. On Tuma, however, no exact abode of the ghost is known. When a Bwaidoga man dies and has been buried, a shark carries his soul to Nuatutu. The parrot-fish then carries the soul to Fatavi, whence the soul makes its way to Wafolo, where it will reside. (These are actual localities.) In Futuma (Home Island) there was differential existence in the next world for good and bad, a happy and an unhappy life, respectively. In the happy land those who found themselves growing old bathed in Lake Vaiola, and thus renewed their youth.

African Negro concepts represent the next world as a continuation of the condition and status enjoyed or suffered in this world. In many areas Mohammedan influence has introduced a paradise in which some enjoy great bliss. Thus some Dahomeans anticipate a delicious sojourn

11. For similar concepts in Iran, see pages 256–259.

where the good live in perpetual prosperity, amid abundant food and alcohol, and women as numerous as they are beautiful. The bad inhabit a land of suffering in which they endure hunger, thirst, cold, blows, and other evils. Between the elect and the unfortunate is an intermediate state, a purgatory, designed for those who deserve neither paradise nor hell. Skertchly speaks of a Dahomean belief in a record kept by Man, the Supreme Being, of good and bad deeds, recorded on two ends of a stick—another suggestion of Mohammedan influence. If at death the good preponderates, the soul is allowed to join Man in Kutomen, or Deadland. If bad deeds outweigh the good, the soul is utterly destroyed. In the earlier aboriginal concept, rewards and punishments are meted out only in this world. If a man can escape punishment in this world, his spirit is released from all consequences of wrongdoing. His social status at death will be his social status for all eternity. Earthly kings are kings in spiritland; the slave on earth is a slave hereafter. Thus the next world is a duplication of this world. Ghosts take an intimate interest in the affairs of surviving kin. "This belief is the one great stumbling-block against the abolition of the human sacrifices at the Customs. The suppression of these would be looked upon by the popular eye as a direct insult to the protecting spirits of the country, and a general revolt would be the inevitable consequence." Since Skertchly wrote, human sacrifices have been suppressed by the French, but his inference is supported by Baudin, who says: "These ideas and beliefs with regard to the future life are the real cause of the human sacrifices which every year imbrue in blood these unfortunate countries of the blacks, as well as the brigandage and continual wars necessary to procure the victims. At the death of the king and chiefs, victims are immolated beside the grave, and their blood gushes forth on the coffin; the women and slaves are massacred that they may accompany the dead, to serve them in the other world. From time to time they send them other women, new servants, and often even messengers to acquaint them with what takes place on the earth. One day the king of Dahomey had thus dispatched several couriers to his predecessors, when he remembered some insignificant detail of his commissions that had escaped his mind. A poor old woman was passing, carrying on her head a pitcher of water. The king called her and gave her his message. The poor wretch, trembling all over, begged and implored for mercy. 'I have done nothing wrong,' she said. 'I know that,' replied the king, 'but I am sending you to my father, go at once.' Resistance was in vain. The poor creature knelt down, drank half a bottle of brandy, and the Mahu cut off her head." Egba and Yoruba dead return to the land of the living; hence survivors frequently take offerings to the graves, consult the departed in affairs of importance, and implore their protection. In Ashanti and on the Gold Coast the ghost continues in ghostland the existence which the man led in this world. The ghost lives in a ghost house and uses the ghosts of the implements placed at his disposal at the grave. Ghostland contains ghost mountains, ghost forests, and ghost rivers. Trees which die in the earthly forest go to join the ranks of the shadow forest in Deadland. Kings, caboceers, and members of the higher class dwell with the Deity and enjoy eternal continuance of their status and luxury on earth. This belief encourages them to kill at the funeral customs a certain number of both sexes to accompany the deceased, announce his distinction, and minister to his pleasures. Spirits of the lower class live in houses, in a state of torpid indolence, a recompense for the drudgery of their lives which Ellis considers "truly congenial to the feelings of the Negro." Men of superior wisdom and experience are endowed with foresight after death, and are appointed to observe and advise those who acknowledge the fetish. "Those whose enormities nullify the mediation of the funeral custom, or whom neglect or circumstances might have deprived of it, are doomed, in the imagination of others, to haunt the gloom of the forest, stealing occasionally to their former abodes in rare but lingering visits. Those who have neglected the custom, or funeral rites of their family, are thought to be accursed and troubled by their spirits." Eastern Ewe tribes locate Deadland to the west, across the river Volta. Natives along the Gold Coast place it to the east of that river; the western Ewe, who live near that stream, locate Deadland in the north. There each man has the position, powers, avocations, and tastes which he enjoyed in this world. He carries with him his bodily imperfections: the hunchback in this world is a ghost hunchback in Deadland. Hence, when a deaf man dies, his kin do not make the usual appeals to the ghost not to desert them, for the ghost is deaf and cannot hear them. Except for change of residence, life after death is about the same as before. Like the living, the dead also die, for nothing can live for ever. The natives seem, however, to be true Weismannians: acquired characteristics are not inherited in the postmortem world. Reproduction of imperfections in Deadland applies only to those which are congenital. For instance, a man who has lost an arm does not become a one-armed ghost; and ghosts of those who have been decapitated are not headless. Natives recognize these imperfections as artificially produced, and not to be confused with those which are congenital. However, aged and infirm individuals who become ghosts do not recover lost vitality. The Kamerun Eghap locate Deadland directly under their tribal area. Life in the home of the dead is a replica of life on earth. Those who have committed suicide or have died of leprosy live on the outskirts of this ghost world and cannot communicate with other ghosts. A broad, deep river separates the habitations of the good from those of the wicked. Souls of the wicked are subject to illness and death. Another Eghap version describes three superimposed planes in the afterworld. In the uppermost live the creator and his attendants. In the lower live other beings. When a man dies, he goes directly to the lowermost stage and interviews the creator. If he has left children, palm oil is poured on his hands and he goes to the middle stage. Otherwise he is sent to the lowest stage, and subsequently back to earth to be reborn.

Among the Timne of Sierra Leone, as the result of Mohammedan influence, the belief now prevails that at death bad men go to Yehenama, or Yehanum, where they remain an indefinite length of time and eventually are forgiven their crimes. The evil include the greedy, robbers, liars, slanderers, the envious, those who are loath to help their fellows, obstinate debtors, those who refuse to lend money, and those who "think bad about God." Among the Ibo of southern Nigeria, men who have not received the death clothes or been given proper burial, or have died of infectious disease, been disowned by their family, killed by leopard, snake, buffalo, or other beast, or have died suddenly without any special illness, are not admitted to the country of the dead but wander about on earth, especially at midnight or midday. On this side of the spirit world there is a river which can be crossed only over a spider's web. The web crumples under the weight of one who as a youth was disobedient to the elders, but supports those who faithfully obeyed their injunctions. The Bachama and Angas, in northern Nigeria, a region which has received much Mohammedan influence, say that at death the great god Nan receives the souls of good men. The souls of the evil become evil spirits which remain near their old homes and plague the living by throwing stones at passers-by, steal children from their mother's satchel, appear as white babies to shepherd boys and carry off their sheep, or infect people with diseases and soon make them also into wandering ghosts. Some people can see such evil ghosts, and drive them off; they squeak like mice when they run away.

Ila souls may become living plants, animals, or human beings. There is a semblance of this concept in the belief of Jamaica Negroes that wicked people are usually born again as savage beasts. A man who goes neither to heaven nor to hell becomes after death a roving calf—and gives the living the *bla*. The Zulu spirit takes up its abode in a species of snake which the natives do not kill. Zulu ancestral spirits, the *ama-Thongo* or *amaDlozi*, "live underground and occupy the same relative position there as they did while alive: an unimportant man has little or no power after death; the head of a family, on the other hand, is the spirit that is invoked for help and that provides for his descendants, while the spirit of a chief has the welfare of the whole tribe at heart and is of far greater importance than any other spirit. He has power even over other spirits in the same way as in life when he could command any one in his tribe, and sometimes when a man's ancestors are not treating him fairly, the departed spirit of a chief is invoked to compel those ancestors to bless him. A man's *iThongo* resembles him in character: if he was good and brave when alive, he will be the same when dead. The spirits of old women and infants are often specially invited to come and eat of the sacrificial meat, because the spirit of an old woman is supposed to be spiteful and malicious and capable of all sorts of harm, while that of an infant is pure and beneficent." Medicine-men divine by the *amaThongo* of infants. The Kagoro of Nigeria have only one afterworld, the sacred grove. To it go all spirits when they leave the body, whether souls of chiefs, of poor men, of good men, or of evil men. The stronger men are on earth, the more influential are their ghosts. Ghosts live the lives of ordinary men. They ride, hunt, eat, and have an unquenchable thirst for palm-beer. They are always hungry and thirsty. They punish surviving kin who neglect them. Feuds are continued, but spirits cannot be destroyed. The Ngala, like the natives of the western coast, sometimes kill slaves and entrust them with messages to deceased influential heads of families. After death the Kongo spirit comes to a parting of the ways. The good reside in the moon; the bad, in the sun. Natives on the lower Congo believe that the spirit of a man who is disagreeable, disobliging, greedy, rude, or discourteous will be punished in the nether region. Such disembodied spirits return to earth to plague their former neighbours.

The Bambuti, Congo pygmies, say that spirits pounce at once upon the departing soul of a wicked man, and cast it into a fire in the interior of the earth. Souls of the good go to God. Schebesta believes this concept is aboriginal. All Kung Bushman souls go to the same realm above, where there is no distinction of fate for good or bad.

The Ganda believe that the ghosts of men who were mutilated in this life are mutilated similarly in the next world. Hence they would rather die in possession of all their limbs than retain life by amputation of a limb and so be without a leg or an arm during postmortem existence. Nandi spirits of the dead live underground and are rich or poor as in this life. The Ruanda say that inferior ghosts, the *bazimu*, haunt their former dwelling-places; the good ones, that is, those who during their lifetime were initiated into the *kubandwa* mysteries, go to join Ryang'ombe in Muhavura; the "profane" are sent to Nyirangongo. This concept may be due to Hamitic influence, for the idea of a future state of rewards and punishments is not a common Bantu attribute. Mba souls of light-complexioned men and of good medicinemen go to heaven, where they live in houses like those on earth and eat much the same kind of food as here. In most of this region there are no rewards for the good, no punishment for the evil.

In many African tribes the death of a chief, king, or other important man brings woe to certain survivors, thanks to belief that the soul of the deceased needs attendants in the next world. In 1670 a traveller to the Congo reported that in that kingdom twelve virgins were buried with a deceased king. A subsequent voyager reports that "they are commonly very cruel to the living, shutting up both together in a tomb with meat and drink, to the end (say they) that the dead lord may want for nothing in his grave. . . . At the death of any of their friends they have been accustomed to kill one of their slaves, to the end that he may go and serve them in the other world." At Benin, when the king's body has been lowered into the huge grave, "his most beloved domesticks of both sexes earnestly beg to be allowed the favour of going into it, to wait and attend on their master in the other life. When a woman dies, if she was a person of distinction, they massacre thirty or forty slaves on the day of her burial; and one has been known to have had seventy-eight slaves sacrificed on her account, which were all her own; and to complete the even number of eighty, as she had ordered before her death, they murdered two young children, a boy and a girl, whom she loved extremely." When the mother of the great Zulu king Chaka died, many men were executed, ten young girls were buried alive with the corpse, and a few thousand people were massacred before the mourning ceremonies terminated. The gory story continues—in Zululand, among the Lunda, Rotse, Yao, Tumbuka, Mba, Lumba, Vyoro, Soga, Kyiga, Nsakara, Ila, Swazi—from equator to Cape.

> Those that in barbarian burials kill'd the slave, and slew the wife,
> Felt within themselves the sacred passion of the second life.

In the higher civilizations of Central America and the Andean region a like practice prevailed. Thus, when an Inca of Peru died, many wives were buried with him. In the tomb of the Inca Huayna Capac, if we can believe de Léon, were buried more than four thousand individuals —women, pages, and other servants. Though this number may be a gross exaggeration, the custom is well attested.

CHAPTER XVI THE LIFE AFTER DEATH: HISTORIC CULTURES

Confucius is reticent regarding life after death. How, he asks, when you do not know about life, can you know about death? Later Chinese scholars, Chu Hi, Yang Chu, and Wang Ch'ung, assert that there is no conscious existence after death. Taoism teaches that length of days in this world and the next depends upon meritoriousness of life on earth. If a man commits a slight fault, a hundred days are subtracted from his life on earth; if he commits a grave fault, twelve years are deducted. "He who wishes to become an immortal of heaven must do a thousand three hundred good works. He who wishes to become an immortal of earth must do three hundred good works." Early Taoism offers immortality only to the few who pursue the exacting course requisite to its achievement. The regimen consists of meditation on Taoist truths and cultivation of Taoist attitudes: notably, inaction and placidity, carefully regulated breathing and diet, discipline, moral living, and partaking of substances which prolong life—such as seeds and resin of evergreens, that is, fir and pine, and certain minerals and jewels. In early Shinto belief, on the plain of high heaven great men, heroes, mikados, wise, virtuous, and heroic men dwell with the gods. Later Shintoism, incorporating Chinese concepts, assigns the positive spirit or *yang* to *ame*, a heaven where the gods dwell, directly over the earth. The belief has no ethical tinge.

The concept that happiness after death depends on a life of virtue and uprightness was, in ancient Egypt, a belief of gradual growth. Ultimately it crystallized into the psychostasia doctrine, the weighing of the heart before Osiris to test the merits of the deceased. It was contemporaneous with a competing, more primitive theory that funerary rites and knowledge of potent formulas were the sole passports to eternal bliss. In the early history of ancient Egypt, as revealed in the Pyramid

Texts of Unas, the dead resided in a celestial region, Aaru, which, apparently, though located in the sky, could be entered from certain places in the Delta, Pe-tep and Tettu. Later, in the *Book of the Dead*, the entrance was located in the north of Egypt. It was an agricultural country, bore abundant crops, was a pleasant and well-watered land in which justified souls might rest from earthly labours, secure in an eternity of bucolic delights. This early paradise of the cult of Osiris, anciently connected with the tillers of the land, antedates the later underworld paradise of Osiris.

According to the Pyramid Texts the "purity" demanded of the deceased was compatible with gross sensuality and flagrant immorality. The Just God, Maat, possessed registers of the deeds of men, kept with care by Thoth and Sesheta. The hearts of men were judged in the afterworld. From the earliest period of history Egyptians entertained belief in post-mortem judgment. The belief, at first vague, later was clearly defined, and became influential. The "Teaching of King Khati" urges that each so live and act that he will be able to prove to the god of the Judgment that he is a righteous man, and justify himself by showing that he has learned the law and obeyed its precepts.

Words and deeds on earth decide one's fate at the Judgment. "Belief that good came to the good and evil to the evil remained unchanged from the days of the Memphite theologians of the Old Kingdom to the Roman period." [1] Many monuments of the Old Kingdom commemorated the virtues of the deceased, evidently to induce passers-by to recite the funerary formulas or, perhaps, bring offerings to the tomb. It was only a step, or a few steps, from this practice to belief that virtue on earth is a necessary precondition to happiness in the afterlife. The *Book of the Dead* describes the many moral tests imposed upon the soul before it reaches the land of shades. In the Land of Double Truth, where Osiris is judge, the soul confronts Maat, goddess of justice, truth, or law, who holds a sceptre and the symbol of life. The scales are set, and the man's heart is placed on one side of the balance, the image of Maat on the other. Horus watches the indicator; Thoth, or Tehuti, god of letters, records the reading of the scales. The ethical standard is high; it requires truth, purity, righteousness, charity, and piety. Above the balance-scale sit forty-two assessors who deal with the forty-two great sins. The soul confesses, that is, asserts that it has not committed the enumerated sins.

1. Sir E. A. Wallis Budge, *From Fetish to God in Ancient Egypt*, 285–286 (London, Oxford University Press, 1934). Reprinted by permission of the publisher.

Its conscience or moral nature is symbolized by the heart in the scales. If the judgment is favourable, the soul regains the use of hands, limbs, and mouth; the functions lost in death are restored. The soul *ka* (double) and the shadow soul are returned to the deceased, and he begins a new life as a post-mortem person. If the judgment is unfavourable, he loses his lifelike functions and suffers pain. A second death and final extinction are the ultimate fate of the sinful.

The declaration made by the soul indicates the kind of acts considered praiseworthy; but the soul's welfare does not depend upon deeds performed in life; it depends upon being able to speak the appropriate words when summoned before the judge of the next world, and especially upon knowing the names of the gods. A portion of the utterance is as follows:

> Hail to thee, great god, lord of truth. I have come to thee, my lord, and am led hither to see thy beauty. I know thy name; I know the names of the forty-two gods who are with thee in the hall of truth, who live on evil-doers and devour their blood on the day of reckoning of character before Wennofre (Osiris). Behold, I come to thee; I bring to thee righteousness and I expel for thee sin. I have committed no sin against people. I have not done evil in the place of truth. I knew no wrong. I did no evil thing. I did not do what the god abominates. I did not report evil of a servant to his master. I allowed no one to hunger. I caused no one to weep. I did not murder. I did not command to murder. I caused no man misery. I did not diminish the food in the temples. I did not decrease the offerings of the gods. I did not take away the food-offerings of the dead. I did not commit adultery. I did not pollute myself in the pure precinct of my city god. I did not diminish the grain measure. I did not diminish the span. I did not diminish the land measure. I did not load the weight of the balances. I did not deflect the index of the scales. I did not take milk from the mouth of the child. I did not drive the cattle away from their pasturage.

And so on, through a notable list of denied vices. But, as mentioned, the denial, rather than the life lived, ensures salvation.

After about 510 B.C. Egyptian concepts are influenced by India, Persia, and Greece. Indian influences come mainly, it seems, through Greek contacts. Thus, in the *Kore Kosmou*, souls are said to be imprisoned in the body; if sinless, they dwell in the fields of heaven; if contaminated by sin, they remain on earth. Continuance in sin brings transformation into animals. After final dissolution of the body, souls resume the happiness of their first estate. Those who lived a blameless life become kings and train to become gods. Later papyri of the fourth century B.C. contain these concepts in modified form.

There developed, probably subsequently, the concept of Duat, the place of punishment which originally, it appears, was merely the place through which the sun god Re passed during the night when returning from west to east to resume his daily journey across the heavens from east to west. It was peopled by powers of night and darkness, natural enemies of the sun. Subsequently these powers were identified with the damned; that is, the damned met the fate generally accorded by later generations to the deities of gloom and chaos. The place of the dead, however, was not a place of retribution, though at the end of Duat infernal goddesses presided over pits of fire where they slew, beheaded, and dismembered the enemies of Re and burned the remains.

Allatu, queen of the Assyrian realm of the underworld of the dead, recompenses or condemns, according to the merits of the individual. She may strike an offender with disease, or imprison him. In this Hades is a region for the souls of the righteous to which are admitted only those who after judgment appear to merit recompense. There ancient prophets, crowned in triumph, sit, amid pleasant fields, under a peaceful silvery sky. Seers quench their thirst from clear rippling streams. Spirits pass from this realm into a firmament above.

Babylonian and Assyrian hymns and prayers indicate that a ritualistic misstep is on a par with ethical transgression. Often the penitent who appeals for divine mercy states that he does not know what wrong he has committed or what deity he has offended. The dismal afterworld pictured by Babylonians and Assyrians could not inspire good conduct or deter from evil. On the contrary, its gloom and chill emphasize the value of the present life and the desirability of extracting therefrom every mortal happiness and privilege ere opportunity for ever passes. Exceptional blessings may be anticipated by a select few, notably by heroes and the semi-divine. The warrior who died in battle and was given honourable burial does not fare badly; but great is the misery of the unburied. The mass of men, good or bad, princes or slaves, lead a meagre existence in an underworld which is a land of forgetfulness, a habitation of shades, uncheered by light of day, with no distinction of lot based on moral worth.

In early Iranian belief, after death the soul wanders three days and is confronted with a beautiful maiden, personification of its good thoughts, good words, and good deeds. In later belief this concept is supplemented with the doctrine that the evil soul is confronted with a personification of its evil deeds in the shape of an old hag. Each man is formally credited with good thoughts, good words, and good actions, and the evil are reckoned against him as debits. After death the soul arrives at the accountant's bridge, over which lies the way to heaven. Here the statement of his life account is made out. If there is a balance of good works in his favour, he forthwith attains paradise and the blessed life. If evil works outweigh the good, he falls finally under the power of Satan, and the pains of hell are his portion for ever. On the day of judgment the evil are parted from the good.

Just and unjust pass through purgatorial fire, made gentle for the righteous and terrible for the wicked, though a restorative to all.

The soul of a righteous man lingers three days and nights near the head of the body, reciting the hymn which begins: "Good comes to him who does good to another; may Mazda, the Almighty, give him his gifts." Mazda's gifts will equal the totality of the goods of this world. At daybreak on the fourth day after death a perfumed zephyr is wafted from the south, and with it comes a beautiful maiden. In response to the soul's inquiries she declares herself his religion, made fair with his virtues and pious observances.

Then, through the three entrance courts of good thoughts, good words, and good deeds, the soul passes into endless light, the company of the good, and the presence of Ahura Mazda. One version states that Sraosha and other good angels conduct the soul to the Cinvat bridge, and protect it *en route* from assaults of demons. At the bridge, Mithra, Sraosha, and Rashnu sit in judgment. Rashnu weighs the soul's merits and demerits in the balance. The balance beam does not deviate from justice by a hair's breadth. It shows no partiality, it deals in the same fashion with the mightiest of kings and the meanest of men.

Religious and moral merits are pitched into the scale. Profession of faith and penitent confession of sins weigh heavily on the side of salvation, as do also funeral masses which friends of the deceased have celebrated for the repose of his soul. The soul, after being weighed in the balance, essays the bridge, which stretches from the peak of Mt. Daitya to the summit of Elburz, and spans the abyss of hell.

For the good, the width of the bridge is nine spear-lengths, or even a parasong, and the soul passes easily to the heavenly mansions at the further end of the span; for the wicked, the bridge is as narrow as a razor-blade, and from its sharp edge the soul pitches headlong into the gulf beneath. For it, "strait and narrow is the path" that leadeth to hell. But heaven is not merely heaven, and it is not reached at a single bound. The soul which has crossed the bridge that leads to the land of bliss arrives first at the limbo inhabited by souls in whom good works and evil exactly balance one another. There they abide until the resurrection. They suffer no pain other than temporary recurring discomforts which result from climatic changes of heat and cold. The soul of the supremely righteous passes from this region into the three regions of good thoughts, good words, and good deeds, which correspond with the spheres of, respectively, stars, moon, and sun. Souls do not reside here, however; they pass through this realm into the highest heaven. In the highest heaven are those who on earth "exercised good sovereignty, rulership, or chieftainship."

The fate of the wicked is correspondingly hard. The soul, greatly perturbed, lingers near the body for three days, murmuring, in the words of the *Gathas*, "To what land shall I turn, O Ahura Mazda, whither direct my prayer?" Meanwhile, it suffers every earthly distress. On the fourth morning after death a cold blast from the north, the abode of demons, brings a foul stench. A demon lassoes the soul in a noose and drags it to the bridge, where Rashnu weighs its wickedness in the balance. The evil deeds of the deceased confront him as a hideous witch, whose ugliness reflects his character. Through the three vestibules of hell, consisting of evil thoughts, evil words, evil deeds, the condemned soul goes to infinite darkness. There, surrounded by souls of other sinners, he is mocked by demons, and Angra Mainyu has loathsome and poisonous food brought to him. Here, until the resurrection, the soul suffers misery and torment. The enveloping darkness is so intense that, although the souls are crowded closely together, each believes it is alone. So intense and agonizing is existence that when three days have passed the soul thinks nine thousand years must have elapsed and the day of relief have dawned.

The unfortunate soul journeys through hell and witnesses the tortures of the wicked, many of which are poetic justice. The man who talked at the dinner-table, did not say grace over meat, greedily devoured his vegetables, and guzzled his portion of water, that man—let us who survive rejoice in the fact—is tormented by hunger and thirst and cries eternally, "I shall die!" The tradesman who gave short measure, who watered his wine, put dust into his grain, sold adulterated food-stuffs, and exacted high prices, that man must spend the millennia in hell measuring dust and ashes in a bushel and having nothing else to eat. The woman who answered her husband snappishly, licks, as is fitting, with her too ready tongue a red-hot stove. And there are many more fine adjustments of the punishment to the crime. Ard a Viraf, who presides over infernal regions, has no sympathy for these stricken souls. He taunts them: "Why did ye eat the bread of Ahura Mazda and do my work, and thought not of your own creator but did my will?" It must be a pleasant question to ask but a queasy one to answer.

Heaven and hell, however, are not the final fate of man but only an era of postmundane existence. At the appointed time Saoshyant, the Saviour, will appear, and the dead be raised, first Gayomard, the archetypal man, and then the first pair of human beings, Mashya and Mashoi. Righteous and wicked will arise where they died; their bones will be demanded of the earth, their blood of the water, their hair of the plants, their life of the fire. The parts will be delivered and the body reconstituted of its original materials. The resurrected dead, assembled in one place, recognize one another. Too well, in fact, for the deeds of all will be manifest, and, reversing our metaphor, the wicked man will be as conspicuous as a white sheep among black.

The wicked will account it a reproach upon his pious friend that the latter did not turn him from his wickedness, and will so declare. The righteous will then be separated from the wicked and go to heaven; the wicked will be cast into hell, there to remain for three days. Meanwhile certain of the monstrously iniquitous will receive exemplary punishment. After these three days the fire will melt the metal in the mountains till it flows like a river. In this stream all shall be made pure. To the righteous the molten metal will be as milk, but the wicked will not be pleasantly deceived: they will know it is molten metal. Father and son, brother and sister, will inquire of one another: "Where hast thou been these many years, and what was the judgment on thy soul? Wast thou righteous, or wicked?" All men will speak the same language; and they will loudly praise Ahura Mazda and the archangels. They will receive the gifts of immortality dispensed as ambrosia by the Saoshyant. Adults will be restored as men and women forty years of age; children, as of fifteen years of age. The life they will then resume will be like the previous earthly life except that in heaven no children will be born, for, as in the New Testament, in heaven there will be no marriages; men and women will claim their former spouses and each will recognize his children. Thus in the end men fare about as they did in the beginning; meanwhile the wicked suffer for their misdeeds.

In one version of Zoroastrian doctrine the soul on its way to the future world must cross a bridge made of a strand of hair. The righteous reach the opposite shore safely; the sinful topple off into a stream of hell-fire. There is a middle place for those who are neither good nor bad, whose fate is not determined until the Last Judgment. This middle place, known as "ever stationary," or "never changing," became the Purgatory of the Roman Catholic Church and Mohammedanism. The darkest hell is located at the centre of the earth. Here an evil spirit mocks and ridicules unfortunate sinners. The first three heavens are, in order, stars, moon, and sun—the fourth and last is the all-glorious Garotman, wherein is the throne of Ahura Mazda. Parsis say that, when the soul arrives at Chinvat Bridge, gods and unclean spirits fight for its possession. If it is righteous, pure souls and the dogs which guard the bridge fight in its behalf. Echoes of the belief survive in a children's game, "London Bridge," played extensively in English-speaking lands.

In Mithraism, if the virtues of the soul outweighed its vices, the soul ascended to celestial realms by a sublime ladder of seven metal steps each associated with a plane. Otherwise it was consigned to a hell the description of which was an inspiration to Dante in depicting the inferno. In some cases the soul was condemned to rebirth in the form of a vile reptile or other base animal, to live a cycle of life in expiation for its previous career. During the ascent of the soul to heaven an angel of Ormazd stood at each of the seven gates, and only by the passwords of the secret mysteries was the soul permitted to ascend to the abode of the blessed where Mithra waited to receive his children. Ultimately there would be a resurrection of the body. The redeemer would return to earth and bring with him the bull for sacrifice. To his risen followers he would give wine prepared from the blood of the bull, and this would seal their immortality. Ormazd the Supreme would send fire to destroy Ahriman and all the minions of darkness. The universe would then roll on through eternity, without sin, stain, or tears.

Mandaeans share a modification of Iranian belief. The soul on the forty-fifth day of its journey reaches the Scales of Abuthur, where its good and evil deeds are weighed in the balance. If the evil deeds counterbalance the good, that is, are equal to or greater than the good, the soul remains in Mataratha, there to receive purification and a punishment adapted to its sin. Thus the soul of a quarrelsome man is sent to the Matarta, or Purgatory, of Nirigh, that is to say, Mars. The soul of a vainglorious man is consigned to Jupiter. Those who were evil are tortured with fire and with ice, are combed with an iron comb, are bitten by snakes, lions, wolves, and dogs. If the soul comes from one who was altogether evil, it is sent into the belly of Ur, a region alternately of ice and of fire. Here it will remain until the end of the world. At this time spirits which are still undergoing purification are carried upward by the forces of life and light; or, mayhap, by Habshaba himself, and, as an act of mercy, are dipped into the heavenly waters of the Frash Ziwa, in a final baptism of purification. The soul of a pious person, on the other hand, is soon purified. After a brief sojourn in Purgatory it returns to the Scales and is weighed against the soul of Shitil, the purest human being. The weighing takes place at the Polar Star. The soul which outweighs the soul of Shitil is sent back for further purification; the soul which does not exceed enters a ship of light which carries it across the river that surrounds the worlds of light. There, on the hither side, it enters that bourne of celestial habitations in which dwell kinsmen long since dead. The ultimate abode of this happy soul, however, may be in one of the worlds of the great spirits of light; and these worlds are countless (the stars?).

The Hindu peasant of the central provinces of India has a vague idea of a future life in which there are a heaven for the good and a hell for the wicked. In the Hindu Veda account of the next world the virtuous sit by the side of Yama, in the abode of light, by sparkling waters, and enjoy unlimited bliss. According to the Upanishads, the soul which has attained the lower knowledge of Brahma goes at death the way of the gods to heavenly joy. It progresses by stages toward true knowledge and final deliverance. The soul which has no knowledge of Brahma and seeks salvation by works, that is, by performing the old Vedic sacrifices and observances, goes the "way of the fathers" to the moon. Those who have neither attained knowledge nor performed good works atone in hell for their misdeeds, and return to earth as beasts, or as men of a caste lower than beasts.

An ethical element is predominant in Hindu concepts of reincarnation. The book of Manu says that men who delight in inflicting injury will be reborn as beasts of prey; those who partake of forbidden food will be worms; those who steal meat will be reborn as vultures; those who steal grain will be rats; those who steal perfume will be muskrats;

those who unlawfully kill an animal will in future reincarnations suffer violent death for each hair of the slain beast. The guilty man will be reborn an idiot, or deaf, or deformed, "all of whom are despised by the virtuous." The Upanishads declare: "As a man consists of this or that, as he acts, as he lives, so will he be born. He who did what was good will be born as a good man; he who did evil, as a bad man. He becomes holy by holy works, wicked by wicked. Therefore it is said, 'Man is altogether fashioned of desire; as his desire is, so is his insight; as his insight, so are his deeds; according to his deeds, so is his destiny.' " Again: "Those who here lead a good life may look forward to being honourably born of a Brahman mother, or a Kshatriya, or a Vaicya [the three high castes]; while those who lead a vile life may expect to enter the womb of a bitch, or a sow, or a Candala," the last mentioned a creature of human form, but lower than an unclean beast.

In the Rig Veda of the early Hindu period there is no concept of hell, but there is distinction of lot in the next world. The good man joins his ancestors in heaven and shares with them a life of happiness. The very evil man ceases to exist, or lingers in the abyss as a woeful shade. From that "pit without a hold" there is no escape. The good man is united with his earthly good works. The nobler his life on earth, the greater his happiness in the hereafter.

In the later Rig Veda period fear of divine retribution hereafter is a prominent factor in the maintenance of ethics. Retribution is exacted with mathematical precision by a god who has become essentially a god of hell who cannot be placated. The wrongdoer is automatically punished in the next world. To plead for pardon is as vain as to ask a machine to weigh motives. The concept is innocent of tenderness, but possibly turned attention to the law of cause and effect and the presumed irrevocability of human destiny. The future life is a glorification of life on earth. The trees are rich in foliage, there are flute-playing, singing, and light everlasting, all desires are fulfilled, and every pleasure abounds. Heaven is attained by warriors who died in battle, the bestowers of a thousandfold largess upon priests, the sages of a thousand songs, the performers of penance: in short, by warriors, rich men, priests. Annihilation is the fate of those who fail to attain heaven; some passages, however, say that those who are false, including women who are unfaithful to their husbands, will fall into a deep abyss. A hymn directed against demons consigns to an abode under the three earths the demon who plots against the singer of sacred formulas. Consignment of the wicked to a pit or the lowest darkness possibly alludes to places of punishment.

After 200 B.C. post-Vedic literature adds to the previous number of heavens and hells. It provides seven of each, or multiples of seven, up to twenty-one. Souls are allocated to these heavens and hells according to their deserts. Chitragupta records the deeds of men; Yama, as judge, consigns men to heaven or to hell according to their deserts. Later, Yama sinks from his rank and becomes merely lord of hell, and the view prevails that heaven is essentially the fruit of divine grace, irrespective of the merit of the recipient.

Subsequently, in theory, the fate of the dead depends on their deeds; but, in practice, it is regarded as dependent also on the actions of descendants. Agastya saw his ancestors hanging head downward in hell, because of his failure to beget sons. Stress is placed on the necessity of due performance of funeral rites and of making the *sraddhas* offerings requisite to secure the welfare of the departed soul. These offerings provide the spirit, disembodied in the process of creation, with a celestial body, and raise it from one state of existence to another. Souls of men who have spat upon a Brahman sit in the middle of a pool and chew hair.

In present-day Hinduism heaven is an immortality of conscious blessedness with Vishnu, Krishna, or Siva. Faith and observance of religious rites ensure immediate entrance into this state. There are twenty-one, or, according to the faith, twenty-eight, hells. Here Yama, formerly ruler of the blessed dead, is judge and executioner. His two messengers bind the soul and hurry it before his judgment-seat. The recorder then produces his book in which are recorded all the man's deeds, meritorious and wicked. Accounts are balanced. Due credit is given for religious devotion and observances, which are reckoned as of great value. Rites performed by a man's relatives after his death are put down to the deceased's credit.

On the thirteenth day the soul is taken to heaven or to hell. The road to hell is eighty-six thousand leagues in length; on it many hardships are encountered. At the end of it the soul is plunged into the hell which the deeds done in the body have merited. This may be a region of heated cauldrons or one of red-hot irons; or the soul may be thrown into a lake of blood and stinking mire; or it may be driven through a jungle in which the leaves of plants are sharp knives, or over a plain paved with sharp spikes; or it may be thrust into a hell of pincers which tear the flesh from the bones.

Other hells there are, but the above will serve as illustrations. Eventually the soul will be reborn in a lower form than that of man; but no earthly misery compares with the horrors of hell. Though many Christian sects have ingeniously refined the doctrines of the New Testament, even Christianity can scarcely boast that it has outdone Hinduism in the devising of hells numerous and discriminatory.

Jains regard attainment of Nirvana as perfection. To secure it right faith, right knowledge, and right conduct are requisite. To this end the five vows are of foremost importance: not to kill; not to lie; not to steal; to abstain from sexual intercourse; to renounce interest in worldly things, and especially to retain no property. Monks take these vows when they enter a monastery. The laity, likewise, to the extent that their condition admits, should observe them, although in their case the rigour of the vows is somewhat mitigated.

Early Buddhism provides reward in heaven or punishment in hell, and rebirth, the type of which depends upon the merits or demerits of the previous life on earth. The wise live in virtue, untarnished by lust for future existence. There are four-and-twenty heavens above Mt. Meru, and as many hells beneath the earth: eight major, and sixteen minor, hells and heavens. In the first hell souls are cut into pieces; and they revive to suffer repeatedly the same fate. In the second hell they are struck down with blazing weapons and while prostrate are cut into sixteen or eighteen pieces. In the third they are on burning mountains and are crushed by blows like sesame seed or sugar cane. In the fourth and fifth they are tortured with smoke. In the sixth they are transfixed on spikes as high as a palm tree and are burned. In the seventh they are cast down from a blazing high mountain upon the ends of stakes. In the eighth they are treated to flames which issue from the four sides of the region.

In the first hot hell are punished those guilty of assault, murder, covetousness, or anger; in the second, slanderers, liars, and those who were undutiful to father, mother, or friends; in the third, those who killed rams, antelopes, or other living beings; in the fourth, those who tormented living things; in the fifth, those who destroyed the property of gods, Brahmans, or their *guru* (priest); in the sixth, those who burned forests and living animals; in the seventh, infidels who reversed right and wrong; in the eighth, those who killed disciple, father, mother, or *guru*.

In minor hells are punished violators of morality. Adulterers climb the thorny simbali tree; destroyers of confidence are cut into pieces; robbers swallow bars of hot iron.

In Burmese Buddhism the fourth infernal region to which unfortunate souls go is Niria, situated in the deepest recesses of the southern island Zabudiba, in the centre of the great stone Silapatavi. This region is divided into eight great hells. On each of its four sides is a gate, and in each gate are four smaller hells. In addition to these, forty thousand and forty smaller hells surround each great hell. They are above and below, to right hand and to left, and each such group extends the length of ten thousand *juzena*.

Tibetans suffer more from cold blasts than from warm; the latter, in fact, generally are comforting. Appropriately, Tibetan Buddhism provides eight cold hells, with as many forms of excruciating torment: immersion in cold water until chilblains result; scarification of the chilblains with jagged knives until open sores are produced; cold so intense that even the tongue is paralyzed and jaws and teeth are clenched. Livid sores develop which become everted until the flesh falls away from the bones, which are continually pecked and gnawed by voracious birds with iron beaks. Fear of the torments of these hells, vividly depicted by priests, should deter evildoers; but the ethical value of the belief is discounted by the fear and the loss of peace of mind inflicted on surviving relatives by the priests' harrowing accounts of intermediate tortures which require masses. Unlike the paradise of the blest in southern Buddhism, which is merely a passing phase of existence followed by ceaseless rebirths, the Tibetan paradise lasts for ever. Good Tibetans look forward to a happier existence in the world beyond death than is vouchsafed the Hindu or southern Buddhist; and their hell, bad as it is, can scarcely be worse than the hells of coreligionists to the south, who depict them as hot places. On the walls of many Chinese Buddhist temples are representations of the ten prisons of hell in the heart of the earth. In each are a prefect and a tribunal before whom the souls are tried, according to the nature of their offences. Punishments are appropriate to the sins. Thus, ecclesiastics who neglected to read masses for the dead for which they had been paid are sent to a dark room where, by the feeble light of a poor lamp, they must read the mass from a book written in minute and illegible hand. Formosan Chinese say that good souls pass over a narrow bamboo bridge to a paradise of sensuous enjoyment; the bad fall from it into a bottomless pit of torment. Belief in the effects of good and bad deeds upon one's future existence is an incentive to the conduct approved by Chinese Buddhism. The acquisition of merit which may later be effective is a strong inducement to the founding and maintenance of the many charitable organizations which characterize Chinese life—societies for supporting nurseries, building bridges, repairing roads, giving medicine to the poor or providing coffins for them, and other enterprises. "Assurance of a happy state in the life beyond the grave is obtained by repeating prayers and observing vegetarianism. Certificates—passports to heaven —may be purchased from Buddhist clergy by those who have performed these acts of devotion. Souls of the dead may be assisted by the living. Services believed to be efficacious in hastening the delivery of the dead from torment are conducted by the monks on payment of a fee." [2]

In Chinese Buddhism the President of the First Court of Hades "keeps the register of the living and the dead, and measures the length of men's lives." When the soul arrives in Hades, "it is taken to the steelyard, a hook is fastened in its back, and its sins are weighed." If its merits outweigh its sins, the President sends it to the Tenth Court, where transmigration takes place. If its sins outweigh its merits, it is placed on the Mirror Tower, "to behold its fate in the next life for the sins of the past—a cow, an ass, a dog, or a reptile." The soul is then sent to the Second Court, where its tortures begin. Thus, in Chinese Buddhism, concern for the post-mortem existence of predecessors may become an incentive to survivors. In Japanese Buddhism paradise awaits the faithful. Their souls are under the charge of Amita, ruler of the blessed dead. "There shall be no distinction, no regard to male or female, good or bad, exalted or lowly; none shall fail to have Pure Life, after having called, with complete desire, on Amita. Just as a great stone, if on a ship, may complete a voyage of myriad miles over the great waters and yet not sink, so we, though our sins are heavy as giant boulders, are borne to the other shore by Amita's primal vows, not sinking in the sea of birth and death."

Ultimately all Mohammedans will be saved, though they will suffer in purgatory for their sins on earth. Infidels will be punished. "Those who disbelieve and call our signs lies, they are fellows of hell," declares the Koran; "they shall dwell therein for ever. And as for those who are wretched—why in the fire they shall groan and sob! to dwell therein

2. Kenneth S. Latourette, *The Chinese, Their History and Culture*, II, 158 (New York, Macmillan, 1934). Reprinted by permission of The Macmillan Company.

for ever as long as the heavens and the earth endure." According to the Koran, Paradise, over which Ridwan presides, has seven named compartments, each built of gold, silver, and precious stones. There are four rivers, of pure water, milk, wine, and honey. (Later, streams of various spices to mix with the water were added.) Black-eyed maidens of perennial virginity are there, also wives and beautiful youths to serve the faithful, who sit under shade-trees or recline on luxurious couches. Between Hell and Paradise is a partisan wall. Upon it are placed those who have worshipped God but have not done good works sufficient to outweigh their evil deeds—intermediates they are called in the Jewish Talmud. They look with envy upon the dwellers in Paradise, and, seeing the unfortunates in Hell, pray that they may be spared those pains and at last by divine grace be admitted to Paradise. Later tradition states that those who in Gehenna pronounce the Mohammedan creed, "There is no God except Allah, and Mohammed is his Prophet," will, at the intercession of the Prophet, be released. They will then bathe in a River of Forgetfulness, be rejuvenated, and be admitted to Paradise.

The fifty-sixth sura of the Koran, which bears the title "The Inevitable," says:

When the inevitable day of judgment shall suddenly come, no soul shall charge the prediction of its coming with falsehood: it will abase some and exalt others, when the earth shall be shaken with a violent shock; and the mountains shall be dashed in pieces, and shall become as dust scattered abroad; and ye shall be separated into three distinct classes: the companions of the right hand (how happy shall the companions of the right hand be!); and those who have preceded others in the faith shall precede them to paradise. These are they who shall approach near unto god: they shall dwell in gardens of delight. (There shall be many of the former religions; but few of the last.) Youths which shall continue in their bloom forever shall go round about to attend them, with goblets, and beakers, and a cup of flowing wine; their heads shall not ache by drinking the same, neither shall their reason be disturbed; and with fruits of the sorts which they shall choose, and the flesh of birds of the kind which they shall desire. And there shall accompany them fair damsels having large black eyes; resembling pearls hidden in their shells; as a reward for that which they shall have wrought. They shall not hear therein any vain discourse, or any charge of sin; but only the salutation, Peace! Peace! And the companions of the left hand (how miserable shall the companions of the left hand be!) shall dwell amidst burning winds and scalding water, under the shade of a black smoke. Ye, O men, who have erred and denied the resurrection as a falsehood, shall surely eat of the fruit of the tree al Zakkum and shall fill your bellies therewith; and ye shall drink thereon boiling water; and ye shall drink as a thirsty camel drinks. This shall be their entertainment on the day of judgment.

Mohammedan commentators recognize the following hells or purgatories: a purgatorial hell for Mohammedans; a blazing fire for Christians; one for Jews; one for Sabaeans; one for Magi; one for idolators; a bottomless pit for hypocrites. Heaven is a place of sensuous delights for men; no post-mortem bliss awaits women. Mohammed said: "Behold I went to the gates of heaven, and it was filled with men; I went to the gates of hell, and it was filled with women." In a Mohammedan tradition of creation, however, the angel Michael declares to Eve: "For the pangs of maternity thou shalt feel, this (recompense) shall be thine: death in childbearing shall be reckoned in heaven as a death of martyrdom." A similar view is found in many preliterate cultures. English lower classes believe that a woman who dies in childbirth, even if unmarried, cannot be "lost."

Those who are to enter the Mohammedan land of bliss take the right-hand way; those destined for hell-fire, the left. All souls must first cross a bridge, *al-Sirat*, which stretches over hell, is finer than a hair, and is sharper than a sword; it is difficult to conceive how one can stand upon it. On each side it is beset with briars and barbed thorns, which, however, do not impede the progress of good souls. These, led by Mohammed and the saints, pass by, like lightning on the wind, with wonderful ease and speed. The wicked cannot cope with the slipperiness of the narrow path and the entanglement of thorns. They are deprived of the light which guides the faithful to Paradise, miss their footing, and tumble headlong into the hell which gapes beneath them. Another legend, which the writer first heard from his Mohammedan guide in the Solomon's Temple area, by the beautiful Omar, or Dome of the Rock, mosque, is to the effect that a bridge, as tenuous as the one described above, will, on the Last Day, extend from the Temple area of Jerusalem to the Mount of Olives on the east. The valley beneath it, the Valley of Jehosophat, will be a Valley of Hell through which will run a river of fire. Souls will pass from the Temple area over this bridge. Mohammed and Christ will sit at the eastern end, on what is now the Mount of Olives. Souls of the faithful, seeing Mohammed, will be of strong heart and pass over safely. Infidels, conscious of shortcomings, will tremble with terror and topple off into the river of fire. A modification of this belief is to the effect that "the pious will be upheld, as they cross, by an angel who will hold them by a single lock of hair, but the wicked will fall into the Valley el-Jehennan (Gehenna) beneath." Another variant of the belief that the resurrection will take place at Jerusalem states that a monster, the Spy, will come out of the earth and mark the foreheads of the faithful by the staff of Moses with the white sign of life, and the noses of evildoers by the signet ring of Solomon with the black sign of perdition. All will then be summoned to the temple-hill at Jerusalem, the highest spot on earth, to await the judgment at the narrow bridge which leads from Hell to Paradise. No intercession, save that of Jesus and Ezra, shall avail. The deeds of men shall be weighed in the scales, and the books containing the records of the faithful, kept in the seventh heaven, and those of sinners, kept in the lowest part of hell, will be read. The former are held in the right hand of the faithful, the latter are placed in the left hand of sinners and tied to their necks. Then Paradise and Gehenna shall descend to earth. The faithful will be welcomed by God and his angels with the greeting, "Peace be on you!" Unbelievers will be ushered into the wretched abode of Hell, and there dwell for ever.

Another account of the bridge describes its length as the equivalent of a journey of three thousand years. Its ascent requires a thousand years, the traversing of the level portion a thousand years, and the descent another thousand years. Fire shoots up about it to a height equivalent to a journey of forty years. The righteous pass over it like a flash of lightning; the time required for the passage of the evil varies with the enormity of their offences, and may be twenty-five thousand years. Another account describes it as composed of seven arches, each of which requires a journey of three thousand years. During the entire journey all except the righteous suffer agonies from hell-fire. Difficult, indeed, "the Brig o' Dread, no brader than a thread."

Moroccan Mohammedans say that as soon as the corpse has been buried the angel Azrael comes to hear the soul's confession. The eyes say: "I have seen such and such a thing, which I ought not to have looked at." The mouth says: "I have lied and have eaten forbidden fruit with enjoyment." Nose, stomach, abdomen, left hand, and feet speak in turn and confess their respective faults. Right eyebrow and right hand, however, defend themselves and deny wrongdoing. Not until the eighth day is the soul set free.

If the dying man has been good, his soul slips out of his body as easily as a strand of hair out of a crumbling cake; but the soul of an evil man sticks to his throat as though his throat were lined with thorns of the jujube tree. During the first three days of its separation from the body the soul visits its mortal home, and for forty days it haunts its tomb. After those forty days it resides in the Barzakh, an enormous hive in the sky where each beelike soul dwells in a cell. Women who have caused abortion are tormented after death in their graves by the souls of all the children whom they have deprived of life on earth. On the Day of Judgment these women will be changed into bitches and sent to howl in hell. The soul of a woman who dies in childbirth or during pregnancy or has given birth to ten sons is not punished but goes directly to Paradise.

Egyptian Mohammedans say that after death the souls of prophets are immediately admitted to Paradise; those of martyrs reside in the crops of green birds, which eat of the fruits and drink of the waters of Paradise. There are various opinions regarding the fate of the souls of other believers. Some say they stay near their sepulchres, free to wander at will; some say they are with Adam in the lowest heaven; some say they remain in a specified well; some say they linger near the grave for seven days; some say they are the trumpet the blast from which will raise the dead; some say they dwell, in the form of white birds, under the throne of God. There are various opinions regarding the fate of souls of the wicked. The strictly orthodox say that souls of the wicked are offered by angels to heaven, whence they are repulsed as stinking and filthy, and are then offered to earth. They are refused a place on earth, are carried down to the seventh underworld and are thrown into a dungeon, under a green rock or under the devil's jaw, to be tormented until summoned back to the surface of the earth to rejoin their bodies. Indian Mohammedans say that when a body is placed in the grave, two black angels with blue eyes, Menkar and Nakir, visit it and interrogate the dead regarding the Prophet of God (Mohammed). If he has been a loyal Mohammedan, he bears witness to the Unity of God and the mission of the Prophet. A light is then given him in the grave. Forthwith the grave expands seventy times seventy yards in length and seventy times seven yards in breadth. The angels then bid the dead sleep until the Resurrection. If, however, the dead has been an unbeliever and has denied the Prophet, the ground will close upon him, break his sides, and cause him great agony until God raises him at the Last Day.

In Homeric Greece the dead are "shadows that drift ineffectually." In

Hades the soul retains the age status of its abandoned body: a babe here is a babe there, a child here is a child in Hades; only those who died in manhood enjoy full maturity of powers in the underworld. Some, however, have a happy fate in the Elysian plain. Thus Menelaus, "cherished by Zeus," was told he would be carried by the Deathless Ones "to the Elysian plain, the place beyond the world, where is fair-haired Rhadamanthus and where the lines of life run smoothest for mortal men. In that land there is no snow-fall, nor much winter, nor any storm or rain: but from the river of earth the west wind ever sings soft and thrillingly to reanimate the souls of men. There you will have Helen for yourself and will be deemed of the household of Zeus." [3] The earliest Greek concept of post-mortem punishment appears to be that of the Erinys, the vengeful Fury, who pursues the guilty soul beyond the tomb. "At death, forthwith," says Pindar, "the helpless souls receive their retribution, and deeds done in this realm of Zeus are judged beneath the earth by one who gives sentence with dire necessity." The abode of the blest the poet describes as a subterranean realm where the sun shines by night as brilliantly as during the day on earth; the good, free from toil and sorrow, dwell with the honoured gods; the evil endure a misery which men cannot countenance. When three lives of purity have been completed on earth, the ancient sin is atoned for. In the ninth year after their final arrival in Hades, souls ascend to the world above for the last time and become incarnate in kings, heroes, and wise men. Freed from the trammels of earth, they find a home in the Island of the Blest—first referred to, among Greek writers, by Homer and Hesiod, but known to Babylonians—where, under the rule of Cronos, they live in communion with earlier heroes, such as Peleus, Cadmus, and Achilles. This Island of the Blest, located by Greeks in the ocean to the west, can be visited only by souls of those who have lived virtuously. "There is," says Empedocles, "an oracle of Necessity, an ancient decree of the gods, eternal, sealed with broad oaths, that when one of the divine beings (*daimones*), who have endless life as their lot, criminally defiles his hands by bloodshed, or when one, in the train of Strife, swears a false oath, he must wander thrice ten thousand seasons far from the blessed, being born through all that time in all manner of forms of mortal creatures, exchanging one grievous path of life for another." The Eumenides thus threaten Orestes: "I'll cling to thee and drag thee down living to pay the penalty of thy mother's murder. Thou shalt see every man who impiously

3. Odyssey, Books IV, X.

wronged a god or a guest or his loving parent suffering each his just deserts; for Hades is a dread judge of men beneath the earth, observing all things with retentive mind." Aeschylus states: "Not even in Hades' realm after death can a man who has done such things escape the penalty of his profane deed. There, as they say, another Zeus among the shades passes final judgment on men's sins." Democritus (c. 460–c. 356 B.C.), a philosophic soul, says: "Some men do not understand that a mortal nature is subject to dissolution, and, being conscious of the evil in life, painfully spend all their days in troubles and fears, inventing lies about the time after death." Pythagoreans teach that souls of the righteous go to a better world, but souls of the unworthy enter other bodies. The worst are punished in Tartarus.

According to Aristophanes (*The Frogs*), the soul, after paying the usual fee to the ferryman, passes over a dreaded bottomless lake, where it encounters serpents, wild beasts, and monsters:

> Then there's an abyss of mire and floating filth,
> In which the damn'd lie wallowing and overwhelm'd;
> The unjust, the cruel, and the inhospitable.
> And the barbarous bilking Cullies that withhold
> The price of intercourse with fraud and wrong;
> The incestuous, and the parricides, and the robbers;
> The perjurers, and assassins.

In the *Republic* Plato refers to beliefs in the punishment of the soul in the next world in terms which indicate that, though the beliefs are not commonly accepted in his day, they yet may trouble the guilty. "For let me tell you, Socrates, that when a man thinks himself to be near death he has fears and cares which never entered into his mind before; the tales of a life below and the punishment which is exacted there of deeds done here were a laughing matter to him once, but now he is haunted with the thought that they may be true; either because of the feebleness of age, or from the nearness of the prospect, he seems to have a clearer view of the other world; suspicions and alarms crowd upon him, and he begins to reckon up in his own mind what wrongs he has done to others. And when he finds that the sum of his transgressions is great, he will many a time like a child start up in his sleep for fear, and he is filled with dark forebodings. But he who is conscious of no sin has in old age a sweet hope which, as Pindar charmingly says, is a kind nurse to him." Cowards and unjust men will be reborn as women, gluttons, or drunkards; the wanton will be asses in the next reincarnation;

the violent will be wolves or hawks. This Pythagorean doctrine is possibly of Hindu origin. The story of the vision of Er, which Plato gives in the *Republic*, implies reward for the righteous and punishment for the wicked. Yet the next world was not a place to be longed for, filled, as it was, with cold, shivering, gibbering ghosts and shades, formless shadows of earthly selves. Indeed, the comfort of the deceased depends to a large extent upon offerings from surviving relatives.

The dead wife of Periander tells her husband in a dream that she is cold because her clothes have not been burned at the funeral pyre. Only after he makes a holocaust of the wardrobes of Corinthian women is she comfortably warm.

The eschatology of ancient Greece seems to have received a stimulus from the Eleusinian mysteries. Before Bacchic and Orphic doctrines entered the Eleusinia, punishment or reward in the next life was not dependent upon good or evil done in the flesh. The mystery cults, however, promised a happy life after death to those who had passed through the initiation ceremonies. The devotee of Isis who kept faith with the divinity was assured a protected life on earth, blessed and glorious. After his earthly existence ended, he dwelt blissfully in Elysian regions where the goddess, shining in the subterranean realm, illuminated the dark Acherontic night. Early in the fourth century A. D. these religions still claimed power to mediate full salvation for the soul, here and hereafter.

Bacchic initiates received assurance that they alone will enjoy "a sun and joyous light" in the next world. Those who passed through the Eleusinian mysteries were promised "a joyous existence (in Hades) while all others suffered evil things." [4] "Happy is he among men upon earth who has seen these [Eleusinian] mysteries; but he who is uninitiate and who has no part in them never has lot of like good things once he is dead, down in the darkness and gloom." [5] Plutarch, referring to beliefs of the mystery religions regarding post-mortem punishments, speaks of "hypocrites who have hidden their wretchedness under the appearance of virtue, obliged to reverse their entrails so that the inner side of them may be seen, haters who devour each other, and misers plunged into and plucked out of lakes of burning gold, icy lead, and jagged iron"—reminders of Buddhist hells. Orphic mysteries represent the wicked as plunged into mud in the next world, the good as enjoying everlasting happiness. The "good" possibly refers to the initiated.

4. Plutarch, *On Hearing Poems,* IV, 21.
5. "To Demeter," *Homeric Hymns.*

Plutarch remarks that "Plato says scornfully of Orpheus, that he makes an eternal debauch hereafter the reward of those who lived well here." [6]

Epicureans considered death the end of sentient existence. Stoics believed a final general conflagration would reduce the universe to primal fire, after which another cycle of evolution would begin.

Romans were little concerned about the next world. Cicero attributed belief in hell and its terrors to "ignorance of philosophy." "Where," he asks, "can we find any old women so silly as to believe the old stories of the horrors of the world below?" Seneca, in similar vein, declares: "Those tales which make the world below terrible to us, are poetic fictions. There is no black darkness awaiting the dead, no prisonhouse, no lake of fire or river of forgetfulness, no judgment-seat, no renewal of the rule of tyrants."

In the earliest recorded Teutonic times there was, it appears, no theory of reward or punishment after death. In the viking age, however, definite places in the future life were assigned to different classes of men dependent upon manner of death. The earliest of these abodes, probably, was the realm of the goddess Hel (whence the English word "hell"), a world of shades similar to the Hades of the Greeks, in which departed spirits, it seems, had only a passive existence, devoid of occupation and interest. Later the view prevailed that only those who died of sickness or old age went to this region. Those who drowned went to the goddess Ran; those who fell in battle went to Odin or to Freyja. (Other evidence indicates that some men went to Thor, and women, to Freyja.) Valhalla, the hall of Odin, was a warriors' paradise, built round the trunk of the tree Laeradhr. In it Teutonic warriors who fell in battle dwelt for ever with the god in feast and fray. On the leaves of the tree browsed the stag Eikthyrmir and the goat Heidbrun, from whose udders flowed inexhaustible streams of mead wherein these heroes quenched their thirst.

Hel's abode, Niflheim, the world of cloud, lay under the third root of the ash tree. The road to Hel's dark dominion was dark and dreary: the descent from heaven was a journey of nine days and nine nights for the gods themselves. The greater part of the way lay through morasses and vast moors overgrown with furze and thorns; to provide protection for the feet of the dead, a pair of shoes was laid in the grave with the corpse. To reach Hel one must pass over the river Gjoll, the Yelling (or Sounding) One; across Gjoll lay a golden bridge, guarded by the

6. Plutarch, "Comparison of Lucullus with Cimon," *Lives*.

maiden Modgud. Terrible rivers through which the sinner must wade flowed hither and yon through the darksome place. Here those who had broken their vows and those who had escaped punishment on earth met their doom. They found the dragon Nid-hogg, which sucked the blood from their corpses, and also the dread Fenris-Wolf, which at the last day would slay even Odin. From that place Darkness came. We are not told whether any of the dead remained on earth, with no special assignment in the next world. "There is no evidence that the ideas of the 'wild hunt' and similar companies of departed spirits, so prevalent in later traditions, go back to the early Teutonic period or reproduce any conception from that time." Not until the time of the Snorri Edda, about 1220, did ethical ideas play a part in assignment of lot in the next world. Then, "all men whose ways are right shall live and be with the highest god, All-father, in the place called Gimle; but wicked men go to Hel and thence to Niffhel, which is down in the ninth world." After the world has been consumed by fire, "it will be best to be in Gimle, in heaven, where there will be abundance of good drink for those who enjoy that in the hall called Brimir. That is also a good hall which stands on Nithafells, made of red gold; its name is *Sindri*. In these halls shall good and righteous men live." Murderers and perjurers are consigned to torment in a great hall on "Corpse-strand," the doors of which open toward the north. Its walls are wattled with snakes, their heads turned inwards; these reptiles spout venom which flows through the hall in streams, in which the wicked are doomed to wade. How much of this concept is genuinely Teutonic, perhaps derived from Indo-Iranian sources, and how much should be credited to medieval Christian concepts, is difficult to determine.

To Valhalla all brave warriors hoped to go, though later tradition suggests that warriors who committed "nithing" actions or lived wickedly were excluded. Thither they were conducted by Valkyries, who later waited upon them in that warriors' bliss. Valhalla was wholly a warriors' paradise, the beatitude of war rather than of peace. In Scandinavian, as in Vedic, belief, the bridge of the dead could be safely crossed by one who, while on earth, had given a cow to the poor. In recognition of this beneficence his soul was provided with a cow which would carry it in comfort across the dreaded gulf. Associated with this belief, whether as cause or as effect, is the funeral custom in Sweden, Denmark, Germany, and England, of leading a cow behind the coffin to the graveyard. Probably the custom is the older, and originally was merely a provision of food for the soul.

In Irish legend the Bridge of Dread or Peril, over which souls must pass on the way to the next world, is connected with the concept that the hero must make his way across a terrible country called the Plain of Ill-luck, a plain infested by monsters. The soul must traverse likewise the Perilous Glen, through which there passes a single narrow path. On the farther side of the plain the feet of men stick fast; and on the farther half the grass rises and holds them fast on the points of its blades. Finally the soul reaches the Bridge of the Cliff, which is low at the ends and high in the middle. If one should leap onto one end of it while a soul was on the other end, the soul would be cast on its back again. Only those who have shown valour can cross this bridge. The concept is probably pre-Christian in Ireland, but underwent considerable modification during Christian times. It plays an important part in later Irish versions of Purgatory and Hell. In most of these later versions the bridge is, for the good, narrow on entry but broadening and made easy toward the end. For the evil, it seems broad at the beginning but strait and narrow when they proceed; and they fall from it into the gaping mouths of serpents and demons which lurk in the abyss below. There is a similar concept in northern England and Scotland, where the belief prevails among the poor that the soul of the dead person goes over Whinny-Moor, or the Moor of Furze. In the early seventeenth century it was common after a death for a woman to sing the Whinny-Moor Dirge. (Sir Walter Scott publishes this dirge in his *Border Minstrelsy*.)

The Chechen of the Caucasus regarded life in the next world as a repetition of the kind of existence lived on earth. The only difference was that in the spirit world men did not work. Indeed, life terminated there, even as on earth.

Early Jewish beliefs regarding life after death are similar to those of the Babylonians. The Old Testament speaks of Sheol and lowest Sheol, but assignment to these realms is not associated with moral rewards. Isaiah says of the righteous man who perisheth: "He entereth into peace; they rest in their beds, each one that walketh in righteousness." The grave is a place of quiet and deliverance from life's troubles and sufferings. There are, indeed, in the entire Old Testament, little more than hints of post-mortem existence, and no suggestion of punishment in Sheol. Sheol was generally regarded with forebodings, as a place in which the soul was hidden from Yahweh and deprived of human fellowship.

Job (10: 21–22) describes this ghostly world as "a land of thick darkness as darkness itself, of the shadow of death without any order and where the light is as darkness." "I perceive that there is nothing better, than that a man should rejoice in his own work; for that is his portion; for who shall bring him to see what shall be after him." [7]

Proverbs, however, voices a different sentiment, and later the Jews adopted belief in personal survival and resurrection. The most rapid development of the Jewish doctrine of immortality, and the roots of Christian theory, are contained in the apocryphal literature which fills the gap between Old Testament and New, and is a connecting link between them.

There were cross-eddies of doubt and faith. *Psalms*, for example, refers to the end of man's earthly career as though it were the end of his existence: "O spare me (look away from me) that I may recover strength, before I go hence, and be no more." "His breath goeth forth, he returneth to his earth; in that very day his thoughts (purposes) perish." *Job* contains a similar plaint: "Man dieth and wasteth away; yea, man giveth up the ghost, and where is he? As the waters fade from the sea, and the river decayeth and drieth up; so man lieth down, and riseth not: till the heavens be no more, they shall not awake, nor be roused out of their sleep."

According to *I Enoch*, written, probably, before 170 B.C., the righteous will not always suffer, nor will the wicked always prosper. Sheol is an intermediate place of punishment to which souls of men are admitted after the first world judgment which metes out punishment to the sinful. Here the wicked are confined for ever. Spirits of the righteous, separated from those of the wicked, live in a region supplied with a bright spring of water. Souls of sinners who have not received merited punishment upon earth dwell apart in great pain and torment and are scourged.

The concept that the fate of the soul is determined solely on moral grounds is recorded also in the earlier books of *Daniel*. All souls go to one of the two abodes in Sheol. There is no distinction between good and better, bad and worse, but merely between the two classes, good and bad. The destiny of each soul is determined at death; its place in Sheol

7. *Ecclesiastes*, 3: 18–22.

is absolutely and irrevocably established by its character on earth. Thus, however long its abode in Sheol, its status there never changes.

Sheol, thus conceived, has been characterized as "a place of petrified moralities and suspended graces. It aims at being moral but ends in being mechanical, and thus constitutes an amalgam formed of heterogeneous elements." There the righteous man will beget a thousand children; each measure sown will yield ten thousand grains; each vine will have ten thousand branches, each branch ten thousand twigs, each twig ten thousand clusters, each cluster ten thousand grapes, and each grape will yield twenty-five measures of wine. Truly the fulfilment does justice to the promise: "And I will open the store-chambers of blessing which are in heaven," and "send them down over the work and labor of the children of men," and "truth and peace shall be associated together throughout all the days of the world."

> But for the elect there shall be light and grace and peace,
> And they shall inherit the earth,
> And they shall not again transgress,
> Nor shall they sin all the days of their life.

The author of Chapters XCI–CIV of *Ethiopic Enoch*, a Pharisee who wrote when his party was suffering severe persecution from Sadducees and the court, and whose personal feelings may have coloured his views, is much concerned over the problem of the sufferings of the righteous. The solution lies in a future life: "I know this mystery, and have read it on the heavenly tables, that manifold good shall be given you in recompense for your labors, and that your lot is abundantly beyond the lot of the living." As for the wicked, "Know ye, that their souls will be made to descend into Sheol, and they will become wicked, and great will be their tribulation." In the first century B. C. the doctrine of future retribution was a bone of contention between Pharisees and Sadducees. *Enoch* and *Psalms of Solomon* deny the views of the Sadducees that retribution in a future judgment will overtake the workers of iniquity. *II Maccabees* and *Wisdom* declare that unrighteousness is punished and righteousness rewarded by adversity or prosperity in the present life—a doctrine repudiated in *Ethiopic Enoch* (XCI–CIV). Resurrection and eternal life is the reward of virtue, eternal punishment the penalty for transgression.

Only in two parts of the *Book of Wisdom*, especially in Part I, is immortality conceived as the crown and culmination of moral development, and moral death as the natural outcome of moral degeneration.

In the *Psalms of Solomon* the reward of virtue is eternal life; the wicked are consigned to eternal torment and irretrievable moral ruin. According to *II Enoch* (1–50 A. D.), the souls of men were created before the foundation of the world. A place of future abode has been prepared for every human soul. The righteous will escape the final judgment and enter paradise as their final abode and eternal inheritance. This paradise, suggesting in some respects the Mohammedan paradise, contains "all the trees of beautiful colours, and their fruits ripe and fragrant, and all kinds of food which they produced, springing up with delightful fragrance." It awaits the righteous who have endured every kind of attack from those who afflict their souls; who turned away their eyes from unrighteousness, accomplished a righteous judgment, gave bread to the hungry and clothes to the naked, raised the fallen, assisted the oppressed orphan, walked without blame before the face of the Lord, and served him only. "Blessed are those who shall go to the mansions of the blessed; for in the evil ones there is no rest nor any means of return from them." The wicked go to a northern region in which there are many tortures, a place of darkness and impenetrable gloom. On all sides are fire and ice; hell both burns and freezes. This is the place prepared for those who do not honour God, who commit evil deeds upon earth, sodomy, witchcraft, enchantments, devilish magic; who boast of their evil deeds, stealing, lying, calumnies, envy, evil thoughts, fornication, murder; who steal the souls of wretched men, oppress the poor, and grow rich by taking other men's possessions; who, when they might feed the hungry, allow them to die of famine; who, when they might clothe them, strip them naked.

Essenes assign to souls of the righteous a blessed immortality; souls of the wicked go to a dark cold region of eternal torment.

In apocryphal literature of the first century A. D. the main sanctions of morality are derived from belief in the retribution which overtakes the individual after death. In some cases, however, the solidarity of the nation is emphasized; the standpoint in *Baruch* (IV, 5; V, 9), for example, is national rather than individual.

The *Assumption of Moses* teaches that individual retribution operates in the present; in the future judgment the nation will be dealt with as a unit.

In the majority of the apocryphal books, however, retribution is visited upon the individual in the future life. The *Psalms of Ezra* revolts against mechanical retribution. If men are to be judged simply by the standard of conformity to the law, then possibly only a few will be saved. From this despairing view the writer appeals to the mercy of God, and expresses a faith that retributive forces will be tempered by divine love. After the Captivity, under Babylonian influence, Sheol becomes a region devoted principally to punishment, and Gehenna a place of especial abasement and torment.

"Ordinary transgressors of Israel, whose merits preponderate," says the Talmud, incorporating Iranian concepts, "though they descend into Hell, do not feel the effects of the flames, and rise at once. Some who sin with their bodies, such as those who put their neighbours to shame publicly and who neglect the phylacteries, are annihilated after twelve months' endurance of hell-fire. Adulterers, though they sin with their bodies, ascend to happiness at the end of the same period. Christians, informers, and those who systematically despise the words of the Rabbis are consigned to eternal punishment. All may escape punishment altogether by repentance in this life." In the first century A. D. liberal Pharisees, as interpreted by Josephus, conceived a Hades of temporary punishment, and an Elysium of light, "Abraham's Bosom." The messiah Logos, as judge, will condemn the wicked to a lake of fire, already prepared but as yet not used for torture, and will reward the righteous in the heavenly kingdom. The wicked will resume their old bodies unchanged, but the righteous will obtain pure and immortal forms fashioned from their old bodies, which have been sowed in the ground. In the future happy age which follows the judgment upon the wicked, there will be dwellers in heaven and on earth, but there will be no births, wild animals, storms, darkness, or change. Man will be able to walk upon the sea, and to ascend into heaven; he will never grow old or die, though he will lead a material or semi-material existence in his spiritual body.

In the *Sohar*, composed perhaps in the twelfth century but almost certainly containing older traditions, the concept of reward of the good and punishment of the evil is clearly expressed, although there are inconsistencies in the respective accounts. According to one account, Adam is surrounded by the just who know how to avoid the path which goes down to hell and have been gathered into paradise. Another account declares that the soul when it leaves this world is stopped by angels who preside over the offices of severity. They do not allow to pass through the door those who have left no son.[8]

Maimonides (twelfth century) says: "The good which is treasured up for the righteous is the life of the world to come; it is a life which is deathless and a happiness free from all adversity. The reward of the righteous is their meriting this bliss and enjoying this happy state. The punishment of the wicked is that they do not merit this higher form of life, but are cut off and die. Whoever does not merit that life suffers death without ever recovering life again; he is cut off in his wickedness and perishes like the beast. . . . All the wicked (of Israel), though their sins be numerous, are judged according to their wrongdoings, but still have a share in the world to come; because all Israel have a share therein, although they have sinned. . . . Likewise the pious of the nations of the world have a share in it. The following (Israelites) have no share in the world to come, but are cut off, perish and are condemned for all eternity because of their great wickedness and sinfulness; viz., infidels and heretics, they who deny the Torah, they who deny the resurrection of the dead and the coming of the Redeemer, apostates, they who cause the public to sin, they who deviate from the accepted practices of the Community, he who commits transgressions presumptuously and openly like Jehoiakim, informers, they who overawe the Community, not for a religious purpose, they who shed blood, slanderers, and he who obliterates the mark of his circumcision. . . . Our statement that none of these sinners has a share in the world to come applies only when he dies without repentance; but if he turn from his wickedness and die a penitent, he is of the sons of the world to come, because there is nothing which can stand against repentance. Even if one denied a fundamental principle of religion all his life but finally repented, he has a share in the world to come." [9]

A rabbinic school of Judaism now supports vigorously belief in life after death with rewards and punishments. Rabbi Stoltz, for example, declares: "Man's personal immortality was always an established belief in Israel. Throughout all his long history we search in vain for a period when this doctrine was not affirmed, believed, or defended by the Jew.

8. A. E. Waite, *The Holy Kabbalah: A Study of the Secret Tradition in Israel as unfolded by Sons of the Doctrine for the Benefit and Consolation of the Elect dispersed through the Lands and Ages of the Greater Exile*, 325–326 (London, Williams and Norgate, 1929).

9. Quoted in A. Cohen, *The Teachings of Maimonides*, 231–232 (London, Routledge, 1927).

The voluminous literature of Judaism is unanimous on the subject."

Eschatological beliefs in Mediterranean and adjacent cultures influenced early Christian concepts. The Persian concept of purgatory, well established in Judaism long before the time of Christ, was adopted by Christianity, as was later the Jewish practice of offering prayers and oblations for the dead. Judas Maccabaeus offered prayers and sacrifices for the sins of his soldiers fallen in battle, "a reconciliation for the dead, that they might be delivered from sin." Shammai taught that, whereas the sins of desperate sinners are punished for ever, others "go down to Gehenna, and moan, and come up again." Christianity adopted this more favourable view of Hades, or purgatory, a view still held by some Christian sects.

The heaven of the righteous, described in the New Testament, promises spiritual goods and discards sensuous elements. The torments of the wicked are perpetual fire, weeping, and gnashing of teeth; the punishment is eternal and repentance availeth nought. Belief in blessings of the next world and adoption of measures to secure them have, however, sometimes taken a perverse course. In some parts of Europe, as late as the last century, universal suicide was preached by fervent missionaries who represented it as the only means of escape from the snares of Antichrist, the only assured way of eluding earthly sins and sorrows and securing the eternal joys of heaven. Communities hailed with enthusiasm the gospel of death and hastened to put its precepts into practice. Through northern and northeastern Russia, as a result of such preaching, there were many suicides. An establishment for the reception of religious suicides, a building without doors or windows, was founded in the forest of Vetlouga. Through a hole in the roof aspirants to heaven were lowered into the building, and the hatch was battened down. Men armed with clubs patrolled the outer walls to prevent the escape of those who might change their minds. Here hundreds of persons perished. At first, sounds of devotion issued from the walls; but later these were replaced by entreaties for food, prayers for mercy, and imprecations on the miscreant who had lured the victims to destruction. Subsequently priests, monks, and laymen preached salvation by flame. They seduced children by promises of gay clothes, apples, nuts, and honey in heaven. Adults who hesitated to comply were assured that troops were then on the way to deliver them to Antichrist, and thus rob them of eternal bliss. Thousands of men, women, and children rushed into the flames and were destroyed.

The general pattern of belief in life after death characteristic of preliterate folk differs from that of historic civilizations. In simple preliterate cultures there is often no distinction of fate for good or evil; though in many simple cultures, as, for example, in many North American tribes, good and wicked go to different regions. In the more highly developed preliterate cultures, however, the character of the post-mortem life of the good and that of the evil may be different, as, for example, in the higher Central American civilizations and in Polynesia.

With the exception of ancient Egypt the early historic civilizations entertain the "squeak and jibber" theory of post-mortem existence, as Aldous Huxley calls it. One might call it with equal verisimilitude the shade and shiver status. Ghosts are mere shadows which cast no shadow, and they shiver in anæmic discomfort.

The next stage in development is a realm of bliss and reward for the righteous in which the wicked, who sometimes are merely the unfortunate, do not share. There then develops a more detailed concept of hell. Heaven remains much the same; but hell develops specialized regions. This is emphatically the case in Iranian, Buddhist, and Mohammedan beliefs. One may observe, too, that whereas Christianity, like Zoroastrianism, Hinduism, Buddhism, and Mohammedanism, has developed only one type of heaven and a single reward for the good irrespective of specific virtues, it has, in theology and poetry, developed a variety of hells. Apparently the sophistications of higher civilizations have been more interested in appropriate punishments for the wicked than in proper rewards for the peculiarities of righteousness. Perhaps the explanation is that there are few ways to be good, but many ways to be wicked; and abstinence from every form of wickedness is itself a virtue of no mean merit.

William McDougall says every vigorous nation has believed in post-mortem existence, and in many instances the loss of it has accompanied the decay of national vigour. Apart from any hope of rewards or fear of punishment after death, the belief has, he thinks, a moralizing influence on thought and conduct. "The admirable Stoic attitude of a Marcus Aurelius or a Huxley may suffice for those who rise to it in the moral environment created by civilization based on a belief in a future life and upon other positive religious beliefs; but I gravely doubt whether whole nations could rise to the level of an austere morality, or even maintain a decent working standard of conduct, after losing those beliefs." [10] A proof that life does not end with death would justify the belief that we have a share in a larger scheme of things than the universe described by physical science; and this conviction would add dignity, seriousness, and significance to our lives, and throw a great weight into the scale against the dangers that threaten an advanced civilization. The solution of the problem of the relation of body to mind must always exert a "determining influence upon man's view of his place in the world, upon his prospects, his hopes, and his deepest purposes, and hence upon his conduct." [11]

Many, like Cicero, think belief in future existence keys men to worthier efforts. Frazer, however, is not sanguine about the benefits which humanity has reaped from belief in immortality of the soul. It has entailed incalculable economic waste—which in itself would horrify a Scot. It has occasioned hostility and warfare through attempts to appease offended ghosts, and fostered religious wars and persecution, or at least furnished an excuse for them. Belief in post-mortem existence of the soul does not always supply a motive for modifying conduct, for the next world may be regarded as affording merely a continuation of the status acquired in this one. Thus the belief may furnish motives for base conduct, inasmuch as the conqueror has at his mercy and service the souls of those whom he subdues or kills. In Fiji, where only the slayer of an enemy is promised the highest post-mortem rewards, belief in life after death furnishes untoward incentives. A religion, such as that of Mohammedans or of Japanese, which promises highest rewards to those who die fighting, affords an incentive to conduct which gives these peoples an apparent advantage over adversaries who lack this martial stimulus. Dahomean belief, which calls for large sacrifice of human life at the death of the king, that messengers or slaves may be sent to spiritland, is scarcely productive of good. Well may the Dahomean lament:

> As the forest trees rock
> When the wild winds blow,
> The King's death is a shock,
> For how bloody the woe!

In Dahomey the greatest offerings of human victims were made at the death of the king or at the annual sacrifice held to supply deceased

10. William McDougall, *Body and Mind: A History and a Defense of Animism*, fifth edition, xiii–xiv (London, Methuen, 1920).
11. *Ibid.*, x.

royalty with new servants. At any time a king might dispatch souls to take messages to the next world. In 1859, when the king of Oyo died, four men were sacrificed and forty-two of his wives poisoned themselves that they might minister to his soul in the Land of the Dead. At the death of the Dahomean king Andezo II, in 1780, five hundred and ninety-five women, in addition to soldiers, eunuchs, bards, and others, were killed. At the death of the Ganda king, four of his closest attendants, four of his widows, and hundreds of slaves and captives were clubbed to death and left in the enclosure in which the king's body rested, that they might minister to his soul. Subsequently hundreds of people were killed to furnish a new retinue for the ghost of the deceased king.

In Ondo about twenty persons were sacrificed when a king died; one was immolated at the place where the corpse was washed, four at different entrances to the palace, one in the market-place. On the day of burial, from eight to ten human victims, and a cat, were killed and interred with the corpse, or were buried alive. "We all went out to meet [the Dahomey king] to accompany him to the town; and when we had met him he bade us sit down. We then took seats. Here a man had his hands tied, and mouth barred, with a fathom of white bast woven about his loins. He pointed him out to us as a messenger that was going to carry private information to his father. The poor creature was taken up to the town, and was sacrificed on the tomb of his father. Another in the same position was sent up to their large market to go and tell the spirits there what he was going to do for his father. About an hour afterwards there were brought forward again four men in the same position, together with one deer, one monkey, and one turkey-buzzard. Here the poor creatures had their heads cut off, save one. One man was to go to all the markets and tell all the spirits what he was about to make for his father; the second man was to go to all the waters, and tell all the animals there, etc.; the third man was to go to all the roads, and tell the spirit-travellers, etc.; the fourth and last man was to go up to the firmament, and tell all the hosts there, etc.; the monkey was to go to all the swamps, to climb all the trees, and tell all the animals there; the turkey-buzzard, fortunate creature, was let loose to fly up to the sky, and tell all the birds there." [12]

Among the Nza of the Congo Free State, thanks to belief in survival of the soul, the deceased man reposed in the lifeless arms of his favourite wife. Around him in a circle lay the corpses of other strangled wives,

12. Sir Richard F. Burton, *Wanderings in West Africa* (London, Tinsley, 1863).

not permitted to survive their husband. Slain slaves who formed a circle about the grave would serve spiritual food to the deceased's invited guests. Among the Rua the crouching body of the chief wife served as a seat for the corpse, a second wife as the footstool; other wives sat in a circle around the body, all buried alive. The Bena Kaniko broke the arms and legs of wives of the deceased to prevent their escape from the grave. A month after the death of a Luba chief, some of his wives were buried alive around his grave that they might join him in the next world. A Kindi chief designated the wives who were to be killed after his death; they were his favourites. In the Lado district, after a chief's death, his widows and slaves were clubbed by a shouting enthusiastic crowd, then stabbed with knives. The victims were thrown into the grave of the deceased chief, that his soul might have company. Comparable practices prevailed in other African tribes. Often at the funerals of Negro chieftains instant steps were taken to counter any feelings of resentment or suspicion on the part of the ghost. People were thrust alive into the burial pit, or put to death in the rooms or courtyard of the deceased, or in other places frequented by him during his lifetime. The roasted body of an Unyoro chief reposed in a deep and spacious grave, on the knees of his living wives. The grave was filled with unwilling victims, seized by the chief's body-guard, and the earth was trampled down upon them. The corpse of the king of Karangue was "sewn up in a cow-hide and floated in a boat on the lake, until it was in an advanced state of decomposition. It was then placed in a hut, together with five virgins and fifty cows; the hut was closed, and the living creatures were left to die. The grave of a Manyema chief was floored with the bodies of ten living women; on these the dead chief was laid, and then men, their limbs, like those of the women, previously broken, were also cast into the pit. Gaga notables were buried sitting on a seat, accompanied by two wives, whose legs were broken; the grave was then filled up, and saturated with oil and blood. The dead king of the Bakitara lay in his tomb on a bed of bark and cow-hides; two of his widows lay on either side of him, covering themselves with bark-cloths; a loose pile of bark-cloths filled up the grave, and the women died, either of starvation or of suffocation." [13]

"A Bantu man, especially a man of consequence, has need of slaves and wives and children to serve and cherish him in the world to which

13. C. E. Vulliamy, *Immortal Man*, 112 (London, Methuen, 1926). Reprinted by permission of Methuen & Co., Ltd.

he is going. There is only one way of providing him with them; they must be killed. This line of thought accounts for one of the cruelest of all the cruel practices of the Bantu." Among the Kuba of the upper Kasai, Congo, on the death of a king or his sister, the funeral might not take place until three hundred slaves had been killed. "Some people give the number at one thousand, but three hundred is a safer figure." [14]

A similar custom prevailed in Sumeria. A poet laureate describes the revelation of the archæologist's spade:

> . . . either side the pole, where lay the harness'd bones
> of the yoke-mated oxen, there beside their bones
> lay the bones of the grooms, and slaughter'd at their post
> all the king's body-guard, each liegeman spear in hand,
> in sepulchred attention; and whereby lay the harp
> the arm bones of the player, as there she had pluck'd her dirge,
> lay mingled with its fragments; and nearby disposed,
> two rows of skeletons, her sisterly audience
> whose lavish ear-pendants and gold-filleted hair,
> the uniform decoration of their young service,
> mark'd them for women of the harem, sacrificed
> to accompany their lord, the day when he set forth
> to enter into the presence of the scepter'd shades
> congregated with splendour in the mansions of death.[15]

At Ur, Mesopotamia, the prehistoric tombs, to which the above lines refer, show that the dead king was carried to his tomb on chariots or sledges, his body dressed in full insignia. Draught animals, drivers, courtiers, ladies-in-waiting, men of the harem, musicians, and armed guards followed their sovereign to the future world. In the chamber with the body of Queen Shuh-ad lay the corpse of an attendant; her ladies-in-waiting, harpist, and grooms reposed in the shaft in which they had been slain. Near the tomb of a king were the bodies of twelve women in court dress, fully armed soldiers, attendants, and grooms.

In Tonga a chief's wives were killed and buried with him. In New Zealand one or more of a chief's wives strangled themselves, and slaves were killed to attend the ghost of the chief. According to Marco Polo, Mongols, when conveying the corpse of the deceased khan to his last resting place, sacrificed all the women they met, "saying to them, 'Depart for the next world, and there attend upon your deceased Lord,' be-

14. Edwin W. Smith, *The Religion of Lower Races,* Chapter V (New York, Macmillan, 1923).

15. From *The Testament of Beauty* by Robert Bridges (Clarendon Press, Oxford). Reprinted by permission of the publisher.

ing impressed with the belief that all whom they thus slay do actually become his servants in the next life. . . . When the corpse of Mongou Kaan was transported to this mountain, the horsemen who accompanied it slew upwards of twenty thousand persons who fell in their way." [16] The statistics may be "a Marco Polo," but the practice is elsewhere well attested.

Among the Natchez the wives of the Great Sun were strangled at his death, and other persons of distinction immolated themselves in order to accompany their lord and master to the next world. The death of the Aztec ruler entailed the sacrifice of many lives. A hundred or even two hundred slaves, men and women, were sacrificed, the number depending upon the position and wealth of the deceased. The victims' breasts were opened, their hearts removed, and their bodies thrown on the funeral pyre. Those slain in this fashion might include some of the deceased's wives, and the dwarfs, hunchbacks, and deformed who had amused him in his palace. They would solace their master in his heavenly abode in the next world. In Peru wives and attendants of a deceased monarch immolated themselves that they might accompany their lord and master in the next world and minister to his spiritual needs. Over the body of their chief the Chibcha of Colombia buried his favourite wives and slaves that they might serve him in the other world as they had served him in this world. The Quimbaya paid similar respect to an important man. In Assam a motive in head-hunting was provision of the dead with slaves in the next world.

"To tell the truth about things of this world is to make of them a terrible satire." Is William McDougall correct in supposing that without belief in life after death the morals of nations will inevitably weaken and decay because their citizens will thereby be deprived of the greatest incentive to moral action, namely, reward in a future life for deeds done in the body?

16. Manuel Komroff (editor), *Travels of Marco Polo*, Kublai Khan edition, 89 (New York, Liveright, 1930).

CHAPTER XVII THE STATUS OF WOMAN IN THE CULT

Tiele refers to the part played by woman in religion and dismisses the topic with the observation that there is no instance of a religion founded by a woman—which is not correct—and with a brief account of the part played by women as priestesses, oracular sibyls, prophetesses, saints; as messengers of divine love who strive with gentle hand to alleviate poverty, sickness, and other miseries of earthly existence; as votaries of calm consecration, who contribute largely to the preservation of the mystic and devotional elements in religion. Farnell, Mrs. Parsons, Hartland, Westermarck, and Hobhouse describe the position of woman in early historic religions; Eckenstein and Emile Lücka recount the part played by women in medieval church history; but an adequate account of woman's place in the religious cult has not been written.

Historic religions have not always been kind to woman. Mohammed said: "I went to the gates of heaven, and behold it was filled with the poor (men); I went to the gates of hell, and behold it was filled with women." In Mohammedan Egypt a century ago some rich men engaged a learned woman to visit the harem daily for the purpose of teaching their daughters and female slaves to say their prayers and recite a few chapters from the Koran. Even among the wealthy, however, few women learned to say their prayers in private, and they were not permitted to say them in the mosque. Though the Prophet did not forbid women to attend public prayers in the mosque, he declared it better that they pray in private. In Cairo females and young boys may not pray with the congregation in the mosque or even be in the mosque during prayer. Formerly women were permitted to come to the mosque, though they must place themselves apart from and behind the men: females inspire a devotion not appropriate in a place consecrated to the worship of God. Sindi (Indian) Mohammedans exclude women when seeking prophetic dreams at the shrine of a saint or elsewhere, reading a charm to cure the sick, attempting to control a spirit, throwing down portions of a sacrificed animal at a cross-roads, reciting charms during an eclipse, sowing, measuring grain, praying as a congregation at *Ids* in a mosque, discussing an important issue, erecting a "Persian wheel," digging a well, putting into place the important beam of a house, laying the foundations of a building, cutting down a tree, or slaughtering an animal. Women may not witness the first equipping of a boat or the efforts to bring rain; may not touch tools, magic herbs, or the first fruits presented to a mullah or sayid; may not join in the prayer for the dead; may not shear sheep; may not enter a garden of plantain or betel; and may not bathe in water used for irrigating plantains, beans, or flowering trees, such as the champha or the moghra tree. Thus the religious restrictions are merely a phase of the social restrictions which hedge her round.

Hindu women may not read the Veda and may not worship a deity with Vedic mantras, or verses. With the exception of the gods known as Puranprasiddh and Svayamblm, a woman may not touch images of deities installed in temples, and may not touch the salagrama stone, though she may worship and touch images temporarily installed for worship. Similarly, Santal women may not participate directly in religious services. Although many Hindu tales picture woman's evil influence over man and interpret her triumph over him as retarding the soul's tedious rise to higher planes, incidentally, in many ways, they depict her as possessing tact and intelligence which far surpass those of the male. The Vedas extol the dignity of motherhood. Women were ordained into the Brahmanic order, but, according to accounts in the Vinaya texts, with much reluctance upon the part of the male contingent; and they were assigned an inferior position in the order. Buddha held that perfection is an inward state attainable by women as well as men. Buddha at first declined to admit women into the order, but was persuaded by the faithful Amada. Among the immortals of Taoism are women who have led an unusually ascetic life. This religion chivalrously declares that woman conquers man by continual quietness. But the assurance is probably ironic. The Tenri Kyokai, a recent Japanese Shinto sect of some four million adherents, was founded by a woman, Omiki. She exercised great personal influence upon her followers. Its doctrines call for the assignment to woman of a more independent position.

In spite of political and social ostracism Greek women sometimes played an important part in the religious life. In the gardens of Adonis were baskets or pots filled with earth, in which wheat, barley, lettuce, fennel, and various kinds of flowers were kept, sown, and tended for eight days, chiefly or exclusively by women. A Greek myth alleges that Zeus, in order to punish Prometheus for his theft of fire and the consequent arrogance of mankind, with the help of the other gods created woman and sent her down to earth. Consonant with Greek thought is the Hebrew doctrine which alleges that the first woman brought upon mankind a pack of insidious and never-ending ills.

After a study of "all the facts bearing upon woman's position in the ancient and later Hebrew cult as contained in the Old Testament," Peritz concludes that the Semites in general, and the Hebrews in particular, exhibit no tendency to discriminate between man and woman in granting permission to participate in religious practices; woman participates in all the essentials of the cult, both as worshipper and as officiant; only at a later time, with progress in the development of the cult, does a tendency appear, not so much to exclude woman from the cult as to make man prominent in it. In ancient Israel, and during the period of Levitical legislation, in the act of sacrifice women enjoyed equal rights with men, he says. Perhaps it is "the position of woman in society that introduces the difference" in the cult, but a difference there is, none the less. In the Hebrew temple, for example, the women were separated from the men. The precedent has been followed in Orthodox Judaism to the present day. In the Middle Ages the women congregated in a room adjoining the synagogue and communicating with it by means of rows of windows, which were carefully curtained. Thus they could follow the service without being seen by the men.

At the present day, in synagogues of Reformed Jews women sit with the men, but in Orthodox Jewish synagogues men and women sit separately, the former in the body of the church, the latter "stowed away up" in a high gallery. The Orthodox Jewish custom at festivals is to decorate only the men's portion of the synagogue; even at Pentecost no flowers are placed in the women's gallery. These distinctions are more marked in European communities than in the freer atmosphere of the New World, but are found also in some American synagogues.

The Christian faith could not flourish amid older faiths and remain uninfluenced by them. Where contact has been closest and has continued longest, outside influence, as one would expect, has been most marked. Egyptian Coptic churches show much oriental influence. Coptic women and children are not entitled to all the formal privileges bestowed upon men and male adolescents. Women are assigned the rearmost places, behind the men, separated from them by a wooden lattice; recently the screen has been removed from some churches.

Several Roman Catholic churches in Rome show similar, Byzantine, influence. The Basilica of St. Agnese fuori la Mura, founded by Constantine, has a gallery for women. In the ninth-century Church of St. Maria in Tavestere the upper galleries were probably at one time reserved for women; until the twelfth century there were women's galleries in the Church of St. Maria in Cosmedin. The galleries in the last-mentioned church, known as *matronaea,* as well as the name of the church (from *Al Meidan,* a Constantinople church), are accounted for by the fact that the church was the possession of a Greek colony in Rome. As a prominent inscription at the door of the chapel states, women are admitted to the Chapel of St. Helena, in the Church of Santa Croce in Gerusalemme, only on the twentieth of March. The Chapel of the Orto del Paradiso, in the Church of St. Prassede, is accessible to men daily; women are admitted only on Sundays during Lent. The first-mentioned chapel contains the inscription from the cross found by St. Helena in Jerusalem; the latter preserves a portion of the column to which Christ was bound while being scourged. These sacred objects invest the chapels with peculiar sanctity. Woman, with her inherent uncleanness, would contaminate these holy spots. Most Christian churches exclude women from the priesthood and from important offices in the church, though a number of Protestant sects officially tolerate women preachers. None of the older Christian sects, however, such as the Orthodox, the Roman Catholic, the Established Church of England, and the Lutheran Church, admit women to the priesthood. In 1936 the Established Church of England gave the following report on the ministry of women: "We maintain that the ministration of women . . . will tend to produce a lowering of the spiritual tone of Christian worship, such as is not produced by the ministrations of men before congregations largely or exclusively female. It is a tribute to the quality of Christian womanhood that it is possible to make this statement; but it would appear to be a simple matter of fact that in the thoughts and desires of that sex the natural is more easily made subordinate to the supernatural, the carnal to the spiritual than is the case with men; and that the ministrations of a male priesthood do not normally arouse that side of female human nature which should be quiescent during the times of the adoration of almighty God. We believe, on the other hand, that it would be impossible for the male members of the average Anglican congregation to be present at a service at which a woman ministered without becoming unduly conscious of her sex." [1] Virginia Woolf remarks, somewhat ironically, that "in the opinion of the Commissioners, therefore, Christian women are more spiritually minded than Christian men—a remarkable, but no doubt adequate, reason for excluding them from the priesthood." [2] The exclusion of women from priesthood, practised by most Christian churches, has its New Testament justification from St. Paul: "Let the women keep silence in the churches: for it is not permitted unto them to speak; but let them be in subjection, as also saith the laws. . . . And if they would learn anything, let them ask their own husbands at home: for it is shameful for a woman to speak in the church."

In many preliterate cultures not only the use of, but also a knowledge of, sacred objects is kept from the women. In tribes in which a sacred significance attaches to the bull-roarer, women may not see it, though in tribes in which it is used only in secular activities it is not taboo to them. Formerly, in Melanesia, the bull-roarer was taboo to women; but when the cause of the sound made by it was ascertained by the women, its use in the secret societies was discontinued and bamboo and a shell were substituted, the women being kept ignorant of the cause of the sound produced by means of these objects. Among the Yorubas of western Africa, the sound of the bull-roarer announced an important ceremony and warned the women to retire into the houses and remain there. Among Zuñis and Eskimos, where no sanctity attaches to the bull-roarer, women and children may use it. Throughout Australia the bull-roarer is sacred and may not be seen by women or children, much less used by them.[3] An exception is the tribe at White Cliffs, Frazer's Island, off the Queensland coast. At their ceremonies held for the purpose of ensuring plentiful supplies of fish and honey both men and women swing the bull-roarer. The participation of the women probably indicates a breaking down of a former ceremonial exclusion and an admission to rites which have lost awe-inspiring sanctity. Some Australian tribes—for example, the Kurnai—have two types of bull-

1. *Women and the Ministry, Some Considerations on the Report of the Archbishops' Commission on the Ministry of Women*, 1936, 24.

2. Virginia Woolf, *Three Guineas*, 245 (New York, Harcourt, 1938).

3. Arunta women do actually see the bull-roarers, though at some distance. Spencer surmises that "perhaps [the women] know a little more than they are given credit for." Baldwin Spencer and F. J. Gillen, *The Arunta*, I, 100 (London, Macmillan, 1927).

roarer: a large and a small one, male and female. Howitt conjectures that these two types of bull-roarer indicate the existence of ceremonies in which women are allowed to participate. The Itchumundi and Turbal, however, though they use two types of bull-roarer, do not allow women to participate in any tribal ceremony. The Parnkalla use two types of bull-roarer, but women play no part in initiation ceremonies. Women and children may not witness tribal ceremonies; while they are in progress, women camp out of sight of men. If it is necessary for women, when procuring food or water, or for any other reason, to go within sight of men, the women cover their heads with a skin rug and walk in stooping posture. Impertinent curiosity merits death, a penalty paid by more than one woman for breach of tribal rules regarding religious ceremonies. Australian males generally keep all knowledge of sacred rites to themselves, though Strehlow says Aruntas have a beneficent "god," Altjira, known only to women. Maori women, however high their rank, when they approach a sacred place must veil their faces. If they disregard this precaution, they are reminded of the fate of a lady of the olden time who saw with open eyes the Sacred Dog, and in consequence was changed into a rock out at sea. Among New Guinea Roro-speaking tribes only the men know that the *harihu*, masked men, are human beings; the women are taught that they are spirits from the bush; they and the uninitiated youths firmly believe this, and are extremely afraid of them. A woman who should venture near a *harihu* would be killed, and a child whose curiosity prompts it to approach a *harihu* is mercilessly beaten.

Toda religious restrictions enforce celibacy in the dairyman priest, who must leave his wife if he is married. Women may not follow the path taken by migrating sacred buffaloes, or may follow it only in part. During the month preceding purification of the dairy, women may not visit it, though they may attend a subsequent feast. They take no part in dairy ritual, the milking of buffaloes, or the churning of milk. Todas say that formerly the women had charge of the buffaloes at the time of calving; they do not have that responsibility now. When women go to the dairy to get buttermilk, they use a prescribed path and stand at an appointed place to receive it. With two exceptions, noted below, women may not enter the dairy. During dairy operations they may enter the outermost room of a dairy used as a funeral hut, while the body of a man is there. Here they sit on one side of the room. At the migration ceremony a girl seven or eight years of age, who has not attained puberty, is given food in the dairy of the village which the buffaloes are leaving; and she sweeps the ground in front of the dairy in the village to which the buffaloes are going. During certain dairy ceremonies women must leave the village. In one Toda village, during the passing of the buffaloes the women leave the village, taking with them pounder, sieve, and broom. The only participation of women in the ceremonies involving the sacred buffaloes is during the ordination of the candidates into the dairy priesthood. On the second day of the ceremony each candidate stands behind an old woman who gives him his portion of food, handing it behind her without looking at the recipient. Previously to this she has bathed and dressed in her best clothes, and donned all the ornaments she can procure: gold earrings, necklaces, bracelets, and rings. The woman chosen for this function must be of the Tartharol exogamous unit, beyond the age of child-bearing, and have had no carnal intercourse with a man of her own clan. South African tribes, similarly, do not allow women to enter the cattle kraals.

Yorubas say that the god Obatala forms the child in the mother's womb; women who desire to become mothers address their prayers to him. On feast days celebrated at the temple of Odudua, patroness of love, women abandon themselves indiscriminately to male worshippers who appear in her honour. At the annual festival of Orisha Oko, the god of agriculture and fertility, general licence prevails. Priestesses give themselves indiscriminately to male worshippers of the god. Theoretically, a man may have sexual intercourse with any woman whom he meets abroad; "social prejudices have, however, restricted the application of the privilege, and it is now only slavegirls, or women of the lowest order, who are at the disposal of the public, and then only if they are consenting parties." When the Edo of southern Nigeria are about to bring out the sacred drum, they shut all doors and with loud cries of "Hoi!" warn the women to keep away. With a few exceptions, women may not witness any of the men's rites. In one village women are warned by the piercing notes of the Oko to keep away when the sweepings of the Egwaibo shrine are being brought out; yet women clean some of the shrines, do the rubbing of the Ovia house, from which ordinarily they are excluded, and in one purificatory ceremony a woman carries the sacred objects of the cult and enters the shrine by the forbidden gate. On the other hand, women are warned to keep their distance when materials for the manufacture of the hats used by one cult are taken through the village.

In Haiti voodoo no woman may enter the chamber set aside for the worship of Erzulie except to clean it and prepare it for the service.

In ancient Mexico certain women were admitted to every sacerdotal function except that of human sacrifice. They were, however, nuns rather than priestesses. The Yahuna, and some other tribes of Brazil, do not allow women or children to see the flutes which the men use at the festivals which celebrate the ripening of fruits. Should the women see the flutes, they would die. The flutes have been in contact with death-spirits, which have entered them, and are therefore infected and highly dangerous to the uninitiated. Tucano women may not look upon the god Yurupari. When the men use the long flutes which they blow in his honour the women must conceal themselves.

PRIESTESS

The priestess is not a common figure in preliterate cultures, unless one includes in that category medicinewomen, who, to be sure, deal with the supernatural. In some Siberian tribes the *shamanka* is a powerful person and has potent spirit-helpers. Among the Eskimos a medicine-woman may induce Sedna to release the souls of seal and walrus, though usually this function is performed by a man. In the Plains area of North America the medicinewoman may deal heroically with the holy; and sometimes she prays to the sun much as do medicinemen. Among Canadian Dakotas and Crees, women are members of the Holy Society, the closest approximation in the Plains area to priesthood.

In tribes of the Southwest in which there is well-defined priesthood, either there is no priestess or she plays, usually, a subordinate rôle; however, in the religious life of Zuñis, Aztecs, and Mayas the priestess is sometimes an important functionary. There were priestesses in ancient Egypt, but not in early Judaism or early Hinduism. They attained high status in the cults of Assyria and Syria. Temple prostitution was in vogue, but the women who served at such temples were otherwise not priestesses.

In Babylonia, Greece, and Rome, celibacy was imposed upon certain classes of priestesses, but women played an important rôle in the cult.

Priestesses served in some Ganda temples. Most temples had in addition to priests or priestesses a corps of virgins, young girls sent to the temple service by parents whose prayers or vows for offspring had been answered. They kept the temple and its grounds in order, guarded the fire, and made sure that visitors observed the taboos. A menstruating woman might not enter a temple; hence at puberty these young female attendants must leave. Among the Herero, as among Peruvians, vestal virgins guard the sacred fires.

In the Nigerian cult of Ebora women had no part or lot with men in worship. Though women were debarred as active participants in the religious rites of Egun, they were eligible for membership in a guild of female dancers and singers, called Ogun, which was a part of the Egun cult. In this cult, however, there was systematic terrorization of women by "dodos."

Among Jaqir Duseens, of Banguey, North Borneo, a priestess acquainted with the ways of the people, knowing the future as well as the past, nominates and trains her successors, who must wear black robes and carry wooden knives. At the harvest festival, if the paddy crop has been a good one, she thanks the chief spirit on behalf of the tribe.

FEMALE DEITIES AND SPIRITS, GOOD AND EVIL

Though woman often is denied participation in the orthodox established religion, she is frequently assigned a place in the pantheon subsidiary to few or no males. Roman Catholicism reached the acme of its Mariology at a time when women were excluded from privileges of the priesthood and womankind was viewed as the source of the sins of the world. Extremes meet also in savagery, where the lowest position of woman is sometimes associated with worship of a female deity or with propitiation of a female spirit. Eskimos assign male and female spirits to different points of the compass. At the north, northwest, and northeast dwell male spirits; female spirits live at the south, southeast, and southwest, perhaps because soft climate suits soft natures. Evil spirits assume the form of women who wear long hair braided into knots. They come from the north, hold a stick in the hand, and give vent to loud and long-drawn-out lamentations. They envelop the spirit of a person in thread and make off with it.

According to the Blackfoot origin myth, the original inhabitants of the world were Old Man and Old Woman. When they decided how people should live, they agreed that Old Man should have the first say in everything and Old Woman the second (and final) decision. Old Man said: "The women are to tan the hides. When they do this, they are to rub brains on them to make them soft, they are to scrape them well with scraping-tools, etc. But all this they are to do very quickly, for it will not be very hard work."

"No, I will not agree to this," said Old Woman. "They must tan the hide in the way you say; but it must be made very hard work, and take a long time, so that the good workers may be found out."

"Well," said Old Man, "let the people have eyes and mouths in their faces, but they shall be straight up and down."

"No," said Old Woman, "we will not have them that way. We will have the eyes and mouth in the faces, as you say, but they shall all be set crosswise."

"Well," said Old Man, "the people shall have ten fingers on each hand."

"Oh, no!" said Old Woman, "that will be too many. They will be in the way. There shall be four fingers and one thumb on each hand."

So they continued until they had provided for everything in the lives of the people who were to be. Then Old Woman asked what they should do about life and death: Should people live for ever, or should they die? They had some difficulty in coming to an agreement upon this matter. Finally Old Man said: "I will tell you what I will do. I will throw a buffalo-chip into the water, and, if it floats, the people die for four days and live again; but if it sinks, they will die forever."

He threw it into the water and it floated.

"No," said Old Woman, "we will not decide in that way. I will throw in this rock. If it floats, the people will die for four days: if it sinks, the people will die forever."

Old Woman threw the rock into the water, and it sank to the bottom.

"There," she said, "it is better for the people to die forever; for, if they did not die forever, they would never feel sorry for one another, and there would be no sympathy in the world."

"Well," said Old Man, "let it be that way." [4]

Takelmas speak of an Acorn Woman, whose flesh appears in the form of acorns. They recognize also a storm-spirit which goes abroad in the form of a supernatural woman, in company with her children, to dig up roots. Instead of uprooting camass with her digging stick, after the manner of mortals, she upturns the trees. Wascos have stories of a stupid, child-stealing ogress, who, in the end, is easily duped and deceived. This creature, known to Upper Chinooks, is of immense size, has a striped body, is fond of children's flesh, and is stupid. She feeds her children frogs, lizards, and other foods repulsive to Indians.

4. Clark Wissler and D. C. Duvall, "Mythology of the Blackfoot Indians," *APAMNH*, 2, Part I: 20–21 (1908). Reprinted by permission of the American Museum of Natural History.

Among Mayas, Xtabai is a wicked, deceitful phantom, which haunts the highways at night. It assumes the form of a beautiful woman who combs her luxuriant locks with a plant which the natives call the "comb of Xtabai." This lovely creature generally runs away when one approaches. If a lovesick youth succeeds in clasping her in his arms, she instantly transforms herself into a sack of thorns which rests on two duck feet. After embracing this prickly deceiver the deluded lover is ill with fever.

The origins of nearly all the customs of the Todas are referred to the goddess Teikirzi. Notirzi, another goddess, is the ruler of two important clans. The hill on which she lives is especially sacred; the Toda who visits it must salute it in all directions, with hand to forehead. In Victoria, Australia, is a *gnulla gnulla gneear*, a fearful female spirit. To be rid of it people present the medicinemen with weapons, rugs, and food; at a threat of a visit from this spirit these presents are forthwith produced. Spirit women make weapons which the Euahlayi medicinemen travel toward the sunset clouds to obtain, for the post-mortem abode of women is in the west. The medicinemen give in exchange animal food and opossum rugs, for there are no animals in this afterworld of the women. The high ridges above the Warrangilla are haunted by two women, who, tradition says, were buried alive. Their spirits have never rested, but come out at any time from the huge fissure in the ridges where their bodies were put. Their anguished cries as the stones and earth fell on them still echo through the scrub; sometimes a man, keener-sighted than his fellows, sees their spirits flitting through the bushes, and hears their strange cries, when they disappear again into the fathomless fissure. The plain of Weawarra is haunted by the widows of two young warriors who disappeared and never returned. If men camp there at night, spirits of these women silently steal into the camp. The men, who think they are women from a strange tribe, speak to them; but they make no answer, and vanish before the dawn of day, to renew their search each night. On Nikman, one of the Gilbert Islands, were both gods and goddesses, to whom certain stone slabs or pillars were dedicated. Those dedicated to goddesses lay on the ground; those dedicated to gods were upright. Dogai is an evil female spirit which troubles the natives of the Torres Straits. A Maori goddess presided over childbirth. Rakataura, a goddess of the air, presided over music, and long ago played on a flute wrought from the tough cocoon of a certain caterpillar, but later lost her flute and was heard only in sudden and unintelligible noises. Among the Musahar, Bansapti, "queen of the wood," is goddess of childbirth and grants offspring to barren women.

In western Africa goddesses flourish. Yemaha, Yoruba goddess of brooks and streams, presides over water ordeal. She is represented by a yellow female figure adorned with blue beads and white cloth. Odudua, the "Mother Who Receives," the chief goddess of the Yorubas, is represented by a woman sitting and nursing a child. Odudua is patroness of love; many stories relate her adventures and amours. Olosa, goddess of the Lagos lagoon, supplies her votaries with flesh; along the shores of the lagoon several temples are dedicated to her at which offerings of fowl and sheep are made. Oya is goddess of the Niger; Oshun, of the Oshun; and Oba, of the Oba, or Ibu, River. The Ganda goddess Nagawomya, wife of Musoke, has power over grain and crops.

In most cultures woman does not share freely in the religious life. This statement applies both to preliterate cultures and to historic civilizations. Knowledge of the sacred has generally been kept from her. Often she has been deceived as to its true nature, or at least deception has been attempted, as, for example, in Australia and western Africa.

The exclusion of women from the religious sphere is in part an extension of the social exclusion of women which characterizes most cultures. It is sometimes due, in part at least, to the concept that woman, because of her physiological function of menstruation, is inherently unclean. Her presence, therefore, would pollute holy things.

CHAPTER XVIII THE IMPACT OF CULTURE

It is not possible to deal within the compass of this volume with all important phases of the religious life. In particular one finds here little regarding the manner in which the religious life is socialized, that is to say, the manner in which a group organizes and utilizes the instrumentalities of the religious life. Nor is there an account of the manner in which the religious life actually functions, with, so to say, all the parts in place.

There are, of course, religious complexes, and each has a specific cultural and historic setting. In a given group priesthood, god, prayer, ritual, ceremony, and all other accompaniments of the religious life are parts of a unified texture of behaviour and belief. The part functions in a specific setting and with regard to the whole. Hence the part can be understood, as specific function, only in relation to that comprehending whole which gives the part its specific character. Religion reflects the spiritual history of a people, thoughts and beliefs about immaterial things, conceptions of the universe and of life, beliefs about birth, death, and the unseen world.

Religion is not a sphere isolated from the culture but is in all respects a part of the culture, and abundantly reflects the culture medium. As Zora Hurston says, "Gods always behave like the people who make them. One can see the hand of the Haitian peasant in that boisterous god, Guede, because he does and says the things that the peasants would like to do and say. You can see him in the market women, in the domestic servant who now and then appears before her employer 'mounted' by this god who takes occasion to say many stinging things to the boss. You can see him in the field-hand, and certainly in the group of women about a public well or spring, chattering, gossiping and dragging out the shortcomings of their employers and the people like him. Nothing in Haiti is quite so obvious as that this *loa* is the deification of common people of Haiti." [1] To cite another instance: The Kotas, of the Nilgiri hills, southern India, have an Elder Father God, a Younger Father God, and a Mother God. "The junior male god shares the wife of the other. It is not so much that 'Younger Father God' is a co-husband, but that Kota deities, like Kota men, have fraternal rights to the wives of their brothers. In this culture as in many others, the attributes and behaviour of the deities are direct projections and elaborations of patterns valid in society." [2]

Comparable observations apply throughout the world. "The mythical beings of the Eskimo are Eskimo; those of the Australians, Australians. The chiefs of the Polynesians have their counterpart in their deities; the gods of the Dahomeans are Dahomeans; and the gods on Olympus lead the life of Greek royalty." [3]

Religion is not a separate compartment of life. It is constituted essentially of attitudes and evaluations which bring the supernatural into alinement with the world of nature and experience. Accounts of origins describe supernatural powers, and myths exploit the creative abilities of the gods. Æsthetic interests influence religious motives, and religion, in turn, affects the trend of æsthetic impulses. Social urge impinges upon religion, and religious motives penetrate tribal activities. "Man is a rationalizing, not a rational animal."

RELIGION AND MYTHOLOGY

In preliterate cultures accounts of creation are embodied in a mythology which constitutes virtually a system of theology and science, and a series of literary episodes. The explanation is not sheer explanation, but is embodied in myth; the myth is not mere myth, but a rounded and elaborated narrative. The account of creation or cosmogony is part of a system of myths and traditional beliefs, and its significance derives in large part from its orientation in a larger intellectual scheme. Frequently recital of myth accompanies specific expression of religious life.

Before the Omaha child is nursed, and later, before it is weaned, the medicineman comes to it and recites the myths which relate the origin of the world and of food, so that the child will not feel estranged on

1. Zora Hurston, *Tell My Horse*, 232 (Philadelphia, Lippincott, 1938). By permission of the J. B. Lippincott Company.
2. David Mandelbaum, "Kota Polyandry," AA, 40: 576 (1938).
3. Franz Boas (editor), *General Anthropology*, 616–617 (Boston, Heath, 1938).

earth, amid unfamiliar surroundings, and, when it is able to eat cooked foods, will duly appreciate them.

In many tribes, during the initiation of the youths, the tribal myths, or a portion of them, are narrated, so that the candidate will know the tribal traditions. Myths frequently embody religious concepts, which usually are implicit rather than explicit. Thus in the Plains area of North America the concept of *wakan* is fully expressed in the myths. Among Wahpeton Dakotas these narrate the adventures of the various animals that possess *wakan* and the origin of the hierarchy of *wakan* beings.[4] Similarly, in the Northwest Coast area, the myths describe the rôles of the totemic animals and their supernatural attributes. In practically all, perhaps one may say in all, preliterate cultures, and in historic civilizations, myth is a vehicle of religious expression.

RELIGION AND ART

In historic civilizations art has been intimately associated with religion. Babylonian and Assyrian artists represented the gods in bas-relief and sculpture. In Egypt portrayal of gods and sacred animals was a leading motive in art. In Greece and Rome sculpture was in large part the representation of gods and goddesses. Mohammed, aware of the intimate relation between art and religion, forbade the representation of any living thing, lest such images lead to idolatry and polytheism. From its beginning, Christian art has had a religious tinge; witness the use of the lamb, the cross, the fish, the labarum, the saints, and Biblical themes. The art of the Renaissance is permeated with religious significance, even though a pagan spirit inspires it, Jove becoming Michelangelo's Moses, and Venus, the Madonna. Its paintings, statuary, and architecture are primarily religious. Almost every theme is designedly religious.[5]

Religious sentiment influences the art of primitive peoples to about the extent that the religious complex dominates the culture. In the Plains area of North America there are representations of the mythic Thunderbird and of the sun; in the Southwest the plumed serpent which rests on the waters of the underworld is an art motive; among Mayas the plumed serpent Quetzalcoatl, and also other gods, are frequently portrayed, especially in statuary and bas-relief. In the Northwest Coast area of North America the totem animals, which play a dominant rôle in the emotional life, are represented in wood carvings.

4. See pages 6–7.
5. See the writer's *Culture and Progress*, 182–185 (New York, McGraw-Hill, 1930).

In religious ceremonial and in ritual conducted at a sacred locality, the art usually has a religious implication. Such is the case in the Southwest of the United States, where altar designs and sand-paintings accompany the religious celebration. It is notably the case among Mayas and Aztecs, at whose altars and temples the gods are depicted.

RELIGION AND WAR

The Lord of Hosts is a figure more familiar to historic cultures than to the preliterate. He guided the Jews in their battles, the Babylonians, Egyptians, Greeks, and Romans in their campaigns. The higher gods, as we have seen, are not a common feature of preliterate religion. But religion may be linked with war through other media. In the Plains area of North America the command to lead a war party was given by a supernatural being through a dream. Directions were usually specific as to time, place, and results of the expedition. In many Plains area tribes the primary purpose of the sun dance was to secure success in warfare. Among Mayas and Aztecs religion was intimately related to war. The victims of sacrifice were principally prisoners of war. Before a fighting expedition was undertaken, offerings were made to the god of war. Aztecs had a god of war, a veritable God of Battles and Lord of Militant Hosts.

RELIGION AND SOCIAL LIFE

In historic cultures religion is intimately related to social life, and social distinctions have influenced every important religious development. Christianity at first was a religion of the poor and oppressed, later of conquerors and the wealthy. Egyptian religion was for royalty, aristocracy, and priesthood. Its blessings eluded the common man, or certainly did not include him.

Religion has been sensitive to social distinctions. In the simpler cultures—for example, those of Australians, Bushmen, Hottentots—there is little social differentiation except along lines of sex and age; and these are about the only social distinctions which invade the religious realm. In many of the more complex preliterate cultures, however, class distinctions have religious emphasis or sanction. This is the case in the higher Mexican and Peruvian civilizations. In these cultures religious activities are reserved largely for the higher classes, and the ruler enjoys some of the prerogatives of a god. In Polynesia, where chieftainship is elaborated and aristocracy flourishes, the religious life centres in the aristocracy. The chief is sacred, that is, taboo, and no one may touch him. The attitude toward him partakes largely of religious awe; the same applies, with modifications, to members of the aristocracy, though they are not instinct with the same amount or degree of the sacred as pertains to the chief or king.

NEW RELIGIONS

Possibly there has not been a time in human culture when man was incapable of initiating a new religion; but he has been more predisposed to launch new religions at some times than at others. Some cultures have produced new religions with amazing facility. Preliterate culture undisturbed by outside influence or internal pressure seems little inclined to develop new religions. We cannot, from the nature of the evidence, know this directly or beyond peradventure of doubt. The fact, however, that no tribe which has remained undisturbed by outside influences supplies evidence of a new religion within its borders suggests that an undisturbed preliterate culture is little given to initiating a new religious movement, though its religious concepts and rituals may, of course, be gradually and constantly modified. The further fact that in such tribes there are no competing cults suggests again the failure of a new religion to appear in undisturbed preliterate cultures within at least the recent past. As far as information extends, new religions have appeared among preliterate folk only after contact with an outside culture has broken down the tribal culture solidarity or, as frequently has been the case, has shattered the culture to its foundations and undermined tribal morale.

Thus about 1870 a Paiute Indian initiated the ghost dance religion. The doctrines of the cult promised resurrection of dead Indians and restoration of the old tribal life, game, and food. Simultaneously the earth would open and swallow the Whites.

Some twenty years later the cult was revived, probably by a son of the founder. Its essential doctrines remained unchanged, but took varying form in the respective tribal areas into which they spread. In the Plains area, for example, the cult assimilated many elements from the sun dance complex. In 1870 the Plains tribes were not prepared to accept the new religion. They had been little disturbed by the encroachments of the Whites. The Paiutes, however, among whom the ghost dance religion originated, were suffering from loss of tribal lands with accompanying loss of food supply. In 1889, when the movement was revived, the situation in the Plains area was very different from the situation there two decades earlier. The buffaloes had been killed or driven away, the Indians had been confined to reservations, and there had been a sudden cramping of the old culture. Culture disintegration made fertile soil for the new ghost dance religion when it was reintroduced into the Plains area in 1889 and 1890.

About 1911 a native of Tufi, New Guinea, climbed alone Mt. Victory. There he encountered a snake from which he received the facts of life and the rules of conduct which led to the establishment of the Baigona cult. Henceforth all snakes were to be called Baigona and were to be treated with respect and affection. The native must hail and welcome all the snakes he saw, and he might neither kill nor eat them. These taboos were extended to all animals which might be reincarnations of men, including lizards, crocodiles, and cuscus. The founder of the cult imparted to others his knowledge of the sacred medicine taboos and rites, and thus, by successive initiations, a group of Baigona men, virtually priests of the new cult, were to be found in villages as far north as the former German boundary. Meanwhile others became adherents of the sect, though most of them comprehended little about it save the taboo on reptiles. The genuine Baigona men practised healing and sorcery, and extorted gifts and fees from the masses, who held them and the founder of the cult in fearsome respect. The healers induced in their patients paroxysms of a peculiarly horrible nature, and finally the local government suppressed the movement. At present some of the practices are continued in secret, but the sect is apparently almost defunct.

The Baigona cult was soon followed and replaced by a more agreeable one, the Taro cult, which originated on the Mambare River, about 1916 or 1917, and spread throughout the Orokaiva peoples. The Taro cult was inspired by the visions of a man who declared himself possessed of the spirits of the taro, the staple food of the Orokaiva. He was in constant communication with these spirits. From them he received instructions regarding the rites which would ensure ample crops. The rites were simple and agreeable, and their appeal to economic motives guaranteed the popularity of the cult. When the movement spread, it underwent many changes. At the present time the emphasis is not upon worship of the taro, but upon worship of the dead, doubtless as a result of this strong motive in the Baigona cult which paved the way to the Taro cult. Through the medicine of the spirits of the dead the rites ensure a bountiful taro crop. Thus the cult is both a fertility cult and a cult of the dead. A secondary activity of the Taro men, as it was a primary activity of the Baigona men, is curing. The drumming and singing by members of the cult is as efficacious in raising the sick from their couches as in raising taro in the gardens. The Taro healers, like the Baigona predecessors, are suspected of indulging in sorcery. Here, as in the Plains area of North America, the infiltration of foreign elements disrupted the native tribal cultures and paved the way for a new religion.

About the middle of the last century a new cult, known as the Hau Hau, arose among the Maoris, the natives of New Zealand. The name was derived from the use of these syllables at the end of the songs. The inspiration to the movement was an attempt to drive the Whites from the land and restore a modified Maori culture. Many elements of English culture, particularly the use of certain English words, seeped into the rituals and songs, as though, by homeopathic magic, the new sect had resolved to fight fire with fire. The sect was exterminated not by suasion but by bullets. Here, as in the above mentioned examples, disintegration of the old culture paved the way to the new cult. Thus in preliterate cultures the successful initiative to organize a new cult seems to exist only when outside influences have become potent and have threatened to destroy or have almost destroyed the old culture.

In historic civilizations many new religions have appeared, some ephemeral, some of considerable duration. The first great religious innovation in history was that of the Egyptian pharaoh Ikhnaton, who established monotheism throughout the land and caused the inscriptions of the names of all gods other than the Sun God to be obliterated. The new religion, however, flourished only during the lifetime of its founder.

Most new religions are compounded largely of elements already present in the older cult from which they take their departure. Such was the case with Christianity, Mohammedanism, Buddhism, and the various sects which have developed within these religions.

The preliterate group which is culturally insulated and self-contained is poor soil for new religions. When outside influences enter, the culture is more likely to produce, or accept, a new religion. In historic civilizations, similarly, the impact of new forces and new ideas, whether arising from within the culture or originating from without, is likely to incite to new religions, or at least to new sects. Without the impact of outside influences, Christianity could scarcely have arisen when it did; without the Renaissance, Protestantism could not have started when it did. Political, social, economic, and scientific forces and ideas stirring in northern and western Europe gave rise to numerous sects, whereas the comparatively stable cultures of southern and eastern Europe produced few sects. In the changeful life of the United States new religions have found, among all lands, the most fertile soil.

The religion of the fathers is good enough while men live the life of the fathers, but new culture situations foster new religious cults which arise to meet new demands. In Germany Nazism revives the Teutonic gods for nationalistic purposes; and, as Ennodius observes, "the gods are never so dangerous as when they awake from sleep." [6]

6. Ennodius, Carmen I, 4.

CHAPTER XIX THE DISTRIBUTION OF RELIGIOUS PATTERNS

Religion, like any phase of life, can be treated without respect to its geographic or cultural occurrence. Belief, ritual, ceremony, or prayer may be said to have a meaning, as expression of hope or despair, irrespective of where it occurs, or when.

Art, one may allege, is art no matter by whom or under what clime or circumstance it is executed; science is science; and religion is religion. Sheer classification of phenomena under appropriate categories is acknowledgment of this fact.

If, however, one is interested in the particularity of phenomena, additional categories must be employed, namely, the categories of place and time. For all events happen somewhere and somewhen; they have geographic placement and historic setting.

Any specific religious complex—Christianity, for example—is a unique historic and cultural phenomenon. It arose at a certain time and in a certain place.

One who searches for the common elements in religion is impressed by the fundamental likenesses in the beliefs of Polynesians, Australians, and tribes of North America; one who is interested in the specific forms of religious life and expression is impressed by the distinctiveness of the religious life and its expression in any selected portion of the globe.

To view religion as concrete expression of belief and practice is to be impressed with the fact that specific religious belief and practice are highly respectful of culture boundaries.

To pass from one culture area to another is, usually, to move from one religious sphere to another. Further, preliterate cultures, unlike many higher cultures (that is, historic civilizations), have, with few exceptions, no competing religious systems. In a given preliterate culture all individuals accept the same religious system, though there may be individual differences in reaction to its implications and compulsions. Yet practically everywhere in preliterate society the religious realm in which one lives is the religious realm of one's culture fellows, save for distinctions based on age or sex. But the Indian of the Plains area of North America, for example, lives in a religious world different from that of the Pueblo Indian of the Southwest of the United States; and the religious world of the native of the Northwest Coast of North America differs from both of these. So it is the world over: the religion in one culture area differs from that in another.

Practically everywhere, it is true, preliterate man is animistic, that is, believes that spiritual beings animate many phases and forces of nature and travel about as disembodied spirits; and the soul survives the body. Practically everywhere there is fear of unusual phenomena such as earthquakes, thunder, and eclipses, and these are given an animistic interpretation. Practically everywhere men have techniques for dealing with these supernatural forces and protecting themselves against encompassing non-human dangers. In most areas there is belief in a supernatural personage or being who ranks as a god. Again, when the religious life becomes complex, certain phases are practically always present, notably, priesthood, ritual, ceremonialism, symbolism. Thus man in his religious life adheres to one great community in which there are contact with the supernatural and similar ways of meeting its hazards and taking advantage of its offerings. All partake of this awe-inspiring medium of inspiration. But the manner in which men respond to the supernatural forces about them and the manner in which they conceive of those forces is institutionalized, that is, standardized. It is standardized in specific fashion for one group and in different fashion for another group. Thus the character and expression of prayer, priesthood, ritual, symbolism, or ceremonial differ from one area to another; moreover, the relation of one phase of the religious life to another differs; and the respective emphases which these receive differ from one culture to another. Hence no general knowledge of religion will enable one to infer the religion of a specific group at a specific period of history. Only ethnology and history give knowledge of specific religious life. Not all the religious systems of the world will tell us the specific form of religion among the Eskimos, or among any other group, as no history will tell us the specific history of a people not included in our survey. What, briefly, are some of the traits of these systems of religious belief and thought which meet the ethnographer as he traverses the globe?

The religious concepts of the Eskimos are intimately related to the food supply, that is, the game of the land and the sea on which his existence depends. Most taboos require avoidance of insults to these animals or their spirits. Hence the most important personage in the supernatural realm is Sedna, who lives at the bottom of the sea and may call the sea animals from the haunts of men, or send the game to men. The moon, too, is a powerful supernatural personage, and is visited by shamans. The air, the sky, and the sea are replete with spiritual beings which are generally malevolent and against which one must constantly be on guard. For the Eskimo, life is one supernatural danger after another; and to jump heedlessly from one danger is likely to land him in one of several other encompassing dangers.

In the Northwest Coast region of North America the religious is the magical, the totemic, or both. There is little or no worship; emotionally charged attitudes toward the totem and conventionalized evaluations of totemic rites, myths, and artistic representations are the closest analogy to the religious. The salmon is respectfully treated; appropriate rites must be performed when or before the first salmon of the season is caught. The shaman is important, but there are neither priests nor religious cults. The religion of the Haidas, Queen Charlotte Islands, reflects their dependence on the sea. They are surrounded by supernatural beings. The "Power of the Shining Heavens" is the source of the powers that inhere in the natural and supernatural world. Prayers and sacrifices are offered mainly to ocean beings which sometimes take the form of fish or of sea mammals and directly affect the food supply. Natives offer these beings tobacco, grease, and feathers of the flicker; they throw the offerings into the water or burn them to release their souls. Tahltans acknowledge a sky god and a sun god. To the latter they offer food by burning it. Parents pray to Day Dawn to ensure the welfare of their children. A supernatural game-mother who controls the supply of birds and animals suggests the rôle of Sedna in Eskimo culture. Carriers offer food to a sky-being to whom they pray for help during famine. Through dreams they communicate with supernatural beings whose aid they entice by appropriate rituals. Some individuals, more highly gifted spiritually than their fellows, gain intimate touch with the supernatural through sickness, by dreaming, or by fasting in a particular locality isolated from their fellows. The power they thus derive enables them by capturing the wandering souls of helpless fellow-tribesmen to inflict or to remove disease. Kutenais worship or respect many supernatural beings, predominantly the sun. Before a fighting expedition they offer to the sun prayers and tobacco smoke, a joint of the first finger, or a piece of flesh from arm or breast.

California tribes have little organized religion, although shamanism is present.

Chipewyans have no deities and make no public prayers, but have individual guardian spirits.

Among Algonquins of the Northeast Woodland area religion is principally an individual affair; there are few organized expressions of the religious life. There is personification of the winds, with fear of the north wind, personified as a giant who blows his breath southward. Those who can obtain mystic power, *manitu*, or *keskamzit*, have an advantage over competitors and may rout even supernatural personages. Among Northern Iroquois there are sacrifices of a white dog, religious New Year and harvest festivals, and the magico-religious concept of *orenda*. Prayer at ceremonials is formal and sometimes elaborate.

In the Central Woodland area the vision induced by fasting and the guardian animal secured thereby are prominent phases of religious life. In the Ojibwa Midewewin ceremony the supernatural is diligently cultivated.

In the Plains area religious concepts hover about *wakaṅ* and its manifestations. The dream is an important means of communication with the spirit world, or the *wakan* world; visions are sometimes induced by fasting in isolation. Prayer is more highly developed here than elsewhere in the non-agricultural areas of the New World, and offerings to the sun are common—a finger or part of a finger, or an albino buffalo skin. In the sun dance, the principal religious rite, self-torture is practised. Vows are common, oath with supernatural sanction is known, ritual purification is emphasized. Pawnees worshipped the sun and each year sacrificed a maiden to it.

In the Southwest of the United States, particularly in the Pueblo and near-by tribes, the sun is sacred, and religious rites and ceremonies are elaborate. These concern natural phenomena, rain, vegetation, the sun, the cardinal points and their respective colours. Thus Dr. Bunzel characterizes Zuñi religious life as a highly developed system of techniques to secure rain and ensure growth of crops. Certain attitudes and behaviours which are socially valuable conduce to the success of these ceremonies, and the ceremonies enhance life by adding an æsthetic element. The primary purpose of the ceremonies is to increase tribal welfare.

Many fundamental phases of the religious pattern of the Southwest—notably, importance of cardinal points and associated colour symbolism, counterclockwise circuits, importance of the Morning Star, importance of the underworld—extend through northern Mexico and characterize also the southeastern Atlantic area.

In the higher civilizations of Mexico there was, with the possible exception of Peru, the highest expression of religion in the New World. Mayas wove myth and legend about Quetzalcoatl, the bird serpent, the feathered snake which dominates much of their art. They had a priesthood and schools for training novices, who entered at the age of seven or eight years. They built and adorned magnificent temples, and with artistic designs, with inlay and precious stones or metal, they beautified the statues of the gods. A similar pattern of religious life characterized the Aztecs. They, too, had temples, priesthood, ceremonies, festivals, and the refinements of human sacrifice. Myths did ample justice to the gods, who were liberally and extravagantly represented in art. The god was eaten in the form of communal cakes.

Chibcha and Peruvian civilizations, like Maya and Aztec, assigned a central position to the sun, which was worshipped in Central American and Andean higher cultures, perhaps most ceremonially by Peruvians. Peruvians had temples and, compared with Mayas and Aztecs, sparse offerings of human sacrifice, which, in Peru, were made to the sun. The priesthood was powerful, and the king was regarded as the son of the sun, as divinity incarnate.

In the remainder of South America there was little organized religion, although beliefs, to be sure, were everywhere institutionalized.

In Negro Africa there are diverse forms of religious expression. In Dahomey and Ashanti there are cult organizations, a pantheon with many local divinities, temples, sacred groves, a priesthood, seminaries for the training of priests, animal and human sacrifices, and offerings. In central eastern Africa the gods are important, and prayer, sacrifice, and offerings are means of appeasing them; and there are temples and a priesthood. Among South African Bantus there are sacrifices, offerings, prayer, and cult of ancestors, but no physical establishment for worship. Practically everywhere in Africa a sky-being is important and the cult of ancestors flourishes.

Madagascar has many high gods, mainly sky-gods, whose culture ancestry is polyglot. They are syncretisms of Mohammedan, Hindu, Christian, and Indonesian influences, compounded in varying proportions.

Dravidians, primitive peoples of India, display various forms of animism. In rice-growing districts the cult of vegetation is dominant. Among Todas the buffaloes are the centre of religious life and, though not worshipped, are sacred. Women may not walk in the path taken by the buffaloes. The animals are herded by priests; their milk is cared for in sacred dairies in charge of a priest and an assistant; they have sacred, *kwarzam*, names; and many taboos and practices testify to their sacred character. In the Malay peninsula there are local gods, and the powers of natural phenomena are personified. The Malay world is peopled with supernatural spirits, as is the entire Indonesian region, in which area animism is highly developed.

Australia is almost innocent of high gods. Some anthropologists, however, regard Daramulum as a sky-being whose attributes are essentially those of a god. For the most part the native is content with spiritual beings of a lesser order, which come from time to time to initiate the medicinemen, or appear in whirlwind or driving storm and bring sickness and physical weakness upon men. Melanesia is imbued with *mana*, which is sometimes resident in men, sharks, or large eels which lie hidden at the bottom of deep water-holes. In Polynesia a species of bird may be sacred to a family or a village, but whether as a totem or merely as a guardian animal is, so far at least as Samoa is concerned, not altogether clear. The supernatural is most pronounced in the form of *taboo*, which sets the sacred apart and invests it with radiant danger. In Siberia, as among Eskimos, shamanism is dominant. Spirits are abroad but are controlled to some extent by shamans who attain their power primarily by virtue of their neurotic dispositions rather than through rite or ceremony.

Ainus, of northern Japan and northeastern Siberia, have a highly developed bear cult, a cult found from Siberian tribes eastward across North America to Labrador and New England. The Ainu use of plumes and altars suggests features in the religious ceremony of the Pueblo tribes of the Southwestern United States.

"The primitive religions of all races, in all places and at all times, have been much alike, in so far as they are known. They have been quite naturally so, for all races have had about them the same world of mystery, and in them the same passions, the same loves and hates, the same hopes and fears."[1] Despite certain common psychic attitudes and reactions, however, the specific expression of the sacred is culturally determined.

There are definite geographic areas of specific religious life, and no one of them is a duplicate of another. There have, of course, been many interculture influences, and also much development within each culture area; but of the specific religious trends in the respective cultures ethnologists are, of necessity, almost entirely ignorant, for, with few exceptions, there are no records of this development, and it cannot be inferred with any confidence. Even where ignorance is not bliss, it is sometimes folly to be wise beyond the assured implications of known facts.

1. W. W. Cochrane, *The Shans*, I, 113 (Rangoon, Burma, Government Printing, 1915).

CHAPTER XX REASON, MOTIVE, AND CAPRICE

RATIONALIZATION

Action and response to stimulus precede rationalization. That this observation applies to reactions to the supernatural is indicated by the behaviour of higher animals toward unusual phenomena and by the universality of a similar human reaction.

Throughout preliterate cultures emotional reaction to an eclipse is similar, though interpretation of the phenomenon differs from one culture to another; men react similarly to ghosts, will-o'-the-wisps, and mirages, though the character of the rationalization of their reaction is culturally determined. Similarity in emotional reaction despite varying rationalistic explanations implies priority of the emotion. If there were no predisposition to heed the supernatural and react to its manifestations, there would be no strong motive to rationalize it. There would be slight interest in the afterlife if there were no interest in living, no hope for happiness if happiness were not valued. Reactions of preliterate man to phenomena deemed supernatural are charged with emotion and are based on fear. They contain, therefore, elements of the irrational or the non-rational. Man, however, rationalizes his fears and hopes into a justification for his responses to the stimuli of the supernatural. Animistic interpretation is an example of such rationalization.

Eclipse, meteor, and earthquake are explained in animistic terms, sometimes zoomorphic, sometimes anthropomorphic. Fear is primary and is responsible for the animism rather than conversely. Rationalization is sequent to attitude and response. "No mortal," Gillen has said of Barama River Caribs, "wishes to have any more dealings with ghosts than are necessary." The remark is applicable to any people. An Eskimo confessed: "We fear those things which are about us and of which we have no sure knowledge; as, the dead, and malevolent ghosts, and the secret misdoings of the heedless ones among ourselves." [1] Ghosts do no physical injury, yet no other phenomenon is so much feared. Many of us can sympathize with the sentiments of the French lady regarding ghosts: "I do not believe in them, but I fear them!" Eclipses, meteors, comets, and rainbows injure no one physically, yet in all parts of the world they are regarded as supernatural, uncanny, and fearsome. Hence, too, the religious significance of dreams, for practically everywhere dreams are regarded as supernatural. Such is the case among Jews, Greeks, and Romans, and in all preliterate cultures. In the Plains tribes of North America supernatural powers convey their wishes through vision or dream. A Freudian, however, finds it difficult to regard the dream as supernatural. When psychology enters by the front door, religion leaves by the back door and seeks more congenial environment.

Man is not fundamentally rational or primarily rationalistic. He acts before he thinks; emotional attitudes precede logic; he behaves and subsequently becomes aware of his behaviour and its import.

Emotional attitudes are primary; cherished logical inductions are secondary and derivative. Reason is profoundly affected by preceding or concomitant emotional attitudes. It is guided by them; their character largely determines rationalized objective and emphasis. Life begins in organisms so simple that one may doubt whether they feel, and is convinced that they do not think. Yet the beasts cling to or fight for life with fierce determination. A will to live infuses all higher animals.

Life at its strongest does not attempt to justify its existence but is content to assert itself. Life is good and needs no apology. Indeed, if you do not live, you cannot discover that life is a failure.

Rationalization is especially evident in fields in which interest centres. These are predominantly economic or other vital concerns. Thus preliterate man acts first and thinks afterward.

But he thinks. He may practise ritual before he formulates belief; but belief follows. His not merely to do and die but also to reason why. His rationalizations focus upon fundamental needs, or at least upon needs which he deems fundamental. They centre upon factors on which he is obviously dependent, as his game, herds, or crops. Hence the frequent sacredness of animals which constitute his food supply and of plants which are his staff of life. The rôles of animals in the religion of In-

1. Knud Rasmussen, *Across Arctic America*, 195, quoted in Edward M. Weyer, *The Eskimos*, 236 (New Haven, Yale University Press, 1932).

dians of tropical South America, for example, "depend on the importance which they have for their practical life. Animals which through their strength and ferocity, their strange appearance or habits of life, or the harm that they do to man, awake feelings of fear and awe in a primitive mind, have, beyond all others, become the objects of superstitious beliefs and practices. Hence the belief which the Ecuadorian Indians hold about the largest carnivora, and which they seem to share with all South American tribes. But the same idea is held of many other and more innocent animals also." [2] The interest of Eskimos centres upon seal and caribou, essential foods in their economy. Sedna, the goddess who lives at the bottom of the sea, may withdraw these animals from the haunts of men, and only spiritual communion with her induces her to send them back. On the Northwest Coast, where the salmon supply is abundant, and there is a "First Salmon" ceremony, interest focuses on the mythic totem animals. Myths, ceremonies, art, dances, and religious emotional attitudes centre upon these animals. In the Plains area buffalo-hunting and fighting are the foci of interest and likewise of religious life. Myths depict the origin of the buffaloes from the underworld; and the albino buffalo is sacred. In agricultural areas dominant religious rationalizations usually concern spirits or gods of vegetation, particularly those which control or typify the mainstay of life. In agricultural areas of the Southwest, Maize, or the spirit of maize, is a goddess; corn pollen is important in religious ceremonies. Vegetation gods are prominent in Maya and Aztec pantheons, and many important religious ceremonies concern vegetation, especially maize. Similar rationalization of motives is common in historic civilizations. The Jews, fighting for national integrity, conceived their god as a god of battles; but agricultural Babylonians, Egyptians, Greeks, and Romans attributed much importance to vegetation gods.

The rationalistic element in sun worship is suggested by its distribution. In the New World the sun cult is highly developed only in areas of intensive agriculture, as in Central America and in the Southwest and Southeast (Natchez) of the United States. In the Old World, similarly, the sun cult flourishes in agricultural areas—Persia, Mesopotamia, Egypt. The Nandi of eastern Africa worship the sun as the benevolent and powerful creator of men and beasts, to whom the whole

2. Rafael Karsten, *The Civilization of the South American Indians*, 284–285 (New York, Knopf, 1926). Reprinted by permission of the publishers: Alfred A. Knopf, Inc.; Kegan Paul, Trench, Trubner & Co., Ltd.; and George Routledge & Sons, Ltd.

world belongs. But one does not find sun worship in unsophisticated cultures, the simple hunting and fishing cultures.

A preliterate culture on the lower levels of intellectual development attributes much importance to moon and little to sun. Only sophisticated cultures become aware of the importance of the sun as life-giving force, bringer of vegetation and sustenance. Hence only in agricultural areas does the sun attain much importance. The North American Plains area sun dance seems to be an exception. Possibly the cult has spread into the Plains from Southwest or Southeast agricultural areas. Moreover, in spite of the designation, in most Plains tribes the sun dance has little reference to the sun. In the Plains area emotional interest centres primarily in fighting. Warfare is the leading motive in stories, dances, decorations, prestige; religious life in almost every phase is associated with fighting. The sun dance is usually held to secure supernatural assistance in a fighting expedition or in fulfilment of a vow made before or after leading a war party. Instigation to lead a war party is usually of supernatural origin, a command conveyed in a dream or vision. Ritualistic preparation for the sun dance follows procedure used in preparation for and conduct of a war party. Thus, among the Crows, although "the Sun is recurrently mentioned, most of the ritualistic performances are not connected with him. Revenge dominates the action. The primary means for gaining the end is the Doll, with its assumed power of stimulating the proper type of revelation. But virtually everyone is trying to help by bringing the universe into accord with this object. Hence the interminable blackening of faces and even of material articles, hence the mention of successful war enterprises, the attempt of the war captains to secure auxiliary visions, the counting of coup on the Lodge pole (and) on returning scouts." [3] However, among the Cœur d'Alêne, a Salish tribe of the Plateau, people prayed to the sun constantly for good health, good luck, success in undertakings, and protection. Symbols of the sun were much used as designs in embroidery and in painting on clothes and utensils, especially on shields and weapons of warriors. Bands and smaller groups of people performed the sun dance at frequent intervals. In some places people danced it once or twice a year, and in others almost every month. "The sun was prayed to directly in this dance." [4]

3. From Robert H. Lowie, *The Crow Indians*, 326 (New York), copyright 1935. Reprinted by permission of the publishers, Farrar & Rinehart, Inc.

4. James A. Teit, "The Cœur d'Alêne," *ABE*, 45: 186 (1927–1928).

PSYCHOLOGY OF PRELITERATE RELIGION

A Kwakiutl says: "You are not an ordinary man, you are a supernatural man." Religion distinguishes between natural and supernatural; ordinary and extraordinary; phenomena and phenomenal.

The one is the world of the profane; the other, the realm of the sacred. Demarcations of these realms are differently drawn in different cultures, and in a given culture boundaries shift with time and circumstance. Some phenomena—for example, earthquakes, eclipses, ghosts—always partake of the sacred and are feared, but events which usually are natural occasionally are charged with supernaturalism.

Thus one who ordinarily attaches no importance to the hoot of the owl may feel uncomfortable if he hears its hoot while a member of the household is dangerously ill or when misfortune threatens. Frightened beast and frightened human being attach significance to trivial sights and sounds which at other times receive scant attention. Primitive religion, as Marett has said, is largely a matter of nerves. The high-strung neurotic individual is more likely to establish contact with the supernatural than is the man whose nerves are leather strings. Most Siberian and Eskimo shamans, for example, are neurotic. In many areas the man given to visions, seeing spirits, or experiencing unusual sights and sounds is, by virtue of his predisposition, selected for the rôle of priest or medicineman. To facilitate contact with the supernatural by enhancing the neurotic state is the main function of fasts, privations, hardships, and self-torture. Conversely, extension of control over the world of phenomena is accompanied by decreased fear of the phenomenal. Science tends to displace religion from those realms of phenomena which science understands even though it cannot control them. The rise of Greek science was the knell of the gods in so far as their interference with natural phenomena was concerned. Epicurean and Stoic, who gave a naturalistic interpretation of all phenomena, dispensed with gods or identified them with the world of phenomena and considered them equally obedient to law. They had, therefore, no motive to placate the gods. When eclipses were predicted and men knew when and why they would occur, the supernaturalism which had seemed inherent in those phenomena waned. When comets and meteors became natural phenomena, and the recurrence of the comet could be foretold, their terrors vanished; men aware of the naturalness of the phenomena no longer trembled.

Lo! from the dread immensity of space
Returning with accelerated course,
The rushing comet to the sun descends;
And as he sinks below the shading earth,
With awful train projected o'er the heavens,
The guilty nations tremble. The enlighten'd few
Whose godlike minds philosophy exalts,
The glorious stranger hail. They feel a joy
Divinely great; they in their powers exult,
That wondrous force of thought, which mounting spurns
This dusky spot, and measures all the sky;
While from his far excursion through the wilds
Of barren ether, faithful to his time,
They see the blazing wonder rise anew.[5]

A naturalistic interpretation of disease brought a change in religious attitude toward disease. Typhoid fever was once the hand of God, who moved in a mysterious way his wonders to perform. When men discovered that only contaminated water or contaminated food brings typhoid fever, its occurrence was attributed to culpable human negligence, and its religious significance disappeared. Syphilis was long regarded as a mysterious affliction which God visited upon men rather indiscriminately; when the cause was apprehended, and especially when a remedy was found, the disease was interpreted as natural rather than supernatural. Now few blame God for the affliction or thank him for its removal.

As Admiral Byrd has said, "men don't fear certainties." [6] The devil one knows is not as much feared as the devil one doesn't know. Men who can face any known danger break down woefully before veiled or mysterious danger. The shell-shock of men at the front during the World War did not afflict those who were going over the top or engaging in the fray; it visited those who were awaiting the zero hour, those who lived amid falling bombs and screaming shells; in a word, not those who knew they were going to be killed, but those who did not know the fate in store for them. The Plains Indian who knew that he would be killed in the fight could face the foe without flinching; but when confronted by a wandering will-o'-the-wisp he would run in terror until he fell unconscious.

Ignorance is the chief source of fear, especially when the phenomena pass human understanding. Preliterate man agrees with Euripides (*Hecuba*) that "the gods toss all things into confusion, . . . that all of us,

5. James Thomson.
6. Richard E. Byrd, *Alone*, 181 (New York, Putnam, 1938).

from our ignorance and uncertainty, may pay them the more worship and reverence." Thus people whose fate depends upon the weather are likely to be religious, or superstitious, at least with regard to the weather, for the weather is capricious and non-human, and therefore is believed to have divine origin. On the rock-bound coast of Brittany, where Atlantic storms make seafaring a constant and imminent peril, the fishermen are among the most religious or superstitious peoples of Europe. Churches dot the coast, being particularly frequent at its most dangerous portions. Every headland has its Calvary, a lofty crucifix visible far from shore. "While the fisherman is at sea, he and his wife pray for his safe return; as soon as he lands, his relief finds expression in drunkenness. A life of this kind, exposed constantly to non-human dangers, is the most favorable to traditional religion. Indeed, the whole of traditional religion may be regarded as an attempt to mitigate the terror inspired by destructive natural forces." [7]

The powerful emotional drives which move man impel or compel his thought. To wish is to hope, to hope is to expect.

Experience and reason are more often cause than result of preference. Man acts in different specific fashion in the various cultures, but the fundamental patterns of behaviour are similar. If the savage is potentially a civilized man, the civilized man is potentially a savage.

In every culture men employ the categories of the everyday and commonplace, the extraordinary and phenomenal. The distinction is based on primary attitudes. The psychology of the rare or aberrant is well expressed by Plutarch (*Lives*, Romulus) in his strained explanation of the importance of the vulture as a bird of omen: "All other birds are, so to say, never out of our eyes; they let themselves be seen by us continually; but a vulture is a very rare sight, and you can seldom meet a man who has seen their young; their rarity and infrequency has raised

7. Bertrand Russell and Dora Russell, *Prospects of Industrial Civilization*, 36–37 (New York, Century, 1923). Reprinted by permission of the publishers, George Allen & Unwin, Ltd. (London), and D. Appleton-Century Company, Inc. (New York). Bertrand Russell regards "all submissiveness as rooted in fear, whether the leader to whom we submit be human or divine."—*Power: A New Social Analysis*, 20 (New York, Norton, 1938). Similarly David Hume: "Infinite unknown evils are dreaded from unknown agents; and where real objects of terror are wanting, the soul, active to its own prejudice, and fostering its predominant inclination, finds imaginary ones, to whose power and malevolence it sets no limits. As these enemies are entirely invisible and unknown, the methods taken to appease them are equally unaccountable, and consist in ceremonies, observances, mortifications, sacrifices, presents, or in any practice, however absurd or frivolous, which either folly or knavery recommends to a blind and terrified credulity."—"Of Superstition and Enthusiasm," *Essays Moral, Political, and Literary*, I, 144–145 (New York, Longmans, 1907), first published in 1742.

a strange opinion in some, that they come to us from some other world; as soothsayers ascribe a divine origination to all things not produced either of nature or of themselves." With the familiar and understood man is on easy terms. Familiarity and understanding bring intellectual accommodation, whether the familiar and understood elicit pleasure or pain. Toward phenomena which fall without this realm man takes highly charged emotional attitudes; he fears them, and "fear has big eyes"; they distress him; they challenge his powers to comprehend or circumvent; they are more likely to control him than he to master them. "The unusual is dangerous, a suggestion of things vague, uncontrollable, and repulsive, whose discomposing intrusion excites the imagination and tries the civilized nerves of the foolish and wise alike." The man who experiences no emotional thrill in the presence of the supernatural does not know religious experience. Though he follows religious forms, subscribes to dogmas, meticulously observes ritual, the forms are empty, the dogmas meaningless, the rituals blind procedure. Preliterate man, however, is ever sensitive to the supernaturalism which bulks large in his culture. Thus Dinkas attribute to ancestral or other spirits "every strange or even slightly unusual happening, such as, for example the appearance of an unusually large gourd in the pumpkin bed." Similarly Caius Marius "very rationally supposed the strangeness of things often makes them seem formidable when they are not so; and by our better acquaintance, even things which are really terrible lose much of their frightfulness." [8] When man can react to danger by a series of purposive and generally highly complex actions of an appropriate kind, to which Rivers applied the term "manipulative activity," there is no great fear, or at least the fear is held in check and does not bring panic, flight, or collapse. When he cannot do so, and the intellectual categories break down, the will is paralyzed. Fear and horror capture the field of consciousness, and, with Ajax, primitive man exclaims:

> If we must perish, we thy will obey,
> But let us perish in the light of day.

"Fear has gone far to shape the moulds into which religious thought has run ever since feeble man began to meditate on the great mysteries by which our little life on earth is encompassed." [9]

8. Plutarch, "Caius Marius," *Lives*.
9. Sir James G. Frazer, *The Fear of the Dead in Primitive Religion*, III, 311 (London, Macmillan, 1936).

"The fear of God is the beginning of wisdom," and it is also the beginning of religion. When no fear enters, there is no religion; but "fear" does not connote "terror." The fear may be mild or intense; in the religious attitude it is always present in at least subdued or concealed form. Knowledge which is thorough, accurate, and precise tends, therefore, to oust the gods from realms which knowledge penetrates. When men can predict eclipses, they are not inclined to give them a supernatural interpretation or to fear them; the man who knows that phosphorescence is the cause of the will-o'-the-wisp is much less likely to fear and propitiate it than is he who does not know the cause and regards the phenomenon as spiritual or supernatural; the gods may dwell on Olympus while its snow-bound or cloud-capped peak is inaccessible to men, but explorers who climb high mountains are less likely to regard these upthrown masses as habitats of supernatural creatures; hail, thunder, and rainbow inspire fear or awe when the cause is unknown, but they are not likely to inspire religious reverence in the meteorologist; the plague is the hand of God until men find that lice on rats or men carry the germs, and then the plague loses religious significance. Miracles arouse little religious awe in men who understand the psychology of belief.

Knowledge, however, is never complete, thorough, and accurate. One may know the cause and course of disease but consider it a mystery that a particular individual was visited with paralysis, typhoid fever, or plague. As a doctor remarked of a "stroke," "Why it's come just now after all these years is known only to the Lord." And if you say, "But if we knew all the facts," the answer is, we do not know and presumably never can know all the facts. No; this "scientific" way out is by formula and faith rather than by demonstrable fact. It is no less formula and faith than is supernaturalism; a superstitious solving of the unknown. One can give the phenomenon an intellectual setting but one does not know why, that is, precisely how, it occurred. One can, therefore, regard it as an act of God if one is predisposed to do so. Hence the paradox of churches flourishing in an age of applied science which accomplishes the impossible and performs more amazing miracles than were proclaimed or imagined by the most credulous religious devotees of even a few decades ago. The scientist, moreover, sometimes lives in watertight compartments. He may think and behave as an open-minded, unprejudiced scientist while repairing his automobile; but when conceiving the creation of the world, or the future life, he may be content to regard as religious faith the myths current among Semites three thousand years ago and accepted then as myths. He readily admits that wireless telephony should be improved, but has apoplexy if one suggests changes in established economic, political, or religious institutions. Many great men have lived in intellectual watertight compartments. The same corporeal Isaac Newton who created the science of celestial mechanics wrote, in theological vein, *Observations on the Prophecies of Daniel and the Apocalypse of St. John; Lexicon Propheticum; and History of the Creation.* "With one part of his mind he believed in the miracles and prophecies about which he had been taught in childhood; with another part he believed that the universe is a scene of order and uniformity." [10] People who explain in primitive fashion phenomena which they do not understand, and who prefer these primitive explanations to the revelations of science, pay tribute to the power of traditional beliefs and ideas. The amazing toughness of tradition is eloquent testimony to the power of culture conditioning.

Supernaturalism flourishes in the modern age not merely because of intellectual inertia, but also because men look beyond verifiable knowledge for a solace and an interpretation which science cannot supply. This attitude may express the despair of ignorance; but men in their ignorance are well acquainted with despair. Moreover, they refuse to accept the impasse which science recognizes. Where knowledge breaks down, faith steps in and gives the faltering soul wings that carry it whither it will. The astronomer locates no heaven, the geodicist no hell; but the soul knows them too well.

Again, like Pascal, the doubter may think that by believing he loses nothing, whereas scepticism may wreck his future. He may believe because it is absurd, for it seems more absurd not to believe. If religion is a confession of weakness through ignorance, it is also an assertion of strength through faith. Those who are steadfast in the faith are invulnerable to assaults of knowledge. Science, therefore, may understand the stimuli to religion but it cannot counter religion, for the realm of religion is essentially the realm that passeth human understanding.

Only when man becomes omniscient will there be no possible place in his mind for religious concepts; and even then there will be room for the religious sentiment which prefers faith to knowledge.

> I know not if the voice of man can reach to the sky;
> I know not if the mighty one will hear as I pray;

10. Aldous Huxley, *Proper Studies*, 5–6 (London, Chatto & Windus, 1927).

I know not if the gifts I ask will all granted be;
I know not if the word of old we truly can hear;
I know not what will come to pass in our future days;
I hope that only good will come, my children, to you.

I now know that the voice of man can reach to the sky;
I now know that the mighty one has heard as I prayed;
I now know that the gifts I asked have all granted been;
I now know that the word of old we truly have heard;
I now know that Tira'wa harkens unto men's prayers;
I now know that only good has come, my children, to you.

Father, unto thee we cry!
Father, thou of gods and men;
Father, thou of all we hear;
Father, thou of all we see;
Father, unto thee we cry!

Father! Thou above, father of the gods,
They who can come near and touch us;
Do thou bid them bring us help.
Help we need; father, hear us! [11]

That is the answer not only of the Pawnee but of many civilized men who cannot solve or cannot bear

The burden and the mystery
Of all this unintelligible world.

PSYCHOLOGICAL ROOTS OF BELIEF IN LIFE AFTER DEATH

Belief in survival of the soul after death is a universal culture phenomenon. Its roots are deep-laid in human nature.

Perhaps, as Hume says, when we become aware of the impossibility of satisfying a desire, the desire vanishes. Frequently, however, we refuse to acknowledge the impossibility of satisfying a deep craving. Before King Edwin's council, according to the Venerable Bede, an English nobleman recommended that the religion brought by Paulinus, the papal legate, be accepted: "Here below the life of man seems tolerable, but of what comes after and of what has gone before we know naught. If the new teaching have some tidings thereof to give us, I think we shall do right to accept it." We wish to be convinced that immortality is a fact. Desire for continued existence makes us welcome a promise which satisfies our demands.

11. Alice C. Fletcher, "The Hako: A Pawnee Ceremony," *ABE*, 22, Part II: 343–344 (1903). Reprinted by permission of the Bureau of American Ethnology.

It is curious that, although life has beginning as well as end, we do not agitate ourselves about our previous non-existence; why, then, are we concerned about post-mortem non-existence? "Before we were born," says Lucretius, "we felt no distress when the Poeni from all sides came together to do battle. For he whom evil is to befall, must in his own person exist at the very time it comes, if the misery and suffering are to have any place at all." "I was not; I was; I am not; I do not care." This sentiment was repeated so often in Roman epitaphs that finally it was indicated by initials.

David Hume found it no more difficult to suppose that he would not exist after this life than that he had not existed before this life; but Samuel Johnson would not accept this sentiment as genuine, inasmuch as all men would cheat death. Most men do not exercise their minds over the past. "To die is only to be as we were before we were born; yet no one feels any remorse or regret or repugnance, in contemplating this last idea." How explain the fact that the idea of a pre-existing state does not excite our longing but the prospect of posthumous existence is enticing? The answer, perhaps, lies partly in the following traits of human behaviour and belief: The more a man busies himself with affairs, the more important to him his objectives and the more remote the realization of his purposes, the more desirable appears the continuance of his life. Things which contribute to the realization of the purposes of the individual have for him value. As the struggle waxes and the issues become more vital, increasing attention is paid to the future. To confine attention to the past is to forgo future opportunities.

Anticipated realization of aims becomes a stimulus to belief in future personal existence. Interest in self-preservation fosters belief in post-mortem existence. The writer of the apocryphal *Book of Wisdom* could say, "Because by mere chance were we born, and hereafter we shall be as though we had never been; because the breath of our nostrils is smoke, and while our heart beateth, reason is a spark, which, being extinguished, the body shall be turned into ashes, and the spirit shall be dispersed as thin air." But this is not the solace of the common man. There is a hard-and-fastness, an inflexibility, to the past, which does not necessarily characterize the future. To wish to live in the past is obviously futile; a wish to have a future existence is not logically absurd. We apply the principle every hour of waking life. Some anticipations are realized; indeed, those who have no will to claim the future are handicapped in the struggle with more imaginatively gifted brethren.

The tendency to view the future as potential realization, the turning of attention forward, and the impulse of self-preservation furnish psychological basis for belief in life after death. The will to live fosters the will to believe. Hope gives a hold on the future which we do not have on a past in which, obviously, we cannot participate. As hope waxes, zest grows and links us with an imagined future. In the game of life there are always moves ahead; and we refuse to believe in a final termination of our existence. "Nice customs curtsey to great beings." Logic bows to man's deeper desires.

Hobhouse suggests that instead of saying, in our traditional way, " 'They believe that the dead continue to live in much the same way and to need the same things: therefore they give them what they will need,' perhaps what we should say is rather, 'The mass of sentiments and emotions stirred by death impels the mourners to acts of respect, affection, and sacrifice. As they come to give to themselves or perhaps to their enquiring children some account of these acts they can express their meaning only by speaking of the dead as continuing to live, so that the practice emerges from a sentiment, and in turn gives rise to the belief that would justify it.' "[12] The "mass of sentiments and emotions stirred by death" Hobhouse takes for granted. The fact, however, that interest and attention focus on the future suggests a reason for the association of intensified sentiments and emotions with death. Indeed, the mere expectation that things will continue as they are, the inertia of thought, creates a tendency to regard former daily companions as still alive, even though we know they no longer live.

ETHICAL VALUE OF BELIEF IN LIFE AFTER DEATH

We cannot accept McDougall's assertion that without belief in survival of the soul the guiding moral principles which keep modern nations intact and vigorous would disappear. In modern civilization people are not much concerned about the fate of the soul after death. To get and beget, to produce and reproduce, are much more thriving concerns. Nor is it clear that disappearance of the belief is accompanied by weakening of the moral fibre. Belief in immortality is not always efficacious as a moral stimulus, even in those areas in which its acceptance is absolute and thoroughgoing. On the contrary, meaning, as frequently it does, merely a continuation of earthly life, with its class

12. Leonard T. Hobhouse, *Development and Purpose*, 98 (London, Macmillan, 1913).

distinctions, class oppression, and social injustices, it offers less occasion for hope than reason for despair. In many cultures it supplies motives to gain personal advantage by force, injustice, or intrigue which will ensure coveted post-mortem supremacy. Leave out of the reckoning the cruder cultures in which immortality is a curse rather than a blessing: Could civilization dispense with belief in immortality without losing a bulwark of morality? The history of penology shows that crime does not diminish as harshness of punishment increases. The more than two hundred crimes once punished in England by death did not increase in frequency when the death penalty was removed. Treason did not become more frequent when the punishment of quartering was mitigated to that of hanging; suicide did not increase with abolition of disgraceful interment, forfeiture of property, and attainder of blood; theft did not become more common when thieves were imprisoned instead of hanged. Facile indebtedness went no faster pace when only property and not the person was seized. It is not true that the greater the reward of virtue and the more severe the punishment of vice, the more moral will people become. The law of nature is not the law of human nature. Often there is marked disparity between threatened punishment and conduct, between promised reward and conduct, because other motives intervene, more powerful than those induced by threat of punishment or promise of reward. Of the Masai, of East Africa, it is said that, though they cannot lay claim to any definite form of religion and their belief "postulates annihilation after death," yet "they possess a more marked ethical instinct than is usually associated with primitive peoples." [13] The weakening of belief in life after death is due in part to higher ethics. "Probably no one outside the China Inland Mission now believes that unbaptized children go to hell because Adam ate an apple. Very few believe in eternal punishment at all, and even those few could not name any particular person who will suffer everlasting torment, with the possible exception of Judas Iscariot. Belief in religion, even where it survives formally, has usually as little vitality or influence upon conduct as belief in the heptarchy and the Merovingian kings." [14]

There is diminishing demand for mere personal survival. The contemplation of aeons upon aeons of time, in which throughout decay of

13. Sidney L. Hinde and Hildegarde Hinde, *The Last of the Masai*, 99 (London, Heinemann, 1901).

14. Bertrand Russell and Dora Russell, *Prospects of Industrial Civilization*, 133 (New York, Century, 1923).

solar systems and crash of universes the soul remains for ever the same unchanging entity, grown but not growing, completed but not completing, discomfits some people rather than attracts them. They suspect that the harp which plays always the same joyous refrain will not afford infinite joy. Some find in social betterment and social service sufficient incentive to good, sufficient deterrent from evil, irrespective of rewards in the next world. An individual influences those with whom he comes into contact, and through them, the social order. A personality which influences one's fellows survives, to that extent, in them. As Buddhism declares, when a man dies, all that survives is the result of his action, speech, and thought; this does not die.

As dreams which have no bearing on life's purposes are inconsequential, so is survival of qualities which do not influence social life. Some would rather dwell unrecognized in the lives of others than dwell for ever as disembodied spirits in a world apart from that in which they struggled to achieve their purposes. As no man liveth to himself, so no man dieth to himself, but each survives in the purposes which he has helped to shape. What matter if these purposes are embodied only in some other habitation of clay than that in which they originated?

Non-existence during the first five hundred thousand years of human history we faced with admirable complacency. Can we not face with equal complacency another five hundred thousand years of non-existence? The child looks out of the window and cries for the moon, which is beyond its reach. Thankful the infant should be that it cannot grasp the lunar orb; the reward would be only a long-lost remnant of earth, a defunct world, cold and lifeless. The child when older reaches out eagerly toward a far-away future where earth's sorrows do not exist and where joy is unalloyed. That postmundane world is a fragment of his culture world, a disjected wilful wish, thrown into regionless, timeless space.

Thankful the older child should be that it cannot enter this realm, for the heaven offered by orthodox tradition is anæmic, vaporous, and tinselled, the creation of a sect of disappointed Jews, who thought heaven must be a fine place because earth was so poor. This concept of heaven was the best the times produced; but it belongs with the astrology, bent-stick ploughs, and ox-carts of two thousand years ago, and deserves a place alongside them in a museum of antiquities. Its present ethical value is on a par with the present intellectual and technological value of these outmoded achievements.

What is man that he should rival God in length of days? Let him have his life and, having lived it, his death. Death is the birthright of all things that live, the reward and penalty of life itself. Birth gives us an opportunity to play our rôles as human nature; death, an opportunity to play our rôles as nature.

BIBLIOGRAPHY

ABBREVIATIONS

AA	*American Anthropologist*, publication of the American Anthropological Association, the Anthropological Society of Washington, and the American Ethnological Society of New York (Washington, D. C.)
ABE	*Annual Report of the Bureau of American Ethnology* (Washington, D. C., Smithsonian Institution)
APAMNH	*Anthropological Papers of the American Museum of Natural History* (New York)
BAMNH	*Bulletin of the American Museum of Natural History* (New York)
BMB	*Bulletin of the Bernice P. Bishop Museum* (Honolulu)
BMM	*Memoirs of the Bernice P. Bishop Museum* (Honolulu)
EB	*Encyclopaedia Britannica*, fourteenth edition (New York and Chicago, Encyclopaedia Britannica Inc., 1929)
ERE	*Hastings' Encyclopaedia of Religion and Ethics* (New York, Scribner, 1908)
ESS	*Encyclopaedia of the Social Sciences* (New York, Macmillan, 1934)
HAI	*Handbook of American Indians* (Washington, D. C., Smithsonian Institution)
INM	*Indian Notes and Monographs* (New York, Heye Foundation of the Museum of the American Indian)
JAI	*Journal of the Royal Anthropological Institute of Great Britain and Ireland* (London)
L'A	*L'Anthropologie* (Paris, Masson)
MAAA	*Memoirs of the American Anthropological Association* (Lancaster, Pa.)
PICA	*Proceedings of the International Congress of Americanists*
SFMV	*Studien und Forschungen zur Menschen- und Völkerkunde* (Stuttgart)
UC	*University of California Publications in American Archaeology and Ethnology* (Berkeley, Calif.)
ZfE	*Zeitschrift für Ethnologie* (Berlin)

GENERAL

Alviella, Count Goblet d', *Lectures on the Origin and Growth of the Conception of God as Illustrated by Anthropology and History* (London, Williams and Norgate, 1897)

Anwander, Anton, *Die Religionen der Menschheit* (Freiburg im B., Herder, 1927)

Benedict, Ruth, "Religion," in Franz Boas and others, *General Anthropology*, Chap. XIV (Boston, Heath, 1938)
Bertholet, Alfred, *Religionsgeschichtliches Lesebuch* (Tübingen, J. C. B. Mohr, 1926–1933)
Bertholet, Alfred, "Religion," *ESS*, XIII, 228–237
Beth, K., *Religion und Magie* (Leipzig and Berlin, Teubner, 1927)
Boas, Franz, "Anthropology," *ESS*, II, 94–97
Boas, Franz, "Religion," *HAI*, II, 365–371
Bohmer, J. (editor), *Die Religionsurkunden der Völker* (Leipzig, 1909)
Boullaye, Father Pinard de la, *Etude comparée des religions*, II, 221–282
Bousset, Wilhelm, *What is Religion?* (New York, Putnam, 1907)
Brinton, Daniel L., *Religions of Primitive Peoples* (New York, Putnam, 1897)
Clark, Richard E., *The Effect of Social Forces upon Religious Rites and Ceremonies* (Philadelphia, privately printed, 1924)
Clemen, Carl (editor), *Die Religionen der Erde* (Munich, 1931)
Clemen, Carl (editor), *Urgeschichtliche Religion* (Bonn, 1932)
Cook, Stanley A., *The Study of Religions* (London, A. & C. Black, 1914)
Cook, Stanley A., "Religion," *ERE*, X, 662–693
Cooper, John M., "The Origin and Early History of Religion," *Primitive Man*, II, 1929 (Quarterly Bulletin of the Catholic Anthropological Conference)—published also as Chap. XIII in Albert Muntsch, *Cultural Anthropology*, 1934
Crooke, W., *The Popular Religion and Folk-Lore of Northern India* (London, Constable, 1896, 1923)
Danzel, Theodor-Wilhelm, *Kultur und Religion des Primitiven Menschen* (Stuttgart, 1924)
Dawson, Christopher, *Progress and Religion*, Chap. V (London, Sheed and Ward, 1929)
Durkheim, Emile, *Elementary Forms of the Religious Life* (London, Allen & Unwin, 1914)
Farnell, L. R., *The Evolution of Religion* (New York, Putnam, 1905)
Frazer, Sir James G., *The Worship of Nature* (New York, Macmillan, 1926)
Frazer, Sir James G., *The Golden Bough*, third edition (New York, Macmillan, 1935)
Frazer, Sir James G., *The Belief in Immortality and the Worship of the Dead* (New York, Macmillan, 1913)
Frazer, Sir James G., *Folklore in the Old Testament*, abridged edition (New York, Macmillan, 1923)
Friers, Horace L., and Herbert W. Schneider, *Religion in Various Cultures*, Chaps. I–II (New York, Holt, 1932)
Gilmore, George W., *Animism or Thought Currents of Primitive Peoples* (Boston, Marshall Jones, 1919)
Gowen, Herbert H., *A History of Religion* (London, Society for Promoting Christian Knowledge, 1934)
Haas, H., *Bilderatlas zur Religionsgeschichte*
Hauer, J. W., *Die Religionen* (Berlin, 1923)
Hume, David, *The Natural History of Religion* (London, 1757)
Karrer, Otto, *Origins of Religion* (New York, Sheed & Ward, 1934)
Karsten, Rafael, *The Origins of Religion* (London, Kegan Paul, 1935)
Kirkpatrick, Clifford, *Religion in Human Affairs* (New York, Wiley, 1929)
Lévy-Bruhl, Lucien, *Le surnaturel et la nature dans la mentalité primitive* (Paris, Alcan, 1931)

Lowie, Robert H., *Primitive Religion* (New York, Boni & Liveright, 1924)
Lowie, Robert H., *Introduction to Cultural Anthropology*, Chap. XVII (New York, Farrar & Rinehart, 1934)
Lowie, Robert H., *Are We Civilized?* Chap. XX (New York, Harcourt, 1929)
Marett, Robert R., *The Threshold of Religion*, second edition (London, Methuen, 1914)
Marett, Robert R., *Faith, Hope, and Charity in Primitive Religion* (New York, Macmillan, 1932)
Marett, Robert R., *Anthropology* (New York, Holt, 1912)
Marett, Robert R., "Religion (Primitive)," *EB*, XIX, 103–107
Mencken, Henry L., *Treatise on the Gods* (New York, Knopf, 1930)
Moore, George F., *History of Religions*, 2 vols. (New York, Scribner, 1913, 1919)
Müller, F. Max, *Lectures on the Origin and Growth of Religion as Illustrated by the Religions of India* (New York, Scribner, 1879)
Muntsch, Albert, *Cultural Anthropology*, Chap. XIII (Milwaukee, Bruce, 1934)
Murdoch, George P., *Our Primitive Contemporaries* (New York, Macmillan, 1934)
Nilsson, Martin P., *Primitive Religion*, second edition (1923)
Oman, John, *The Natural and the Supernatural*, Chap. XXII (New York, Macmillan, 1931)
Perry, W. J., *Gods and Men* (New York, Morrow, 1929)
Pettazzoni, Raffaele, *Dio: Formazione e sviluppo del monoteismo nella storia delle religioni* (Rome, 1922)
Pettazzoni, Raffaele, "La formation du monothéisme," *Revue de l'histoire des religions*, 88 (1923)
Pettazzoni, Raffaele, "Allwissende höchste Wesen bei primitivsten Völkern," *Archiv für Religionswissenschaft*, 29: 108–129 (1931)
Plischke, Hans, *Kukailimoku, ein Kriegsgott von Hawaii* (Berlin, *Studien zur Völkerkunde*, 1929)
Preuss, Konrad Th., *Glauben und Mystik im Schatten des höchsten Wesens* (Leipzig, 1926)
Preuss, Konrad Th., "Die höchste Gottheit bei den kulturarmen Völkern," *Psychologische Forschung*, 2 (1922)
Preuss, Konrad Th., "Die Hochgottidee bei den Naturvölkern," *Africa*, 4 (1931)
Preuss, Konrad Th., *Lehrbuch der Völkerkunde*, 57–123 (Stuttgart, Enke, 1937)
Quellen der Religionsgeschichte (Göttingen and Leipzig, 1909–1926)
Radin, Paul, *Monotheism among Primitive Peoples* (London, Allen & Unwin, 1924)
Radin, Paul, *Primitive Religion* (New York, Viking, 1937)
Radin, Paul, *Primitive Man as Philosopher*, Chaps. XVII–XVIII (New York, Appleton, 1927)
Radin, Paul, *Social Anthropology*, Part IV (New York, McGraw-Hill, 1932)
Radin, Paul, *The Story of the American Indian* (New York, Boni & Liveright, 1927)
Radin, Paul, "Religion of the North American Indians," *Anthropology in North America*, 259–305 (New York, Stechert, 1915)
Ratzel, Friedrich, *The History of Mankind*, I, 38–65 (London, Macmillan, 1896–1898)
Reik, Theodor, *Der eigene und der fremde Gott* (Leipzig, Internationaler psychoanalytischer Verlag, 1923)
Reik, Theodor, *Probleme der Religionspsychologie* (Leipzig, Internationaler psychoanalytischer Verlag, 1928)

Die Religion in Geschichte und Gegenwart, encyclopedia (Tübingen, Mohr, 1909–1913)
Saussaye, Chantepie de la, *Lehrbuch der Religion* (Tübingen, Bertholet und Lehmann, 1925)
Schmidt, Pater W., *Der Ursprung der Gottesidee*, 6 vols. (Münster, Aschendorff, 1912–1935)—English translation, *The Origin and Growth of Religion* (New York, Dial Press, 1931)
Schmidt, Pater W., "Heilbringer bei den Naturvölkern," *Semaine d'ethnologie religieuse*, 4
Science and Religion: A Symposium (New York, Scribner, 1931)
Söderblom, Nathan, *Das Werden des Gottesglaubens* (Leipzig, J. C. Hinrichs, 1926)
Swift, Arthur L. (editor), *Religion Today*, Chap. II (New York, McGraw-Hill, 1933)
Toy, Crawford H., *Introduction to the History of Religions* (Boston, Ginn, 1913)
Tylor, Sir Edward B., *Primitive Culture*, sixth edition (London, Murray, 1920)
Wissler, Clark, *An Introduction to Social Anthropology*, Chaps. XII–XIII (New York, Holt, 1929)
Wundt, Wilhelm, *Völkerpsychologie*, IV (Leipzig, W. Engelmann, 1911)

CHAPTER I

Abbott, J., *The Keys of Power: A Study of Indian Ritual and Belief* (London, Methuen, 1932)
Arbman, Ernst, "Seele und Mana," *Archiv für Religionswissenschaft*, 29: 293–394 (1931)
Bendann, Effie, *Death Customs*, Chap. XIV (New York, Knopf, 1930)
Beth, Karl, *Religion und Magie*, Chap. IV (Leipzig and Berlin, 1927)
Briffault, Robert, *The Mothers*, II, Chap. XVII (New York, Macmillan, 1927)
Burrill, Eli E., *Taboo, Magic, Spirits* (New York, Macmillan, 1932)
Burstein, Sona Rosa, "Tabu," *EB*, XXI, 732–733
Campbell, Ivy G., "Manaism, A Study in the Psychology of Religion," *American Journal of Psychology*, 29: 1–49 (1918)
Capell, A., "The Word 'Mana': A Linguistic Study," *Oceania*, 9: 79–88 (1938)
Clodd, Edward, *Magic in Names and in Other Things* (London, Chapman & Hall, 1920)
Codrington, R. H., *The Melanesians* (Oxford, Clarendon Press, 1891)
Codrington, R. H., "Melanesians," *ERE*, VIII, 530–534
Collocott, E. E. V., "The Supernatural in Tonga," *AA*, 23: 415–424 (1921)
Dawson, Christopher, *Progress and Religion*, Chap. IV (London, Sheed and Ward, 1929)
Fletcher, Alice C., "Wakonda," *HAI*, II, 897–898
Fletcher, Alice C., "Manito," *HAI*, II, 800–801
Goldenweiser, Alexander A., "Spirit, Mana, and the Religious Thrill," *Journal of Philosophy, Psychology, and Scientific Method*, 12 (1915)
Hewitt, J. N. B., "Orenda and a Suggestion towards the Origin of Religion," *AA*, 4 (1902)
Hewitt, J. N. B., "Orenda," *HAI*, II, 147–148
Hocart, A. M., "Mana," *Man*, 46 (1914), 79 (1922), 78 (1932)
Hocart, A. M., *The Progress of Man*, Chap. XV (London, Methuen, 1933)
Hodson, T. E., "The 'Genna' amongst the Tribes of Assam," *JAI*, 36: 94 ff. (1906)

Hopkins, E. Washburn, "Manitu," *ERE*, VIII, 403–405
James, E. O., *The Old Testament in the Light of Anthropology* (London, Society for Promoting Christian Knowledge, 1935)
Jones, William, "The Algonkin Manitou," *Journal of American Folk-Lore*, 18 (1905)
Karrer, Otto, *Origins of Religion*, Chap. I (New York, Sheed & Ward, 1934)
Karsten, Rafael, *The Civilization of the South American Indians* (New York, Knopf, 1926)
King, John H., *The Supernatural: Its Origin, Nature, and Evolution* (London, Williams and Norgate, 1892)
Kirkpatrick, Clifford, *Religion in Human Affairs* (New York, Wiley, 1929)
Lehmann, Friedrich R., *Mana: Eine Begriffsgeschichtliche Untersuchung auf ethnologischen Grundlagen* (Leipzig, 1915)
Lehmann, Friedrich R., *Mana: Der Begriff des 'ausserordentlich Wirkungsvollen' bei Südseevölkern* (Leipzig, O. Spanner, 1922)
Lehmann, Friedrich R., *Die polynäischen Tabusitten* (Leipzig, 1930)
Lévy-Bruhl, Lucien, *Le surnaturel et la nature dans la mentalité primitive* (Paris, Alcan, 1931)
Lévy-Bruhl, Lucien, *Primitives and the Supernatural* (New York, Dutton, 1935)
Linton, Ralph, *Ethnology of Polynesia and Micronesia*, 146–151 (Chicago, Field Museum, 1926)
Maitra, S., "Religion and Magic," *Journal, Department of Letters*, University of Calcutta, 27 (1935)
Marett, Robert R., *The Threshold of Religion*, second edition (London, Methuen, 1914)
Marett, Robert R., *Man in the Making*, Chap. IV (London, Benn, 1928)
Marett, Robert R., *Sacraments of Simple Folk*, Chap. VII (London, Oxford University Press, 1933)
Marett, Robert R., "Mana," *ERE*, VIII, 375–380
Marett, Robert R., "Mana," *EB*, XIV, 770–771
Marett, Robert R., "Supernaturalism," *EB*, XXI, 576–577
Marett, Robert R., "Supernaturalism," *ERE*, XII, 119–120
Marett, Robert R., "Tabu," *ERE*, XII, 181–185
Marett, Robert R., *The Raw Material of Religion* (London, Oxford University Press, 1929)
Moore, George F., *The Birth and Growth of Religion*, Chap. I (New York, Scribner, 1923)
Oesterley, W. O. E., and Theodore H. Robinson, *Hebrew Religion, Its Origin and Development*, 56–57 (New York, Macmillan, 1930)
Otto, Rudolf, *The Idea of the Holy*, translation (London, Oxford University Press, 1937)
Pfister, F., *Die Religion der Griechen und Römer* (Leipzig, 1930)
Platt, Charles, *Popular Superstitions*, Chap. I (London, Jenkins, 1925)
Radin, Paul, "Religion of the North American Indians," *Journal of American Folk-Lore*, 27: 344–351 (1914)
Reinach, Salomon, *Cults, Myths and Religions*, Chap. III (London, Nutt, 1912)
Rohr, "Das Wesen des Mana," *Anthropos*, 14–15: 97–124 (1919–1920)
Schneff, Gerald J., "The Concept of Mana," *Primitive Man*, 5: 53–60 (1932)
Singer, Jacob, *Taboo in the Hebrew Scriptures* (Chicago, Open Court, 1928)
Sneath, E. Hershey (editor), *The Evolution of Ethics*, Chap. VI (New Haven, Yale University Press, 1927)

Soares, Theodore G., *The Social Institutions and Ideals of the Bible*, Chap. XIV (New York, Abingdon Press, 1915)
Söderblom, Nathan, *Das Werden des Gottesglaubens* (Leipzig, 1915)
Söderblom, Nathan, "Holiness," *ERE*, VI, 731–741
Swain, Joseph W., *The Hellenistic Origins of Christian Asceticism*, Chap. I (New York, Ph.D. thesis, Columbia University, 1916)
Thomas, William I., *Primitive Behavior*, Chap. XI (New York, McGraw-Hill, 1937)
Thomson, Donald F., "Hero Cult, Initiation and Totemism on Cape York," *JAI*, 63: 510–513 (1933)
Thurnwald, Richard, "Neue Forschungen zum Mana-Begriff," *Archiv für Religionswissenschaft*, 27: 93–112 (1929)
Toy, Crawford H., *Introduction to the History of Religions*, 99–104, 239–264 (Boston, Ginn, 1913)
Walker, J. R., "The Sun Dance and Other Ceremonies of the Oglala, Division of the Teton Dakota," *APAMNH*, 16 (1916)
Wallis, Wilson D., "The Element of Fear in Religion," *Journal of Religious Psychology* (1912)
Wanninger, Joseph, "Das Heilige in der Religion der Australier: Eine Untersuchung über den Begriff 'Tjuringa' bei den Aranda," *Abhandlungen zur Philosophie und Psychologie der Religion*, 14–15 (Würzburg, Becker, 1927)
Webster, Hutton, *Rest Days* (New York, Macmillan, 1916)
Westermarck, Edward, *The Moorish Conception of Holiness* (Helsingfors, Abo Akademie, 1916)
Westermarck, Edward, *Ritual and Belief in Morocco*, 2 vols. (London, Macmillan, 1926)
Westermarck, Edward, *Marriage Ceremonies in Morocco* (London, Macmillan, 1914)
Westermarck, Edward, *The Goodness of Gods*, Chap. I (London, Watts, 1926)
Williamson, Robert W., *Religion and Social Organization in Central Polynesia*, Chap. V (Cambridge, Cambridge University Press, 1937)
Williamson, Robert W., "Polynesia," *ERE*, X, 108–109

CHAPTER II

PRELITERATE CULTURES

Balfour, Henry, "Concerning Thunderbolts," *Folk-Lore* (1929)
Boas, Franz, "Kwakiutl Culture as Reflected in Mythology," *Memoirs of the American Folk-Lore Society*, 28: 98–148 (1935)
Bonnerjea, Biren, "Eclipses among Ancient and Primitive Peoples," *Scientific Monthly*, 40: 63–69 (1935)
Brown, A. R., "The Rainbow-Serpent Myth of Australia," *JAI*, 56: 19–25 (1926)
Brown, A. R., "The Rainbow-Serpent Myth in South-east Australia," *Oceania*, 1: 342–347 (1930)
Crooke, W., *The Popular Religion and Folk-Lore of Northern India*, I, Chap. II (London, Constable, 1896, 1923)
Dexter, T. F. G., *The Sacred Stone* (Treberran, Perranporth, Cornwall, 1930)
Elkin, A. P., "The Rainbow-Serpent Myth in North-west Australia," *Oceania*, 1: 349–352 (1930)
Evans-Pritchard, E. E., *Witchcraft, Oracles and Magic among the Azande*, Chap. IV (Oxford, Clarendon Press, 1937)

Fallaize, E. N., "Sun, Moon, and Stars (Primitive)," *ERE*, XII, 62–65
Foucart, George, "Sky and Sky-Gods," *ERE*, XI, 580–585
Frazer, Sir James G., *The Worship of Nature* (New York, Macmillan, 1926)
Herskovits, Melville J., and Frances S. Herskovits, "An Outline of Dahomean Religious Belief," *MAAA*, 41 (1933)
Hodson, T. C., "The 'Genna' amongst the Tribes of Assam," *JAI*, 36: 92–103 (1906)
Karsten, Rafael, *The Civilization of the South American Indians*, Chaps. XV–XVI (New York, Knopf, 1926)
Karsten, Rafael, *The Origins of Religion*, Chap. VII (London, Kegan Paul, 1935)
McConnel, Ursula, "The Rainbow-Serpent in North Queensland," *Oceania*, 1: 347–349 (1930)
Marett, Robert R., *Head, Heart and Hands in Human Evolution*, Chap. XIV (London, Hutchinson, 1935)
Marett, Robert R., "Supernaturalism," *ERE*, XII, 119–120
Oefele, F. von, "Sun, Moon, and Stars (Introductory)," *ERE*, XII, 48–62
Opler, M. E., "The Concept of Supernatural Power among the Chiricahua and Mescalero Apaches," *AA*, 37: 65–70 (1935)
Owen, D. C., *The Infancy of Religion*, Chap. II (London, Oxford University Press, 1914)
Piddington, Ralph, "The Water-Serpent in Karadjeri Mythology," *Oceania*, 1: 352–354 (1930)
Roth, Walter E., "An Inquiry into the Animism and Folk-Lore of the Guiana Indians," *ABE*, 30 (1908–1909)
Schaafhausen, Hermann, "The Struggle of Man with Nature," *Anthropological Review*, 5: 278 (1867)
Schmidt, Pater W., *Der Ursprung der Gottesidee*, V, 837–840 (Münster, Aschendorff, 1934)
Transactions of the Asiatic Society of Japan, 16, Part I (1887)
Wallis, Wilson D., "The Element of Fear in Religion," *Journal of Religious Psychology* (1912)
Wallis, Wilson D., "Prodigies and Portents," *ERE*, X, 362–376

HISTORIC CULTURES

Abou Bekr Abdesselam ben Choib, "La divination par le tonnerre d'après le manuscript marocain intitulé Er-Ra' adiva," *Revue d'ethnographie et de sociologie publiée par l'Institut ethnographique internationale de Paris* (1913)
Case, Shirley J., *Experience with the Supernatural in Early Christian Times* (New York, Century, 1929)
Dukes, Edwin J., "Feng-Shui," *ERE*, V, 533–535
Emmons, S. B., *The Spirit Land*, 274–276 (Philadelphia, Evans, 1859)
Foucart, George, "Sky and Sky-Gods," *ERE*, XII, 580–585
Foucart, George, and others, "Personification," *ERE*, IX, 781–803
Groot, Jan Jacob de, *The Religions in China* (New York, Putnam, 1912)
Lewis, Isabel M., *A Handbook of Solar Eclipses*, Chap. I, 20–21 (New York, Duffield, 1924)
New China Review, 1: 179–208 (1919)
Revon, M., and others, "Nature," *ERE*, IX, 233–253
Wallis, Wilson D., "Prodigies and Portents," *ERE*, X, 362–376
White, Andrew D., *A History of the Warfare of Science with Theology in Christendom* (New York, Appleton, 1910)

CHAPTER III

Armstrong, W. E., *Rossel Island: An Ethnological Study*, Chap. XII (Cambridge, Cambridge University Press, 1928)

Basset, Henri, *Le culte des grottes au Maroc* (Alger, Ancienne Maison Bastide-Jourdan, 1920)

Briffault, Robert, "Holy Places," *ESS*, VII, 419–422

Burriss, Eli E., *Taboo, Magic, Spirits: A Study of the Primitive in Roman Religion*, 119–123, 196–202 (New York, Macmillan, 1931)

Codrington, R. H., "Melanesians," *ERE*, VIII, 532–533

Crooke, W., *The Popular Religion and Folk-Lore of Northern India*, new edition, I, 60–65 (London, Constable, 1896)

Donaldson, Dwight M., *The Shi'ite Religion: A History of Islam in Persia and Irak* (London, Luzac, 1933)

Duncan, J. Garrow, *New Light on Hebrew Origins*, 31–32, 192–193, 202, 216–217, 227–233, 253–259 (New York, Macmillan, 1936)

Fison, Lorimer, "The Nanga, or Sacred Stone Enclosure of Wainimala, Fiji," *JAI*, 14: 14–30 (1885)

Hasluck, F. W., *Christianity and Islam under the Sultans* (Oxford, Clarendon Press, 1929)

Hobley, C. W., *Bantu Beliefs and Magic*, Chap. III (London, Witherby, 1922)

Lods, Adolphe, *Israel from Its Beginnings to the Middle of the Eighth Century*, 83–97, 230–236, 258–269 (New York, Knopf, 1932)

Madden, R. R., *Shrines and Sepulchres of the Old and New World*, 2 vols. (London, Newby, 1851)

Moore, George F., "High Places," *Encyclopaedia Biblica*, II, 2064–2070 (New York, Macmillan, 1901)

Oesterley, W. O. E., and Theodore H. Robinson, *Hebrew Religion, Its Origin and Development*, 8–12, 157–159 (New York, Macmillan, 1930)

Ponsonby-Fane, R., *The Kamo Mioya Shrine: An Account of the Shrine, Its History and Festivals* (London, Kegan Paul)

Ramsay, Sir William M., "The Permanence of Religion at Holy Places in Western Asia," in his *Pauline and Other Studies in Early Christian History*, second edition, 161–168 (London, Hodder and Stoughton, 1908)

Rhys, Sir John, *Lectures on the Origin and Growth of Religion as Illustrated by Celtic Heathendom* (London, Williams and Norgate, 1888)—the Hibbert Lectures of 1886

Roscoe, John, *The Banyankole* (Cambridge, Cambridge University Press, 1923)

Spencer, Baldwin, and F. J. Gillen, *The Arunta*, I, Chap. VI (London, Macmillan, 1927)

Squier, E. G., *The Serpent Symbol, and the Worship of the Reciprocal Principles of Nature in America*, Chap. III (New York, Putnam, 1851)—American Archaeological Researches, No. 1

Starr, Frederick, *Fujiyama: the Sacred Mountain of Japan* (Chicago, Covici-McGee, 1924)

Toy, Crawford H., *Introduction to the History of Religions*, 528–532 (Boston, Ginn, 1913)

Van Valkenburgh, Richard F., and Scotty Begay, "Sacred Places and Shrines of the Navajo," *Museum Notes*, Museum of Northern Arizona, 11, No. 3 (1938)

White, G. E., "A Primitive Cattle Shrine in Asia Minor," *Records of the Past*, 6: 99 ff. (1907)
Williamson, Robert W., *Religion and Social Organization in Central Polynesia*, Chaps. VI–VII (Cambridge, Cambridge University Press, 1937)
Williamson, Robert W., "Polynesia," *ERE*, X, 107–108

CHAPTER IV

Alviella, Count Goblet d', "Images and Idols," *ERE*, VII, 110–116
Bastian, A., "Zum westafrikanischen Fetischdienst," *ZfE*, 6: 1–16, 8–98 (1874)
Baudin, P., *Fétichisme et féticheurs* (Lyon, 1884)
Briault, M., *Polytheism and Fetishism* (London, Sands, 1931)
Brosses, Charles de, *Du culte des dieux fétiches, ou parallèle de l'ancienne religion de l'Egypte avec la religion de nigritie* (Paris, 1760)
Budge, Sir E. A. Wallis, *From Fetish to God in Ancient Egypt* (New York, Oxford University Press, 1934)
Budge, Sir E. A. Wallis, *Amulets and Superstitions* (London, Oxford University Press, 1930)
Codrington, R. H., "Melanesians," *ERE*, VIII, 532–533
Crawley, A. E., "Dress," *ERE*, V, 40–72
Crooke, W., *The Popular Religion and Folk-Lore of Northern India*, new edition, I, 60–65 (London, Constable, 1896, 1923)
Haddon, Alfred C., *Magic and Fetishism* (London, Constable, 1906)
Hiroa, Te Rangi (Peter H. Buck), "Material Representations of Tongan and Samoan Gods," *Journal of the Polynesian Society*, 44: 48–53, 85–96, 153–162 (1935)
Hocart, A. M., "Idolatry," *ESS*, VII, 575–577
Hull, Ernest R., *Studies in Idolatry* (Bombay, 1912)
Ignace, Etienne, "Le fétichisme des nègres du Brésil," *Anthropos*, 3: 881–904 (1908)
Kingsley, Mary H., *Travels in West Africa*, Chaps. XII–XVI (London, Macmillan, 1904)
Lods, Adolphe, *Israel from Its Beginnings to the Middle of the Eighth Century*, 258–264, 424–435 (New York, Knopf, 1932)
Lowie, Robert H., "The Religion of the Crow Indians," *APAMNH*, 25: 391–401 (1922)
Rattray, Robert S., *Religion and Art in Ashanti*, Chap. II (Oxford, Clarendon Press, 1927)
Rivers, William H. R., *The Todas* (London, Macmillan, 1906)
Schultze, Fritz, *Fetichism: A Contribution to Anthropology and the History of Religion* (New York, Humboldt, n.d.)
Spencer, Baldwin, and F. J. Gillen, *The Arunta*, I, Chap. VI (London, Macmillan, 1927)
Talbot, P. Amaury, *The Peoples of Southern Nigeria*, II, Chap. XVII (London, Oxford University Press, 1926)
Talbot, P. Amaury, *In the Shadow of the Bush*, Chaps. IV–V (London, Heinemann, 1912)
Torday, E., "Le fétichisme, l'idolatrie et la sorcellerie des Bantou occidentaux," *L'A*, 39: 431–452 (1929)
Toy, Crawford H., *Introduction to the History of Religions*, 535–538 (Boston, Ginn, 1913)

Weyer, Edward M., *The Eskimos*, Chap. XVIII (New Haven, Yale University Press, 1932)

Williamson, Robert W., *Religion and Social Organization in Central Polynesia*, Chap. VII (Cambridge, Cambridge University Press, 1937)

Willoughby, W. C., *The Soul of the Bantu*, Chap. IV (Garden City, Doubleday, 1928)

CHAPTER V

PRELITERATE CULTURES

Abbott, John, *The Keys of Power: A Study of Indian Ritual and Belief*, Chap. XV (London, Methuen, 1932)

Allen, Grant, *The Evolution of the Idea of God* (New York, Holt, 1897)

Barbar, Leo, "Baumkult der Bulgaren," *Anthropos*, 30: 797–802 (1935)

Burriss, Eli E., *Taboo, Magic, Spirits: A Study of Primitive Elements in Roman Religion*, 202–212 (New York, Macmillan, 1931)

Crooke, W., *The Popular Religion and Folk-Lore of Northern India*, new edition, II, Chap. II (London, Constable, 1896, 1923)

Dallas, Douglas, "The Sacred Tree of Ol Donyesha," *Man*, 31: 39–41 (1931)

Fletcher, Alice, "The Emblematic Use of the Tree in the Dacotan Group," *Proceedings of the American Association for the Advancement of Science* (1896)

Frazer, Sir James G., *The Spirit of the Wild and of the Corn*, third edition (New York, Macmillan, 1935)

Greene, Katherine G., *The Evolution of the Conception of God* (Boston, Christopher, 1934)

Hasluck, F. W., *Christianity and Islam under the Sultans* (Oxford, Clarendon Press, 1929)

Holmberg, Uno, "Der Baum des Lebens," *Annales Academiae Scientiarium Fennicae*, 16 (1922)

Hopkins, E. Washburn, *Origin and Evolution of Religion*, Chap. II (New Haven, Yale University Press, 1923)

Jeremias, Alfred, *The Old Testament in the Light of the Ancient East*, I, 207–217 (New York, Putnam, 1911)

Kagarow, Eugen, "Der umgekehrte Schamanen-Baum," *Archiv für Religionswissenschaft*, 29: 183–185 (1929)

Karsten, Rafael, *The Civilization of the South American Indians*, Chap. X (New York, Knopf, 1926)

Karsten, Rafael, *The Origins of Religion*, Chap. VI (London, Kegan Paul, 1935)

Lake, J. W., *An Essay on the Mythological Significance of Tree and Serpent Worship* (1870)

MacKenzie, Donald A., *The Migration of Symbols and Their Relations to Beliefs and Customs*, Chap. IV (New York, Knopf, 1926)

McCown, Chester C., "Muslim Shrines in Palestine," *Annals of American School of Oriental Research at Jerusalem*, Nos. 2–3 (1921–1922)

Mitra, Sarat C., "On the Cult of the Tree-Goddess in Eastern Bengal," *Man in India*, 2: 230–240

Parker, K. L., *Australian Legendary Tales* (London, Nutt, 1897)

Philpot, Mrs. J. H., *The Sacred Tree, or the Tree in Religion and Myth* (London, Macmillan, 1897)

Porteous, Alexander, *Forest Folklore, Mythology, and Romance* (New York, Macmillan, 1928)

Schroeder, L. von, "Lebensbaum und Lebenswasser," *Festschrift für E. Kulna*, 60 ff. (1916)

Skinner, Charles M., *Myths and Legends of Flowers, Trees, Fruits, and Plants in All Ages and in All Climes* (Philadelphia, Lippincott, 1925)

Toy, Crawford H., *Introduction to the History of Religions*, 112–123 (Boston, Ginn, 1913)

Weusinck, A. J., "Tree and Bird as Cosmological Symbols in Western Asia," *Verhandelingen den Akademe von Wetenschappen ta Amsterdam*, 22 (1921)

HISTORIC CULTURES

Astley, H. J. D., *Biblical Anthropology*, Chaps. XVI–XVII (London, Oxford University Press, 1929)

Barns, Thomas, "Trees and Plants," *ERE*, XII, 448–457

Barton, George A., "Poles and Posts," *ERE*, X, 91–98

Boetticher, C., *Baumkultus der Hellenes und Römer*

Conway, Moncure D., "Mystic Trees and Flowers," *Frazer's Magazine* (1870)

David, T. W. Rhys, "Wisdom Tree," *ERE*, XII, 747–749

Evans, A. J., "The Mycenaean Tree and Pillar Cult," *Journal of Hellenic Studies*, 21 (1901)

Fergusson, Adam, *Tree and Serpent Worship*, second edition (1873)

Frazer, Sir James G., *Attis, Adonis, and Osiris*, third edition (New York, Macmillan, 1935)

Grierson, G. A., "Gaya," *ERE*, VI, 184

Henderson, George, *Survivals in Belief among the Celts*, 179–198 (Glasgow, MacLehose, 1911)

Hornblower, G. D., "The Sacred Grove in Egypt," *Man*, 29: 17–19 (1929)

Hull, Eleanor, *Folklore of the British Isles*, Chap. VI (London, Methuen, 1928)

Lods, Adolphe, *Israel from Its Beginnings to the Middle of the Eighth Century*, 230–235 (New York, Knopf, 1932)

MacCulloch, J. A., *The Religion of the Ancient Celts*, Chap. XII (Edinburgh, Clark, 1911)

MacCulloch, J. A., "Branches and Twigs," *ERE*, II, 831–833

Mannhardt, Wilhelm, *Baumkultus* (1875)

Mannhardt, Wilhelm, *Wald- und Feldkulte*, second edition (Berlin, 1904)

Mills, L. H., and L. H. Gray, "Barsom," *ERE*, II, 424–425

Oesterley, W. O. E., and Theodore H. Robinson, *Hebrew Religion, Its Origin and Development*, 6–8, 18–21 (New York, Macmillan, 1930)

Platt, Charles, *Popular Superstitions*, Chap. V (London, Jenkins, 1925)

Ralston, W. R. S., "Forest and Field Myths," *Contemporary Review*, 31 (1878)

CHAPTER VI

Briffault, Robert, *The Mothers*, II, Chap. XXI (New York, Macmillan, 1927)

Budge, Sir E. A. Wallis, *From Fetish to God in Ancient Egypt*, 67–100 (London, Oxford University Press, 1934)

Crooke, W., *The Popular Religion and Folk-Lore of Northern India*, new edition, II, Chaps. II, IV (London, Constable, 1896)

De Kay, Charles, *Bird Gods*, Chap. VI (New York, Barnes, 1898)

Ellis, Alfred B., *The Yoruba-speaking Peoples of the Slave Coast of West Africa* (London, Chapman and Hall, 1894)
EB, "Animal Worship," I, 972–973
Fabre, Jean F., *The Sacred Beetle* (New York, Dodd, 1918)
Firth, Raymond, "Totemism in Polynesia," *Oceania*, 1: 291–321, 377–398 (1930–1931)
Franciscan Fathers, *An Ethnologic Dictionary of the Navaho Language*, 171–178 (Saint Michael, Arizona, The Franciscan Fathers, 1910)
Frazer, Sir James G., *Totemism and Exogamy*, 4 vols. (London, Macmillan, 1910)
Frazer, Sir James G., *Totemico: A Supplement to "Totemism and Exogamy"* (New York, Macmillan, 1937)
Frazer, Sir James G., *The Scapegoat*, third edition (New York, Macmillan, 1935)
Hasluck, F. W., *Christianity and Islam under the Sultans* (Oxford, Clarendon Press, 1929)
Hull, Eleanor, *Folklore of the British Isles*, Chap. VI (London, Methuen, 1928)
Karsten, Rafael, *The Origins of Religion*, Chap. V (London, Kegan Paul, 1935)
King, John H., *The Supernatural: Its Origin, Nature, and Evolution*, I, Chap. V (London, Williams and Norgate, 1892)
Laing, Gordon J., *Survivals of Roman Religion*, Chap. III (New York, Longmans, 1931)
Lasch, Richard, "Der Eid, seine Entstehung und Beziehung zu Glaube und Brauch der Naturvölker," *SFMV*, 5: 44–51, 84–88 (1908)
Lods, Adolphe, *Israel from Its Beginnings to the Middle of the Eighth Century*, 108–113, 243–249 (New York, Knopf, 1932)
MacCulloch, J. A., *The Religion of the Ancient Celts*, Chap. XIV (Edinburgh, Clark, 1911)
Mond, Sir Robert, and Oliver H. Myers, *The Bucheum*, 3 vols. (London, Oxford University Press, 1934)
Platt, Charles, *Popular Superstitions*, Chap. IV (London, Jenkins, 1925)
Ransome, Hilda M., *The Sacred Bee* (Boston, Houghton Mifflin, 1937)
Singer, Jacob, *Taboo in the Hebrew Scriptures*, Chap. I (Chicago, Open Court, 1928)
Smith, W. Robertson, "Animal Worship and Animal Tribes among the Arabs and in the Old Testament," *Journal of Philology*, 9: 70 (1880)
Smith, W. Robertson, *Lectures on the Religion of the Semites*, third edition (London, A. & C. Black, 1927)
Sternberg, Leo, "Der Adlerkult bei den Völkern Sibiriens," *Archiv für Religionswissenschaft*, 28: 125–153 (1930)
Thomas, Northcote W., "Animals," *ERE*, I, 483–535
Toy, Crawford H., *Introduction to the History of Religions*, 104–112 (Boston, Ginn, 1913)
Wales, H. G. Quaritch, *Siamese State Ceremonies*, Chap. XXIII (London, Quaritch, 1931
Wallis, Wilson D., "Divinations and Omens in Borneo and in Ancient Rome," *Classical Journal* (1914)
Wallis, Wilson D., "Prodigies and Portents," *ERE*, X, 362–376
Weissenborn, J., *Tierkult in Afrika* (Leiden, 1904)
Wiedemann, "Der Tierkult der alten Aegypter," *Der alte Orient*, 14. Jahrgang, Heft 1
Williams, Joseph J., *Voodoos and Obeahs* (New York, Dial Press, 1932)

CHAPTER VII

Abbott, John, *The Keys of Power: A Study of Indian Ritual and Belief*, 94–102 (New York, Dutton, 1932)
Bastian, A., *Ueber die priesterlichen Functionen unter Naturstämmen*, dissertation (1888)
Bertholet, Alfred, "Priesthood," *ESS*, XII, 388–395
Briffault, Robert, *The Mothers*, II, Chap. XIX (New York, Macmillan, 1927)
Brown, J. Tom, *Among the Bantu Nomads: A Record of Forty Years Spent among the Bechuana*, Chap. XV (London, Seeley, 1926)
Drower, E. S., *The Mandaeans of Iraq and Iran*, Chaps. IX–X (Oxford, Clarendon Press, 1937)
Greenbie, Sydney, "Man-God of Japan," *American Mercury* (1936)
Hasluck, F. W., *Christianity and Islam under the Sultans* (Oxford, Clarendon Press, 1929)
James, E. O., *Origins of Sacrifice*, Chap. VIII (London, Murray, 1933)
Landtman, Gunnar, *The Origin of Priesthood* (Ekenaes, Finland, 1905)
Landtman, Gunnar, and others, "Priest, Priesthood," *ERE*, X, 278–325
Lods, Adolphe, *Israel from Its Beginnings to the Middle of the Eighth Century*, 102–103, 296–307, 440–450 (New York, Knopf, 1932)
Mencken, H. L., *Treatise on the Gods*, 104–111 (New York, Knopf, 1930)
Montet, Eduard L., *Le culte des saints musulmans dans l'Afrique du nord et plus spécialement au Maroc* (Geneva, Georg, 1909)
Oesterley, W. O. E., and Theodore H. Robinson, *Hebrew Religion, Its Origin and Development*, 146–147, 163–166 (New York, Macmillan, 1930)
Rattray, Robert S., *Religion and Art in Ashanti*, Chap. IV (Oxford, Clarendon Press, 1927)
Russell, Bertrand, *Power: A New Social Analysis*, Chap. IV (New York, Norton, 1938)
Seler, Eduard, "Mexicans (Ancient)," *ERE*, VIII, 612–617
Spence, Lewis, and others, "Prophecy," *ERE*, X, 381–393
Swanton, John R., "Shamans and Priests," *HAI*, II, 522–524
Thalbitzer, Wm., "The Heathen Priests of East Greenland," *PICA*, 16: 447–464 (1910)
Thomas, E. J., and others, "Saints and Martyrs," *ERE*, XI, 49–82
Thompson, J. Eric, *Mexico before Cortez*, Chap. VII (New York, Scribner, 1933)
Toy, Crawford H., *Introduction to the History of Religions*, 512–528 (Boston, Ginn, 1913)
Williamson, R. W., "Polynesia," *ERE*, X, 107–108
Willoughby, W. C., *The Soul of the Bantu*, 112–135 (Garden City, Doubleday, 1928)
Woolley, R. M., "Sacerdotalism," *ERE*, X, 894–896

CHAPTER VIII

Alt, Albrecht, *Der Gott der Vater* (Stuttgart, Kohlhammer, 1929)
Arndt, Deva, "Das höchste Wesen der Ngadha," *Anthropos*, 32: 195–209, 347–377, 894–909 (1937)
Baentsch, Bruno, *Altorientalischer Monotheismus* (Tübingen, Mohr, 1906)

Barbeau, C. Marius, "Supernatural Beings of the Hurons and Wyandot," AA, 16: 288–313 (1914)
Bosch, G. van den, "Quelques notes sur le nom et la notion de l'Etre Suprême et d'un dieu-vengeur chez les Balendu," *Anthropos*, 23: 987–999 (1928)
Boullaye, P. P. de la, "L'origine du monothéisme," *Rivista di filosofia neo-scholastica* (1925)
Breysig, K., *Die Entstehung des Gottesgedankens und der Heilbringer* (Berlin, G. Bondi, 1905)
Brown, J. Tom, *Among the Bantu Nomads: A Record of Forty Years Spent among the Bechuana*, Chap. XIV (London, Seeley, 1926)
Budge, Sir E. A. Wallis, *Egyptian Literature: the Language of the Gods* (London, Kegan Paul, n.d.)
Budge, Sir E. A. Wallis, *From Fetish to God in Ancient Egypt* (New York, Oxford University Press, 1934)
Cathrein, V., "Der Gottesbegriff der Sulus," *Anthropos*, 10: 307–322 (1915)
Clemen, Carl, "Der sogenannte Monotheismus der Primitiven," *Archiv für Religionswissenschaft*, 27: 290–333 (1929)
Cook, A. B., *Zeus: A Study of Ancient Religion* (Cambridge, Cambridge University Press, 1914)
Cooper, John M., "The Northern Algonquian Supreme Being," *Primitive Man*, 6: 41–111 (1933)
Correia, I. A., "L'animisme Ibo et les divinités de la Nigeria," *Anthropos*, 16–17: 360–366 (1921–1922)
Crawley, A. E., "Hearth, Hearth-Gods," *ERE*, VI, 559–561
Crooke, W., *The Popular Religion and Folk-Lore of Northern India*, new edition, I, Chap. II (London, Constable, 1896, 1923)
Curtin, Jeremiah, *Creation Myths of Primitive America* (Boston, Little, 1898, 1903)
Dangel, Richard, "Tirawa, der höchste Gott der Pawnee," *Archiv für Religionswissenschaft*, 17: 113–144 (1929)
Deursen, A. van, *Der Heilbringer: Eine ethnologische Studie* (Groningen, 1931)
Dirr, A., "Der kaukasische Wild- und Jagdgott," *Anthropos*, 20: 139–147 (1925)
Dubois, H. M., "L'idée de Dieu chez les anciens Malagaches," *Anthropos*, 24: 281–311 (1929), 29: 757–774 (1934)
Ehrenreich, Paul, "Götter und Heilbringer," *ZfE* (1906)
Evans, Ivor H. N., *The Negritos of Malaya*, Chaps. XIV–XV (Cambridge, Cambridge University Press, 1937)
Farnell, L. H., *The Attributes of God* (Oxford, Clarendon Press, 1905, 1925)
Foucart, George, "Sky and Sky-Gods," *ERE*, 12: 580–585
Fox, C. E., *The Threshold of the Pacific*, Chaps. VI, VIII, X (New York, Knopf, 1925)
Funke, E., "Der Gottesname in den Togosprachen," *Archiv für Anthropologie*, 43: 161–163 (1917)
Golther, Wolfgang, *Götterglaube und Göttersagen der Germanen* (Berlin, 1910)
Graebner, Fritz, "Thor und Maui," *Anthropos*, 14–15: 1099–1119 (1919–1920)
Gunsaulus, Helen C., *Gods and Heroes of Japan* (Chicago, Field Museum of Natural History, 1924)
Gusinde, Martin, "Das höchste Wesen bei den Selk'nam auf Feuerland," in *Festschrift: Publication d'hommage offerte au Pater W. Schmidt*, 269–274 (Vienna, 1928)
Hackin, J., and others, *Asiatic Mythology* (London, Harrap, 1932)

Haddon, A. C., and others, "Heroes and Hero-Gods," *ERE*, VI, 633–668
Herskovits, Melville J., *Dahomey, an Ancient West African Kingdom*, II, Part VI (New York, Augustin, 1938)
Hull, Eleanor, *Folklore of the British Isles*, Chap. I (London, Methuen, 1928)
James, E. O., "Primitive Monotheism," *Sociological Review*, 27: 328–343 (1935)
James, E. O., "The Idea of God in Early Religions," *Anthropos*, 22: 793–802 (1927)
Karsten, Rafael, *The Origins of Religion*, Chap. X (London, Kegan Paul, 1935)
Kunike, Hugo, "Indische Götter, erläutert durch nichtindische Mythen," *Anthropos*, 12–13: 152–186 (1917–1918)
Lang, Andrew, and others, "God," *ERE*, VI, 243–247
Pearson, A. C., "Mother of the Gods," *ERE*, VIII, 847–851
Preuss, K. Th., "Die Hochgottidee bei den Naturvölkern," *Africa*, 4: 287–301 (1931)
Preuss, K. Th., *Glauben und Mystik im Schatten des höchsten Wesens* (Leipzig, 1926)
Preuss, K. Th., "Die oberste Gottheit bei den Naturvölkern," *ZfE*, 54: 123–129 (1922)
Rahmann, Rudolf, "Gottheiten der Primitivstämme im nordöstlichen Vorderindien," *Anthropos*, 31: 37–96 (1936)
Rhys, Sir John, *Lectures on the Origin and Growth of Religion as Illustrated by Celtic Heathendom* (London, Williams and Norgate, 1888)—the Hibbert Lectures of 1886
Rose, Herbert J., *Primitive Culture in Greece*, Chap. IV (London, Methuen, 1928)
Roy, Sarat Chandra, *Oraon Religion and Customs*, Chap. II (Ranchi, Man in India Press, 1928)
Schumacher, Peter, "Gottesglaube und Weltanschauung der zentralafrikanischen Kivu-Pygmäen Bagesera-Bazihaba," *Festschrift: Publication d'hommage offerte au Pater W. Schmidt*, 677–692 (Vienna, 1928)
Sikes, E. E., "Hearth, Hearth-Gods," *ERE*, VI, 562–563
Talbot, P. Amaury, *The Peoples of Southern Nigeria*, II, Chaps. III–VIII (London, Oxford University Press, 1926)
Tessmann, Günter, *Die Indianer Nordost-Perus* (Hamburg, Friederichsen, de Gruyter, 1930)
Thalbitzer, William, "The Cultic Deities of the Innuit (Eskimo)," *PICA*, 22: 367–393 (1926)
Thrämer, E., "Health and Gods of Healing," *ERE*, VI, 540–556
Wanger, W., "The Zulu Notion of God according to the Traditional Zulu God-names," *Anthropos*, 18–19: 656–687 (1923–1924), 20: 558–578 (1925), 21: 351–385 (1926)
Williams, Joseph J., "Africa's God: I, Gold Coast and Its Hinterland," *Anthropological Series*, Boston College Graduate School, I, No. 1, Series 1 (Chestnut Hill, Mass., Boston College Press, 1936)
Williamson, Robert W., *Religion and Social Organization in Central Polynesia*, Chaps. II–IV (Cambridge, Cambridge University Press, 1937)
Williamson, Robert W., "Polynesia," *ERE*, X, 107–108
Wissowa, G., "Hearth, Hearth-Gods (Roman)," *ERE*, VI, 563–565

CHAPTER IX

Abbott, J., *The Keys of Power: A Study of Indian Ritual and Belief*, Chap. XXV (New York, Dutton, 1932)
Ames, Edward S., "Confession," *ESS*, IV, 181–183
Ba, C. Hayavadana Rao, "Indian [i. e., India] Ceremonial Baths," *Anthropos*, 12–13: 84–88 (1917, 1918)
Baikie, J., "Confession (Egyptian)," *ERE*, III, 827–829
Coats, R. H., "Sanctification," *ERE*, X, 181–184
Crawley, A. E., and others, "Anointing," *ERE*, I, 549–557
Crooke, W., *The Popular Religion and Folk-Lore of Northern India*, new edition, I, 164–174 (London, Constable, 1896, 1923)
Drower, E. S., *The Mandaeans of Iraq and Iran, Their Cults, Customs, Magic, Legends, and Folklore*, Chap. VII (Oxford, Clarendon Press, 1937)
Fallaize, E. N., and others, "Purification," *ERE*, X, 455–504
Farnell, L. R., *The Evolution of Religion*, Lecture III (New York, Putnam, 1905)
Feltoe, C. L., "Consecration," *ERE*, IV, 58–64
Frazer, Sir James G., *The Fear of the Dead in Primitive Religion*, II (London, Macmillan, 1934)
Gomme, Laurence, "Need-Fire," *ERE*, IX, 263–264
Hartland, E. Sidney, "Sin-Eating," *ERE*, XI, 573–576
Henshaw, Henry W., "Sweating and Sweat-Houses," *HAI*, II, 660–662
Hobley, C. W., *Bantu Beliefs and Magic, with Particular Reference to the Kikuyu and Kamba Tribes of Kenya Colony*, Chap. VII (London, Witherby, 1922)
Hoernle, A. W., "The Expression of the Social Value of Water among the Nama of South-west Africa," *South African Journal of Science*, 20 (1923)
James, E. O., *Origins of Sacrifice*, Chap. VII (London, Murray, 1933)
Karsten, Rafael, *The Origins of Religion*, Chap. XIV (London, Kegan Paul, 1935)
Laing, Gordon J., *Survivals of Roman Religion*, Chap. XXVIII (New York, Longmans, 1931)
Landtman, G., and others, "Priests, Priesthood," *ERE*, X, 278–336
Lane, Edward W., *The Modern Egyptians*, 69–73 (London, Everyman's Library, n.d.)
Lawlor, H. J., "Confirmation," *ERE*, IV, 1–8
Lévy-Bruhl, Lucien, *Le surnaturel et la nature dans la mentalité primitive*, Chaps. VIII, XI–XII (Paris, Alcan, 1931)
Lods, Adolphe, *Israel from Its Beginnings to the Middle of the Eighth Century*, 269–276 (New York, Knopf, 1932)
MacCulloch, J. A., "Austerites," *ERE*, II, 225–325
MacCulloch, J. A., and others, "Fasting," *ERE*, V, 759–771
MacCulloch, J. A., and others, "Sacraments," *ERE*, X, 897–915
Maclean, A. J., and others, "Ordination," *ERE*, IX, 540–555
Maspero, G., *Life in Ancient Egypt and Assyria*, Chap. IV (New York, Appleton, 1892)
Pettazzoni, Raffaele, *La confessione dei peccati* (Bologna, N. Zanichelli, 1929, 1934–1935)
Pettazzoni, Raffaele, *La confession des péchés*, 2 vols. (Paris, E. Leroux, 1931–1932)
Pinches, T. G., "Confession (Assyro-Babylonian)," *ERE*, III, 825–827
Srawley, J. H., and Hugh Watt, "Eucharist," *ERE*, V, 540–570

Suffrin, A. E., "Confession (Hebrew)," *ERE*, III, 829–831
Toy, Crawford H., *Introduction to the History of Religions*, Chap. III (Boston, Ginn, 1913)
Willoughby, W. C., *The Soul of the Bantu*, 373–379 (Garden City, Doubleday, 1928)
Woodhouse, W. J., and J. D. Prince, "Scapegoat," *ERE*, XI, 218–223

CHAPTER X

Addison, James T., *Life beyond Death in the Beliefs of Mankind*, Chap. III (Boston, Houghton Mifflin, 1932)
Basden, George T., *Among the Ibos of Nigeria*, Chap. XXI (Philadelphia, Lippincott, 1921)
Bunzel, Ruth L., "Introduction to Zuñi Ceremonialism," *ABE*, 47: 498–501 (1929–1930)
Codrington, R. H., "Melanesians," *ERE*, VIII, 530–534
Crawley, A. E., and others, "Human Sacrifice," *ERE*, VI, 840–867
Creel, Herrlee G., *The Birth of China*, Chap. XIV (London, Jonathan Cape, 1936)
Crooke, W., *The Popular Religion and Folk-Lore of Northern India*, new edition, II, 167–179 (London, Constable, 1896, 1923)
Duncan, J. Garrow, *New Light on Hebrew Origins*, 196–201 (New York, Macmillan, 1936)
EB, "Sacrifice," XIX, 801–803
Fox, C. E., *Threshold of the Pacific*, Chap. IX (New York, Knopf, 1925)
Gray, George Buchanan, *Sacrifice in the Old Testament* (London, Oxford University Press, 1925)
Hamilton-Grierson, P. J., "Gifts," *ERE*, VI, 197–209
Hartland, E. Sidney, "Foundation, Foundation Rites," *ERE*, VI, 109–115
Hewitt, J. N. B., "White Dog Sacrifice," *HAI*, II, 939–944
Hobley, C. W., *Bantu Beliefs and Magic*, 40–68 (London, Witherby, 1922)
Hocart, A. M., "Sacrifice," *ESS*, XIII, 501–503
Hubert, H., and M. Mauss, "Essai sur le sacrifice," *L'année sociologique*, 2
Hull, Eleanor, *Folklore of the British Isles*, Chap. VIII (London, Methuen, 1928)
Ivens, W. G., *Melanesians of the Southeast Solomons*, Chap. XI (London, Kegan Paul, 1927)
Ivens, W. G., *The Island Builders of the Pacific*, Chap. VII (Philadelphia, Lippincott, 1932)
James, E. O., *Origins of Sacrifice* (London, Murray, 1933)
James, E. O., and others, "Sacrifice," *ERE*, XI, 1–39
Jolly, J., "Gifts (Hindu)," *ERE*, VI, 213–214
Karsten, Rafael, *The Civilization of the South American Indians*, Chap. XII (New York, Knopf, 1926)
Karsten, Rafael, *The Origins of Religion*, Chap. XV (London, Kegan Paul, 1935)
Knight, G. A. F., "Bridge," *ERE*, II, 848–857
Krige, Eileen J., *The Social System of the Zulus*, 289–296 (London, Longmans, 1936)
Landtman, Gunnar, "The Origins of Sacrifice as Illustrated by a Primitive People," in *Essays Presented to C. G. Seligman*, 103–112 (London, Kegan Paul, 1934)
Linton, Ralph, "The Origin of the Skidi Pawnee Sacrifice to the Morning Star," *AA*, 28: 457–466 (1926)

Lippert, Julius, *The Evolution of Culture*, Chap. XI (New York, Macmillan, 1931)
Lods, Adolphe, *Israel from Its Beginnings to the Middle of the Eighth Century*, 97–101, 276–289 (New York, Knopf, 1932)
Loeb, Edwin M., "Mentawei Religious Cult," *UC*, 24: 185–247 (1929)
Loisy, Alfred F., *Essai historique sur le sacrifice* (Paris, E. Nourry, 1920)
MacCulloch, J. A., "Sacraments," *ERE*, X, 897–902
MacLeod, William C., "Child Sacrifice in North America, with a Note on Suttee," *Journal de la Société des Americanistes*, 23: 127–138 (1931)
Mencken, H. L., *Treatise on the Gods*, 150–173 (New York, Knopf, 1930)
Money-Kurle, R., *The Meaning of Sacrifice* (London, Hogarth Press, 1930)
Moore, George F., "Sacrifice," *Encyclopaedia Biblica*, IV, 4183–4233 (New York, Macmillan, 1903)
Moss, Rosalind, *The Life after Death in Oceania and the Malay Archipelago*, Chap. XVI (Oxford, Clarendon Press, 1925)
Parry, N. E., *The Lakhers*, Part IV (London, Macmillan, 1932)
Pearson, A. C., "Gifts (Greek and Roman)," *ERE*, VI, 209–213
Reinach, Salomon, *Cults, Myths, and Religions*, Chaps. II, VI (London, Nutt, 1912)
Roy, Sarat Chandra, *The Birhors*, Chap. IX (Ranchi, Man in India Press, 1925)
Seler, Eduard, "Mexicans (Ancient)," *ERE*, VIII, 612–617
Soares, Theodore G., *The Social Institutions and Ideals of the Bible*, Chap. XV (New York, Abingdon Press, 1915)
Talbot, P. Amaury, *The Peoples of Southern Nigeria*, III, Chap. XXXIV (London, Oxford University Press, 1926)
Toy, Crawford H., "Mexican Human Sacrifice," *Journal of American Folk-Lore*, 28 (1905)
Willoughby, W. C., *The Soul of the Bantu*, 336–368 (Garden City, Doubleday, 1928)

CHAPTER XI

Bell, H. Chalmers, "The Revival of Prayer," *Contemporary Review*, 143: 211–219 (1933)
Boas, Franz, *The Religion of the Kwakiutl Indians*, II (New York, Columbia University Press, 1930)
Boas, Franz, "Prayer," *HAI*, II, 303–304
Bunzel, Ruth L., "Introduction to Zuñi Ceremonialism," *ABE*, 47: 494 (1929–1930)
Bunzel, Ruth L., "Zuñi Ritual Poetry," *ABE*, 47: 615–836
Burriss, Eli E., *Taboo, Magic, Spirits: A Study of Primitive Elements in Roman Religion*, Chap. VI (New York, Macmillan, 1931)
Burriss, Eli E., "The Magic Elements in Roman Prayers," *Classical Philology*, 25: 47–55 (1930)
Case, Shirley J., *Experience with the Supernatural in Early Christian Times*, Chap. V (New York, Century, 1929)
Codrington, R. H., "Melanesians," *ERE*, VIII, 531
Fallaize, E. N., and others, "Prayer," *ERE*, X, 154–205
Farnell, L. R., *The Evolution of Religion*, Lecture IV (New York, Putnam, 1905)
Fox, C. E., *The Threshold of the Pacific*, Chap. VII (New York, Knopf, 1925)
Frost, Fr. Bede, *The Art of Mental Prayer* (Milwaukee, Morehouse, 1931)

Hamberger, Alois, "Religiöse Ueberlieferungen und Gebräuche der Landschaft Mkulwe (Deutsch-Ostafrika)," *Anthropos*, 4: 306–309 (1909)
Haver, J. W., *Die Religionen* (Berlin, 1923)
Heiler, F., *Das Gebet* (Munich, 1923)
Hollis, A. C., *The Nandi*, 40–48 (Oxford, Clarendon Press, 1909)
Holmes, William, "Prayer Sticks," *HAI*, II, 304
Karsten, Rafael, *The Origins of Religion*, Chap. XVI (London, Kegan Paul, 1935)
Lane, Edward W., *The Modern Egyptians*, 73–93 (London, Everyman's Library, n.d.)
Lippmann, Walter, *A Preface to Morals*, Chap. VIII (New York, Macmillan, 1929)
Loeb, Edwin M., "Mentawei Religious Cult," *UC*, 25: 183–247 (1929)
Lowie, Robert H., "Crow Prayers," AA, 35: 433–442 (1933)
Marett, Robert R., *The Threshold of Religion* (London, Methuen, 1912)
Marett, Robert R., "Prayer," *EB*, XVIII, 419–420
Mason, J. Alden, "Tepecano Prayers," *International Journal of American Linguistics*, 1: 91–155 (1918)
Owen, D. C., *The Infancy of Religion*, Chap. V (London, Oxford University Press, 1914)
Paulitschke, Philipp, *Ethnographie Nordost-Afrikas*, II, 40–46 (Berlin, D. Reimer, 1893–1896)
Puglisi, Mario, *La Preghieras* (Turin, Fratelli Bocca, 1928)
Roy, Sarat Chandra, *Oraon Religion and Customs*, Chap. VI (Ranchi, Man in India Press, 1928)
Schmidt, Pater W., *High Gods in North America* (Oxford, Clarendon Press, 1933)
Schultze, Leonhard S., *Indiana*, 2 vols. (Jena, G. Fischer, 1933–1935)
Spier, Leslie, "Havasupai Ethnography," *APAMNH*, 29: 285–287 (1928)
Spier, Leslie, *Yuman Tribes of the Gila River*, 293–296 (Chicago, University of Chicago Press, 1933)
Van Wing, J., "Bakongo Incantations and Prayers," *JAI*, 60: 401–423 (1930)
Willoughby, W. C., *The Soul of the Bantu*, 368–373 (Garden City, Doubleday, 1928)

CHAPTER XII

Alexander, H. B., and others, "Worship," *ERE*, XII, 752–812
Allcroft, A. Hadrian, *The Circle and the Cross* (London, Macmillan, 1930)
Allen, John Romilly, *Early Christian Symbolism* (London, Whiting, 1887)
Alviella, Count Goblet d', *The Migration of Symbols* (London, Constable, 1894)
Alviella, Count Goblet d', *Origin and Growth of the Conception of God*, 264–277 (London, Williams and Norgate, 1892)
Alviella, Count Goblet d', "Cross," *ERE*, IV, 324–329
Benson, George W., *The Cross, Its History and Symbolism* (Buffalo, privately printed, 1934)
Blish, Helen H., "The Ceremony of the Sacred Bow of the Oglala Dakota," *AA*, 36: 180–187 (1934)
Brown, W. Norman, *The Swastika: A Study of the Nazi Claims of Its Aryan Origin* (New York, Emerson Books, 1934)
Budge, Sir E. A. Wallis, *Amulets and Superstitions*, Chaps. XVII–XIX (London, Oxford University Press, 1930)

Cressman, L. S., "Ritual the Conserver," *American Journal of Sociology*, 35: 564–572 (1930)
Dorsey, George A., "Ceremony," *HAI*, I, 226–229
EB, "Ritual," XIX, 323–325
Farnell, Lewis R., *Greece and Babylon: A Comparative Sketch of Mesopotamian, Anatolian and Hellenic Religions*, Chap. XIII (Edinburgh, Clark, 1911)
Fewkes, J. W., "The Growth of Hopi Ritual," *Journal of American Folk-Lore*, 11 (1898)
Gamble, J., and others, "Symbolism," *ERE*, XII, 134–151
Guardini, Romano, *Vom Geist der Liturgie* (Freiburg im B., Herder, 1934)
Hartland, E. Sidney, *Ritual and Belief* (London, Williams and Norgate, 1914)
Hodge, F. W., "Color Symbolism," *HAI*, I, 325–326
Hooke, S. H. (editor), *Myth and Ritual* (London, Oxford University Press, 1933)
Hull, Eleanor, *Folklore of the British Isles*, 72–80 (London, Methuen, 1928)
Karsten, Rafael, *The Origins of Religion*, Chap. XI (London, Kegan Paul, 1935)
Lang, Andrew, *Myth, Ritual and Religion*, new edition (New York, Longmans, 1887)
Lods, Adolphe, *Israel from Its Beginnings to the Middle of the Eighth Century*, 269–307 (New York, Knopf, 1932)
Lowie, Robert H., *The Crow Indians*, Chap. XII (New York, Farrar & Rinehart, 1935)
MacIver, R. M., *Society: Its Structure and Changes*, 257–260 (New York, Long & Smith, 1931)
MacKenzie, Donald A., "Colour Symbolism," *Folklore*, 33: 136–169 (1922)
MacKenzie, Donald A., *The Migration of Symbols and Their Relations to Beliefs and Customs* (New York, Knopf, 1926)
Marett, Robert R., *Head, Heart, and Hands in Human Evolution*, Chap. VII (London, Hutchinson, 1935)
Marett, Robert R., *Sacraments of Simple Folk* (London, Oxford University Press, 1933)
Mills, J. P., "The Effect of Ritual upon Industries and Arts in the Naga Hills," *Man*, 35 (1935)
Mortillet, Gabriel de, *Le signe de la croix avant le christianisme* (Paris, 1866)
Newell, William W., "Ritual Regarded as the Dramatization of Myth," in C. Staniland Wake (editor), *Memoirs of the International Congress of Anthropology*, 237–245 (Chicago, Schulte, 1894)
Oesterley, W. O. E., and Theodore H. Robinson, *Hebrew Religion, Its Origin and Development*, 148–150 (New York, Macmillan, 1930)
Parsons, Elsie C., "Hopi and Zuñi Ceremonialism," *MAAA*, 39 (1933)
Parsons, Elsie C., "Isleta, New Mexico," *ABE*, 47: 274–288 (1929–1930)
Platt, Charles, *Popular Superstitions*, Chaps. III, VI (London, H. Jenkins, 1925)
Reik, Theodor, *Das Ritual: Psychoanalytische Studien* (Leipzig, 1928)
Roy, Sarat Chandra, *Oraon Religion and Customs*, Chap. III (Ranchi, Man in India Press, 1928)
Toy, Crawford H., *Introduction to the History of Religions*, 507–512 (Boston, Ginn, 1913)
Whitehead, Alfred N., *Symbolism, Its Meaning and Effect*, Chap. III (New York, Macmillan, 1927)
Wilson, T., *The Swastika* (Washington, Government Printing Office, 1896)

Wissler, Clark, "The Functions of Primitive Ritualistic Ceremonies," *Popular Science Monthly*, 200–203 (1915)

CHAPTER XIII

Benedict, Ruth, "The Concept of the Guardian Spirit in North America," *MAAA*, 29 (1923)
Benedict, Ruth, "The Vision in Plains Culture," *AA*, 24: 1–23 (1922)
Blumensohn, Jules, "The Fast among North American Indians," AA, 35: 451–469 (1933)
Lowie, Robert H., "The Religion of the Crow Indians," *APAMNH*, 25: 323–344 (1922)
Lowie, Robert H., *The Crow Indians*, Chap. XII (New York, Farrar & Rinehart, 1935)
Macler, F., and others, "Festivals and Fasts," *ERE*, V, 835–894
Parry, N. E., *The Lakhers*, Part IV (London, Macmillan, 1932)
Radin, Paul, "The Winnebago Tribe," Chaps. XV–XVII, *ABE*, 37 (1915–1916)
Roy, Sarat Chandra, *Oraon Religion and Customs*, Chap. VI (Ranchi, Man in India Press, 1928)
Seler, Eduard, "Mexicans (Ancient)," *ERE*, VIII, 612–617
Spier, Leslie, *Yuman Tribes of the Gila River*, 236–249 (Chicago, University of Chicago Press, 1933)

CHAPTER XIV

Abbott, J., *The Keys of Power: A Study of Indian Ritual and Belief*, Chaps. XXII–XXIII (New York, Dutton, 1932)
Alviella, Count Goblet d', *Lectures on the Origin and Growth of the Conception of God*, Lecture IV (London, Williams and Norgate, 1897)
Beauchamp, Philip, *The Analysis of the Influence of Natural Religion on the Temporal Happiness of Mankind* (1822)
Beech, Meryn W. H., *The Suk*, 28–29 (Oxford, Clarendon Press, 1911)
Boas, Franz, "Religion," *HAI*, II, 365–371
Bouglé, C., *The Evolution of Values*, Chap. VII (New York, Holt, 1926)
Breasted, James H., *The Dawn of Conscience* (New York, Scribner, 1933)
Bredon, Juliet Hill, "A la Chinoise," *Asia*, 25: 138–141 (1925)
Bruce, W. S., *The Ethics of the Old Testament* (Edinburgh, Clark, 1895)
Carty, P., "Moralité, sanction, vie future dans le Védanta," *Anthropos*, 3: 1030–1046 (1908)
Charles, R. H., *Religious Development between the Old Testament and the New* (New York, Holt, 1914)
Charles, R. H., *The Apocrypha* (Oxford, Clarendon Press, 1913)
Clodd, Edward, *Magic in Names* (New York, Dutton, 1921)
Crawley, E., *Oath, Curse, and Blessing* (London, Watts, n.d.)
Dawson, Christopher, *Progress and Religion*, Chap. IV (New York, Macmillan, 1929)
Dickinson, G. Lowes, *Is Immortality Desirable?* (Boston, Houghton Mifflin, 1909)
Dickinson, G. Lowes, *Religion and Immortality* (London, Dent, 1911)
Farnell, Lewis R., *Greece and Babylon: A Comparative Sketch of Mesopotamian, Anatolian and Hellenic Religions*, Chap. VIII (Edinburgh, Clark, 1911)

Fortune, Reo F., *Manus Religion: An Ethnological Study of the Manus Natives of the Admiralty Islands*, Chap. III (Philadelphia, American Philosophical Society, 1935)

Frazer, Sir James G., *The Belief in Immortality and the Worship of the Dead* (London, Macmillan, 1913)

Garvie, A. E., "Eschatology," *EB*, VIII, 702–704

Glotz, Gustave, *L'ordalie dans la Grèce primitive*, thesis (Paris, 1904)

Gorham, Charles T., *Religion as a Bar to Progress*

Gutmann, B., "Flüche und Segen im Munde der Wadschagga," *Globus*, 93: 298–302 (1908)

Guyau, Marie Jean, *The Non-religion of the Future* (New York, Holt, 1897)

Hall, T. C., *History of Ethics within Organized Christianity* (New York, Scribner, 1910)

Hambly, W. D., *Origins of Education among Primitive People*, 382–391 (London, Macmillan, 1926)

Hippolytus, Père, "The Relations between Religion and Morality among the Bhils," *Primitive Man*, 4: 49–53 (1931)

Hobhouse, Leonard T., *Morals in Evolution* (London, Chapman and Hall, 1906)

Hobley, C. W., *Bantu Beliefs and Magic*, 103–154 (London, Witherby, 1922)

Hobson, J. A., *God and Mammon: The Relations of Religion and Economics* (New York, Macmillan, 1931)

Hodson, T. C., *The Nāga Tribes of Manipur* (London, Macmillan, 1911)

Holbach, Paul H. T., *Système de la nature* (London, 1770)

Holbach, Paul H. T., *Lettres à Eugénie* (London, 1768)

Holbach, Paul H. T., *Christianisme dévoilé* (London, 1761)

Holbach, Paul H. T., *La contagion sacrée* (London, 1768)

Holbach, Paul H. T., *Essai sur les préjugés* (London, 1770)

Holbach, Paul H. T., *Système social*, I, Chap. III (London, 1773)

Hollis, A. C., *The Masai* (Oxford, Clarendon Press, 1905)

Hughes, T. Maldwyn, *The Ethics of the Apocrypha*

Hume, David, *The Natural History of Religion*, Chaps. XIII–XV (London, 1757)

Indian Notes, "Oath-taking among the Dakotas," 4: 81–83 (1927)

Ivens, W. G., *Melanesians of the Southeast Solomons*, Chap. XII (London, Kegan Paul, 1927)

Ivens, W. G., *The Island Builders of the Pacific*, 241–242 (Philadelphia, Lippincott, 1932)

Lake, Kirsopp, *Immortality and the Modern Mind* (Cambridge, Harvard University Press, 1922)

Lasch, Richard, "Der Eid, seine Entstehung und Beziehung zu Glaube und Brauch der Naturvölker," *SFMV*, 5 (1908)

Lazarus, *Die Ethik des Judentums* (Frankfurt am Main, Kauffmann, 1911)

Lea, H. C., *Superstition and Force*, fourth edition (Philadelphia, Lea, 1892)

Leuba, James H., *God or Man: A Study of the Value of God to Man* (New York, Holt, 1933)

Lévy-Bruhl, Lucien, *Primitive Mentality*, Chap. VIII (London, Allen & Unwin, 1923)

Lods, Adolphe, *Israel from Its Beginnings to the Middle of the Eighth Century*, 476–481 (New York, Knopf, 1932)

MacCulloch, J. A., "Eschatology," *ERE*, V, 373–390

MacCulloch, J. A., and others, "Blest, Abode of the," *ERE*, II, 680–710

McDougall, William, *Body and Mind* (New York, Macmillan, 1911)
McDougall, William, *An Introduction to Social Psychology*, fourteenth edition (Boston, Luce, 1921)
MacIver, R. M., *Society: Its Structure and Changes*, Chap. XIV (New York, Long & Smith, 1931)
Malinowski, Bronislaw, *The Foundations of Faith and Morals* (London, Oxford University Press, 1936)
Marett, Robert R., *Sacraments of Simple Folk*, Chap. VII (Oxford, Clarendon Press, 1933)
Mitchell, H. G., *The Ethics of the Old Testament* (Chicago, University of Chicago Press, 1912)
Moore, George F., *The Birth and Growth of Religion*, Chap. IV (New York, Scribner, 1923)
Muntsch, A., "Relations between Religion and Morality among the Plains Indians," *Primitive Man*, 4: 22–29 (1931)
Parsons, Elsie C., "Links between Religion and Morality in Early Culture," *AA*, 17: 41–57 (1915)
Pedersen, Johannes, *Israel, Its Life and Culture*, 182–212 (London, Oxford University Press, 1926)
Rattray, Robert S., *Ashanti Law and Constitution* (Oxford, Clarendon Press, 1929)
Rose, Herbert J., *Primitive Culture in Greece*, Chap. IX (London, Methuen, 1925)
Schmidt, Pater W., in Edward Eyre (editor), *European Civilization*, I, 56–74 (New York, Oxford University Press, 1934)
Sneath, E. Hershey (editor), *The Evolution of Ethics as Revealed in the Great Religions* (New Haven, Yale University Press, 1927)
Stülpner, Kurt, *Der Tote in Brauch und Glauben der Madagassen* (Leipzig, 1929)
Talbot, P. Amaury, *In the Shadow of the Bush*, Chap. XVI (London, Heinemann, 1912)
Turner, J. E., "Personal Immortality as an Ethical Principle," *International Journal of Ethics*, 34: 59–68 (1923–1924)
Tyler, J. E., *Oaths* (London, Parker, 1835)
Wales, H. G. Quaritch, *Siamese State Ceremonies*, Chap. XV (London, Quaritch, 1931)
Wallis, Wilson D., *Messiahs: Christian and Pagan* (Boston, R. G. Badger, 1918)
Wasserzug, D., *The Messianic Idea and Its Influence on Jewish Ethics* (London, Myers, 1913)
Weeks, John H., *Among Congo Cannibals*, Chap. XXI (London, Seeley, 1913)
Westermarck, Edward, *Origin and Development of the Moral Ideas*, second edition (London, Macmillan, 1912, 1917)
Westermarck, Edward, *Early Beliefs and Their Social Significance* (London, Macmillan, 1932)

CHAPTERS XV–XVI

CULT OF ANCESTORS

Addison, James T., *Life beyond Death in the Beliefs of Mankind* (Boston, Houghton Mifflin, 1932)
Addison, James T., "The Modern Chinese Cult of Ancestors," *Journal of Religion*, 4: 492–503 (1924)

Ankermann, B., "Totenkult und Seelenglaube bei afrikanischen Völkern," *ZfE*, 50 (1918)
Bendann, Effie, *Death Customs*, Chap. XXII (New York, Knopf, 1930)
Bösch, F., "Le culte des ancêtres chez les Banyanwesi," *Anthropos*, 20: 200–209 (1925)
Bovinais et Paulus, *Le culte des morts dans l'Annam et l'Extrême-Orient* (Paris, Musée Guimet)
Brown, G. Gordon, and A. M. Bruce Hutt, *Anthropology in Action: An Experiment in the Iringa District of the Iringa Province, Tanganyika Territory*, 166–172 (London, Oxford University Press, 1935)
Bryant, A. T., "The Zulu Cult of the Dead," *Man*, 17 (1917)
Bunzel, Ruth L., "An Introduction to Zuñi Ceremonialism," *ABE*, 47: 509–511 (1930)
Camerling, Elisabeth, *Ueber Ahnenkult in Hinterindien und auf den grossen Sunda-Inseln* (Rotterdam, Nijgh & van Ditmar, 1928)
Clarke, Edith, "The Sociological Significance of Ancestor-worship in Ashanti," *Africa*, 3: 431–470 (1930)
Crazzolara, J. P., and Yoinyang, "Beitrag zur Kenntnis der Religion und Zauberei bei den Schilluk," *Anthropos*, 27: 183–211 (1932)
Crooke, W., *The Popular Religion and Folk-Lore of Northern India*, I, Chap. IV (London, Constable, 1896, 1923)
Crooke, W., and others, "Ancestor Worship and Cult of the Dead," *ERE*, I, 425–467
Fewkes, J. W., "Ancestor Worship of the Hopi Indians," *Smithsonian Institution, Annual Report for 1921*, Part I (1922)
Frazer, Sir James G., *The Belief in Immortality and the Worship of the Dead* (London, Macmillan, 1913)
Garnier, J., *The Worship of the Dead or the Origin and Nature of Pagan Idolatry* (London, Chapman & Hall, 1904)
Gilhodes, Ch., "La religion des Katchins (Birmanie)," *Anthropos*, 4: 710–722 (1909)
Hartland, E. Sidney, and others, "Death and Disposal of the Dead," *ERE*, IV, 411–511
Hasluck, F. W., *Christianity and Islam under the Sultans*, I, Chap. XVII (Oxford, Clarendon Press, 1929)
Hocart, A. M., "The Cult of the Dead in Eddystone of the Solomons," *JAI*, 52
Hofmayr, W., "Religion der Shilluk," *Anthropos*, 6: 123–127 (1911)
Joyce, Thomas A., *South American Archaeology*, Chap. VII (New York, Macmillan, 1912)
King, John H., *The Supernatural: Its Origin, Nature, and Evolution* (London, Williams and Norgate, 1892)
Krige, Eileen J., *The Social System of the Zulus*, Chap. XIII (London, Longmans, 1936)
Latourette, Kenneth S., *The Chinese: Their History and Culture*, II, 143–148 (New York, Macmillan, 1934)
Lévy-Bruhl, Lucien, *Le surnaturel et la nature dans la mentalité primitive* (Paris, Alcan, 1931)
MacCulloch, J. A., *Religion of the Ancient Celts*, Chap. X (Edinburgh, Clark, 1911)
MacKenzie, D. R., *The Spirit-Ridden Konde*, Chaps. XV–XVI (Philadelphia, Lippincott, 1925)

Malcolm, L. W. G., "Notes on the Ancestral Cult of the Egap Central Cameroons," *JAI*, 55: 373–404 (1925)
Marzan, J. de, "Le culte des morts aux Fiji, Grand Ile-Intérieur," *Anthropos*, 4: 87–98 (1909)
Meek, C. R., *Law and Authority in a Nigerian Tribe*, 61–79 (London, Oxford University Press, 1937)
Moore, George F., *History of Religions*, I, Chap. XXII (New York, Scribner, 1928, 1929)
Oesterley, W. O. E., and Theodore H. Robinson, *Hebrew Religion, Its Origin and Development*, 58–61 (New York, Macmillan, 1930)
Owen, D. C., *The Infancy of Religion*, Chap. VI (London, Oxford University Press, 1914)
Radin, Paul, *Social Anthropology*, Chap. XXXI (New York, McGraw-Hill, 1932)
Reinach, Salomon, *Cults, Myths, and Religions*, Chap. VII (London, Nutt, 1912)
Rohde, Erwin, *Psyche: Seelencult und Unsterblichkeitsglaube der Griechen* (Freiburg im B. and Leipzig, Mohr, 1894)
Rose, H. J., "Ancestor Worship," *EB*, I, 887–889
Roy, Sarat Chandra, *Oraon Religion and Customs*, Chap. II (Ranchi, Man in India Press, 1928)
Smith, Edwin W., *The Religion of Lower Races*, Chap. VI (New York, Macmillan, 1923)
Stade, B., *Die alttestamentlichen Vorstellungen vom Zustande nach dem Tode*
Talbot, P. Amaury, *The Peoples of Southern Nigeria*, II, Chap. XVI (London, Oxford University Press, 1926)
Thomas, William I., *Primitive Behavior*, Chap. XI (New York, McGraw-Hill, 1937)
Thurnwald, Richard, and Hilde Thurnwald, *Black and White in East Africa, the Fabric of a New Civilization: A Study in Social Contact and Adaptation of Life in East Africa*, 298–300 (London, Routledge, 1935)
Toy, Crawford H., *Introduction to the History of Religions*, 147–160 (Boston, Ginn, 1913)
Tylor, Sir Edward B., *Primitive Culture*, sixth edition (London, Murray, 1920)
Vulliamy, C. E., *Immortal Man*, Chap. II (London, Methuen, 1926)
Weyer, Edward M., *The Eskimos*, Chap. XV (New Haven, Yale University Press, 1932)
Williamson, R. W., "Polynesia," *ERE*, X, 108–109
Willoughby, W. C., *The Soul of the Bantu* (New York, Doubleday, 1928)

BELIEF IN LIFE AFTER DEATH

Addison, James T., *Life beyond Death in the Beliefs of Mankind* (Boston, Houghton Mifflin, 1932)
Alexander, H. B., and others, "Soul," *ERE*, XI, 725–755
Alger, William R., *A Critical History of the Doctrine of a Future Life* (Boston, Roberts, 1889)
Alviella, Count Goblet d', *Lectures on the Origin and Growth of the Conception of God*, 187–200 (London, Williams and Norgate, 1892)
Amyraut, Moïse, *Estate des fidèles après la mort* (1646)
Ankermann, B., "Totenkult und Seelenglaube bei afrikanischen Völkern," *ZfE*, 50 (1918)
Bell, W. Crosby, *If a Man Die* (New York, Scribner, 1934)
Bendann, Effie, *Death Customs*, Chaps. XII, XXI (New York, Knopf, 1930)

Benedict, Laura W., "Bagobo Ceremonial, Magic and Myth," *Annals of the New York Academy of Sciences*, 25: 49–65 (1916)
Best, Elsdon, "Maori Eschatology," *Transactions of the New Zealand Institute*, 38: 228–229 (1905)
Bevan, Edwyn, *The Hope of a World to Come Underlying Judaism and Christianity* (London, Allen & Unwin, 1930)
Boas, Franz, "The Central Eskimo," *ABE*, 6: 588–591 (1884–1885)
Böklen, *Die Verwandtschaft der jüdisch-christlichen mit der parsieschen Eschatologie* (1902)
Bonnet, Charles, *La palingénésie philosophique* (Ghent and Lyons, 1770)
Breasted, James H., *The Dawn of Conscience*, Chaps. XIII–XIV (New York, Scribner, 1933)
Budge, Sir E. A. Wallis, *The Egyptian Heaven and Hell*, 3 vols. (London, Kegan Paul, 1903)
Budge, Sir E. A. Wallis, *From Fetish to God in Ancient Egypt*, Chaps. XII–XV (London, Oxford University Press, 1934)
Burton, Sir Richard, *The Kasidah of Haji Abdu El-Yezdi*, Book Eight (New York, Knopf, 1924)
Case, Shirley J., *Experience with the Supernatural in Early Christian Times*, Chap. VIII (New York, Century, 1929)
Charles, R. H., *A Cultural History of the Doctrine of a Future Life in Israel, in Judaism, and in Christendom* (London, Black, 1913)
Clemen, Carl, *Das Leben nach dem Tode im Glauben der Menschheit* (Leipzig, Teubner, 1920)
Codrington, R. H., "Melanesians," *ERE*, VIII, 530–534
Cole, F. T., "Santal Ideas of the Future Life," *Indian Antiquary*, 6 (1878)
Cumont, F., *After Life in Roman Paganism* (New Haven, Yale University Press, 1923)
Dalgat, Baschir, "Die alte Religion der Tsetschenen," *Anthropos*, 3: 731–734 (1908)
Dorsey, James O., "A Study of Siouian Cults," *ABE*, 11: 419–422 (1889–1890)
Edkins, Joseph, *The Early Spread of Religious Ideas, Especially in the Far East*, Chap. VII (London, Religious Tract Society, 1893)
Elbe, Louis, *Future Life in the Light of Ancient Wisdom and Modern Science* (London, Oxford University Press, 1927)
Evans, Sir Arthur, *The Ring of Nestor: A Glimpse into the Minoan Afterworld* (New York, Macmillan, 1925)
Evans, Ivor H. N., *The Negritos of Malaya*, Chap. XXIV (Cambridge, Cambridge University Press, 1937)
Evans-Wentz, Walter Y., *The Tibetan Book of the Dead* (London, Oxford University Press, 1927)
Falconer, Robert A., *The Idea of Immortality in Western Civilization* (Cambridge, Harvard University Press, 1930)
Farnell, Lewis R., *Greek Hero Cults and Ideas of Immortality* (Oxford, Clarendon Press, 1921)
Frazer, Sir James G., *The Belief in Immortality and the Worship of the Dead*, 3 vols. (London, Macmillan, 1913)
Frazer, Sir James G., *Fear of the Dead in Primitive Religion*, 3 vols. (London, Macmillan, 1934–1936)
Freudenthal, Herbert, *Das Feuer im deutschen Glauben und Brauch*, 451–469 (Berlin, de Gruyter, 1931)

Galloway, George, *The Idea of Immortality* (Edinburgh, Clark, 1919)
Gardiner, Alan H., *The Attitude of the Ancient Egyptians to Death and the Dead* (Cambridge, Cambridge University Press, 1935)
Garvie, A. E., "Immortality," *EB*, XIII, 111–113
Godden, Gertrude M., "Naga and Other Frontier Tribes," *JAI*, 26: 200–201 (1897)
Griffin, Nathaniel E., and Lawrence Hunt, *The Farther Shore* (Boston, Houghton Mifflin, 1934)
Guise, R. E., "Tribes North of the Wanigela River," *JAI*, 28: 216 (1899)
Herder, Johann G. von, *Ideen zur Philosophie der Geschichte der Menschheit*, Book IV, Chap. VII (Berlin, G. Hempel, 1879)
Hoffman, Frank S., *The Sphere of Religion: A Consideration of Its Nature and of Its Influence upon the Progress of Civilization*, Chap. X (New York, Putnam, 1908)
Hogbin, H. Ian, *Law and Order in Polynesia*, Chap. IV (New York, Harcourt, 1934)
Hose, C., "Natives of Borneo," *JAI*, 23: 165 (1894)
Hose, C., *Natural Man: A Record from Borneo*, Part V, Chap. II (London, 1926)
Howell, James, *The Parly of Beasts; or, Morphandra Queen of the Inchanted Iland*, 40–46 (London, 1660)
Ivens, Walter G., *The Island Builders of the Pacific*, Chap. VI (Philadelphia, Lippincott, 1932)
Jackson, A. V. William, "The Ancient Persian Doctrine of a Future Life," *Biblical World*, 8: 149–163 (1896)
Jardine, John, *The Burmese Empire a Hundred Years Ago as Described by Father Sangermano*, Chap. IV (London, Constable, 1893)
Jastrow, Morris, Jr., *Hebrew and Babylonian Traditions*, Chap. IV (New York, Scribner, 1914)
Karsten, Rafael, *The Origins of Religion*, Chap. XII (London, Kegan Paul, 1935)
Knight, G. A. F., "Bridge," *ERE*, II, 848–857
Kohler, Kaufmann, *Heaven and Hell in Comparative Religion* (New York, Macmillan, 1923)
Laing, Gordon J., *Survivals of Roman Religion*, Chap. XXX (New York, Longmans, 1931)
Lamont, Corliss, *The Illusion of Immortality* (New York, Putnam, 1935)
Landan, Marcus, *Hölle und Fegefeuer in Volksglaube, Dichtung und Kirchenlehre* (Heidelberg, 1909)
Landtman, Gunnar, *The Kiwai Papuans of British New Guinea*, Chap. XX (London, Macmillan, 1927)
Lawton, George, *The Drama of Life after Death* (New York, Holt, 1932)
Leuba, James H., *The Belief in God and Immortality* (Boston, Sherman, 1916)
Lister, J. J., "Notes on the Natives of Fakaofu," *JAI*, 21: 50–53 (1892)
Lodge, Rupert C., *Plato's Theory of Ethics*, Chap. XVI (New York, Harcourt, 1928)
Lods, Adolphe, *Israel from Its Beginnings to the Middle of the Eighth Century*, 219–230, 475–476 (New York, Knopf, 1932)
Lyman, Eugene W., *The Meaning of Selfhood and Faith in Immortality* (Cambridge, Harvard University Press, 1928)
MacCulloch, J. A., and others, "Blest, Abode of the," *ERE*, II, 680–710
MacCulloch, J. A., and others, "State of the Dead," *ERE*, XI, 817–854
Marchant, Sir James (editor), *Immortality* (New York, Putnam, 1924)
Marett, Robert R., *Sacraments of Simple Folk*, Chap. X (Oxford, Clarendon Press, 1933)

Marshall, Frank H., *The Religious Backgrounds of Early Christianity*, Chaps. XVIII–XIX (St. Louis, Bethany Press, 1931)
Mencken, H. L., *Treatise on the Gods*, 180–199 (New York, Knopf, 1930)
Moore, Clifford H., *Ancient Beliefs in the Immortality of the Soul* (New York, Longmans, 1931)
Moore, Clifford H., *Pagan Ideas of Immortality during the Early Roman Empire* (Cambridge, Harvard University Press, 1918)
Moore, Clifford H., *Theories Regarding the Immortality of the Soul*
Moore, George F., *Metempsychosis* (Cambridge, Harvard University Press, 1914)
Moore, George F., *The Birth and Growth of Religion*, Chap. VI (New York, Scribner, 1924)
Moss, Rosalind, *The Life after Death in Oceania and the Malay Archipelago* (Oxford, Clarendon Press, 1925)
Newberry, John S., *The Rainbow Bridge: A Study of Paganism*, Chap. IV (Boston, Houghton Mifflin, 1934)
Oesterley, W. O. E., *Immortality and the Unseen World* (New York, Macmillan, 1921)
Ostwald, Wilhelm, *Individuality and Immortality* (Boston, Houghton Mifflin, 1906)
Palmer, Edward, "Notes on Some Australian Tribes," *JAI*, 13: 290 (1884)
Paton, Lewis B., *Spiritism and the Cult of the Dead in Antiquity* (New York, Macmillan, 1921)
Pavry, Dastur C., *The Zoroastrian Doctrine of a Future Life from Death to the Individual Judgment* (New York, Columbia University, Indo-Iranian Series, 1926)
Pedersen, Jons, *Israel, Its Life and Culture*, 453–470 (London, Oxford University Press, 1926)
Petrie, Sir W. Flinders, *Doctrine of the Future Life in Egypt Prior to Christianity* (1930)
Powdermaker, Hortense, *Life in Lesu*, Chap. VIII (New York, Norton, 1933)
Preuss, K. Th., *Tod und Unsterblichkeit in Glauben der Naturvölker* (Tübingen, Mohr, 1930)
Pringle-Pattison, A. Seth, *The Idea of Immortality* (Oxford, Clarendon Press, 1922)
Reisner, George A., *The Egyptian Conception of Immortality* (Boston, Houghton Mifflin, 1912)
Rohde, Erwin, *Psyche: The Cult of Souls and Belief in Immortality among the Greeks* (London, 1925)
Santayana, George, *The Life of Reason or the Phases of Human Progress*, Series III, second edition (New York, Scribner, 1922)
Santayana, George, *Reason in Religion*, Chaps. XIII–XIV (New York, Scribner, 1926)
Schebesta, P., "Jenseitsglaube der Semang auf Malakka," *Festschrift: Publication d'hommage offerte au Pater W. Schmidt*, 635–644 (Vienna, 1928)
Schmidt, Pater W., *Der Ursprung der Gottesidee*, V, 760–762, 851–852 (Münster, Aschendorff, 1934)
Schwally, F., *Das Leben nach dem Tode nach den Vorstellungen des alten Israel* (Giessen, J. Ricker, 1892)
Seler, Eduard, "Mexicans (Ancient)," *ERE*, VIII, 612–617
Seligman, C. G., "The Ideas of Primitive Man," in *The Future Life* (London, Hopkinson, 1933)
Smith, Edwin W., *The Religion of Lower Races*, Chap. V (New York, Macmillan, 1923)

Sneath, E. H. (editor), *Religion and the Future Life* (New York, Revell, 1922)
Söderblom, Nathan, *La vie future d'après le mazdéisme* (Paris, 1901)
Somerville, Boyle T., "Notes on Some Islands of the New Hebrides," *JAI*, 23: 9–10 (1894)
Spence, Lewis, *An Introduction to Mythology*, Chap. VII (New York, Farrar & Rinehart, 1931)
Spencer, F. A. M., *The Future Life* (New York, Harper, 1935)
Spier, Leslie, *Yuman Tribes of the Gila River*, 296–299 (Chicago, University of Chicago Press, 1933)
Steinman, Th., *Der religiöse Unsterblichkeitsglaube* (Göttingen, 1912)
Strong, Eugénie, *Apotheosis and After Life* (New York, Dutton, 1916)
Stülpner, Kurt, *Der Tote in Brauch und Glauben der Madagassen* (Leipzig, 1929)
Swanton, John R., "Creek Religion and Medicine," *ABE*, 42: 510–515 (1928)
Talbot, P. Amaury, *Peoples of Southern Nigeria*, II, 259–278 (London, Oxford University Press, 1926)
Tempeller, B., *Die Unsterblichkeitslehre bei den jüdischen Philosophen des Mittelalters* (Vienna, 1895)
Toy, Crawford H., *Introduction to the History of Religions*, Chap. II (Boston, Ginn, 1913)
Vulliamy, C. E., *Immortal Man* (London, Methuen, 1926)
Warneck, Lic. Joh., *Die Religion der Batak*, Chap. III (Göttingen, Vandenhoeck & Ruprecht; Leipzig, J. C. Hinrichs; 1909)
Watt, G., "The Aboriginal Tribes of Manipur," *JAI*, 16: 356 (1887)
Whitley, John, *Life Everlasting* (1846)
Williams, F. E., *Orokaiva Society*, Chap. XVI (London, Oxford University Press, 1930)
Williamson, R. W., "Polynesia," *ERE*, X, 108–109
Woodthorpe, R. G., "Notes on the Wild Tribes Inhabiting the so-called Naga Hills, on Our North-East Frontier of India," *JAI*, 11: 69 (1882)
Zimmerman, Jeremiah, *Faith in God and Heaven* (New York, Revell, 1934)

CHAPTER XVIII

RELIGION, ART AND MYTHOLOGY

Jochelson, Waldemar, *Peoples of Asiatic Russia*, 215–216 (New York, American Museum of Natural History, 1928)
Lang, Andrew, *Myth, Religion and Ritual*, new edition (New York, Longmans, 1887)
Lowie, Robert H., *Primitive Religion*, Chap. XII (New York, Boni & Liveright, 1924)
Preuss, K. Th., *Religion und Mythologie der Uitoto* (Göttingen, 1923)
Seta, Alessandro della, *Religion and Art: A Study in the Evolution of Sculpture, Painting, and Architecture* (New York, Scribner, 1914)
Toy, Crawford H., *Introduction to the History of Religions*, Chap. VII (Boston, Ginn, 1913)
Wundt, W., *Mythus und Religion*, second edition (1910)

NEW RELIGIONS

Breasted, James H., *The Dawn of Conscience*, Chap. XV (New York, Scribner, 1933)
Chamberlain, Alexander F., "New Religions among the North American Indians," *Journal of Religious Psychology*, 6: 1–49 (1913)

Kroeber, Alfred L., *Handbook of the Indians of California*, Bulletin 78 of the Bureau of American Ethnology (Smithsonian Institution, Washington, D. C., 1925)
Lowie, Robert H., *Primitive Religion*, Chap. XI (New York, Boni & Liveright, 1924)
Métraux, A., "Les hommes-dieux chez les Chiriguano et dans l'Amérique du Sud," *Revista del Instituto de Etnología de la Universidad Nacional de Tucumán* (Argentina), 2: 61–91 (1931)
Parker, A. C., *The Code of Handsome Lake*, Bulletin 163 of the New York State Museum
Petrullo, Vicenzo, *The Diabolic Root: A Study of Peyotism, the New Indian Religion, among the Delawares* (Philadelphia, University of Pennsylvania Press, 1934)
Radin, Paul, *The Winnebago Tribe*, Chap. XVI, *ABE*, 37 (1915–1916)
Radin, Paul, "A Sketch of the Peyote Cult of the Winnebago: A Study in Borrowing," *Journal of Religious Psychology*, 7: 1–22 (1914)
Söderblom, N., and others, "Incarnation," *ERE*, VII, 183–201
Wallis, Wilson D., *Messiahs Christian and Pagan* (Boston, R. G. Badger, 1918)
Williams, F. E., *Orokaiva Magic*, 3–101 (London, Oxford University Press, 1928)

CHAPTER XIX

General

Bertholet, Alfred, *Religionsgeschichtliches Lesebuch* (Tübingen, Mohr, 1932)
Beth, Karl, *Religion und Magie*, Chap. IV (Leipzig and Berlin, 1927)
Clemen, Carl, *Religions of the World: Their Nature and Their History* (New York, Harcourt, 1931)
Cook, Stanley A., "Religion," *ERE*, X, 662–693
Gowen, Herbert H., *A History of Religion* (Milwaukee, Morehouse, 1934)
Haas, H., *Bilderatlas zur Religionsgeschichte*
Schmidt, Pater W., *Der Ursprung der Gottesidee*, 6 vols. (Münster, Aschendorff, 1912–1935)

Primitive Cultures

NORTH AMERICA

Harrington, M. R., "Religion and Ceremonies of the Lenape," *INM*, 19 (1921)
Jenness, Diamond, *The Indians of Canada*, Chap. XII (Ottawa, National Museum of Canada, 1932)
Loewenthal, John, *Die Religion der Ostalgonkin*, inaugural dissertation (Berlin, 1913)
Parsons, Elsie C., *Pueblo Indian Religion* (Chicago, University of Chicago Press, 1939)
Radin, Paul, "Religion of the North American Indians," *Journal of American Folk-Lore*, 27: 335–373 (1914)
Reid, A. P., "Religious Beliefs of the Ojibway or Sauteux Indians," *JAI*, 3: 106–113 (1874)

NORTHWEST COAST

Boas, Franz, *The Religion of the Kwakiutl Indians* (New York, Columbia University Press, 1930)
Boas, Franz, "Die Ausdrücke für einige religiöse Begriffe der Kwakiutl Indianer," *Festschrift Meinhof*, 386–392

Jones, Livingston F., *A Study of the Thlingets of Alaska*, Chaps. XVII, XXIII (New York, Revell, 1914)

Locher, S. W., *The Serpent in Kwakiutl Religion* (Leyden, 1932)

ESKIMOS

Boas, Franz, "Religious Beliefs of the Central Eskimo," *Popular Science Monthly*, 57: 624–631 (1900)

Thalbitzer, William, "The Cultic Deities of the Inuit (Eskimo)," *PICA*, 22: Part II, 367–391 (1928)

Weyer, Edward M., *The Eskimos*, Chaps. XIV–XXVI (New Haven, Yale University Press, 1932)

CALIFORNIA

Dixon, Roland B., "The Shasta," *BAMNH*, 17: 471–491 (1907)

Kroeber, Alfred L., "The Religion of the Indians of California," *UC*, 4: 319–356 (1907)

Kroeber, Alfred L., *Handbook of the Indians of California*, Bulletin 78 of the Bureau of American Ethnology (Smithsonian Institution, Washington, D. C., 1925)

SOUTHEASTERN UNITED STATES

Swanton, John R., "Creek Religion and Medicine," *ABE*, 42 (1924–1925)

SOUTHWESTERN UNITED STATES

Bunzel, Ruth L., "Introduction to Zuñi Ceremonialism," *ABE*, 47 (1929–1930)

Parsons, Elsie C., "Isleta, New Mexico," *ABE*, 47 (1929–1930)

Spier, Leslie, *Yuman Tribes of the Gila River*, Chap. IX (Chicago, University of Chicago Press, 1933)

Spier, Leslie, "Havasupai Ethnography," *APAMNH*, 29: 275–287 (1928)

PLAINS AREA

Dorsey, J. O., "A Study of Siouan Cults," *ABE*, 11: 351–544 (1889–1890)

Goddard, Pliny E., and others, "The Sun Dance," *APAMNH*, 16 (1919)

Lowie, Robert H., "The Religion of the Crow Indians," *APAMNH*, 25: 315–444 (1922)

Lowie, Robert H., *Primitive Religion*, Chap. I (New York, Boni & Liveright, 1924)

Mead, Margaret, *The Changing Culture of an Indian Tribe*, Chap. VI (New York, Columbia University Press, 1932)

Wallis, Wilson D., "Beliefs and Tales of the Canadian Dakota," *Journal of American Folk-Lore*, 36, No. 139: 36–101 (1923)

MEXICO

Dieseldorff, *Kunst und Religion der Mayavölker* (Berlin, 1931)

Thompson, J. Eric, *Mexico before Cortez*, Chap. V (New York, Scribner, 1933)

SOUTH AMERICA

Joyce, Thomas A., *South American Archaeology*, Chap. VII (New York, Macmillan, 1912)

Karsten, Rafael, *The Civilization of the South American Indians* (New York, Knopf, 1926)

Karsten, Rafael, "La religión de los Indios Mataco-Nocténes," *Anales del Museo Nacional de Historia Natural de Buenos Aires*, 24 (1913)

Karsten, Rafael, "Religion of the Jibaro Indians of Eastern Ecuador," *Boletín de la Academia Nacional de Historia*, Quito, 3 (1922)

Métraux, A., *La religion des Tupinamba et ses rapports avec celle des autres tribus Tupi-Guarani* (Paris, Leroux, 1928)

AFRICA

Basden, George T., *Among the Ibos of Nigeria*, Chaps. XX–XXI (Philadelphia, Lippincott, 1921)

Bleek, D. F., *The Mantis and His Friends* (London, Blackwell, 1923)

Bleek, D. F., *The Naron, a Bushman Tribe of the Central Kalahari*, 25–27 (Cambridge, Cambridge University Press, 1928)

Bleek, D. F., "Ueber die Religion der Zulukaffern," *Das Ausland*, 30 (1857)

Braner, E., *Züge aus der Religion der Herero* (Leipzig, 1925)

Brown, J. Tom, *Among the Bantu Nomads: A Record of Forty Years Spent among the Bechuana*, Chaps. X–XVII (London, Seeley, 1926)

Bullock, Charles, *The Mashona*, 116–165 (Capetown and Johannesburg, Juta, 1927)

Callaway, R. H., *The Religious System of the Amazulu and Other Tribes of South Africa* (London, 1868–1870)

Campbell, Dugold, *In the Heart of Bantuland*, 244–252 (London, Seeley, 1922)

Cardinal, Allan Wolsey, *Tales Told in Togoland* (London, Oxford University Press, 1931)

Collection de monographies ethnographiques, 11 vols. (Brussels, Institut international de bibliographie, 1907–1913)

Cooksey, J. J., and Alexander McLeish, *Religion and Civilization in West Africa* (London, World Dominion Press, 1931)

Culwick, A. T., and G. M. Culwick, *Ubena of the Rivers*, Chap. V (London, Allen & Unwin, 1935)

Cureau, A. L., *Savage Man in Central Africa*, Chap. V (London, Unwin, 1915)

Ellis, George W., *Negro Culture in West Africa*, Chap. VI (New York, Neale, 1914)

Evans-Pritchard, E. E., "Zande Theology," *Sudan Notes and Records*, 19 (1936)

Field, M. J., *Religion and Medicine of the Ga People* (New York, Oxford University Press, 1937)

Hamberger, A., "Nachtrag zu den religiösen Ueberlieferungen and Gebraüchen der Landschaft Mkulwe (Deutsch-Ostafrika)," *Anthropos*, 5 (1910)

Herskovits, Melville J., *Dahomey, an Ancient West African Kingdom*, 2 vols. (New York, Augustin, 1938)

Herskovits, Melville J., and Frances S. Herskovits, "An Outline of Dahomean Religious Belief," *MAAA*, 41 (1933)

Hobley, C. W., "Further Researches into Kikuyu and Kamba Religious Beliefs and Customs," *JAI*, 41: 406–457 (1911)

Hobley, C. W., *A-Kamba and Other East African Tribes*, Chap. XVIII (Cambridge, Cambridge University Press, 1910)

Lindblom, Gerhard, *The Akamba*, 177–214 (Uppsala, Appelbergs, 1916)

Lowie, Robert H., *Primitive Religion*, Chap. II (New York, Boni & Liveright, 1924)

Luttig, H. P., *The Religious System and Social Organization of the Herero* (Utrecht, Kemmik, 1933)

Mair, L. P., *An African People in the Twentieth Century*, Chap. IX (London, Routledge, 1934)

Meek, C. K., "A Religious Festival in Northern Nigeria," *Africa*, 323–346 (1930)

Meek, C. K., *The Northern Tribes of Nigeria*, II, Chap. VII (London, Oxford University Press, 1925)

Meek, C. K., *Law and Authority in a Nigerian Tribe*, Chaps. II–III (London, Oxford University Press, 1937)

Meinhof, Carl, "Afrikanische Religionen, 1923–1929," *Archiv für Religionswissenschaft*, 28: 304–317 (1930)

Meinhof, Carl, *Religionen der Afrikaner in ihrem Zusammenhang mit dem Wirtschaftsleben* (Oslo, Instituttet for Sammenlignende Kulturforskning, 1926)

Nalder, L. F. (editor), *A Tribal Survey of Mongalla Province*, Chap. IV (London, Oxford University Press, 1937)

Roscoe, John, *The Bakitara*, Chap. III (Cambridge, Cambridge University Press, 1923)

Roscoe, John, *The Baganda*, Chap. IX (London, Macmillan, 1911)

Roscoe, John, *The Bagesu*, Chaps. II, IX, XVI (Cambridge, Cambridge University Press, 1924)

Routledge, W. Scoresby, and Katherine Routledge, *With a Prehistoric People, the Akikuyu of British East Africa*, 225–248 (London, Edward Arnold, 1910)

Schapera, I., *The Khoisan Peoples of South Africa*, Chap. VII (London, Routledge, 1930)

Schneider, W., *Die Religion der afrikanischen Naturvölker* (Münster, 1891)

Seligman, C. G., "The Religion of the Pagan Tribes of the White Nile," *Africa*, 4: 1–22 (1931)

Seligman, C. G., *Pagan Tribes of the Nilotic Soudan*, 74–105, 122–130 (London, Routledge, 1932)

Shooter, Joseph, *The Kafirs of Natal and the Zulu Country*, Chap. VI (London, Stanford, 1857)

Smith, E. W., and A. Murray Dale, *The Ila-speaking Peoples of Northern Rhodesia*, II (London, Macmillan, 1920)

Soga, John Henderson, *The Ama-Xosa: Life and Customs*, 353–367 (Lovedale, South Africa, Lovedale Press, 1931)

Spieth, J., *Die Religion der Eweer in Süd-Togo* (Göttingen, Vandenhoeck & Ruprecht; Leipzig, J. C. Hinrichs; 1911)

Stayt, Hugh A., *The Bavenda*, Chap. XX (London, Oxford University Press, 1931)

Talbot, P. Amaury, *In the Shadow of the Bush* (London, Heinemann, 1912)

Talbot, P. Amaury, *Peoples of Southern Nigeria*, II, 14–154 (London, Oxford University Press, 1926)

Thomas, Northcote W., *Anthropological Report on the Ibo-speaking Peoples of Nigeria*, Part I, 26–45; Part IV, 12–35 (London, Harrison, 1913)

Thomas, Northcote W., *Anthropological Report on the Edo-speaking Peoples of Nigeria*, Part I, Section 2 (London, Harrison, 1910)

Thomas, Northcote W., *Anthropological Report on Sierra Leone: Part I, Law and Custom of the Timne and Other Tribes*, Chaps. IV–V (London, Harrison, 1916)

Weeks, John H., *Among Congo Cannibals*, Chap. XVIII (London, Seeley, 1913)

Williams, Joseph J., *Africa's God* (Chestnut Hill, Mass., Boston College Press, 1936)

AUSTRALIA

Basedow, Herbert, *The Australian Aboriginal*, Chap. XXVII (Adelaide, Preece, 1925)

Durkheim, Emile, *Elementary Forms of the Religious Life* (London, Allen & Unwin, 1915)

INDIA

Biswas, P. C., "Primitive Religion, Social Organization, Law and Government amongst the Santals," *Journal, Department of Letters, University of Calcutta*, 26, No. 4 (1935)

Grigson, W. V., *The Maria Gonds of Bastar*, Part IV (London, Oxford University Press, 1938)

MacKenzie, D. R., *The Spirit-Ridden Konde*, 178–214 (Philadelphia, Lippincott, 1925)

Mills, J. P., *The Rengma Nagas*, Part IV (London, Macmillan, 1937)

Parry, N. E., *The Lakhers*, Part IV (London, Macmillan, 1932)

Roy, Sarat Chandra, *Oraon Religion and Customs* (Ranchi, Man in India Press, 1928)

Roy, Sarat Chandra, *The Birhors*, Chap. IX (Ranchi, Man in India Press, 1925)

INDO-CHINA

Milne, Mrs. Leslie, *The Home of an Eastern Clan: A Study of the Palaungs of the Shan States*, Chap. XV (Oxford, Clarendon Press, 1924)

Wales, H. G. Quaritch, *Siamese State Ceremonies, Their History and Function* (London, Quaritch, 1931)

INDONESIA

Clifford, Sir Hugh, "Borneo," *EB.*, III, 910–911

Evans, Ivor H. N., *Studies in Religion, Folklore and Custom in British North Borneo and the Malay Peninsula* (Cambridge, Cambridge University Press, 1923)

Evans, Ivor H. N., *The Negritos of Malaya* (Cambridge, Cambridge University Press, 1937)

Evans, Ivor H. N., "Notes on the Religious Beliefs, Superstitions, Ceremonies and Tabus of the Dusuns of the Taura and Tenpassuh Districts, British North Borneo," *JAI*, 42: 380–396 (1912)

Gomes, Edwin H., *Seventeen Years among the Sea Dyaks of Borneo*, Chap. XV (London, Seeley, 1911)

Grandidier, A., and G. Grandidier, "De la religion des Malagaches," *L'A*, 28: 93–128 (1917)

Hagen, B., "Beiträge zur Kenntnis der Battareligion," *Tijdschrift voor Indische Taal-Land-en Volkenkunde*, 28 (1883)

Hose, Charles, *Natural Man: A Record from Borneo*, Part V, Chap. I (London, Macmillan, 1926)

Loeb, Edwin M., "Mentawei Religious Cult," *UC*, 25: 185–247 (1929)

Roth, Henry Ling, *Natives of Sarawak and British North Borneo*, I, Chaps. VIII–IX; II, 284–287 (London, Truslore & Hanson, 1896)

Schebesta, P., *Die religiösen Anschauungen der Sensang-Zwerge von Malaya* (Bonn, n.d.)—Religiöse Quellenschriften, 52

Skeat, W. W., "Malay Peninsula," *ERE*, VIII, 348–372

Skeat, W. W., and C. O. Blagden, *Pagan Races of the Malay Peninsula*, 2 vols. (London, Macmillan, 1906)

Warneck, Lic. Joh., *Die Religion der Batak: Ein Paradigma für die animistischen Religionen des indischen Archipels* (Göttingen, Vandenhoeck & Ruprecht, 1909)

MELANESIA

Codrington, R. H., "Religious Beliefs and Practices in Melanesia," *JAI*, 10 (1881)

Codrington, R. H., *The Melanesians* (Oxford, Clarendon Press, 1891)

Codrington, R. H., "Melanesians," *ERE*, VIII, 530–534

Fortune, Reo Franklin, *Manus Religion: An Ethnological Study of the Manus Natives* (Philadelphia, American Philosophical Society, 1935)

Jenness, Diamond, and A. Ballantyne, *The Northern D'Entrecasteaux*, Chap. XII (Oxford, Clarendon Press, 1920)
Landtman, Gunnar, *The Kiwai Peoples of British New Guinea*, Chap. XXI (London, Macmillan, 1927)
Lowie, Robert H., *Primitive Religion*, Chap. III (New York, Boni & Liveright, 1924)
Peekel, P. G., *Religion und Zauberei auf dem mittleren Neumecklenburg* (Münster, 1910)
Rivers, W. H. R., *The History of Melanesian Society*, II, Chap. XXXVI (Cambridge, Cambridge University Press, 1914)
Thomson, Basil H., "Fiji," *ERE*, VI, 13–17

POLYNESIA

Brown, J. Macmillan, *The Riddle of the Pacific*, Chaps. XII–XIII (London, Unwin, 1925)
Handy, E. S. C., "Polynesian Religion," *BMB*, 34: 1–342 (1927)
Hogbin, H. Ian, *Law and Order in Polynesia*, Chaps. V, VIII (New York, Harcourt, 1934)
Lowie, Robert H., *Primitive Religion*, Chap. IV (New York, Boni & Liveright, 1924)
Stimson, J. Frank, "Tuamotuan Religion," *BMM*, 103 (1933)
Stimson, J. Frank, "Cult of Kiho-Tumu," *BMM*, 111 (1933)
Williamson, Robert W., *Religion and Social Organization in Central Polynesia* (Cambridge, Cambridge University Press, 1936)

AINUS

Batchelor, J., "Ainus," *ERE*, I, 239–252

SIBERIA

Sternberg, L., "Die Religion der Giljaken," *Archiv für Religionswissenschaft*, 8 (1905)

HISTORIC CULTURES

JAPAN

Griffis, William E., *Religions of Japan* (New York, Scribner, 1904)

CHINA

Latourette, Kenneth S., *The Chinese, Their History and Culture*, II, Chap. XVI (New York, Macmillan, 1934)

INDIA

Banerjee, Guaranga N., *Hellenism in Ancient India*, Chap. XI (Calcutta, Butterworth, 1920)
Dubois, Abbé J. A., *Hindu Manners, Customs, and Ceremonies*, third edition, Part III (Oxford, Clarendon Press, 1936)
Mackay, Ernest, *The Indus Civilization*, Chap. III (London, Lovat Dickson & Thompson, 1935)—prehistoric

JEWS

Soares, Theodore C., *The Social Institutions and Ideals of the Bible* (New York, Abingdon Press, 1915)

PERSIA

Dhalla, Maneckji Nusservanji, *History of Zoroastrianism* (London, Oxford University Press, 1938)

BABYLONIA

Delaparte, L., *La Mésopotamie: Les civilisations babylonienne et assyrienne* (Paris, 1923)—L'évolution de l'humanité, synthèse collective

Jastrow, Morris, *Die Religion Babyloniens und Assyriens* (Giessen, J. Ricker, 1905–1912)

King, Leonard W., *Babylonian Religion and Mythology* (London, Kegan Paul, 1899)

Pinches, Theophilus G., *The Religion of Babylonia and Assyria* (London, Constable, 1906)

Ungnad, A., *Die Religion der Babylonier und Assyrier* (Jena, 1921)

CHAPTER XX

Calverton, V. F., *The Passing of the Gods*, Chap. VII (New York, Scribner, 1934)

Radin, Paul, *Primitive Man as Philosopher* (New York, Appleton, 1927)

Radin, Paul, "Economic Factors in Primitive Religion," *Science and Society*, 1: 310–325 (1937)

INDEX